# Bolivia: Geopolitics of a Landlocked State

*Bolivia: Geopolitics of a Landlocked State* goes beyond the traditional focus on inter-American relations, territorial issues and the maritime question to provide the first comprehensive study of Bolivian foreign policy from independence to the present day. It aims to redress the balance between the often overstated importance of external determinants – actors and forces outside Bolivia which have influenced the foreign policy process – and the understated impact of internal determinants, similar actors and forces within Bolivia.

Drawing on 50 years of research and study, the author focuses on the five interrelated goals of sovereignty, national security, territorial integrity, continental solidarity and economic independence, which have characterized Bolivian foreign policy from the outset. In so doing, the negative impact which poor governance, weak state capacity and a fixation on the seaport issue had on the achievement of those five goals is centre stage in the discussion. In acknowledging the geopolitical ramifications of being landlocked, the singular nature of Bolivia's approach to the problem also is detailed.

An examination of foreign policy today can no longer be confined to intergovernmental relations; instead, it must consider the full range of internal and external forces which have influenced its scope and direction. In addition to bilateral relations, boundary disputes and the seaport issue, this volume explores the impact of foreign capital and multinational companies, together with the effects of domestic entrepreneurs, political parties, labour unions and social movements. It also assesses the overlap or linkage between domestic and foreign variables when the two combined to influence Bolivian foreign policy.

**Ronald Bruce St John** first conducted research in Bolivia in 1968 under the auspices of a Shell Foundation grant for research in developing countries. Since that time, he has published 24 monographs and contributed to 27 others with a threefold focus on Andean America, North Africa and the Middle East, and Southeast Asia. Recent publications include *Libya: Continuity and change* (Routledge 2015), *Toledo's Peru: Vision and Reality* (University Press of Florida 2010), and *Revolution, Reform and Regionalism in Southeast Asia: Cambodia, Laos and Vietnam* (Routledge 2006). Dr St John has served as a consultant for a variety of Fortune 500 companies, US government agencies, BBC World Service, CNN News, *New York Times*, and *Washington Post*, among others. He currently resides in Albuquerque, New Mexico, USA.

# Europa Country Perspectives

The *Europa Country Perspectives* series, from Routledge, examines a wide range of contemporary political, economic, developmental and social issues from areas around the world. Complementing the *Europa Regional Surveys of the World series*, *Europa Country Perspectives* is a valuable resource for academics, students, researchers, policymakers, business people and anyone with an interest in current world affairs.

While the *Europa World Year Book* and its associated Regional Surveys inform on and analyse contemporary economic, political and social developments at the national and regional level, Country Perspectives provide in-depth, country-specific volumes written or edited by specialists in their field, delving into a country's particular situation. Volumes in the series are not constrained by any particular template, but may explore a country's recent political, economic, international relations, social, defence, or other issues in order to increase understanding.

**Political Change in Switzerland: From Stability to Uncertainty**
*Clive H. Church*

**Russian Nationalism and Ethnic Violence: Symbolic Violence, Lynching, Pogrom, and Massacre**
*Richard Arnold*

**Beyond the Drug War in Mexico: Human rights, the public sphere and justice**
*Wil G. Pansters, Benjamin T. Smith, Peter Watt*

**Greece in the 21st Century: The Politics and Economics of a Crisis**
*Edited by Constantine Dimoulas and Vassilis K. Fouskas*

**The Basque Contention: Ethnicity, Politics, Violence**
*Ludger Mees*

**Bolivia: Geopolitics of a Landlocked State**
*Ronald Bruce St John*

For more information about this series, please visit: www.routledge.com/Europa-Country-Perspectives/book-series/ECP.

# Bolivia: Geopolitics of a Landlocked State

Ronald Bruce St John

LONDON AND NEW YORK

First published 2020
by Routledge
2 Park Square, Milton Park, Abingdon, Oxon OX14 4RN

and by Routledge
711 Third Avenue, New York, NY 10017

*Routledge is an imprint of the Taylor & Francis Group, an informa business*

First issued in paperback 2021

© 2020 Ronald Bruce St John

The right of Ronald Bruce St John to be identified as the author of this work has been asserted in accordance with sections 77 and 78 of the Copyright, Designs and Patents Act 1988.

All rights reserved. No part of this book may be reprinted or reproduced or utilised in any form or by any electronic, mechanical, or other means, now known or hereafter invented, including photocopying and recording, or in any information storage or retrieval system, without permission in writing from the publishers.

*Trademark notice*: Product or corporate names may be trademarks or registered trademarks, and are used only for identification and explanation without intent to infringe.

Europa Commissioning Editor: Cathy Hartley

Editorial Assistant: Lucy Pritchard

*British Library Cataloguing-in-Publication Data*
A catalogue record for this book is available from the British Library

*Library of Congress Cataloging-in-Publication Data*
Names: St. John, Ronald Bruce, author.
Title: Bolivia : geopolitics of a landlocked state / Ronald Bruce St John.
Description: First edition. | Abingdon, Oxon ; New York, NY : Routledge, 2019. | Series: Europa country perspectives | Includes bibliographical references and index.
Identifiers: LCCN 2019012307 | ISBN 9781857439694 (hardback)
Subjects: LCSH: Geopolitics--Bolivia. | Geopolitics--South America. | Bolivia--Foreign relations--South America. | South America--Foreign relations--Bolivia.
Classification: LCC F3321.2 .S7 2019 | DDC 327.8408--dc23
LC record available at https://lccn.loc.gov/2019012307

ISBN: 978-1-85743-969-4 (hbk)
ISBN: 978-1-03-209117-4 (pbk)
ISBN: 978-0-429-26257-9 (ebk)

Typeset in Times New Roman
by Taylor & Francis Books

**To Our Grandchildren**

**Kaley Maya, Louise Frances, Maxime Robert**

**"Make Your Own Way"**

# Contents

| | | |
|---|---|---|
| *List of figures* | | viii |
| *Acknowledgements* | | ix |
| *Acronyms* | | xi |
| 1 | Introduction | 1 |
| 2 | Setting the Stage, 1809–41 | 8 |
| 3 | Rivalry on the Pacific Coast, 1841–79 | 31 |
| 4 | War and Peace, 1879–1904 | 52 |
| 5 | Landlocked, Dependent, Challenged, 1904–30 | 74 |
| 6 | War, Revolution, Water, 1930–70 | 97 |
| 7 | New Horizons, Old Constraints, 1971–90 | 123 |
| 8 | Bilateral Issues, Multilateral Initiatives, Trilateral Solutions, 1990–2005 | 146 |
| 9 | Evo Morales, 2006– | 168 |
| 10 | Conclusions | 198 |
| | *Bibliography* | 211 |
| | *Index* | 236 |

# Figures

| | | |
|---|---|---|
| 1 | Bolivia at Independence and Today | xiv |
| 2.1 | Audiencia of Charcas, 1810 | 12 |
| 2.2 | Early Claims in the Atacama Desert | 14 |
| 2.3 | Treaty of San Ildefonso, 1777 | 15 |
| 3.1 | Treaty of Mutual Benefits, 1866 | 39 |
| 4.1 | Atacama Littoral, 1883–1929 | 59 |
| 5.1 | Northern Sector, 1909–12 | 89 |
| 5.2 | Failed Treaties, 1879–94 | 92 |
| 6.1 | Bolivia–Paraguay Boundary, 1938 | 99 |
| 6.2 | Territorial Losses, 1867–1938 | 100 |
| 6.3 | Silala River Dispute | 112 |
| 6.4 | Lauca River Dispute | 113 |
| 7.1 | Chilean Proposal 1975 | 133 |
| 7.2 | Peruvian Proposal, 1976 | 135 |
| 9.1 | Proposed Bioceanic Railway Corridor Project | 178 |

# Acknowledgements

This book is the product of five decades of study and research which began when I first visited Bolivia in 1968. Since that time, I have been fortunate to have been an active observer and occasional participant in some of the central issues of Andean foreign policy. In recent years, considerable progress has been made in dealing with long-standing, complicated, and difficult questions. Examples include a peaceful end to the Ecuador–Peru boundary dispute in 1998, final resolution in 1999 of the issues outstanding from the Treaty of Ancón (1883) and Treaty of Lima (1929), and the Chile–Peru maritime settlement in 2014. The one issue which has remained intractable is Bolivia's quest for a sovereign outlet to the Pacific Ocean, a central issue of the present work.

Over time, a large number of people have encouraged and assisted my research and writing, and I want to acknowledge their generosity and support. I will not attempt to name all of them here as it would take far too much time and space, and in any case, most of them prefer to remain anonymous. I would like to recognize the long-time counsel and support of one individual, Ambassador Jorge Gumucio Granier, scholar, diplomat, and friend. In addition to serving as the Bolivian ambassador to Peru and the United Nations, he was the Vice Minister of Foreign Affairs on three separate occasions. I first met Ambassador Gumucio in 1999 when I was in Lima, Peru for the launch of the Spanish language edition of my book, *The Foreign Policy of Peru* (*La política exterior del Perú*), and he was serving as the Bolivian ambassador to Peru. In our initial conversation, he encouraged me to write a similar book on Bolivia, and over much of the ensuing 20 years, he was gracious in providing me with documents, articles, and other materials about Bolivian foreign policy. The publication of this book is due in no small measure to his encouragement and support. I would also like to acknowledge the assistance of a long-time friend and colleague, Waltraud Queiser "Trudi" Morales, the preeminent US scholar of Bolivia of her generation. Trudi was kind enough to read early drafts of the manuscript, offering invaluable insight and comment along the way. While her counsel and guidance has made for a much better book, she is not responsible for any of its shortcomings.

Some of the material herein has appeared in one form or another in the multiple monographs and dozens of articles on Andean America which I have published since 1976. Any material in the present work which has been published previously has been thoroughly revised and updated, condensing or expanding it as appropriate.

On a personal level, I would like to thank my wife, Carol, and our two sons, Alexander and Nathan, for their support over our many years together. In addition, I offer a special thanks to Nathan, an architect and graphic artist, for drawing many of the sketch maps.

# Acronyms

| | |
|---|---|
| ACE | *Acuerdo de Complementación Económica* (Complementary Economic Agreement) |
| ALADI | *Asociación Latinoamericana de Integración* (Latin American Integration Association) |
| ALALC | *Asociación Latinoamericana de Libre Comercio* (Latin American Free Trade Association) |
| ALBA | *Alianza Bolivariana para los Pueblos de Nuestra América* (Bolivarian Alliance for the Peoples of Our America) |
| ALCA | *Área de Libre Comerico de las Américas* (Free Trade Area of the Americas) |
| ALC-UE | *Cumbre de América Latina, el Caribe y la Unión Europea* (Summit of Latin America, the Caribbean, and the European Union) |
| APEC | Asia-Pacific Economic Cooperation |
| ATPDEA | Andean Trade Promotion and Drug Enforcement Act |
| CAN | *Communidad Andina de Naciones* (Andean Community of Nations) |
| CELAC | *Comunidad de Estados Latinoamericanos y Caribeños* (Community of Latin American and Caribbean States) |
| CEPAL | *Comisión Económica para la América Latina* (Economic Commission for Latin America) |
| CIDOB | *Confederación de Pueblos Indígenas de Bolivia* (Confederation of Indigenous Peoples of Bolivia) |
| CMAA | Customs Mutual Assistance Agreement |
| COB | *Central Obrero Boliviano* (Bolivian Labor Central) |
| COMIBOL | *Corporación Minera de Bolivia* (Bolivian Mining Corporation) |
| CONAMAR | *Consejo Nacional Marítimo* (National Maritime Council) |
| CSCIB | *Confederación Sindical de Comunidades Interculturales de Bolivia* (Confederation of Unions of Inter-cultural Communities of Bolivia) |
| CSN | *Comunidad Sudamericana de Naciones* (South American Community of Nations) |

## Acronyms

| | |
|---|---|
| CSUTCB | *Confederación Sindical Única de Trabajadores Campesinos de Bolivia* (Confederation of Peasant Unions of Bolivia) |
| DEA | Drug Enforcement Agency |
| EU | European Union |
| EXIM | Export–Import Bank of the United States |
| FCAB | *Ferrocarril (Chili) Antofagasta-Bolivia* (Antofagasta (Chili) and Bolivia Railway Co. Ltd.) |
| FEJUVE | *Federación de Juntas Vecinales* (Federation of Neighborhood Councils) |
| FSB | *Falange Socialista Boliviana* (Bolivian Falange Party) |
| FSTMB | *Federación Sindical de Trabajadores Mineros de Bolivia* (Bolivian Mine Workers' Federation) |
| GATT | General Agreement on Tariffs and Trade |
| GDP | Gross Domestic Product |
| GNP | Gross National Product |
| G-Río | Grupo Río (Rio Group) |
| G-77 | Grupo de los 77 (Group of 77) |
| IACHR | Inter-American Commission on Human Rights |
| ICC | International Criminal Court |
| ICJ | International Court of Justice |
| IDB | Inter-American Development Bank |
| IMF | International Monetary Fund |
| MAS | *Movimiento al Socialismo* (Movement toward Socialism) |
| MERCOSUR | *Mercado Común del Sur* (Southern Common Market) |
| MIP | *Movimiento Indígena Pachakuti* (Pachakuti Indigenous Movement) |
| MNR | *Movimiento Nacionalista Revolucionario* (Nationalist Revolutionary Movement) |
| MRTKL | *Movimiento Revolucionario Tupac Katari de Liberación* (Tupac Katari Revolutionary Liberation Movement) |
| NAM | Non-Aligned Movement |
| OAS | Organization of American States |
| OTCA | *Organización del Tratado de Cooperación Amazónica* (Amazon Cooperation Treaty Organization) |
| PBEC | Pacific Basin Economic Council |
| PECC | Pacific Economic Cooperation Council |
| PDVSA | *Petróleos de Venezuela, S.A.* (Venezuelan State Petroleum Agency) |
| PIR | *Partido de la Izquierda Revolucionaria* (Party of the Revolutionary Left) |
| POR | *Partido Obrero Revolucionario* (Revolutionary Workers' Party) |
| PRC | People's Republic of China |
| RADEPA | *Razón de Patria* (Reason of the Fatherland) |
| SELA | *Sistema Económico Latinoamericano y del Caribe* (Latin American and Caribbean Economic System) |

| | |
|---|---|
| UN | United Nations |
| UNASUR | *Unión de Naciones Suramericanas* (Union of South American Nations) |
| UNCLOS | United Nations Conference on the Law of the Sea |
| UNCTAD | United Nations Conference on Trade and Development |
| UNESCO | United Nations Educational, Scientific and Cultural Organization |
| USAID | United States Agency for International Development |
| WHINSEC | Western Hemisphere Institute for Security Cooperation |
| WTO | World Trade Organization |
| YPFB | *Yacimientos Petrolíferos Fiscales Bolivianos* (Bolivian State Petroleum Agency) |

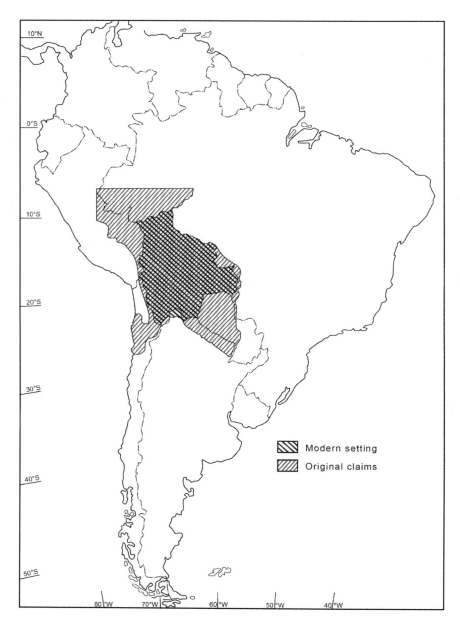

*Figure 1* Bolivia at Independence and Today
Source: Nathan Bailey St John.

# 1 Introduction

The Andes Mountains split into two great branches at around latitude 14° south, dividing Bolivia from north to south. The largest part of the country is located east of the slopes of the Cordillera Oriental, also known as the Cordillera Real, the eastern arm of the Andes. Here we find deep valleys lining the mountainside, forest lands, and eventually, an extensive prairie which borders on Brazil and Paraguay. At independence in 1825, the bulk of the population of Bolivia lived in the *altiplano*, nestled between the Cordillera Oriental to the east and the Cordillera Occidental to the west. The Cordillera Occidental or coastal range obstructed travel between the *altiplano* and the coast. Consequently, it proved difficult for Bolivians to establish east–west links between the highlands and the coast, a challenge which contributed to the failure of Bolivia to retain its Pacific littoral as part of the national domain (Pike 1977, 75, 119). Bolivia borders on Argentina, Brazil, Chile, Paraguay, and Peru, and it survived as an independent state "largely upon terms dictated elsewhere" (Fifer 1972, 252). Although it endured as a sovereign state, modern-day Bolivia includes less than half the territory it claimed at independence.

The inherent disadvantages of an interior location were evident long before Bolivia became independent. The central Andean cordilleras were primary sources of wealth in the Spanish colonial era, but they were never real centers of power. Lima, not Cuzco, became the City of Kings, and the coast, not the plateau or high mountain basin, was the focus of Spanish authority and prestige in South America. Furthermore, the mining centers of the Viceroyalty of Peru were serviced for the most part by Pacific ports (Fifer 1972, 1–2, 253). The transfer of Upper Peru, the territorial basis for nineteenth century Bolivia, to the Viceroyalty of Río de la Plata in the latter half of the eighteenth century temporarily realigned traditional trading patterns; however, the long-standing economic dependence of Upper Peru on the most accessible Pacific ports remained unchanged. Under the principle of *uti possidetis de jure de 1810*, which generally stated that each new state was entitled to the territory formerly under the jurisdiction of the colonial administrative unit from which it was formed, Bolivia inherited the Atacama littoral at independence (Checa 1936). In this isolated, desert region far from traditional trade routes, there was no port of any consequence and no real prospect of developing one; therefore, Bolivia at independence was in effect landlocked. The Treaty of Peace, Friendship, and Commerce which was signed by Bolivia and Chile in 1904 to end the War of the Pacific (1879–84) ratified the landlocked status of Bolivia.

From the beginning, newly independent but landlocked states like Bolivia were at a distinct disadvantage when it came to economic development (Hausmann 2001; Faye et al. 2004). Dependent on the goodwill of neighboring states for maritime rights, the Bolivian economy failed to reach its full potential (Morales 2010, xxix–xxx). In an effort to attract foreign investment and overseas immigration, Bolivia after 1825 promoted various colonization projects, often involving settlement or homesteading schemes, but they attracted little interest in Europe or the United States. In addition, Bolivia's landlocked position isolated it from two of the most important technological advances bearing on the growth of state organization and state power in the nineteenth century. With no seaport, it was unable to reap the advantages of direct contact with new ocean steamship routes and the effective reduction in global distances they initiated. At the same time, it largely failed to benefit from the increased mobility resulting from the first phase of railway construction in South America (Fifer 1972, 2–4, 30–1).

Given the obvious disadvantages of being landlocked, access to the sea was an immediate priority for Bolivian foreign policy. In the nineteenth and twentieth centuries, Bolivia attempted to attain improved access to the sea, if not a sovereign outlet, in a variety of creative ways, including proposed exchanges of territory, improved access to navigable portions of international waterways, demands for a corridor to the sea, and negotiated free port and transit agreements (St John 2001, 2–9). Eventually, it placed the issue before the International Court of Justice (ICJ) at The Hague (St John 2015c). Diplomacy, protracted effort, and legal argument over almost 200 years yielded little tangible achievement; nevertheless, the issue of sovereign access to the sea remained at the center of the external policy of Bolivia.

With the seaport issue central to Bolivian foreign policy, it was not surprising that Bolivian preoccupation with this question had a substantial and often negative impact on the achievement of wider, more permanent foreign policy goals. The accomplishment of core objectives central to the well-being of any independent state, including sovereignty, national security, continental solidarity, territorial integrity, and economic independence, were compromised due to Bolivia's quest for sovereign access to the sea. Bolivia's numerous and protracted territorial disputes with neighboring states often were linked to its efforts to achieve a Pacific port. With the attitudes of its immediate neighbors an important consideration in its quest for a seaport, enclosure by five newly created states proved a debilitating burden. Invariably, Bolivia found itself negotiating with its neighbors from a position of weakness. Often involving vast tracts of land and considerable potential wealth, many of these territorial disputes were in reality boundary disputes which resulted from Spain's failure to delineate carefully its administrative units during the colonial era. Other irredentist issues arose from challenging the validity of treaty settlements previously ratified by the parties to a dispute. Emotionally charged and highly involved, territorial issues with neighboring states complicated and disrupted inter-American relations in general and Bolivian foreign policy in particular throughout much of the period under discussion.

Bolivia is a land of enormous geographical and socioeconomic contrasts, profoundly fragmented by territorial identity, cultural and linguistic variance, and social stratification. On the one hand, "political and social dynamics are not just regional," and "regionalism can encompass ethnic oppositions, class conflict, and political projects of different orders" (Barragán 2008, 83). On the other hand, Bolivia is a land in which regionalism was encouraged by geographical barriers, cultural diversity, economic activity, and primitive communication and transportation networks, undermining the very concept of a nation-state (Querejazu 1979, 224). "The same natural barriers that divided Bolivia into regions also split the nation into separate linguistic and cultural groups," and "this unhappy convergence of geographic obstacles and language differences fostered a strong sense of identification with a region rather than with the nation-state" (Sater 2007, 12).

Nineteenth and early twentieth century histories of Bolivia tended to focus on domestic events at the expense of a broader treatment of the complex interrelationship of domestic and foreign policies (Arguedas 1922; Morales 1925; Finot 1980; Arguedas 1981). When foreign affairs were addressed, it was generally in the context of the War of the Pacific and Bolivia's loss of its Pacific littoral (Vaca 1879; Lucas 1893). In the first half of the twentieth century, Miguel Mercado Moreira (Mercado Moreira 1916) and Carlos Alberto Salinas Baldivieso (Salinas 1938) initiated a wider discussion of Bolivian external affairs with publications on the international history of Bolivia; however, it was only in the second half of the twentieth century that a dedicated treatment of Bolivian diplomacy and foreign policy began to be available. The first edition of the *Historia diplomática de Bolivia* (Escobari 1982) was published in 1975 followed by *Las relaciones internacionales en la historia de Bolivia* (Abecia 1986) in 1979, *Las relaciones internacionales de Bolivia, 1825–1990* (Arze 1991) in 1991, and *Hacía una nueva política exterior boliviana* (Salazar 2000) in 2000. In this time frame, we also see the publication of a growing number of country and policy specific monographs like *Momento internacional: Desviación de las aguas del rio Lauca* (Moya 1962), *La desviación del rio Lauca* (Iturralde 1963), *El desvio del rio Mauri: Integración y reintegración marítima 3 conferencias* (Escobari 1969), *Bolivia y los ingleses (1825–1948)* (Querejazu 1973), *Bolivia, Colombia, Chile y el Perú* (Pérez del Castillo 1980), *Bolivia y la integración andina* (Camacho 1981), *Las relaciones económicas de Bolivia con Alemania, 1880–1920* (Bieber 1984), *Para una historia de los límites entre Bolivia y el Brasil* (Vásquez-Machicado 1990), *Masamaclay: historia, política, diplomática y militar de la Guerra del Chaco* (Querejazu 1992), *El mito del Silala* (Bazoberry 2003), and *Pugna por influencia y hegemonía: La rivalidad germano-estadounidense en Bolivia, 1936–1946* (Bieber 2004).

The respected Bolivian scholar and former foreign minister, Jorge Escobari Cusicanqui, in his pioneering work, *Historia diplomática de Bolivia*, identified three broad periods in the diplomatic history of Bolivia. In the first, which stretched from independence in 1825 to the end of the Chaco War in 1935, he noted that Bolivia largely resorted to legal arguments and documents in its efforts to resolve territorial and related issues. In the second much shorter period, which stretched from 1935 to 1952, Bolivian diplomacy focused on improved railroad access to the Atlantic Ocean, concluding related agreements with Argentina and Brazil. After 1952, the third and final period identified by Escobari, Bolivia looked to enhanced regional cooperation and integration as a means to achieve its foreign policy goals, notably sovereign access to the Pacific Ocean (1982, I, 42–4).

These general divisions remain useful today; however, as the reader will find, a closer examination suggests Bolivian foreign policy varied considerably in content, approach, and goals within each period. In the 15 years after independence in 1825, for example, the central concern of Bolivian foreign policy was the very existence of the state as an independent entity with intractable territorial issues related concerns. For the next 30 years, a period dominated by the so-called Age of the Caudillos, Bolivia fought a losing battle to retain control of the Pacific littoral it had inherited at independence. In this period, the main threat to Bolivian sovereignty came from the south; however, Bolivian diplomacy toward Chile often involved neighboring states, especially Argentina and Peru. In the wake of the War of the Pacific, Bolivia once again fended off aggressive behavior from its neighbors as it searched for a peace with Chile which included a sovereign port on the Pacific Ocean. Once Bolivia had signed the 1904 peace treaty with Chile, successive Bolivian governments spent much of the next three decades attempting to escape the landlocked condition which the treaty ratified. After 1930, Bolivia experienced a traumatic war with Paraguay followed by a short period of consolidation and a longer period in which its foreign policy expanded in scope and purpose. As the twentieth century drew to a close, the external interests of Bolivia continued to increase as successive governments participated in a growing number of subregional, regional, and international bodies. At the same time, the United States was increasingly involved in the domestic and foreign policies of Bolivia, highlighting its dependence on others. After 2005, Bolivia abandoned the neoliberal policies of the previous 20 years, implementing dramatic changes to the direction, tone, and content of its foreign policy. In pursuit of enhanced political sovereignty and economic independence, Bolivia totally revamped its long-standing relationship with the United States and sought legal recourse against Chile at the International Court of Justice at The Hague.

The early work of respected Bolivian academics reflected a traditional focus on inter-American relations, territorial questions, and the maritime issue.

These scholars generally approached their subjects chronologically and emphasized regional or bilateral relations. In the second half of the twentieth century, the literature on the foreign policy of Bolivia became increasingly abundant; however, much of it continued to be largely descriptive or polemical in approach. Examples include *La cuestión portuaria y las negociaciones de 1950* (Guachalla 1976), *Litoral andino: retrospección y perspectivas en torno al problema marítimo* (Galindo 1977), and *Geopolítica chilena y mar boliviano* (Ponce 1998). Often legalistic or moralistic in tone, issue-oriented monographs also suffered from being unnecessarily narrow in scope while frequently containing little or no documentation. With a few notable exceptions like *Bolivia: Temas de la Agenda Internacional* (Zelada 2000) and *Bolivia, país de contactos: Un análisis de la política vicinal contemporánea* (Orias, Seoane and Torres 2001), Bolivian scholars provided little assistance or guidance in the form of policy studies on the nation's external relations. In turn, the literature by non-Bolivian scholars made only a modest contribution to this generally unsatisfactory situation. Frequently oriented toward bilateral relations or specific events or policy issues, most of these studies addressed topics like the War of the Pacific (Farcau 2000; Sater 2007), United States diplomatic and commercial relations with Bolivia (Lehman 1999; Dorn 2011; Siekmeier 2011; Field 2014), the seaport issue (Glassner 1964; St John 1977, 1992b, 2001; Shumavon 1981), or the drug war (Ledebur 2002; Ledebur and Walsh 2009).

As the scope of Bolivian foreign policy broadened in the second half of the twentieth century, Bolivian scholars increased the range and depth of their study of external affairs but generally continued to concentrate on familiar issues and concerns, a focus which amplified ongoing problems of direction and balance. In particular, studies often overstated the importance of external determinants – actors and forces beyond the territorial boundaries of Bolivia which influenced the foreign policy process – and understated the impact of internal determinants, similar actors or forces within the nation. This tendency was especially prevalent among Bolivia scholars but also gained some acceptance among European and North American academics. Like most small to mid-sized states, external influences have long been important to Bolivia because its domestic structures often have proved sensitive to actions taken by outside centers of decision-making authority; however, in-depth analysis should not ignore or disparage the equal or greater influence of internal forces. In Bolivia, the latter became increasingly numerous and complex as the twentieth century progressed, and played a correspondingly larger role in the determination and execution of its foreign policy. In recent years, high quality publications on Bolivian foreign policy have proliferated, but many remain focused on the maritime issue (Guzmán Escobari 2015a; Agramont and Peres-Cajías 2016; Mesa Gisbert 2016).

Given the above state of affairs, the author has pursued what many readers will consider to be a revisionist approach to the study of Bolivian foreign policy. Government interactions with a variety of nongovernmental bodies have become increasingly important in the twentieth century; therefore, the subject of foreign policy can no longer be confined to the study of intergovernmental relations. On the contrary, a thorough study of Bolivian foreign policy necessitates the analysis and assessment of the total range of internal and external forces that have influenced its scope and direction. Although this approach does not exclude boundary disputes and bilateral relations, it embraces the impact of foreign capital and multinational companies as well as the effects of domestic entrepreneurs, political parties, labor unions, and social movements. Therefore, the ensuing study analyzes both the internal and external determinants of Bolivian foreign policy, the substantive content of individual foreign policies, and the subsequent consequences of foreign policy behavior.

In particular, the author has tried to assess the overlap or linkage that has often occurred between foreign and domestic determinants when the two types of variables combined to influence foreign policy. He also has endeavored to place Bolivian foreign policy in the context of events in the outside world, especially its relationship to United States foreign and domestic policy. Although this has seldom been done, it is an essential aspect of a deeper understanding of Bolivian external affairs. It is also important to recognize fully the freedom of choice often open to Bolivian decision-makers on specific foreign policy issues. The failure to do so has produced distorted analyses which overemphasize the limited policy alternatives faced by Bolivians rather than to recognize and explore the wider options actually available. In particular, the occasional claim that the Bolivian ruling class was often only a shadow of the US government and North American investors seems exaggerated. On the contrary, there is limited evidence to suggest that external powers or forces dictated major policy decisions for any prolonged period. Such assertions appear to be mostly an attempt to lighten whatever responsibility the native ruling class may have had for the country's present state of affairs.

From the opposite angle, foreign policy has occasionally been used by Bolivian decision-makers to advance domestic political goals. In common with their counterparts in other small to medium-sized developing states, Bolivian decision-makers have generally viewed domestic well-being as the central policy issue; consequently, attempts to influence external events have often been shaped by domestic issues, problems, and concerns. Lacking popular support, opportunistic politicians have emphasized foreign policy issues to direct attention away from internal political crises. Political advantage also has been sought and gained by both government and opposition leaders who underscored issues like the territorial disputes, external intervention, or imperialism by foreign entrepreneurs. The nationalization or expropriation of foreign enterprises also has been designed not only to further domestic economic development but to gain popular political support. Because of Bolivia's limited resources, questions of internal economic growth and development have long had far more salience for Bolivians than the latest round in the Cold War. Finally, Bolivian foreign policy has been intimately connected with domestic policy and ideologies, explicit or implicit that determined internal policy.

International economics and national economic development have often represented the clearest nexus between the foreign and domestic policies of Bolivia. For that reason, the author has spent a substantial amount of time and effort analyzing the development of Bolivian financial and economic policies since independence. As will become clear, domestic and international economic and financial policies have often played a central role in the formulation and execution of Bolivian foreign policy. Post-independence policy makers debated the relative merits of mercantilist policies which sought to protect home industries and markets vis-à-vis free trade policies and international investment. In the process, the Age of Caudillos proved to be "the great age of expansion of the Bolivian economy" (Klein 2011, 123). In the run up to the War of the Pacific, domestic and foreign economic interests were at the center of Bolivian policy in what was essentially a contest over who would control and develop the natural resources in the Atacama Desert. Thereafter, economic and financial policy frequently exerted a strong if not dominant influence on Bolivian foreign policy throughout the twentieth and twenty-first centuries. The successful pursuit of Bolivia's policy objectives, either foreign or domestic, has often been the consequence of the more or less efficient utilization of the state's productive economic resources. The crucial importance of this variable is only now being acknowledged by many of the scholars who devote themselves to Bolivian affairs.

Another theme of the following chapters is the degree to which the conflicting demands of independence and interdependence, as determined by a constellation of internal and external forces, have determined the content and direction of Bolivian foreign policy. Systematic analysis will reveal the full extent to which the foreign policy of Bolivia has been distinguished by a strong linkage between external and internal concerns, with both domestic objectives and domestic political considerations strongly influencing, if not actually dictating, many aspects of the nation's international posture. Because violence is integral to the Bolivian political system, internal conflict in particular has frequently disrupted external policy with the latter often a reflection of the former. Other factors such as the size and location of Bolivia, the export-led nature of its economy, and the socioeconomic and political relationships which developed with regional and extra-regional powers also have strongly influenced its foreign affairs.

# 2  Setting the Stage, 1809–41

Governed from Lima, the Viceroyalty of Peru was a Spanish colonial administrative district created in 1542 and originally containing most of Spanish-ruled South America. The Audiencia of Charcas, decreed in 1559 and later known as Upper Peru, was an administrative division under the Viceroyalty of Peru which expanded over time to become the territorial basis of nineteenth century Bolivia (Abecia 1986, I, 81–106; Cajías 1975, 12–15). As part of an ongoing program of sweeping administrative and economic reform, the Spanish Crown in 1717 created the Viceroyalty of New Granada from the northern territories of the Viceroyalty of Peru, and in 1776, it created the Viceroyalty of Río de la Plata from its southern territories. The creation of the Viceroyalty of Río de la Plata, which included the Audiencia of Charcas, separated Upper Peru, location of rich silver mines, from the Viceroyalty of Peru and shifted the lucrative mining trade to Buenos Aires (Mesa and Gisbert 2001, 265–7, 281–3, 292–3). The economic and political competition between Buenos Aires and Lima which arose from the creation of the Viceroyalty of Río de la Plata dominated events in Upper Peru in the decades before Bolivia achieved independence in 1825, and ambitions and rivalries in Argentina, Chile, and Peru influenced events in Bolivia for years after independence.

## Creation of the Republic

In late 1806, Napoleon Bonaparte's armies invaded Spain, leading in March 1808 to the abdication of King Charles IV in favor of his son, Ferdinand VII. In May 1808, the residents of Madrid rose up against the French-controlled Spanish government, establishing a formal resistance structure which proclaimed itself the legitimate government of the Bourbon dynasty. Controlling parts of southern Spain, the rebel regime demanded the loyalty of the colonial viceroyalties in the Americas (Gisbert 2001, 310–11). The turmoil in Spain created a climate of indecision in South America which resulted in power struggles between royal officials and local municipal councils and between individual governors and local bishops and judges (Guzmán 1998, 84–5; Klein 2011, 89–92).

Upper Peru was the first region in South America to be severely impacted by events in Spain and the first center of an independence movement. The nineteenth century opened with a prolonged, severe depression in Upper Peru which had a profound impact on both the urban elite and the mining export economy. The prevailing economic uncertainty formed a crucial background to Upper Peru's response to the collapse of the imperial government in Madrid. Tensions within the bureaucracy of the Audiencia of Charcas, together with limited mob activity and a call for independence in Chuquisaca (modern-day Sucre) in late May 1809, were followed by popular unrest in La Paz in July. Events in La Paz led to a proclamation of independence in the name of Ferdinand VII (Escobari 1982, I, 49–54). This was the first declaration of independence by an American colony of Spain, and it initiated the prolonged period of American wars of independence which lasted until 1825. In response to the declaration of independence, the Viceroyalty of Peru dispatched an army from Cuzco and the Viceroyalty of Río de la Plata sent troops from Buenos Aires, and by the beginning of 1811, they had put an end to the revolt (Arguedas 1981, I, 21–70; Klein 2011, 89, 93–6). Upper Peru was the first region to declare independence from Spain, but it was the last to achieve it.

In September 1820, the Argentinian José de San Martín landed troops on the Peruvian coast, entering Lima in July 1821. By 1823, the Venezuelan Antonio José de Sucre, chief lieutenant of the celebrated Venezuelan liberator, Simón Bolívar, and the Bolivian Andrés Santa Cruz also had arrived in Lower Peru, the territorial basis for nineteenth century Peru. At this point, General Santa Cruz convinced the other rebel leaders that a major armed force could take Upper Peru (Klein 2011, 97). After he had occupied his native city of La Paz in August 1823, Santa Cruz defeated royalist forces sent to oppose him at the battle of Zepita. Meanwhile, rebel forces under the command of the guerrilla General José Miguel Lanza seized Cochabamba. When the liberation of Upper Peru seemed finally at hand, developments in Lower Peru left Santa Cruz's lines of communications dangerously exposed, and he was forced to evacuate La Paz, enabling the royalists to reestablish control over the entire region (Arnade 1957, 109–11; Abecia 1986, I, 251–3). The retreat of Santa Cruz and the subsequent defeat of Lanza on the plains of Falsuri left the royalists in undisputed control of Upper Peru until Sucre in early December 1824 destroyed the Spanish armies at the battle of Ayacucho (Arguedas 1981, 183–6). The battle of Ayacucho ended Spanish power on the continent after 16 years of bitter civil war, considerable loss of life, and severe socioeconomic dislocation (Arze 1991, 151–9).

In late 1824, Simón Bolívar directed Antonio José de Sucre to proceed to Upper Peru and subdue any pockets of royalist resistance. Sucre's advance became a triumphal march through the Andean *altiplano*, and when he reached La Paz, he issued a decree calling upon the provinces to elect a council of delegates to decide the region's future. Given the strong likelihood that Upper Peru would vote for independence, Sucre's February 1825 decree, which unequivocally stated the right of the region to self-determination, clearly violated the widely accepted principle of *uti possidetis de jure de 1810* (Salazar 2000, 485–8; Andaluz 2002, 41–7). In a letter later in the month, Bolívar admonished Sucre for exceeding his authority. Upper Peru was a dependency of the former Viceroyalty of Río de la Plata; consequently, its independence depended on the negotiation of a treaty between the parties concerned (Fifer 1972, 14–15). Three months later, as the provinces of Upper Peru elected delegates, it was clear that only independence would satisfy the most determined group of Upper Peruvians (Escobari 1982, I, 78; Roca 2008. 71–2). In the interim, Sucre set about the remainder of his official task, defeating the last remnants of royalist resistance at the battle of Tumusla on 1 April 1825.

The liberation of Upper Peru did not immediately resolve the issue of the ultimate fate of the region. Initially, the mere thought that Upper Peru would become an independent state was anathema to Bolívar who hoped to form a continent-wide republic (Querejazu 1979, 11). Fearing the presence of a strong, unified state south of the Confederation of Gran Colombia, Bolívar later changed his mind and moved to create a buffer between Argentina and Peru. His vision of a Federation of the Andes called for Bolivia and Peru to be maintained as separate states with Gran Colombia divided into Colombia and Venezuela to ensure the balance required for harmonious federation (Henderson 2013, 133–5). Not as concerned as Bolívar with continental visions, Sucre was more influenced by an Upper Peruvian elite whose wartime experiences left them hostile to an amalgamation with Argentina. Among this group, there was some sympathy for a union with Peru although the level of that support was limited (Arnade 1957, 191–202). In turn, the Lower Peruvian elite, focused on an uneasy relationship with Bolívar and his Colombian armies, showed little interest in the incorporation of Upper Peru into their national borders. They were more concerned with a definition of the jurisdictions of highland Puno and the Atacama coastal borders, especially Tarapacá. Like Bolívar, the Lower Peruvian elite viewed Upper Peru as a buffer against the aggressiveness of the Río de la Plata regimes, but beyond that, they were mostly indifferent to its fate as long as it did not become part of Argentina (Klein 2011, 98–100).

On 6 August 1825, the Constituent Assembly issued a declaration of independence. Hoping to gain Bolívar's official approval, it named the new republic after him (Salazar 2000, 489–92). Two days after the declaration of independence, Bolívar was welcomed in La Paz where he would serve for five months as the first president of Bolivia. Before departing for Peru, never to return to Bolivia, Bolívar handed the government over to Antonio José de Sucre, his handpicked successor. Sucre ruled Bolivia by fiat until May 1826 when the Constituent Assembly formally elected him president. By this time, Bolívar had accepted the inevitability of Upper Peruvian independence (Guzmán 1998). For the next two and a half years, Sucre ruled Bolivia, struggling to rebuild the country, implement a series of sweeping liberal reforms, and lay the foundations for a successful buffer state. Increasingly unpopular due to his open partiality in appointing foreigners to senior positions, Sucre's attempts to attract British capital to revitalize the silver mines were a total failure, and his tariff reductions resulted in a flood of British and French goods that ruined local artisans (Pike 1977, 95–6; Klein 2011, 100–1, 109–10). Following an assassination attempt and an abortive *golpe de estado* in August 1828, Sucre resigned and returned to his native Caracas.

## Bolivia at Independence

The newly formed Republic of Bolívar, soon renamed the Republic of Bolivia, was a war-weary and economically depressed state which faced economic stagnation for almost half a century. From around 1803 to the late 1840s, Bolivia experienced a progressive decapitalization of its mining industry, a severe crisis in its international economy, and the greatest decline in its urban population since the great depression of the seventeenth century (Millington 1992, 11–18, 46–102; Gisbert 2001, 352–3). Throughout South America, the destruction of the mercantilist colonial customs union that was the Spanish American empire had a profoundly negative impact on the national and international economies of the newly independent republics. The creation of multiple new states led to an era of protectionism in which most of them rushed to set up tariff barriers against each other and the dominant English traders (Gootenberg 1989, 7–8). In Bolivia, independence seriously restricted most of Upper Peru's traditional economic ties with Argentina, Chile, and Peru, pushing the Bolivian economy toward subsistence. The depression that Bolivia experienced in the early nineteenth century left the Bolivian economy in the 1840s more rural-dominated and subsistence-oriented than at any pervious time (Klein 2011, 102–10).

Under the principle of *uti possidetis de jure de 1810*, Bolivia was entitled to the territory formerly known as the Audiencia of Charcas which consisted of an irregularly shaped mass of land approximately 850,000 square miles, twice the size of contemporary Bolivia. Its only outlet to the Pacific Ocean was a narrow corridor in the Atacama Desert inherited from the Intendencia of Potosí. With almost no irrigated settlement and no port of any consequence, this awkward panhandle ran south-westwards to the sea across 300 miles of the most inhospitable part of the Atacama Desert. It was an inauspicious beginning for a fledging republic hoping to develop an overseas trading economy (Guzmán 1998, 147; Fifer 1972, 19, 22; Bustos 2003, 19–29).

In pressing for independence, the Upper Peruvian elite, consciously or unconsciously, discounted the dependence of Upper Peru on Lower Peru and its links with the Pacific coast. The mining centers of the former Viceroyalty of Peru were serviced for the most part by Pacific ports. Despite centuries of reliance upon colonial trade routes, Upper Peruvians largely failed to take into account that the ports upon which Upper Peru had long depended, Arica in particular, did not lie within the Audiencia of Charcas (Cajías 1975, 12–25; Escobari 1982, I, 98). Granted, the political and trade reorganizations imposed

12  *Setting the Stage, 1809–41*

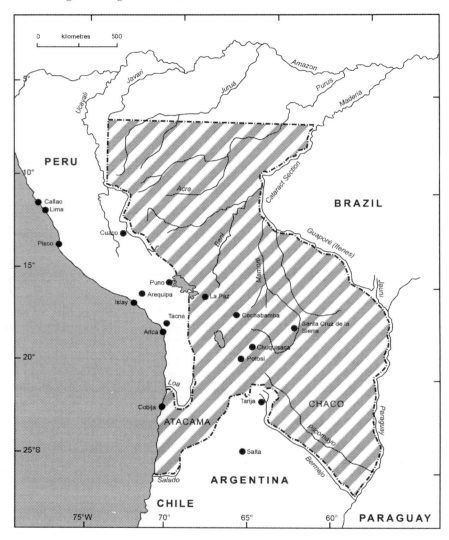

*Figure 2.1* Audiencia of Charcas, 1810
Source: IBRU, Durham University, UK.

by the Spanish crown in the second half of the eighteenth century temporarily obscured the importance of Pacific routes; however, after independence, Bolivia's trade links with Buenos Aires quickly declined while those with Peru, which were never completely severed, regained their importance. Moreover, Sucre and the Bolivian elite believed that Peru would cede the Pacific coast from Arica southward to Bolivia, in effect regularizing the long-established colonial circulation pattern (Gumucio 2005, 62–5; Fifer 1972, 22–5). Such hopeful thinking failed to take into account Bolívar's opposition to any distortion of the former boundaries between Upper Peru and Lower Peru. Determined that Bolivia should not rearrange its borders to suit itself, he insisted that any violation of Lower Peru's rightful territorial claims was out of the question (Novak and Namihas 2013, 60). With Peru unwilling to relinquish its claim to Arica despite continuous Bolivian entreaties, the Republic of Bolivia in 1825–26, while not yet technically landlocked, was immediately confronted with the seaport issue.

In the western sector, Bolivia's frontier with Peru was extensive and varied, beginning with Lake Titicaca, encompassing cordilleran peaks, and descending through the Atacama Desert to the Pacific Ocean. The northern boundary in the Atacama Desert was generally accepted to be the mouth of the Loa River although Peru had laid claim to the coast as far south as Tocopilla. North of the Loa River, the old border between Lower Peru and Upper Peru followed the central chain of peaks and the principal watershed in the Cordillera Occidental before it descended to the Desaguadero River. The general agreement which existed between Bolivia and Peru over the location of the northern boundary never existed between Bolivia and Chile over the southern boundary. Chile did not advocate a specific boundary in the early years of independence, and its 1833 constitution simply stated that Chile's territorial limits stretched from the Atacama Desert to Cape Horn (St John 1977, 42–3). With the most effective Chilean settlement in the well-watered valley of the Copiapó River, Bolivia's southern boundary in the Atacama Desert was indefinite but generally considered to be the Salado River. Bolivia thus claimed a broad desert corridor between the Loa and Salado rivers, approximating 350 miles of the 5,000-mile Pacific coast of South America (Gumucio 2005, 36–8; Dennis 1931, 6–7, 15). With the discovery of rich guano and nitrate deposits in the Atacama, Chilean historians and publicists later argued that obscure colonial documents indicated the entire Atacama Desert was a part of Chile at independence (Barros 1924, 46–54; Abecia 1986, I, 528–31).

Even as Sucre advocated for the acquisition of Arica, Bolívar designated Cobija, a tiny seamen's sanctuary in an especially inhospitable stretch of shoreline, as Bolivia's Pacific port (Cajías 1975, 45–65). By the early 1830s, Cobija had become the point of entry for almost one-third of Bolivia's foreign trade; however, two decades later, a US envoy reported that 90 percent of Bolivian imports were again coming through Peru. The difficult journey from Cobija to the major population centers of Bolivia tripled the price of imported goods. As a result, Arica remained the key port of entry until the second half of the nineteenth century when newly constructed railroads temporarily shifted much of Bolivia's foreign trade to the Puno-Mollendo route, also through Peru (Abecia 1986, I, 535–40; Fifer 1972, 36–44, 48–51; 240–1; Mesa Gisbert 2016, 48–9, 65–6).

In the northern sector, Bolivia's frontier plunged to the north-northeast from the summits of the Andean Cordillera Oriental or Cordillera Real to the rain forests of the interior. Beginning with its border with Peru and

14  Setting the Stage, 1809–41

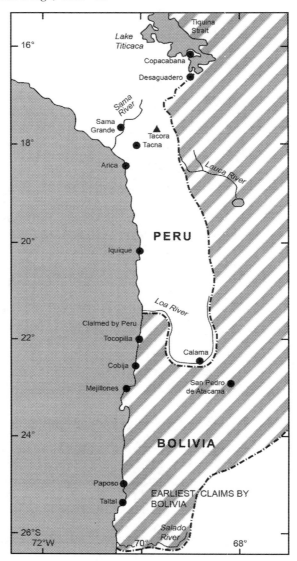

*Figure 2.2* Early Claims in the Atacama Desert
Source: IBRU, Durham University, UK.

continuing for the greater part with its border with Brazil, Bolivia's northern frontier swept over some 1,800 miles of central South America, constituting almost half of its total frontier at independence (Fifer 1972, 92–8). In the eighteenth century, notably in the Treaty of Madrid (1750) and the Treaty of San Ildefonso (1777), Spain and Portugal attempted to define the borders of their respective possessions; however, with the exception of the Peru sector

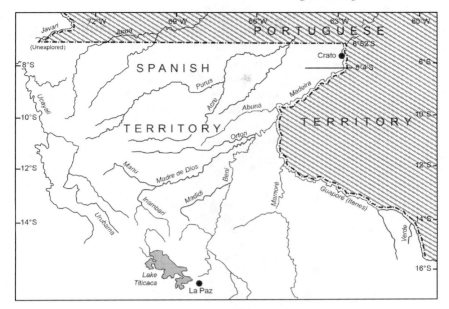

Figure 2.3 Treaty of San Ildefonso, 1777
Source: Nathan Bailey St John.

which was defined by the Audiencia of Charcas and the Intendencia of Puno, the frontier remained mostly a *terra incognita* in 1825 (Novak and Namihas 2013, 26–7). Despite Bolivian efforts to conclude a treaty of limits with Brazil, the region remained largely unexplored for years to come (Vázquez-Machicado 1990, 56–86; Abecia 1986, I, 494–6).

In late 1824, Sebastián Ramos, governor of the Bolivian province of Chiquitos, asked Brazilian authorities in the neighboring province of Mato Grosso to send troops to defend Chiquitos against insurgent forces in Upper Peru. The Ramos initiative advanced to the point that Brazilian troops occupied Chiquitos for a brief period, and in April 1825, Chiquitos and Mato Grosso were joined to form the short-lived United Province of Mato Grosso. In the end, the brief annexation of Chiquitos by monarchist Brazil proved to be a local affair. At the time, it was no threat to the territorial integrity of Bolivia, but it was a harbinger of future conflict on its borderlands (Seckinger 1974; Vázquez-Machicado 1990, 87–94).

In the southern sector, almost one-third of the approximately 850,000 square miles of territory claimed by Bolivia lay within the Paraguay Basin. The Paraguay River marked the boundary between Spanish and Portuguese colonial claims in the region, and subsequently, between those of Bolivia, Brazil, and Paraguay. In the years following independence, little change occurred in this area with one exception. The economic orientation of the province of Tarija had always been toward Potosí and Chuquisaca, but in

February 1807, a royal *cédula* removed Tarija from the Intendencia of Potosí and placed it under the jurisdiction of the Argentine province of Salta. Consequently, it lay outside the limits which Bolivia could inherit under *uti possidetis de jure de 1810*. In July 1825, Tarija sent deputations to President Sucre and the governor of Salta to express the determination of *tarijeños* to be linked to Upper Peru and not Argentina (Roca 1980, 21). When approached in October 1825 for guidance on the issue, Bolívar in line with his strict interpretation of *uti possidentis de jure de 1810* reminded *tarijeños* that Tarija was under the sovereignty of the United Provinces of the Río de la Plata. Later in the same month, Sucre publicly upheld the principle of self-determination for Tarija, and when Argentina failed to take action to retain it, *tarijeños* rose up in August 1826, deposed the governor, and announced their incorporation with Bolivia. Tarija's future was settled in 1837–38 when Bolivia repelled an invading Argentine army (Escobari 1982, II, 267–9; Fifer 1972, 161–70).

## End of the Bolivarian Regime

When Simón Bolívar returned to Colombia in September 1826, he installed Andrés Santa Cruz as president of the council of government and commander of the armed forces of Peru. With vague dreams of rebuilding the old Inca Empire, Santa Cruz favored some form of union between Bolivia and Peru (Crespo 1979, 199–200). In late August 1825, after the delegates assembled in Sucre to decide the fate of Upper Peru had chosen independence, Santa Cruz stated in a letter to a friend that he believed Charcas (Bolivia) should not separate from Peru. In October 1826, he wrote a friend in Chuquisaca that he would only be satisfied if he could reunite Peru and Bolivia because the two regions should never have been separated (St John 1999, 18–19). Before assuming the presidency of Bolivia in May 1829, Santa Cruz founded a pseudomasonic lodge to support his plans to reunite Peru and Bolivia (Arguedas 1981, II, 56–7; Navarro 1968, 58).

The Peruvian council of government in June 1826 appointed Ignacio Ortiz de Zevallos its diplomatic representative to Bolivia and instructed him to pursue the reunification of the two republics. With a merger of the two states viewed as the optimal solution, Ortiz de Zevallos was told that federation was preferable to continued separation. To encourage Bolivian support for its plan, Peru declared its willingness to remove the capital of a united Peru–Bolivia from Lima to another location if the Bolivians insisted. It also indicated that it would consider ceding to Bolivia the ports and territories of Arica and Iquique if necessary to achieve federation (Abecia 1986, I, 307–9; Ortiz de Zevallos 1956, V, xxv–xxix, 3–13; Basadre 1968, I, 130–1).

On 15 November 1826, Ortiz de Zevallos succeeded in concluding treaties of federation and limits with Bolivia. The first treaty established the Federación Boliviana with Simón Bolívar as lifetime president. Once the treaty had been ratified, it called for the new federal government to send ministers to

Bogotá to negotiate Colombian adherence to the pact. In the treaty of limits, Peru ceded Tacna, Arica, and Tarapacá to Bolivia in exchange for the territories of Copacabana on Lake Titicaca and Apolobamba in the northern part of the Department of La Paz. Bolivia also agreed to assume five million pesos of its debt to Peru with the understanding that both states would renounce the right to seek further indemnities (Ortiz de Zevallos 1956, V, 25–38, 75–86; Escobari 1982, I, 100–1). The Bolivian National Assembly approved the treaties with the stipulation that Colombia must become part of the federation, but the Peruvian council of government rejected them outright. Santa Cruz opposed the treaties on the grounds they were vague, subordinated Peru to Colombia, involved inequitable concessions, and dismembered national territory (Abecia 1986, I, 309–16; Crespo 1979, 77–82).

The 1826 treaty of limits marked a decisive moment in Bolivian foreign policy as it proved to be the only time a Peruvian government would agree to give Arica to Bolivia. As Fifer noted, "the failure to incorporate Arica within its own territory at the time of independence must be regarded as Bolivia's greatest single impediment to subsequent progress" (1972, 253). If Arica had become a part of Bolivia at this point, Bolivia would have been better able to resist Chilean expansion in the Atacama Desert, possibly avoiding the War of the Pacific (1879–84). Moreover, it almost certainly would have ended at independence the issue of a sovereign Pacific port which dominated Bolivian foreign policy from that point forward.

When the Constituent Assembly convened in Lima in June 1827 to choose a successor to Bolívar, Santa Cruz hoped it would confirm him in the presidency; instead, the convention elected José de la Mar. The elevation of La Mar marked the beginning of the end of the Bolivarian regime. La Mar was a weak chief executive whose election encouraged regional chieftains with presidential ambitions (Pike 1967, 70–1). Both Agustín Gamarra in Cuzco and Antonio Gutierrez de la Fuente in Arequipa opposed La Mar's election, and they joined Santa Cruz in an informal alliance to bring down the La Mar government and make peace with Gran Colombia. For Santa Cruz, the overthrow of La Mar was a step toward the union of Bolivia and Peru under his leadership (Basadre 1968, I, 275–82; Abecia 1986, I, 322–4). The Gamarra–La Fuente–Santa Cruz alliance was one of convenience as there was nothing to suggest that either Gamarra or La Fuente intended to allow Santa Cruz to take power in Peru or to unite Bolivia and Peru under his leadership. Gamarra and La Fuente were ambitious rivals, and they considered Santa Cruz as the most serious threat to their respective aspirations.

At the beginning of 1827, Bolivia and Peru were divided by ideological, border, and trade disputes. With the Venezuelan Sucre, supported by Colombian and Venezuelan troops, presiding over Bolivia, the La Mar government considered itself flanked by a Colombian satellite which was likely to hurry to Colombia's aid in the event of a war between Peru and Colombia (St John 1992a, 24; Abecia 1986, I, 316–20, 334–8). To counter this threat, Peru in mid-1827 undertook a search for new allies, stifling a recent rapprochement with Brazil and courting Argentina. In February 1828, Javier Mariátegui, the foreign minister of Peru, instructed defeated presidential aspirant Santa Cruz to improve ties with Argentina. At the same time, Santa Cruz was told to resist any Argentine requests for military assistance against Brazil for fear of attracting a powerful enemy (Seckinger 1976, 256–61).

On 1 May 1828, a Peruvian army under the command of General Agustín Gamarra invaded Bolivia. The principal objective of the Peruvian invasion was to eliminate an enemy in the south before Peru had to face a more dangerous one in the north. A secondary objective was to secure the support of the Bolivian armed forces which necessitated the replacement of Sucre with a president more sympathetic to Peru. Ideological differences and personal rivalries, notably the animosity which Gamarra felt for Sucre, contributed to the decision to invade Bolivia (Basadre 1968, I, 302–3; Abecia 1986, I, 342–3). After the Bolivian armed forces offered minimal resistance, Bolivia and Peru signed the Treaty of Piquiza in early July 1828, providing for the departure of Sucre and all foreign-born troops from Bolivia and for the abrogation of the Bolivian constitution (Salazar 2000, 90, 495–8). The Treaty of Piquiza largely ended Bolívar's dream of uniting Bolivia, Colombia, and Peru; nevertheless, Bolivia and Peru would be deeply involved in each other's domestic politics for most of the next decade.

After Santa Cruz assumed the presidency of Bolivia in May 1829, he suggested that Gamarra, elevated to the presidency of Peru in September 1829, send a diplomatic representative to La Paz to discuss outstanding issues between Bolivia and Peru. President Gamarra named Mariano Alejo Álvarez, a personal friend of Santa Cruz, as the Peruvian minister plenipotentiary to Bolivia. Álvarez was instructed to negotiate a defensive alliance and a commercial treaty, obtain guarantees that Bolivia would no longer interfere in the internal affairs of Peru, and discuss with Santa Cruz the question of reunification (Abecia 1986, I, 377–8). At the same time, the Peruvian envoy worked to foment a revolt against Santa Cruz with the goal of making Bolivia an integral part of Peru. When Santa Cruz realized the perfidy of Álvarez, he suspended all communication with the Peruvian legation in La Paz, leading to the recall of Álvarez in August 1830 (Basadre 1968, II, 17–19).

In mid-December 1830, presidents Gamarra and Santa Cruz commenced an inconclusive three-day conference at Desaguadero. The Peruvian delegation opened the meeting by suggesting a bilateral alliance and a commercial treaty which would reduce duties on goods imported from one country to the other. In addition, the Peruvians proposed a treaty of limits in which Peru would cede to Bolivia territory in the province of Tarapacá in return for Copacabana and the Bolivian side of the Desaguadero River. The Bolivian delegation responded that any alliance must include Colombia and any treaty of limits must include the cession of the port of Arica to Bolivia. The Peruvian delegation rejected both Bolivian demands, and the conference ended on a sour note (Abecia 1986, I, 384–6; Basadre 1968, II, 19–20).

In the wake of the inconclusive Desaguadero conference, bilateral talks continued in Arequipa between the newly appointed Bolivian minister to Peru, Casimiro Olañeta, and the Peruvian minister to Bolivia, Manuel Ferreyros y de la Mata. With the Gamarra government insisting on a defensive alliance as an essential condition for additional negotiations, the Olañeta-Ferreyros talks also were unsuccessful (Abecia 1986, I, 386–8; Basadre 1968, II, 20–3). Santa Cruz feared a bilateral pact with Peru would enable Gamarra to dismember Colombia, seize Guayaquil, and annex Bolivia; consequently, the Bolivian president continued to insist on a tripartite agreement that included Colombia. After the Gamarra administration refused to deal with Colombia, Olañeta countered with a proposal centering on the cession of Tacna and Tarapacá to Bolivia. Not surprisingly, Ferreyros refused to consider making Arica a Bolivian port because that would be the end of the Peruvian stranglehold on Bolivian commerce (Novak and Namihas 2013, 60; Escobari 1982, II, 22–3).

President Gamarra's motives at Desaguadero and during the Olañeta-Ferreyros talks remain a subject of debate; however, the most likely explanation is that the Peruvian chief executive was stalling as opposed to pursuing a negotiated solution to his dispute with Santa Cruz. Gamarra likely explored an alliance with Bolivia, together with a reduction in the size of the Bolivian army, as a means to forestall a bilateral alliance between Bolivia and Colombia. In this regard, it is important to remember that Gamarra, when negotiating with Bolivia, was also negotiating with the Peruvian Congress and other political forces in Lima for agreement to invade Bolivia. In the wake of the failed Desaguadero talks, President Gamarra continued to plan for war, at one point directing the head of the Peruvian navy to be prepared to raze the port of Cobija if war broke out. At the end of 1830, President Santa Cruz informed Ecuadorian President Juan José Flores that Peru planned to invade Bolivia, warning that Gamarra intended to annex Guayaquil in addition to Potosí. At the same time, Santa Cruz proposed a defensive alliance between Ecuador and Bolivia, but Flores refused to act (St John 1992a, 27).

In 1831, the Santa Cruz government focused its attention on the absence of an adequate outlet to the sea. Pursuing a two-fold policy, it worked to develop Cobija while continuing its efforts to acquire Arica (Cajías 1975, 51–9, 173; Roca 1980, 85–6). In pursuit of the first goal, Bolivia minimized the tariffs on trade through Cobija while increasing duties on goods entering Bolivia through Peruvian ports (Gootenberg 1989, 31). The Gamarra administration took strong exception to the trade measures of the Santa Cruz government, charging they were designed to harm Peruvian trade with Bolivia and to reduce Peruvian revenues derived from the port of Arica. In response, Peru increased duties on Bolivian goods passing through Peruvian territory (Novak and Namihas 2013, 47). Faced with a widening trade war, both sides tried to resolve the issue in the Olañeta-Ferreyros talks, and when that failed, Bolivia requested Chilean mediation. Welcoming the good offices of Chile, the Peruvian Congress rejected Gamarra's petition for a declaration of war and directed him to begin negotiations with Bolivia (Abecia 1986, I, 394–5).

In August 1831, Bolivia and Peru concluded a preliminary peace treaty at Tiquina which provided for a reduction in their armed forces and their mutual withdrawal from the frontier. This agreement was followed by a definitive treaty of peace and friendship signed at Arequipa on 8 November 1831. The Treaty of Arequipa, in which Bolivia agreed to reduce its army to 1,600 men and Peru to reduce its army to 3,000 men, committed the signatories to a policy of non-intervention, prohibited seditious activities by political exiles residing in either republic, and recognized existing borders until a boundary commission could resolve any differences (Burr 1967, 26–7). A commercial agreement concluded on the same day lowered the duties paid on the goods of one country imported by the other. In addition, it reduced the duties charged by Bolivia on foreign goods imported through Peru to the same level as those charged by Peru on goods imported for its own consumption. Bolivia and Peru asked Chile to guarantee the November 1831 pacts, but the latter declined on the grounds it was unwilling to compromise its neutrality (Abecia 1986, I, 394–8; Basadre 1968, II, 25).

Peru achieved all of its goals in the Treaty of Arequipa and the associated commercial agreement. The latter pact abolished discriminatory tariffs, lowered duties on Peruvian products and on the duties of the products of other nations imported by Bolivia through Peru, and ensured Arica would remain the principal outlet for Bolivian foreign trade. In destroying the tariff wall Santa Cruz had erected to promote Cobija, the commercial treaty undercut Bolivia's only port, perpetuating the Peruvian stranglehold on Bolivian external trade. Understandably, Bolivian public opinion strongly opposed both agreements, and the Bolivian National Assembly later rejected the commercial pact (Kendall 1936, 35). On 17 November 1832, Bolivia and Peru concluded a new treaty in Chuquisaca which gave Bolivia more freedom to regulate its tariffs without menacing its highly vulnerable port at Cobija (Novak and Namihas 2013, 48).

In 1833–34, a rebellion centered in the southern departments of Peru led the military commander of Arequipa to request Bolivian support to put down the revolt, a request repeated by Peruvian President Luís José de Orbegoso one month later. Santa Cruz sent Bolivian troops to the border but refused to intervene unless Peru agreed to enact a federation plan. In the end, Bolivian intervention proved unnecessary as the rebel forces capitulated at Maquinhuayo on 24 April 1834 (Abecia 1986, I, 411–14). In early 1835, Santa Cruz again sought to reunify Bolivia and Peru by creating an independent state in southern Peru which would federate with Bolivia. Eventually, President Orbegoso accepted this approach, agreeing to convoke an Assembly of Southern Departments and then attack the rebellious General Felipe Santiago Salaverry in the north. Once peace was restored, Orbegoso also agreed to convoke an Assembly of Northern Departments and then retire to private life (Kendall 1936, 37–8).

In mid-June 1835, Bolivia and Peru signed the Treaty of La Paz. The agreement called for a Bolivian army to move into Peru to restore order and to protect an Assembly of Southern Departments convened to establish the bases of their reorganization. The Bolivian army was to remain in Peru until the nation was pacified and the northern departments had assembled and determined a course of action (Ortiz de Zevallos 1972, IX, 17–19; Novak and Namihas 2013, 36–7). In mid-June 1835, well before the treaty had been ratified, the Bolivian army crossed the Desaguadero River into Peru. When Santa Cruz and Orbegoso met three weeks later, Orbegoso again promised to convoke the two assemblies and then retire from public life. While Santa Cruz hoped to maintain Gamarra's support, the latter refused to work with Orbegoso, defecting to the rebels in late July 1835. The long-anticipated clash between Santa Cruz and Gamarra came at Yanacocha in August 1835. After a two-hour battle, Santa Cruz emerged victorious, and Gamarra fled to Lima where he was arrested and exiled. In February 1836, Santa Cruz and Salaverry clashed in a pitched battle at Socabaya, a few miles south of Arequipa. Once again, Santa Cruz emerged victorious. With the obstacles and opponents blocking his unionist dreams eliminated, Santa Cruz was now master of Peru (Abecia 1986, I, 415–18; Cayoja 1998, 36–40).

## Peru–Bolivia Confederation

As provided for in the Treaty of La Paz, delegates from the southern Peruvian departments of Arequipa, Ayacucho, Cuzco, and Puno assembled in Sicuani on 16 March 1836. On the next day, the newly formed Assembly of Southern Departments proclaimed their independence from Peru and established the state of South Peru with Santa Cruz as its supreme protector. The delegates further declared their intention to unite with Bolivia and a state to be created in northern Peru to form a three-member confederation whose bases would be drawn up in a joint congress named by the three states. Having approved the Treaty of La Paz, the assembly adjourned on 22 March 1836 (Querejazu 1996, 117–18; Basadre 1968, II, 131).

The convening of the Assembly of Northern Departments, scheduled by General Orbegoso for 15 July 1836, was delayed until early August. Resistance to the new order was growing in northern Peru, and *santacrucista* agents needed additional time to solidify public opinion in favor of the confederation. Installed in the village of Huaura on 3 August 1836, the Assembly of Northern Departments followed the Sicuani pattern. Delegates representing the four northern Peruvian departments of Amazonas, Junín, Libertad, and Lima declared independence, created the state of North Peru with Santa Cruz the supreme protector, and empowered a congress of plenipotentiaries to develop the bases for confederation (Crespo 1979, 209; Querejazu 1996, 176–7). In a surprise move, the assembly also elected General Orbegoso president of North Peru, invalidating his spring 1835 pledge to Santa Cruz to retire to private life after convening the northern assembly (Basadre 1968, II, 135–6).

Santa Cruz decreed the establishment of the Peru–Bolivia Confederation on 28 October 1836, and the three member states, North Peru, South Peru, and Bolivia, were asked to name representatives to meet in Tacna on 24 January 1837, to draft a charter of confederation (Salazar 2000, 517–18). The assembly eventually convened in mid-April 1837, and the Treaty of Tacna was signed two weeks later. The treaty created a federal republic consisting of the three nominally sovereign states. Each would have its own government, but all three would be subordinate to a powerful central government. Headed by Santa Cruz, the central government exercised control over the armed forces, foreign affairs, and economic matters of general interest. In turn, the three member states retained control over their internal affairs and were to deal with one another through their respective foreign ministries. Santa Cruz was named provisional supreme protector pending the opening of the first general congress (Abecia 1986, I, 418–19). The Peru–Bolivia Confederation, which bore a remarkable similarity to Bolívar's projected Federation of the Andes, represented the most serious effort at South American regional integration from the collapse of Gran Colombia to the present time.

Santa Cruz's military conquest of Peru left no one in either Bolivia or Peru who could effectively dispute his will; nevertheless, internal opposition to the confederation existed in both countries. Bolivians were concerned about their independence, fearing the confederation would subordinate them to Peru. They also worried that Peru, divided into two states, would receive more economic advantages and exercise a greater moral and physical force in the confederation than Bolivia. Bolivians and Peruvians alike argued that the treaty gave too much power to Santa Cruz and thus was proof of his alleged authoritarianism. Latent regionalism also fueled internal opposition. Residents of Lima and North Peru feared they would lose their hegemony over Peru while the mining-bureaucratic oligarchies of Chuquisaca and South Peru feared they would lose their influence over Bolivia (Crespo 1979, 107–8, 202; Fifer 1972, 8, 10–11). Moreover, a consensus never developed, even among unionists, as to the optimum form the Peru–Bolivia Confederation should take (Guzmán 1998, 150–1; St John 1992a, 32).

Chile led external opposition to the Peru–Bolivia Confederation. In the colonial period, haughty *limeños* looked down on their parochial neighbors to the south, and the colonial economic system concentrated coastal trade on Lima-Callao, discriminating against Chile in favor of Peru. During the wars of independence, Chile sent an army under San Martín to fight for Peru's liberation, and in the minds of Chileans, Peru showed its ingratitude by treating the Chilean troops shabbily and refusing to compensate Chile for their expense. The treaty covering war costs, together with a one million peso Chilean loan to Peru after San Martín's departure, were pigeonholed by successive Peruvian governments, none of which sought to honor the nation's obligations (Encina 1956, 895–900). After independence, Chile attempted to regularize commerce with Peru; however, trade remained a problem after 1830 when Chile failed to negotiate a treaty, together with a loan repayment, which would have rationalized commercial relations with Peru. In the ensuing decade, the trade issue became increasingly important as the Chilean elite sought to replace Lima-Callao with Valparaiso as the major South American port on the Pacific. Chilean officials rightly feared the Peru–Bolivia Confederation could tip the scales in the favor of its northern neighbors, constraining the Chilean economy and permanently eclipsing Valparaiso. The concerns of the Chilean elite were confirmed when Santa Cruz enacted discriminatory tariffs which favored ships rounding Cape Horn, bypassing Valparaiso, and proceeding directly to Lima-Callao (Basadre 1968, II, 143–4; Burr 1967, 25–6, 28–30).

In May 1836, General Orbegoso further irritated Chile when he declared null and void a Chile–Peru commercial treaty celebrated in Santiago in January 1835 and ratified by the Salaverry government in June of that year (Delaney 1962, 231; Burr 1967, 36–7). Two months later, Chilean exiles living in Peru, including former President Ramón Freire, launched an armed expedition against Chile in an attempt to overthrow the government. In response, the Chilean government accused Santa Cruz and Orbegoso of complicity in the abortive *golpe de estado* and broke diplomatic relations (Arguedas 1981, II, 143; Loveman 2001, 112). Earlier, Peru had leased two allegedly deactivated ships to the Chilean exiles, albeit through a third party; consequently, there was little doubt that some elements of the Peruvian government, possibly including Orbegoso, were aware of the plot. That said, the available evidence did not substantiate Chilean accusations, largely rejected by Peruvians, that Santa Cruz was directly involved in the Freire expedition or even knew of it. Nevertheless, the Chilean government considered the Freire conspiracy a harbinger of future Peru–Bolivia involvement in Chilean affairs if it allowed the confederation to be established (Abecia 1986, I, 431–3; Kendall 1936, 42–3).

Determined on a forceful response to the Freire affair, the Chilean warship *Aquiles* entered the port of Callao on 21 August 1836, and seized three Peruvian naval vessels. In an attempt to preserve the peace until he had consolidated the Peru–Bolivia Confederation, Santa Cruz dispatched Casimiro Olañeta to Santiago in search of a diplomatic solution. At the time, Olañeta was en route from Europe so his arrival in Chile was delayed. In turn, the Chilean government sent Mariano Egaña, a member of the Chilean Senate, to Lima (Abecia 1986, I, 437–8, 443–4). Egaña was instructed to negotiate a peace if he could secure agreement on a variety of controversial issues, including satisfaction for the jailing of the Chilean chargé d'affaires during the *Aquiles* incident, recognition of the Peruvian debt to Chile, naval limitations, a reciprocal trade treaty, exemption of Chilean nationals from forced loans and service in the Peruvian army, and most importantly, dissolution of the Peru–Bolivia Confederation. Egaña reached Callao on 30 October 1836 and departed less than two weeks later, concluding further attempts to negotiate with Santa Cruz would be fruitless. Rejecting third-party offers of mediation, the Chilean Congress on 24 December 1836 ratified the government's request for a declaration of war (Encina 1956, 901–3; Burr 1967, 39–41).

The initial stage of the conflict centered on a search for allies. As early as March 1836, Bolivian diplomats reported that official opinion in Argentina opposed Bolivian intervention in Peru, and Santa Cruz's assertions that he desired peace did not reassure Argentina any more than they reassured Chile. Argentina and Chile opened negotiations for an anti-Santa Cruz pact in February 1837, but those talks failed, largely because the parties could not agree on the postwar status of Bolivia. For Chile more so than Argentina, it was important that Bolivia emerge from the war independent and sufficiently strong to constitute a counterpoise to Peru (Burr 1967, 45–7). On the other hand, the failure of the Argentina–Chile talks did not deter Argentine President Juan Manuel de Rosas from his determination to destroy the confederation. In February 1837, President Rosas terminated all communications with the Peru–Bolivia Confederation, and in May 1937, his government declared war (Navarro 1968, 64–6; Parkerson 1979, 223–8).

In the immediate aftermath of Santa Cruz's successful bid for power in Peru, Chile and the Peru–Bolivia Confederation both dispatched envoys to Ecuador in search of an alliance. From the outset, Ecuadorian President Vicente Rocafuerte had maintained a friendly attitude toward the confederation, and in November 1836, he agreed to a treaty of friendship and defensive alliance. This pact was later rejected by the Ecuadorian Congress which also refused an alliance with Chile, preferring to remain neutral in the dispute. In May 1837, the confederation accepted an Ecuadorian offer of mediation; however, after Chile refused the offer, Ecuador returned to its neutral position (Abecia 1986, I, 448–9; Delaney 1962, 233–4).

## Dissolution of the Peru–Bolivia Confederation

With diplomatic efforts to resolve the dispute at a standstill, Chile resorted to military force. In mid-September 1837, a Chilean expeditionary force embarked at Valparaiso under the command of Admiral Manuel Blanco Encalada, a former Chilean president and veteran of the wars of independence (Abecia 1986, I, 450–2). Chile's minimum peace terms continued to be those presented by Egaña in the fall of 1836. In addition, Admiral Blanco and his special negotiator, Antonio José de Irisarri, had instructions to remove Santa Cruz from the presidency of Bolivia. In return for Argentine support, Chile offered to support its claim to Tarija, compensating Bolivia with a port through the Peruvian department of Arequipa (Basadre 1968, II, 150). This was the first time Chile sounded a policy that would recur again and again in Chilean diplomacy, the solution to Bolivian problems was the appropriation of Peruvian territory (Burr 1967, 49–50).

Once the Chilean expeditionary force reached Iquique, it disembarked and marched on Arequipa. Arriving short of supplies and with men and horses exhausted, Admiral Blanco found himself in an untenable position, surrounded by a hostile force growing daily. Fearful a fight would prove disastrous, Blanco concluded a peace treaty with Santa Cruz on 17 November

1837. Given the plight of the Chilean army, the terms of the Treaty of Paucarpata were generous albeit far short of the expectations of the Chilean government. In addition to allowing the expeditionary force safe passage to Chile, the agreement established perpetual peace and friendship between Chile and the Peru–Bolivia Confederation. It also recognized the principle of non-intervention, renounced the use of force, and established trade relations on a most-favored-nation basis pending the negotiation of special commercial treaties. Santa Cruz assumed with interest the Peruvian debt to Chile, and accepting Chilean mediation, he agreed to make peace with Argentina. In turn, Admiral Blanco agreed to return the three Peruvian naval vessels seized in Callao in mid-August, a move which would give the confederation naval superiority (Salazar 2000, 519–22; Pérez del Castillo 1980, 152–6). In signing the peace treaty, Admiral Blanco granted diplomatic recognition to the Peru–Bolivia Confederation, a body whose destruction had been the primary objective of the Chilean intervention.

Pleased with the terms of the Treaty of Paucarpata, Santa Cruz immediately ratified the agreement. He mistakenly believed the treaty would end the quarrel with Chile and allow him to consolidate the Peru–Bolivia Confederation. The Chilean government thought differently. Given its war aims, Chile considered the treaty an unmitigated disaster, and in mid-December 1837, it rejected the agreement, notifying Santa Cruz that a state of war still existed (Arguedas 1981, II, 175–6; Loveman 2001, 113). Instead of being the bloodless victory Santa Cruz desired, the Treaty of Paucarpata marked the beginning of the end for the Peru–Bolivia Confederation.

With the Chilean threat temporarily neutralized, Santa Cruz focused on the southern border of Bolivia where fighting with Argentina had erupted in August 1837. Santa Cruz planned to round out Bolivia's southern border at the expense of Argentina by seizing Humahuaca which lay well within Argentine territory. Following an indecisive engagement on 13 September 1837, the southern front remained relatively quiet until the coming year. In the meantime, Chile made another effort to secure an alliance with Argentina, proposing that Argentina invade Bolivia while Chile invaded Peru. The Argentine government countered with a proposal that both Argentina and Chile invade Bolivia, setting aside the question of Peru (Burr 1967, 52). Unable to reach a compromise, bilateral talks between Argentina and Chile were suspended, leaving Argentina to fight alone. The Argentine threat to the Peru–Bolivia Confederation ended in June 1838 with the defeat of the Argentine army at Montenegro (Basile 1943, II, 146, 164–6, 192–4; Abecia 1986, I, 453–5).

In rejecting the Treaty of Paucarpata, Chile emphasized that it intended to continue the struggle until Santa Cruz and the Peru–Bolivia Confederation were destroyed. In response, Santa Cruz prepared for a second invasion, declaring martial law and increasing the strength of the army to 17,000 men, 7,000 in North Peru, 5,000 in South Peru and northern Bolivia, and 5,000 on the Argentine border. He also declared a blockade of Valparaiso, but this effort was even less effective than an earlier Chilean blockade of Callao, Chorrillos, and Ancón (St John 1992a, 36). As Santa Cruz struggled to improve the effectiveness of his army, he faced growing dissent within the confederation. Opposition to the Treaty of Tacna was widespread in Bolivia, especially in Chuquisaca, and in June 1838, the Bolivian National Assembly agreed to guidelines for a more liberal pact which reduced the powers of the supreme protector. Opposition to the confederation in Peru, particularly in North Peru, also centered on the high degree of centralization called for in the Tacna accords. The continuation of the war and a mounting sense of rivalry with Bolivia added to widespread discontent in Peru (Basadre 1968, II, 155–6, 161–2; Querejazu 1973, 191, 241).

The approach of a second Chilean invasion force off Callao brought matters to a head in Peru. On 30 July 1838, General Orbegoso declared North Peru free and independent albeit still at war with Chile. Orbegoso's concerns centered on Santa Cruz's near-absolute power, alleged Bolivian domination of the confederation, the subjugation of Peru to foreign influence, and the failure to give Peruvians adequate opportunity to voice their opinion of the confederation (Arguedas 1981, II, 184–5; Basadre 1968, II, 156). Given the fact that Orbegoso had been deeply involved in the formation of the Peru–Bolivia Confederation, personal ambition also appeared to have played a part in his eventual rejection of it. Orbegoso appeared willing to support Santa Cruz only until the power of the latter was threatened at which point Orbegoso deserted the supreme protector (Parkerson 1979, 291–307).

With the Peru–Bolivia Confederation in crisis and as many as seven aspirants to the presidency of Peru, the second restoration expedition, commanded by General Manuel Bulnes, arrived off Callao on 6 August 1838. The Chilean expeditionary force, which included a Peruvian complement led by Agustín Gamarra, disembarked at Ancón, north of Lima. When the Chilean force edged closer to Lima, hostilities commenced. After a pitched battle, the Chileans occupied Lima and declared Gamarra the provisional president of Peru, an announcement which generated little popular support (Pérez del Castillo 1980, 157–60; Arguedas 1981, II, 186–8). Because it threatened Valparaiso's commercial hegemony, Gamarra immediately overturned the provisions of the Santa Cruz commercial code which established double duties on foreign goods touching other Pacific ports before arriving at a confederation port. In addition, Gamarra agreed to provision the Chilean expeditionary force and to assume the total cost of the war against Santa Cruz. Gamarra hoped to persuade Orbegoso, besieged in Callao, to unite with the Chilean army against Santa Cruz, but Orbegoso continued to oppose both the Chilean invaders and Santa Cruz, demanding they all withdraw from Peru (Novak and Namihas 2013, 41–2).

With the assistance of Orbegoso, Santa Cruz on 10 November 1838 recaptured Lima where he was greeted with a tumultuous welcome. Thereafter, Santa Cruz and Orbegoso failed to reach agreement on further cooperation, and Orbegoso sailed into exile on 4 December 1838. Once he had reoccupied Lima, Santa Cruz sought a negotiated settlement with Chile even if it meant the dissolution of the Peru–Bolivia Confederation (Novak and Namihas 2013, 42). In mid-November 1838 talks at the Chilean headquarters in Huacho, Santa Cruz authorized the British chargé d'affaires, Belford H. Wilson, to abandon the confederation in order to make peace as long as North Peru and South Peru were not united. Santa Cruz hoped South Peru would remain independent or be annexed by Bolivia. To achieve this result, he wanted the armies of Chile and the Peru–Bolivia Confederation to withdraw from Peru, leaving the governments of North Peru and South Peru, both named by him, to decide the fate of the confederation. In response, the Chilean representative, Mariano Egaña, argued that the Peruvian authorities would not allow freedom of choice, suggesting the Peruvian people instead elect a national congress to decide the future of the federal pact. Egaña also opposed a proposal by Wilson to limit the army and naval forces of Chile and the Peru–Bolivia Confederation, and he rejected a separate Wilson proposal that Chile renounce its right to establish differential tariffs on foreign imports, a measure which could be used to punish both Bolivia and Peru (Basadre 1968, II, 161–5; Burr 1967, 56). Unable to make any progress toward a diplomatic settlement, the negotiators broke off talks, and military operations resumed.

On 20 January 1839, Bulnes and Santa Cruz resolved the issue outside Yungay, a village north of Lima. Santa Cruz was almost victorious in what is widely considered to be one of the bloodiest battles fought on Peruvian soil, but at a crucial moment, a cavalry charge led by Ramón Castilla, a future president of Peru, turned the tide in favor of the expeditionary forces (Novak and Namihas 2013, 42). Santa Cruz was determined to continue the struggle and retired to Lima and then to southern Peru; however, the walls of the Peru–Bolivia Confederation were collapsing around him. A revolt by the Army of the South was followed by pronouncements repudiating the confederation in Chuquisaca, Potosí, La Paz, Oruro, Cochabamba, Santa Cruz, and Tarija. On 18 February 1939, a rebellion broke out in Puno followed by uprisings in Cuzco, Tacna, and elsewhere in southern Peru later in the month. Faced with the obvious, Santa Cruz on 20 February 1839 resigned his authority as supreme protector of the Peru–Bolivia Confederation, and president of Bolivia and dissolved the confederation (Basadre 1968, II, 166–70, 173–6). On 28 February 1839, he sailed into exile, stopping first at the Ecuadorian port of Guayaquil. When Santa Cruz returned to Peru in October 1843, he was detained and later interned in Chile. In October 1845, Bolivia, Chile, and Peru concluded the Treaty of Santiago, a tripartite agreement which granted Santa Cruz a pension and sent him into European exile for a period of no less than six years (Arguedas 1981, II, 194–9, 316–18; Crespo 1979, 356). In 1850, Santa Cruz was appointed minister plenipotentiary to Belgium, France, Great Britain, and the Vatican, occupying that position until 1853 (Querejazu 1973, 341–6).

## Aftermath

On 14 August 1839, Bolivia and Peru concluded a preliminary peace agreement in which Bolivia agreed to compensate Peru for a wide range of alleged offenses and damages incurred after 1835 (Arguedas 1981, II, 224–5). When the Bolivian government rejected the treaty on the grounds its terms were burdensome and unfair, the agreement was renegotiated in April 1840. In the 1840 treaty, Bolivia officially repudiated the Santa Cruz regime and agreed to return all flags and prisoners taken in battle. Both signatories also agreed to limit their armed forces; however, the question of indemnity was left to Colombian arbitration (Basadre 1968, II, 219–21; Novak and Namihas 2013, 44–5, 48–9). The 1840 treaty returned Bolivia–Peru affairs to 1835 with several commercial clauses turning the clock back to 1832.

Agustín Gamarra was proclaimed the president of Peru for a second time in August 1838. With the goal of annexing the department of La Paz if not all of Bolivia to Peru, he sent Juan Bautista Arguedas on a secret mission to Bolivia in July 1840 to secure signatories to a petition in which Bolivian cities would request annexation to Peru (Novak and Namihas 2013, 45). President Gamarra also maintained the Peruvian army on a wartime footing and reminded Congress that Peru had numerous reasons for attacking Bolivia. Intrigue by Santa Cruz combined with a June 1841 revolution in Bolivia to provide Gamarra with a pretext to act. Peru declared war on Bolivia in early July 1841, and the Peruvian army invaded Bolivia in early October, occupying La Paz before the end of the month. After peace negotiations broke down, the two armies clashed at Ingavi on 18 November 1841, and in a short but intense battle, Gamarra was killed and the Peruvian army routed (Abecia 1986, I, 476–80; Basadre 1968, II, 222–7).

Following the battle of Ingavi, a Bolivian force occupied Tacna, and on 22 December 1841, a Bolivian column occupied the port of Arica, marking the first and last time Bolivian forces would occupy Arica. One week later, an army commanded by José Ballivián, who had been proclaimed provisional president of Bolivia on 22 September 1841, crossed the Desaguadero River and marched toward Puno. The Chilean government, alarmed when Gamarra's defeat at Ingavi was followed by a Bolivian invasion of Peru in which Ballivián seemed likely to demand the port of Arica as the price for peace, instructed its chargé d'affaires in Lima to seek a Bolivian withdrawal followed by a peace treaty guaranteeing the *status quo ante bellum* (Abecia 1986, I, 480–1; Novak and Namihas 2013, 46). Around this time, Bolivia offered to buy Arica from Peru and even requested a British guarantee in the event of outside intervention. Bolivian efforts in this regard were frustrated both by Great Britain's refusal to provide any guarantee and Peru's refusal to sell Arica (Querejazu 1973, 275–6; St John 1977, 44–5). After lengthy negotiations, both antagonists accepted Chilean mediation, and a peace treaty was signed at Acora on 7 June 1842 which provided for a Bolivian withdrawal from Peru (Burr 1967, 66–8; Arguedas 1981, II, 287–8). The 1842 treaty did not end Bolivian aspirations for Arica, but it marked the end of any probability that Arica would ever become a Bolivian port.

Outside the Americas, France in 1831 was the first country to recognize the independence of Bolivia (Querejazu 1973, 238–9). In 1834, Bolivia concluded a treaty of friendship, commerce, and navigation with France, and a replacement treaty was negotiated in August 1850. Bolivia did not ratify the 1850 agreement, and an additional treaty was concluded in June 1864. Political turmoil in Bolivia resulted in the 1864 treaty also not being ratified; consequently, Bolivia did not establish a legation in France until after the War of the Pacific. Following the Assembly of Southern Departments in March 1936, Great Britain recognized the Peru–Bolivia Confederation, concluding a treaty of friendship, commerce, and navigation in June of that year. In July 1847, Bolivia and Spain concluded a treaty of peace and friendship in which Spain recognized Bolivian independence; however, a debt clause in the agreement delayed the exchange of treaty ratifications until 1861 (Querejazu 1973, 187, 238–9; Crespo 1979, 128, 137–8; Abecia 1986, I, 420–1, 574–5, 587–8, 593).

On 30 November 1836, the Peru–Bolivia Confederation signed a general convention of peace, friendship, commerce, and navigation with the United States (Abecia 1986, I, 420–1; Crespo 1979, 216). In 1838, the United States recognized the Peru–Bolivia Confederation, 12 years after it had recognized Peru; however, the United States did not recognize Bolivia as a sovereign state until 1848. Moreover, Bolivia was the last country in South America to be visited by a diplomatic or consular agent of the United States. In his 1848 letter of instruction to John Appleton, the first US chargé d'affaires accredited to Bolivia, Secretary of State James Buchanan stated the reason for the delay was not disinterest or ill will but the lack of a seaport which kept Bolivia isolated in the interior of South America. Noting in his instructions to Appleton that Cobija was the only Bolivian port, Secretary Buchanan added that Arica seemed naturally to belong to Bolivia, and he instructed Appleton, should the opportunity arise, to promote the cession of Arica to Bolivia. In May 1858, Bolivia and the United States concluded a treaty of peace, friendship, commerce, and navigation, articles four and eight of which recognized Bolivian sovereignty over the Atacama littoral. The Bolivian National Assembly ratified the treaty in mid-1861 (Lehman 1999, 29, 35–6; Gumucio 2005, 43–5, 72–3; Siekmeier 2011, 13–14).

## End of the Beginning

The Bolivian victory at Ingavi was of considerable long-term significance to the foreign affairs of the new republic. Ending Gamarra's dreams of dismemberment, it confirmed Bolivian independence, defined its northwestern frontier, and relieved Bolivia of the economic obligations to Peru imposed as a result of the fall of the Peru–Bolivia Confederation. After Ingavi, Peru never again involved itself directly in Bolivian politics, and no Bolivian politician ever again sought to become a potential contender in Peruvian politics.

The end of the Santa Cruz era also resulted in Argentina and Chile abandoning their intense involvement in Bolivian affairs, allowing Bolivia to focus on national issues and interests. Finally, it marked the end of Bolivia as a major power of contention in the Southern Hemisphere of Latin America (Klein 2011, 117).

For a decade and a half after independence, the overriding concerns of Bolivian foreign policy were three-fold. The first concern was the future of the newly independent state. Would Bolivia unite with Peru to form a single state, become part of a wider three-state confederation, or remain an independent entity? This question dominated relations with neighboring Chile and Peru and to a lesser extent with Argentina and Ecuador until the end of the 1830s. The Bolivian victory at Ingavi confirmed Bolivian independence, but national security remained an open issue. The second concern was the so-called "Problem of the Pacific." The failure to secure a Pacific port at independence would have enormous consequences for the economic development of the new state. After 1825, successive Bolivian governments tirelessly pursued a sovereign outlet to the Pacific Ocean, a desperate search which continues to the present time. Third, Bolivia at independence inherited often intractable boundary disputes with all of its neighbors; consequently, territorial integrity remained a central concern of Bolivian foreign policy well into the next century. Ostensibly bilateral issues, boundary disputes often assumed multilateral dimensions as Bolivia and its neighbors formed alliances to achieve their foreign policy goals.

# 3 Rivalry on the Pacific Coast, 1841–79

From the 1840s to the 1870s, a succession of military strongmen or *caudillos* fought over who would rule the country. *Caudillismo* was so pervasive that the Bolivian historian, Alcides Arguedas, distinguished between the barbarous *caudillos* (*los caudillos bárbaros*) and the cultured *caudillos* (*los caudillos letrados*) in his five-volume history of post-independence Bolivia (1981). In this period, Bolivian foreign policy was generally the handmaiden of domestic policy, especially fiscal and trade policy. Successive governments debated the relative merits of protectionism versus free trade and the role of foreign investment in economic development. Bolivia suffered a constant deficit in its balance of trade well into the 1850s, and public expenditures, especially military ones, regularly outstripped the resources of the state (Klein 2011, 122–3). In a milieu in which money was always short, the *caudillo* leadership of Bolivia often sacrificed the national interest for personal gain.

## Continental Solidarity

Simón Bolívar was a strong proponent of Pan-Americanism, broadly defined as permanent cooperation among the American states, and he worked hard to implement his dream. In December 1824, Bolívar extended an invitation to virtually every country in Latin American to attend a congress of American states in Panama. The goal of the congress was to create a federation which would reduce discord among its members, defend the independence of Latin America, and counteract the influence of the Holy Alliance. The Panama Congress opened in June 1826 with delegations from Central America, Colombia, Mexico, and Peru in attendance. Bolivia was invited to send delegates, but its two plenipotentiaries failed to arrive. Brazil, Chile, and Argentina declined to attend. The United States also was invited to attend; however, one of its envoys died en route and the other arrived late. Four conventions were concluded, including a treaty of perpetual union, league, and confederation. Colombia was the only state to ratify the conventions, and it did not do so until mid-1827 (Yepes 1955, I, 42–52; Barrenechea y Raygada 1942). The Panama Congress failed to meet its goals; nevertheless, it was noteworthy because it marked the formal beginning of the inter-American movement (Rivera 2014, 34–83).

Facing dual threats to the Americas, Spanish designs on the west coast of South America and the United States incursion into Mexico, a second Latin American conference convened in Lima in December 1847. Official delegations from Bolivia, Colombia, Ecuador, and Peru were in attendance with the US representative, an unofficial observer. The Lima Conference aimed to guarantee the independence and territorial integrity of the participating states, shape them into a league of nations capable of resisting aggression, and codify a uniform body of international law applicable to all states in the hemisphere. The delegates to the Lima Conference concluded four agreements, including a treaty of union and confederation, a treaty of commerce and navigation, a consular convention, and a postal convention (Cuevas 1976, 222–8). In many respects, the provisions of the treaty of union and confederation were similar to those of the Panama Congress. When the conference reconvened in December 1848, the Bolivian delegate proposed to strengthen the treaty of union and confederation by adding a clause allowing the confederacy to intervene in the internal affairs of a member state if a *golpe de estado* was undertaken in that state. The majority of the delegates rejected the Bolivian proposal in part because they viewed any form of intervention as a denial of their sovereignty (Rivera 2014, 101–7). New Granada's ratification of the consular convention marked the only one of the four agreements to be ratified by any government (Barrenechea y Raygada 1947, 27–8).

Bolivia, Chile, Colombia, Guatemala, Peru, and Venezuela attended the Second Lima Conference which opened in the Peruvian capital in November 1864. Before the conference convened, the foreign minister of Bolivia, Mariano Rafael Bustillo Montesinos, circulated a letter in support of political union, citing "the growth in commerce between them as a reason for seeking a new mode of relations" (Rivera 2014, 113–19, quote 116). Chile agreed to attend the Second Lima Conference only after the other conferees agreed not to include its territorial issues with Argentina and Bolivia on the agenda. The issue of European intervention in Latin America, notably Spanish intervention in general and Spain's April 1864 occupation of the Chinchas Islands in particular, was center stage throughout the conference. The Second Lima Conference continued into March 1865 but failed to conclude any agreements regarding foreign intervention. It did draft a treaty of political union, but it was not implemented (Abecia 1986, I, 594–5).

## Age of Caudillos

Following the overthrow of President Santa Cruz, the administration of General José Ballivián (1841–47) ruled for six years, initiating the so-called Age of Caudillos, an era of repeated military *golpes de estado* and illegal successions which endured until the last quarter of the nineteenth century

(Klein 1969, 11). President Ballivián advocated constitutional reform and increased civilian participation in national life, and his government focused on economic development and territorial exploration in what proved to be the final stable government in a prolonged period of mounting socioeconomic and political unrest (Morales 2010, 58–9). One of Ballivián's most controversial policies was his encouragement of free trade, reversing the protectionist policies of Santa Cruz (Pike 1977, 97–8). When a revolt forced Ballivián to resign, General Manuel Isidoro Belzu (1848–55) seized the presidency in December 1848. The ouster of President Ballivián ended the era designated by Arguedas as the cultured *caudillos* and began the period known as the barbarous *caudillos* (Pérez del Castillo 1980, 203). Known as Tata (Father) Belzu by the indigenous masses, President Belzu was a larger-than-life *caudillo* who faced some 40 revolts in almost seven years in office. The populist policies of the Belzu government favored the oppressed masses and included mercantilist economic policies designed to protect home markets and industries (Querejazu 1973, 335–6; Mesa and Mesa Gisbert 2001, 396–405).

Following the short-lived presidency of General Jorge Córdova (1855–57), José María Linares (1857–61) interrupted the pattern of *caudillo* rule to become the first civilian president of Bolivia. The Linares government upended the economic policies of the Belzu administration in a victory for advocates of free trade and foreign investment (Guzmán 1998, 137–9; Pike 1977, 101–2). President Linares made the mining industry a central focus of his government, but he also pursued sweeping fiscal, administrative, and judicial reforms, catering to foreign capitalists interested in investing in Bolivia. In 1857, the first nitrate deposits were discovered in Mejillones, an isolated and desolate spot in the Atacama Desert. Chilean capitalists and workers had been active in the Bolivian littoral since the 1840s when large deposits of guano, the ossified droppings of sea birds, were discovered. The unearthing of substantial nitrate deposits increased the activity of Chilean and allied British interests to the point that they soon established de facto control over the area (Guzmán Escobari 2015b, 24–5, footnote 11). Faced with incessant plotting, Linares established a formal dictatorship in September 1858 which only increased the opposition to his government (Klein 2011, 128–30, 140; Abecia 1986, I, 566).

Eventually, President Linares was ousted by the minister of war, General José María Achá, who became president in 1861. The Achá administration (1861–64), which continued many of the domestic policies of its predecessor, was unique in that it was the most violent of nineteenth century Bolivian governments in terms of its repression of the opposition (Morales 2010, 64). In foreign affairs, the Achá government also was noteworthy in that Bolivia moved closer to war with Chile in this period. With Chilean and allied British interests increasingly aggressive in their pursuit of the guano and nitrate deposits along the Bolivian coast, Chile extended its territorial claims northward to include Mejillones (Dennis 1931, 40–1). As tensions escalated, the

Bolivian National Assembly in 1863 granted the Achá administration discretionary powers to declare war; nevertheless, President Achá was unable to mount an effective defense against Chilean incursions into the area (Querejazu 1979, 36–9; Klein 2011, 130–2).

General Mariano Melgarejo (1864–70) seized power in December 1864, initiating one of the longest and most controversial dictatorships in South American history (Gómez 1980, 42–7; Henderson 2013, 148–50). Renowned for selling the most lucrative national resources to the highest bidder, the Melgarejo government in 1866 signed the Treaty of Mutual Benefits which set the boundary with Chile at latitude 24° south, hastening the War of the Pacific (Abecia 1986, I, 628–32). The following year, President Melgarejo ceded much of the rich Matto Grosso to Brazil (Gómez 1980, 101–30). After it overthrew the Melgarejo government, the regime of General Agustín Morales (1870–72) attempted to reset some of the more disastrous agreements concluded by its predecessor. Unfortunately, President Morales promised to be as unpredictable and authoritarian as his predecessor, and his assassination in November 1872 likely prevented another despotic ruler from consolidating his grip on power (Morales 2010, 68–9).

The civilian governments of Tomás Frías Ametller (1872–73, 1874–76), which bracketed the short regime of Adolfo Ballivián (1873–74), hoped to overcome military rivalries and resolve the looming crisis with Chile. Unfortunately, the Frías governments were largely impotent in the face of a hawkish army and a popular mood increasingly restive with past agreements (Morales 2010, 70). In May 1876, the minister of defense, General Hilarión Daza, deposed President Frías to become the last *caudillo* to rule Bolivia before the War of the Pacific. In 1878, the Daza government (1876–79) violated the 1874 Treaty of Sucre which had exempted Chilean firms operating in Bolivian territory from any new taxes for 25 years. Through his support for the imposition of a ten centavos per quintal (hundredweight) tax on nitrate exports by the Antofagasta Nitrate and Railroad Company, President Daza provided Chile and its allied foreign capitalists with a pretext for war (Mesa and Mesa Gisbert 2001, 440–5; Klein 2011, 139–42).

**Andean Rivalries**

When Bolivia and Peru concluded the Treaty of Acora in June 1842, there remained in place a February 1842 Bolivian decree which put a 20 percent duty on Peruvian agricultural and manufactured goods entering Bolivia and a duty of at least 25 percent on alcoholic beverages. When Bolivia in 1844 increased its duties on Peruvian goods, Peru responded, establishing new duties on Bolivian imports. At the same time, it signaled a willingness to compromise on the issue. A clause in the Peruvian decree indicated Peru was willing to rebate Peruvian duties to the same level agreed to by Bolivia (Garibaldi 2003, 156–7; Basadre 1968, II, 245). After 1844, political intrigue and mercantile conflict combined to keep tensions high, and by 1847, Bolivia and Peru were mobilizing troops and moving them toward their common border (Novak and Namihas 2013, 49). Armed conflict was averted only after Bolivia, faced with popular opposition to war and a National Assembly which refused to authorize military action, proposed a new commercial treaty (Arguedas 1981, II, 322–3).

In November 1847, representatives of Bolivia and Peru met in Arequipa and concluded a comprehensive treaty of peace and commerce, generally known as the Treaty of Arequipa. In the agreement, the signatories agreed to arbitrate the Bolivian debt to Peru and to form a commission to fix their territorial limits on the basis of natural frontiers (Novak and Namihas 2013, 31, 50; Arguedas 1981, II, 327–9). In addition, Bolivia agreed to stop the flow into southern Peru of so-called weak money, money whose silver content was less than its face value. Both parties also agreed to lower or eliminate duties on goods imported from the other party as well as goods transshipped to third parties (Garibaldi 2003, 158–60). After the Treaty of Arequipa had been amended by both signatories, a second treaty was negotiated in Sucre in October 1848. Both the 1847 and 1848 treaties affirmed the right of free transit of Bolivian exports and imports through the Peruvian port of Arica (Gumucio 2005, 71–2; Novak and Namihas 2013, 50–1).

The treaties of Arequipa and Sucre improved mercantile relations between Bolivia and Peru and also led to a number of minor settlements covering commerce and duties in several locations. Unfortunately, these agreements proved to be the last general treaties of peace and commerce to be concluded by the two states for well over a decade. In the interim, Bolivia failed to live up to its treaty obligations in regards to the issuance of weak money. Contraband between Bolivia and Peru also continued to flourish. In December 1850 and again in January 1851, armed Bolivians entered Peru, giving rise to a Peruvian decree demanding indemnification for the damages arising from such incursions (Novak and Namihas 2013, 52; Vargas Ugarte 1962, 141).

When Bolivia failed to honor its commitment to check the flow of weak money into Peru, commercial relations between the two states degenerated into another trade war. After Peru occupied the Bolivian port of Cobija and broke diplomatic relations with Bolivia, war seemed inevitable (Pérez del Castillo 1980, 206–8; Arguedas 1981, III, 207–8). In the end, domestic disturbances in Bolivia and a civil war in Peru combined to prevent an outbreak of hostilities between the two states. In Peru, Domingo Elías, a wealthy landowner, rose in revolt against President José Rufino Echenique at the end of 1853, and former President Castilla joined the rebellion in early 1854. The civil war ended in January 1855 when Echenique was defeated at the battle of La Palma, and Castilla again was named president of Peru (Vargas Ugarte 1962, 152–4; Novak and Namihas 2013, 52–3).

At this point, bilateral relations between Bolivia and Peru looked set to improve; however, long-standing, deep-seated problems frustrated any real progress. In September 1855, President Castilla decreed that commerce between Bolivia and Peru, together with the passage of Bolivian goods through Peruvian territory, would now be regulated by a May 1852 statute approved by the Echenique administration. In October 1855, President Córdova responded positively to the decree, according special facilities to Peruvian commerce (Basadre 1968, IV, 283–4). Nevertheless, commercial issues and the issuance of underweight currency continued to hamstring bilateral relations, especially after President Linares abolished former President Belzu's protectionist policies in a move to increase foreign investment (Dunkerley 2007, 263–4). The departure from Tacna of an abortive expedition of Bolivian dissidents, backed by Peruvian money and recruits and intent on overthrowing the Linares regime, complicated the situation. President Linares lodged sharp protests with the Castilla government in Lima which in turn complained about the safe haven Bolivia offered former Peruvian President Echenique (Abecia 1986, I, 569–70). On 21 November 1860, the Peruvian Congress authorized war with Bolivia; however, armed conflict was averted largely because President Linares required the full services of the Bolivian armed forces to suppress internal insurrections (Pike 1977, 125–6).

With the installation of the Achá government, bilateral relations with Peru looked set to improve, but a series of border episodes once again inflamed old passions (Garibaldi 2003, 165–6). Eventually, Bolivia and Peru in November 1863 concluded a treaty of limits, peace, and friendship, an agreement whose significance was best measured by the 25 years of bad relations which preceded it. In the agreement, Bolivia once more agreed to halt the issuance of weak money, and Peru reaffirmed the right of free transit for Bolivian goods through the port of Arica. Both states also agreed to monetary policies based on similar principles and conditions. The 1863 pact was followed in May 1864 by a postal convention and in September 1864 by a commerce and customs agreement which sought to reduce a burgeoning trade in contraband by expanding commerce between Bolivia and Peru. In return for tariff concessions, Peru agreed in the September 1864 treaty to credit Bolivia annually with a fixed amount of pesos. Over the next decade, Bolivia and Peru concluded at least six additional agreements in an ongoing effort to regularize their commercial relations (Novak and Namihas 2013, 53–6).

As Peru and Bolivia worked to resolve a variety of long-standing issues, newly found riches along the Pacific coast of South America added a strong economic dimension to the territorial dispute in the Atacama Desert. Well before the Spanish conquest, Peruvians had begun exploiting in a modest way the coastal deposits of guano, but it was not until the 1830s that studies in Europe suggested the value of the substance as a commercial fertilizer (Pérez del Castillo 1980, 186–7; Dennis 1931, 27–8). Previously, Chile had not seriously challenged Bolivian claims to a boundary as far south as the Salado River, but with the discovery of the commercial value of the guano deposits, Chilean indifference to its northern boundary ended (Espinosa 1965, 29–30, 35–6). Following the Peruvian discovery of particularly rich deposits of guano in 1842, Chile quickly dispatched an exploratory survey team into the Atacama Desert as far north as Mejillones near the 23rd parallel (Barros 1924, 50–1). When the results of the survey proved highly promising, Chilean President

Manuel Bulnes Prieto declared the northern boundary of Chile was now latitude 23° south, adding that all guano deposits south of that parallel were Chilean and exploitable only under concession (Encina 1963, 31). In support of its claim to latitude 23° south, Chile argued that a desert was like a river between two countries and thus should be divided along their median line (Vaca 1879, 21). Bolivia protested the expanded territorial pretensions of Chile, demanding the latter continue to recognize Bolivian sovereignty north of the Salado River along latitude 26° south (Dennis 1931, 30–2; Fifer 1972, 53).

Over the next two decades, Bolivia sent no less than five separate diplomatic missions to Chile in an abortive effort to resolve the controversy in the Atacama Desert (Fifer 1972, 53–5). At the same time, Bolivia continued its efforts to secure a Pacific port, notably the port of Arica. In 1842, Casimiro Olañeta was accredited as Bolivian minister to Chile with instructions to secure a Peruvian port for Bolivia, either Pisagua or another port south of Camarones. Instead, Olañeta's unsuccessful mission focused on Arica as the optimum port for Bolivia (Abecia 1986, I, 498–500, 527–8). In October 1845, the Bolivian ambassador to Chile, Joaquín Aguirre, presented the Chilean foreign minister, Manuel Montt, with a memorandum detailing Bolivian grievances with Peru, outlining the Bolivian case for a Pacific port, and requesting Chilean assistance in securing the cession of Tacna and Arica to Bolivia (Encina 1963, 173–4). At the same time, Bolivian scholars engaged in exhaustive archival research in an effort to prove the Bolivian legal case under the doctrine of *uti possidetis de jure de 1810* was more conclusive that the growing de facto case of Chile. In 1861, the Bolivian authorities in Mejillones were replaced by Chilean officials, the permission of the Chilean government to exploit the guano deposits was made mandatory, and a Chilean warship was stationed in Mejillones Bay to protect the loading of Chilean vessels bound for Europe (Mesa and Mesa Gisbert 2001, 452–3; Sater 2007, 17). When a flurry of negotiations and mediation efforts proved unproductive, war appeared a distinct possibility until the Spanish intervention in 1866 distracted the attention of first Peru and later Bolivia and Chile (Burr 1967, 89–90).

## Spanish Intervention

In the four decades after independence, Spanish involvement in Latin American politics, often in concert with other European powers, led to a growing tide of anti-Spanish sentiment throughout the region. In 1864, Eusebio de Salazar y Mazarredo, a former member of the Spanish Chamber of Deputies, was appointed resident minister to Bolivia and special commissioner to Peru and instructed to obtain the satisfaction due Spain for Peru's alleged mistreatment of Spanish nationals (St John 1999, 65). When Peru refused to accept Salazar y Mazarredo in the capacity of special commissioner, a title reminiscent of the arbitrary powers of the royal commissioners during the colonial era, Spain responded by occupying the Chincha Islands, guano-rich islands off the coast of Peru which were an irreplaceable source of government income, and seizing the Peruvian naval vessel *Iquique* (Davis 1950, 51–4) Various negotiations led to the establishment of a tenuous peace; however, a Spanish squadron remained in the Pacific region, and its presence afforded new opportunities for conflict. In May 1865, Spain felt compelled to chastise Chile for alleged hostile acts, including public insults to the Spanish flag, leading Chile to declare war on Spain in September 1865 (Burr 1967, 97–8).

Having declared war on Spain, Chile moved quickly to bring its Andean neighbors into the fray. After Chile concluded a treaty of offensive and defensive alliance with Peru in late 1865, Ecuador adhered to the agreement in January 1866, and Bolivia joined later in the year to form the Quadruple Alliance (Espinosa 1965, 92–3; Basadre 1968, V, 311). Two years earlier, Bolivia had broken diplomatic relations with Chile over the latter's aggressive policies in the Atacama Desert; therefore, Bolivia actually concluded separate treaties with Chile in March 1866 and with Peru in June 1866 (Salazar 2000, 525–7; Querejazu 1979, 36–9). The addition of Bolivia to the alliance did not increase allied naval strength opposed to the Spanish squadron, but it did close the Bolivian port of Cobija to Spain.

At the beginning of May 1866, the Spanish squadron bombarded the Peruvian port of Callao, causing considerable damage. Prepared for the attack, Peruvian guns succeeded in inflicting some damage on the Spanish fleet albeit not as much as Peruvian publicists later claimed. At the conclusion of the bombardment, the Spain squadron declared victory and sailed for Spain. The battle proved a major political victory for the Peruvian government as it solidified the Peruvian people in their opposition to Spanish intervention and united them against any form of compromise with Spain. Elsewhere in South America, the Battle of Callao was considered a great victory for Peru and the Quadruple Alliance. Extensive celebrations were the order of the day in La Paz, Santiago, and Quito, and the Melgarejo government declared the second of May a permanent Bolivian holiday (Basadre 1968, V, 323–36; Davis 1950, 314–21).

In the second half of 1866, Great Britain and France were persistent in their efforts to persuade the belligerents to accept their good offices. In the case of Spain, this proved fairly easy, but when it came to the four allies, mediation was more complicated. Negotiations were conducted simultaneously in Lima and Santiago with Bolivia and Ecuador disposed to go along with whatever position Chile and Peru took. Frustrated with the lack of progress, Great Britain and France eventually abandoned their mediation efforts at which point the United States offered its friendly offices to resolve the dispute. The United States proposed a peace conference in Washington in April 1867; however, another four years passed before the conference took place (Abecia 1986, I, 678–9). After the belligerents agreed to an armistice in April 1871, Spain negotiated separate pacts with each of them, concluding treaties with Peru in April 1879, Bolivia in August 1879, Chile in June 1883, and Ecuador in January 1885 (Davis 1950, 330–2).

Seizing on a moment of anti-Spanish solidarity, Bolivia and Chile signed a treaty in August 1866 in which both parties renounced some of the territorial

Rivalry on the Pacific Coast, 1841–79   39

*Figure 3.1* Treaty of Mutual Benefits, 1866
Source: IBRU, Durham University, UK.

and mining rights they claimed in the Atacama Desert (Salazar 2000, 529–32; Ríos 1963, 205–8). Referred to as the Treaty of Mutual Benefits, the benefits in the agreement were anything but mutual as the treaty was a generous settlement for Chile. The 1866 treaty placed the boundary between Bolivia and Chile at latitude 24° south. In the zone between latitudes 23° and 25° south,

Bolivian and Chilean businesses were assured equal rights, and the signatories agreed to split equally tax revenues realized from the production and sale of mineral resources. In addition, the treaty called for Bolivia to open the bay and port of Mejillones and to establish a customs house there (Vaca 1879, 35–9; Escobari 1982, I, 127–8; Querejazu 1979, 60–5). The establishment of the frontier at 24° south advanced earlier Chilean claims by some three degrees, and the condominium provision was also favorable to Chile. Under the agreement, Bolivia would receive half the tax revenues from minerals exported between latitudes 24° and 25° south and Chile would receive the same consideration from exports between latitudes 23° and 24° south. These terms were advantageous for Chile because the richest mineral deposits were located above latitude 24° south (Abecia 1986, I, 612–32; Espinosa 1965, 96–9). Even more important, the terms of the 1866 treaty encouraged aggressive, efficient Chilean business interests to exploit the region, and they quickly created a mining-industrial complex far superior to anything the Bolivians could have hoped to achieve in the foreseeable future (Burr 1967, 118–19).

During the negotiations for the Treaty of Mutual Benefits, Chile offered to help Bolivia appropriate Peruvian territory from the Loa River to the Morro de Sama, including Iquique, Tarapacá, Tacna, and Arica. In return, Chile expected Bolivia to renounce its claim to the territory between the coastal settlements of Paposo and Mejillones or even as far north as the Loa River. Although Bolivia declined the offer, the terms of the Chilean proposal were significant because they were an accurate reflection of Chilean ambitions in the Atacama Desert. The Chilean proposal marked a resurgence of the old argument that Arica was the natural port for Bolivia, a notion which had surfaced as early as the independence era (Escobari 1982, I, 128–9; Querejazu 1979, 9–12). The Arica-for-Bolivia doctrine would take on a life of its own in the aftermath of the War of the Pacific.

Opponents of the Melgarejo administration and the few Bolivians knowledgeable about the littoral region strongly criticized the 1866 treaty. Earlier Chilean advocacy of an extreme claim to latitude 23° south coupled with its subsequent acceptance of latitude 24° south with an air of compromise smacked of hypocrisy to those Bolivians who believed they were entitled to a border down to latitude 27° south. Moreover, the new agreement allowed Chilean activity as far north as latitude 23° south, and this region soon became the area of primary Chilean interest because the richest guano deposits were located around Mejillones in the zone between latitudes 23° and 24° south (Espinosa 1965, 96–102; Escobari 1982, I, 127–9). Most Bolivian historians reported the 1866 treaty provoked widespread protests in Bolivia, but Querejazu took a contrary view, suggesting most Bolivians greeted it with a sense of relief because they believed the agreement would prevent war with Chile. In support of this argument, he noted that the National Assembly voted unanimously to approve the 1866 treaty (1979, 66).

As the Spanish intervention drew to a close, representatives of Bolivia and Brazil in March 1867 signed a treaty of amity, limits, navigation, commerce, and extradition, known as the Muñoz-Netto convention (Vázquez-Machicado

1990, 250–7). The 1867 agreement accepted the principle of *uti possidetis de jure de 1810* as the basis for the delimitation of post-independence boundaries with effective settlement, *uti possidetis de facto*, regulating the demarcation of the Bolivia–Brazil frontier (Abecia 1986, I, 637–40, 643–5). The boundary outlined in the Muñoz-Netto convention began in the south with the Paraguay River, moving generally north before making an abrupt turn to the west just north of San Matías and later continuing north to the headwaters of the Verde River. The boundary then continued up the Verde River to its junction with the Mamoré River and up the Mamoré to its junction with the Beni River which was the source of the Madeira River. From the source of the Madeira, the east-west boundary initially followed latitude 10° 20' south until the Javary (Yávari) River was reached; however, this straight line was soon replaced by an oblique line from the confluence of the Mamoré and Beni rivers to the unknown source of the Javary River (Salazar 2000, 541–8). Over much of the next 40 years, attempts to locate the source of the Javary River failed; consequently, no official demarcation of the Muñoz-Netto line was possible beyond the erection of boundary monuments at both of its ends (Fifer 1972, 100–2).

Earlier, Peru had made extravagant claims as far east as the Madeira River, and when it learned of the 1867 Bolivia–Brazil agreement, it delivered a strong protest to the Melgarejo government, stating Bolivia was ceding land to Brazil over which Bolivia had no legal title (Fifer 1972, 100–2). Adding it could not allow Bolivia to compromise its territorial rights, the Peruvian foreign minister, José Antonio Barrenechea, insisted on the observance of an 1851 Brazil–Peru treaty as reinforced by a fluvial agreement between the two states in 1858. The Bolivian foreign minister, Mariano Donato Muñoz, replied to the Peruvian protest in February 1868, assuring his Peruvian counterpart that Bolivia would respect Peruvian rights in the region. At the same time, Muñoz reminded Barrenechea that the 1851 treaty stipulated that the left bank of the Javary River was Peruvian and the right bank was Brazilian. In the mind of the Bolivian foreign minister, this feature effectively excluded Peru from any legitimate interest in the territory in question (Abecia 1986, I, 649; Vázquez-Machicado 1990, 272–80).

The Muñoz–Netto convention was heavily criticized in Brazil, primarily because the introduction of the oblique line from the confluence of the Mamoré and Beni rivers to the source of the Javary River left large areas settled by Brazil on the Bolivian side of the border. With Brazil at war with Paraguay at the time, Brazil likely accepted the terms of the convention because it hoped to avoid antagonizing international opinion by driving too hard a bargain with another weak neighbor (Fifer 1972, 101). That said, the Muñoz–Netto convention ceded to Brazil some 58,000 square miles of territory which many Bolivians believed to be part of Bolivia, and for this reason, it was widely criticized in Bolivia (Gómez 1980, 101–30). Bolivian critics charged the Brazilian representative, Felipe López Netto, took advantage of the vanity and ignorance of President Melgarejo to negotiate an agreement which ceded to Brazil territory rightfully Bolivian (Escobari 1982, II, 306–7;

Arguedas 1981, V, 155). Although the National Assembly eventually approved the agreement by a slim majority, the terms of the Muñoz–Netto convention contributed to the downfall of the Melgarejo government (Querejazu 1979, 66).

## Tension along the Pacific Coast

In the wake of the Spanish intervention, the question of Pacific coast hegemony was at the center of renewed competition between Chile and Peru. In both naval power and defensive installations, the end of the Spanish intervention left Peru in a militarily superior position to Chile (Espinosa 1965, 95). At the same time, the war inflicted serious damage on the Peruvian economy; therefore, Peru lacked the economic resources necessary to maintain its temporary military advantage (Basadre 1968, V, 337, 347–8). In this sense, the war clarified the relative military strength of Bolivia and Peru vis-à-vis Chile, highlighting both the weakness of the Bolivian army and the vulnerability of the Peruvian navy. During the war with Spain, Great Britain had impounded two corvettes, the *O'Higgins* and the *Chacabuco*, being built for Chile. When Chile in February 1868 petitioned for their release, Peru protested the sailing of the two vessels on the grounds their liberation violated the spirit of the Quadruple Alliance (Abecia 1986, I, 718–19). After Chile ignored the Peruvian protest, the Peruvian government of José Balta Montero proceeded with a reorganization of the army and created a military college and naval school. The Balta administration also sought to acquire additional warships, but President Balta died before a deal could be consummated (Basadre 1968, VI, 240–2).

With the end of the Spanish intervention, Bolivian relations with Peru also deteriorated. Following six years of harsh, incompetent rule, opposition in Bolivia to President Melgarejo was considerable. In 1870, Bolivian exiles crossed from Peru into Bolivia in an effort to coalesce that opposition and overthrow the government. The response of the Melgarejo administration was both swift and savage, and the resultant campaign of terror in the Bolivia–Peru borderland threatened war with Peru. Tensions only relaxed after Peru concentrated troops along the border, and the Melgarjeo government assured Peru of its pacific intent. In a March 1870 protocol, Bolivia agreed to pay damages to Peruvians living near the border and to return Peruvian nationals sequestered in the Bolivian army (Gómez 1980, 93–100; Novak and Namihas 2013, 65). In July 1870, Bolivia and Peru signed a new treaty of commerce and tariffs which included a most-favored-nation clause and which replaced an earlier agreement concluded in September 1864. The new agreement was approved by the Peruvian Congress in October 1872, but it later lapsed after the Daza government rejected it in October 1876 (Basadre 1968, VI, 242–3).

Around the time of the negotiation of the 1866 treaty, Chilean prospectors discovered rich nitrate deposits in the Atacama Desert near Moreno Bay south of the Mejillones Peninsula and north of the future port of Antofagasta, founded by Bolivia in 1870–71 (Querejazu 1979, 127–9, 135–6). The economic and political ramifications of this new discovery proved more far-reaching than the earlier discovery of the now increasingly depleted guano deposits. The value of the newly discovered nitrate holdings and the silver deposits discovered around Caracoles in 1870 invigorated the nascent resource war in the Atacama Desert and the resultant competition for hegemony on the west coast of South America (Bonilla 1980, 140–3; Galindo 1977, 46). Moreover, Bolivia's claim to a Pacific port became inextricably intertwined in the growing rivalry between Chile and Peru in the region.

Instead of calming the intense rivalry on the Pacific coast, the terms of the 1866 treaty became a source of renewed controversy. The treaty did not specify by name the individual items from which Chile was to derive half the tax revenues under the condominium provision, and the Melgarejo government attempted to restrict their number with predictably acrimonious results. In addition, Bolivia sought to export minerals extracted from the shared zone through the port of Cobija in a related effort to avoid sharing customs receipts. A further controversy developed when Bolivia argued that the highly valuable silver deposit at Caracoles lay outside the zone of condominium (Burr 1967, 118–19; Abecia 1986, I, 686–8). After the newly installed Bolivian government of Agustín Morales approached Chile in early 1871 to renegotiate the objectionable provisions of the 1866 treaty, Bolivia and Chile signed the Lindsay–Corral protocol in December 1872 (Ríos 1963, 209–13). The new agreement granted Chile the right to name customs officials who would cooperate with those of Bolivia in the condominium zone, stipulated that no unilateral changes could be made to tax rates, and affirmed Bolivian acceptance of borax and nitrates as products falling within the provisions of the 1866 treaty (Escobari 1982, I, 129–30; Peñaloza 1984, IV, 145–7). While Chile viewed the 1872 protocol as nothing more than a clarification of the 1866 treaty, Bolivians argued it extended Chilean influence in the littoral, and the National Assembly refused to ratify it (Abecia 1986, I, 684; Mercado 1979, 23–5).

During the Bolivia–Chile talks leading to the Lindsay–Corral protocol, Bolivia initiated discussions with Peru regarding terms for a possible defensive alliance. In early November 1872, a secret session of the National Assembly authorized the Morales government to negotiate and ratify an alliance with Peru without submitting the agreement to the Assembly for approval (Querejazu 1979, 114–16; Abecia 1986, I, 718–21). On 19 November 1872, the Peruvian government agreed to support the Bolivian government in opposing Chilean demands which Peru considered unjust and threatening to Bolivian independence (Phillips 1973, 35–6). Why Peru agreed to an alliance with Bolivia at this time remains unclear, especially a pact not conditioned on Argentine adherence. The Peruvian decision was likely driven, at least in part, by ongoing concerns that Bolivia would ally with Chile at Peru's expense if Peru did not first ally with Bolivia (Bonilla 1980, 153–4; Novak and Namihas 2013, 66–72).

On 6 February 1873, Bolivia and Peru concluded a treaty of defensive alliance which guaranteed their sovereignty, independence, and territorial integrity.

The pact provided for them to ally if a third party attempted to deprive one of them of its territory, form of government, or sovereignty. It also gave the party appealed to as opposed to the party allegedly aggrieved the right to decide if the treaty should be invoked. Moreover, it called for the conciliatory settlement of all disputes, where possible, with arbitration highlighted as an often successful approach. Bolivia and Peru also agreed not to celebrate a treaty of limits or territories without first notifying the other signatory (Lecaros 1983, 17–20; Pinochet de la Barra 2000, 24). An additional article called for the treaty to remain secret as long as the contracting parties, by common accord, agreed its publication was unnecessary (Barros 1924, 28–31).

Widely discussed, the 1873 treaty was poorly understood. Peruvians generally agreed that there was nothing in the agreement which could justifiably alarm a neighboring state (García Salazar 1928, 166–7, 174). Bolivians also argued that it was a purely defensive alliance (Pérez del Castillo 1980, 254–5; Oblitas 2001, 182–4). Chilean politicians and polemists, on the other hand, argued the treaty was really an offensive instrument aimed at Chile (Barros 1924, 26–31, 40–4; Bustos 2003, 39–53; Miguel 2011, 43–4). Efforts on the part of Bolivia and Peru to enlist Argentina as a party to the treaty were soon at the center of the argument over whether it was a defensive or offensive pact. Seeking to take advantage of anti-Chilean sentiment in Argentina which stemmed from its boundary dispute with Chile, the Peruvian minister to Argentina, Manuel Irigoyen, opened negotiations with the Argentine government in early 1973. The Peruvian diplomat hoped to represent both Peru and Bolivia in the talks; however, he never received the necessary authorization from the Frías government. Consequently, the negotiations in Buenos Aires were hamstrung from the start by the ongoing need for Irigoyen to consult with Bolivia (Peñaloza 1984, 152–3). Argentina expressed interest in adhering to the 1873 treaty, but it insisted that Bolivia first settle its boundary dispute with Argentina and also that a Bolivian rupture of relations with Chile not be considered a *casus foederis* for the alliance. Bolivia agreed to the first condition but rejected the second (Burr 1967, 124–6; Novak and Namihas 2013, 71–2).

Peru hoped to secure Argentine adherence to the 1873 treaty before Chile could take delivery of the two ironclads it had on order, warships which threatened to cancel the temporary naval advantage enjoyed by Peru during the Spanish intervention. Recognizing a threat to its naval strategy, Chile ordered the *Almirante Cochrane*, the ironclad nearest completion, to put to sea before it was properly fitted out. At this point, Peru lost any initiative it had enjoyed in the diplomatic arena because Chile was increasingly in possession of the military means necessary to impose its own conditions (Mercado 1979, 28–9, 31–2; Pinochet de la Barra 2000, 24). In the interim, Peru continued its efforts to secure Argentine adherence to the 1873 treaty. The lower house of the Argentine legislature approved the treaty in September 1873, but the upper house delayed approval, pending further study and progress in the resolution of its boundary dispute with Bolivia. At that point, the negotiations in Buenos Aires largely became a holding action, collapsing in the summer of 1874 (Crosby 1949, 24–5; Novak and Namihas 2013, 71–3).

Brazilian concerns complicated the Bolivia–Peru negotiations with Argentina. War between Argentina and Brazil had been narrowly averted as recently as 1872 after Brazil violated the terms of the Triple Alliance, concluding an agreement with Paraguay. Given the tension between Argentina and Brazil, the trilateral negotiations in Buenos Aires in the fall of 1873 naturally raised concerns in Brazil. In October 1873, the Brazilian ministry of foreign affairs asked its representatives in Bolivia, Chile, and Peru to investigate whether Argentina, Bolivia, and Peru might be forming an alliance against Brazil. Argentine negotiations with Bolivia and Peru thus threatened to provide the basis for a new accord between Brazil and Chile, a prospect which worried the government in Buenos Aires. Brazil and Chile failed to conclude a formal entente, but the mere prospect of one added to Argentina's hesitancy to adhere to the Bolivia–Peru alliance. Concurrently, Peru had begun to worry that the inclusion of Argentina in the Bolivia–Peru alliance might compromise Peruvian relations with Brazil, endangering expanding Peruvian interests in the Amazon Basin (Burr 1967, 129–30; Novak and Namihas 2013, 72–4). Heightened Brazilian and Chilean interest in the negotiations in Buenos Aires in 1873–74, after the 1873 treaty had passed through three chancelleries and three national congresses, also increased the likelihood that Chile was aware of the general contents of the 1873 treaty. In fact, it may have received a copy of the agreement as early as the spring of 1874 (Basadre 1968, VIII, 19; Dennis 1931, 65–6).

## Casus Belli

When the 1872 Lindsay–Corral protocol failed to resolve the outstanding problems between Bolivia and Chile, the signatories to the agreement reopened negotiations in the fall of 1873, and following a year of difficult talks, they signed a new treaty in August 1874 (Salazar 2000, 533–5; Ríos 1963, 215–16). The Treaty of Sucre recognized latitude 24° south as the boundary between Bolivia and Chile, but with the exception of its claim to 50 percent of the region's guano deposits, Chile relinquished its former rights of condominium. These provisions favored Bolivia. In return, Chile received a 25 year guarantee against tax increases on Chilean commercial interests and their exported products (Espinosa 1965, 160–7; Peñaloza 1984, IV, 153–6). This concession was consistent with a contract Bolivia had signed earlier with the Antofagasta Nitrate and Railroad Company, an extensive industrial complex formed at the beginning of the decade, stating that no new taxes would be levied for a period of 15 years, beginning 1 January 1874. Bolivia also agreed in the new pact to establish Mejillones and Antofagasta as permanent ports on the Pacific coast (Abecia 1986, I, 768–9). The Treaty of Sucre, as amended in an 1875 agreement providing for arbitration if disagreements arose, abrogated in its entirety the 1866 Treaty of Mutual Benefits (Salazar 2000, 537–9).

The Treaty of Sucre strengthened the relative power position of Chile vis-à-vis Bolivia and Peru because it largely neutralized their 1873 defensive alliance, eliminating a potential challenge to Chilean diplomacy. At the same time, related developments on the Pacific coast of South America further enhanced the Chilean position. In January 1875, the ironclad *Valparaíso* joined the *Almirante Cochrane* which meant the Chilean navy now enjoyed parity with, if not supremacy over, the Peruvian navy. Moreover, Peruvian public finances were in a wretched shape, eliminating any likelihood Peru could regain naval superiority in the foreseeable future. Finally, with the conclusion of the Treaty of Sucre, the Antofagasta Nitrate and Railroad Company, owned jointly by British and Chilean interests, formed the nucleus for reinvigorated commercial expansion in the Atacama with other Chilean concerns actively involved (Querejazu 1979, 138–45). In the process, the well-financed, efficient, and aggressive industrial and mining interests of Chile no longer restricted their operations to the Bolivian littoral but expanded north into the Peruvian littoral as well. By the end of the decade, European and Chilean interests had acquired almost half of the productive capacity of the Tarapacá nitrate fields (St John 1999, 94).

Initially, the newly elected Peruvian government of Mariano Ignacio Prado pursued a conciliatory policy toward Chile. Shortly after his inauguration, Peru dispatched a diplomatic mission to Santiago in search of compromise, and in late December 1876, a treaty of friendship, commerce, and navigation was signed. Well-meaning, the diplomatic overtures of the Prado administration lacked direction and commitment; consequently, they failed to contribute to a regional climate conducive to peace. In part, this failure was due to the ongoing concern in Peru that Bolivia, if divested of its alliance with Peru, might come to terms with Chile and align with the latter in despoiling the Peruvian province of Tarapacá. Aware that Chile had approached Bolivia on previous occasions with such a proposal, Peru remained concerned that Bolivia under different circumstances might be tempted to accept (Burr 1967, 140–3). Torn by uncertainty, the Prado government frittered away opportunities to obtain Argentine adherence to the 1873 treaty, and the government in Buenos Aires elected to remain neutral. Argentine neutrality was not entirely the product of Peruvian diplomacy as Argentina continued to fear that an alliance with Bolivia and Peru might precipitate an alliance between Brazil and Chile (Basadre 1968, VIII, 55–6). At the same time, the foreign minister of Chile, Adolfo Ibáñez y Gutierrez, had concluded that the unreliable *caudillos* ruling Bolivia made the Treaty of Sucre a dead letter. Believing war with Peru was highly likely if not inevitable, Chile removed Argentina from the diplomatic equation by concluding two agreements with the latter in 1878–79 which provided for a resolution of the Argentina–Chile territorial dispute in Patagonia (Burr 1967, 144–6; Querejazu 1979, 241–3; Miguel 2011, 49–54). With the conclusion of those pacts, Peru lost any opportunity to secure an ally who might have prevented the War of the Pacific or altered its outcome.

The financial mismanagement and currency debasement of the Megarejo administration, together with the effects of a worldwide depression, left the Bolivian economy in a perilous state when Hilarión Grosole Daza took office in May 1876. Moreover, the municipal authorities in Antofagasta, the principal export port of Bolivia, soon needed fresh funds to repair the damage caused by a May 1877 earthquake and tidal wave (Querejazu 1979, 177–81). In response to a proposal from the Antofagasta city council, the Daza administration on 14 February 1878 authorized a tax of ten centavos per quintal on all nitrates exported by the Antofagasta Nitrate and Railroad Company. At the time, the vast majority of the population of Antofagasta was Chilean with only a small minority Bolivian, and there were no Bolivians on the Antofagasta city council (Guzmán Escobari 2015b, 24–5, footnote 11). In reality, the new tax, which superseded all other taxes, was only slightly higher than the tax the company had been paying; nevertheless, it clearly violated the terms of the 1874 treaty (Espinosa 1965, 183–9; Abecia 1986, II, 14–16). When Chile protested the ten centavo tax, the official position of the authorities in Antofagasta was that the new tax was a purely internal affair which did not affect Chile, a position supported by the Daza government (Arguedas 1922, 373–5; Peñaloza 1984, 172–3, 181).

The Daza administration did not expect the Chilean government of Aníbal Pinto Garmendia to respond aggressively to the tax increase; unfortunately, its judgment proved faulty as Chile refused to accept the new assessment (Sater 2007, 35). Reflecting the Chilean attitude that the unruly *caudillos* ruling Bolivia made the Treaty of Sucre a dead letter (Ross 2016, 203–4), the Pinto administration viewed the ten centavo tax as a clear violation of the compromise reached in 1872–74 in which Chile recognized latitude 24° south in return for Bolivia's promise to renounce new taxes for 25 years. Over the next year, Bolivia expressed a willingness to submit the issue to arbitration as provided for in the Treaty of Sucre or to allow it to be settled in the courts, but Chile refused to accept any solution short of a cancellation of the proposed tax (Ortega 1984, 350–2, 356–8; Dennis 1931, 70–1). Frustrated with the attitude of the Chilean government and the foreign concessionaires in the littoral, President Daza took decisive action, ordering the new law to be enforced with retroactive collection to 18 February 1878. In December 1878, the Antofagasta Nitrate and Railroad Company was told to pay the new assessment, and when George Hicks, the company's English manager refused, he was arrested. Chile responded with a degree of restraint, continuing to negotiate even as it stationed the *Blanco Encalada* in the Bay of Antofagasta (Sater 2007, 31–2; Querejazu 1983, 51–3).

The next step taken by President Daza was poorly conceived if Bolivia entertained any hope of preventing war. In what Bolivian authorities viewed as an attempt to eliminate the cause of the trouble in the Atacama Desert, the Daza administration cancelled the concession of the Antofagasta Nitrate and Railroad Company and proposed to sell its assets at public auction (Ortega 1984, 356–7, 362). In addition to the cancellation order, President Daza sent the prefect of Antofagasta a letter which outlined the 1873 defensive treaty with Peru and detailed Bolivia's position in the dispute. In the letter, Daza indicated that he did not expect Chile to resort to force over the issue because it had earlier displayed weakness and a lack of resolution in its dispute with Argentina. He added that the cancellation of the Antofagasta Nitrate and Railroad Company contract would demonstrate that right was on the side of Bolivia which intended to exploit the resources of the littoral in its own best interests. Finally, Daza told the prefect of Antofagasta that Serapio Reyes Ortiz, the new Bolivian minister to Peru, would soon travel to Lima to confirm Peruvian support for the 1873 treaty (Querejazu 1983, 58; Encina 1963, 119).

President Daza's letter was intercepted by Chilean authorities who demanded it be rescinded. If not, they promised a Chilean occupation of the Bolivian littoral. After the Daza administration proceeded to set 14 February 1879 as the date for the sale of Antofagasta company assets, the Pinto government ordered Colonel Emilio Sotomayor, commandant of the Chilean military college, to prepare for the occupation of the Bolivian littoral to latitude 23° south. Once the *Almirante Cochrane* and the *O'Higgins* had joined the *Blanco Encalada* in the Bay of Antofagasta, Chilean troops landed on 14 February 1879 and occupied the port of Antofagasta (Peñaloza 1984, 186–7; Espinosa 1965, 195). Further north, Chilean troops also seized the port of Mejillones and the silver mines at Caracoles, and when Bolivia reinforced its army and moved to activate the 1873 treaty, they occupied the ports of Cobija and Tocopilla. Finally, Chilean forces seized the Calama Oasis to prevent Bolivia from moving troops from the interior to the coast (Querejazu 1983, 61–74; Arguedas 1922, 375, 377–80).

The Chilean occupation of the Bolivian littoral found Peru completely unprepared for war. A general lack of military preparedness was compounded by ongoing financial difficulties and the high level of political unrest which plagued Peru after 1876 (Pike 1967, 139–42). Faced with a seemingly impossible situation, the Prado administration adopted a two-fold strategy. On the one hand, it accelerated preparations for war, and on the other, it attempted to avoid war altogether by urging Bolivia and Chile to find a peaceful settlement (Phillips 1973, 77–8). When Serapio Reyes Ortiz arrived in Lima on 16 February 1879, the Prado administration informed him that it considered the 1873 treaty null and void. Peruvian officials argued that the 1873 agreement was no longer active because Bolivia had concluded the 1874 treaty with Chile without first notifying Peru as it was bound to do so under the terms of the 1873 pact (Peñaloza 1984, 200; Pinochet de la Barra 2000, 24). As Peru continued its diplomatic efforts to forestall an outbreak of general hostilities, it worked to derail the Reyes Ortiz mission by refusing to discuss the 1873 treaty with the Bolivian envoy (Querejazu 1979, 314–18).

In late February 1879, President Prado dispatched the historian and diplomat José Antonio de Lavalle to Chile as the head of a Peruvian delegation whose goal was to find a peaceful solution to the dispute. While most Peruvians in and out of government expected Lavalle's mission to fail, it offered the secondary advantage of giving Peru additional time to prepare for war (Phillips 1973, 80; St John 1999, 98). Fearful the 1873 treaty would compromise the Lavalle mission, Peruvian Foreign Minister Pedro Irigoyen instructed Lavalle to admit to the existence of the agreement only if pressed and then to stress that its terms did not call for the automatic intervention of Peru in support of Bolivia. Within days of Lavalle's arrival in Santiago, the Pinto government began raising embarrassing questions about the existence of a military alliance between Bolivia and Peru (Basadre 1968, VIII, 43–8). Fully aware of the terms of the 1873 treaty, Lavalle responded with little conviction that to his knowledge no such treaty existed (Espinosa 1965, 201–2; Abecia 1986, II, 66–7). The issue of the secret treaty quickly eroded Lavalle's credibility, reinforcing speculation in the Chilean press that his mission was nothing but a ploy to give Peru time to rearm (Sater 1986, 11)

Once its forces had occupied the Bolivian littoral, the position of the Chilean government hardened. When Lavalle proposed that Bolivia suspend the ten centavo tax in return for a Chilean evacuation of the area, the Pinto administration responded that the current state of Chilean public opinion made any thought of withdrawal impossible (Peñaloza 1984, 198; Sater 1986, 11). Turning the clock back to 1866, Chilean officials told Lavalle that Chile had agreed to Bolivian occupation of the area under certain conditions, and when Bolivia failed to meet those conditions, Chile was now free to reclaim its territory (Ross 2016, 198–9). Although Chile rejected the terms of the Lavalle mediation, it did so in a conciliatory mood that left Lavalle hopeful that a peaceful settlement was still possible (García Salazar 1928, 184–5; Abecia 1986, II, 68–9, 71). All hopes in this regard were soon dashed by events in Bolivia and Peru.

After Bolivia declared war on Chile on 14 March 1879, the Chilean government demanded a declaration of neutrality from Peru, together with a categorical denial that a Bolivia–Peru alliance existed. In response, the Prado administration detailed the terms of the 1873 treaty to Chilean officials, arguing it was strictly a defensive alliance which was not directed at Chile (Espinosa 1965, 201–2; Encina 1963, 147–9). In so doing, Peru stressed that the terms of the agreement left each signatory free to decide whether a specific situation necessitated its active support on behalf of the other signatory; consequently, the 1873 treaty left Peru free to mediate in good faith. Unimpressed, Chile demanded Peru abrogate the alliance, cease preparations for war, and issue a declaration of neutrality (Novak and Namihas 2013, 75–6). Continuing to fear that Bolivia might resolve its differences with Chile and join the latter in despoiling Peruvian nitrate deposits in Tarapacá, the Prado administration refused to disavow the 1873 treaty (Pike 1967, 142). This decision left Chile convinced that further negotiations would be pointless, and on 5 April 1879, it declared war on both Bolivia and Peru.

With the end to diplomatic efforts to find a peaceful solution to the rivalry on the Pacific coast of South America, the central role played by nitrates in the march to war became clear (Ortega 1984, 366–7). In a circular to the diplomatic corps in Santiago, Chile accused Peru of fomenting the conflict to eliminate competition for the Peruvian nitrate monopoly. While no credible evidence directly linked Peru either to the ten centavo tax or the Bolivian decision to confiscate Chilean holdings in Antofagasta, influential Peruvian interests clearly had deep-seated economic and political reasons for going to war. By the end of the 1870s, Peru had a near monopoly on the nitrate trade, and the ten centavo tax imposed by Bolivia in 1878 supported this position. On the other hand, the consolidation of Chilean control over the Atacama Desert promised ruinous competition for Peru (Mercado Jarrín 1979, 42–5). Finally, where Peru remained concerned that Bolivia, if abandoned by Peru, could ally with Chile and despoil the Peruvian nitrate fields in Tarapacá, Chile viewed Peruvian nitrate revenues as a means to indemnify itself for the expense of any war (O'Brien 1979).

By 1879, guano and nitrates had become important to the global economy; therefore, with the war threatening to disrupt trade in both commodities, European interest in the conflict was high. Peruvian nitrate bonds were held widely in Europe, particularly in France, Holland, and Italy, and the creditors in those countries also were concerned that events in the Atacama Desert did degrade the value of Peruvian guarantees. European investment in Bolivia, on the other hand, was relatively modest with mines, lands, public utilities, and manufacturing the major categories of British investment (Rippy 1953, 38–9, 41–3). With British financial interests centered on Chile, British financiers and businessmen, in particular, openly supported Chile throughout the conflict. European support for Chile during the war facilitated the development by Chile of a master narrative in which it depicted itself as a culturally, morally, and racially superior nation compared to Bolivia and Peru with a duty to civilize its neighbors (Guzmán Escobari 2015b, 16–17, 56). The concentration of European investment in the nitrate industry in general and in Chile in particular also helped spawn a foreign conspiracy thesis which argued European interests influenced events during the war to the disadvantage of Bolivia and Peru (Francaviglia 2018, 215–16). While no firm evidence surfaced to support suggestions of foreign influence or foreign intervention, the British government clearly had no impetus to pressure Chile to forego any territorial gains. With Chile occupying large swaths of Bolivian and Peruvian territory, any status quo agreement was to Chile's advantage, and that is how British policy was interpreted both in Bolivia and Peru (Kiernan 1955; Bonilla 1980, 157–8, 167–75, 183–4).

## Conclusions

Throughout this period, Bolivia engaged in a losing struggle to maintain control of the Pacific littoral it inherited at independence. Sandwiched between Peru to the north and Chile to the south, the main threat to Bolivian sovereignty came from the south. The dispute with Chile intensified after 1840 following the discovery of guano and nitrates in the Atacama Desert with clashes over competing claims leading to conflict in 1857 and 1863. Too weak to defend itself militarily, Bolivia resorted to questionable policies and largely ineffective diplomacy in a series of agreements with Chile and Peru, none of which slowed the inexorable march to war. Along the way, the Bolivarian goal of continental solidarity was undermined both by economic and political power struggles within Bolivia and geopolitical rivalries with its neighbors.

While the 1873 treaty and the imposition of the ten centavo tax proved to be a convenient *casus belli*, there were deeper, more fundamental reasons for the outbreak of hostilities in 1879. On one side, there was the power, prestige, and relative economic and political stability of Chile compared to the economic deterioration and political discontinuity of Bolivia and Peru. On the other, there was the ongoing competition for economic and political dominance on the west coast of South America, complicated by a deep antipathy between Chile and Peru. In this milieu, the vagueness of the boundaries between the three states, coupled with the discovery of valuable deposits of guano, nitrates, and other minerals in the disputed territories, combined to produce a diplomatic conundrum of insurmountable proportions. Bolivia was in the middle of the growing competition between Chile and Peru because the richer mineral deposits were in areas Bolivia claimed after 1825. As the tragedy unfolded, Bolivia and to a lesser extent Peru found it increasingly difficult to establish a solid economic and political footing in the littoral or to formulate a foreign policy capable of dealing with Chilean encroachments. Chile in turn was increasingly unhappy with what it viewed as the ineptitude of Bolivia and Peru to develop the valuable mineral holdings in the Atacama Desert, together with their alleged harassment of Chilean citizens working in the region.

The origins of the War of the Pacific were the 1866 and 1874 treaties between Bolivia and Chile as opposed to either the 1873 treaty between Bolivia and Peru or the ten centavo tax. Bolivia's agreements with Chile opened the door for Chilean exploitation of the mineral riches in the Bolivian littoral, and once the door was open, Bolivia could not close it. In this context, the dispute with the Antofagasta Nitrate and Railroad Company was both symptomatic of wider, deeper conflicts and a convenient pretext for war. Ironically, six months after Chile seized Antofagasta, it levied a 40 centavo tax per quintal of nitrates in order to help pay for a war caused in part by Bolivia's levy of a ten centavo tax. If the dispute with the Antofagasta Nitrate and Railroad Company had not arisen or been resolved peacefully, some other event would in all likelihood have led to the same end result. In this sense, the War of the Pacific was a natural consequence of the aggressive growth of global capitalism in the nineteenth century together with competition between Chile and Peru for hegemony on the Pacific coast of South America. Bolivia's quest for a Pacific port was not central to the events leading up to the War of the Pacific, but the outcome of the war had a decisive impact on its future objectives in that regard.

# 4 War and Peace, 1879–1904

For Bolivia, the War of the Pacific was a relatively short conflict with enormous long-term consequences. Fourteen months after Bolivia declared war on Chile, the Bolivian army withdrew into the highlands and for all purposes was out of the war. Bolivia and Chile signed a truce agreement in April 1884, but it would be another two decades before they concluded a peace treaty. When they did, the agreement left Bolivia landlocked, threatening national security, sovereignty, and economic independence. Between 1884 and 1904, Bolivian diplomacy worked to secure a sovereign Pacific port even as it fended off aggressive initiatives from neighboring states. This search for an outlet to the sea repeatedly impacted on central elements of Bolivian foreign policy. This was clearly the case with Chile and to a lesser extent with Peru, but it was also true of Brazil with whom Bolivia traded vast tracts of land in the Upper Amazon in return for tenuous access to the Atlantic Ocean via the Amazon and Paraguay rivers.

## Hostilities Commence

Despite the success Chile enjoyed eventually in the War of the Pacific, the outcome of the conflict at the outset was far from certain. Bolivia and Peru collectively drew on approximately twice the population of Chile although the citizens of the latter were more homogenous, educated, and motivated. In addition, the Chilean populace was endowed with a sense of national identity which was almost completely lacking in the ill-equipped and poorly trained soldiery of Bolivia and Peru (Encina 1963, 152–3; Querejazu 1979, 339–40; Guzmán Escobari 2015b, 16–18). Initially, Chileans offered only tepid support for the war, and political strife in Chile, as well as in Bolivia and Peru, complicated the war effort. If Chile enjoyed any advantage, it was the military strategy it pursued as opposed to the size or composition of its armed forces. Knowing control of the sea was an imperative, Chile over the previous decade had doggedly pursued a successful naval buildup (Abecia 1986, II, 90–2; Sater 2007, 44–115).

In the wake of Chile's declaration of war, Bolivia and Peru concluded three protocols designed to coordinate the allied war effort. In the first, dated 15

April 1879, Bolivia promised to contribute 12,000 men and Peru 8,000 men plus its navy. In addition, Bolivia agreed to loan Peru 100,000 soles interest free and to reimburse it for its war-related expenses by allowing the latter to retain 50 percent of Bolivian customs revenues at Arica and Mollendo and 50 percent of all receipts from nitrate exports. In the event the allies won the war and Chile paid an indemnity, the protocol stated Bolivia's financial obligations to Peru would be forgiven. The terms of this first protocol clearly favored Peru, and Bolivia reluctantly agreed to it on the assumption the allies would win the war and Chile would pay all war-related expenses. After Bolivia made clear its displeasure with the terms of the first protocol, the allies concluded a second protocol on 7 May 1879 in which Peru agreed to extend a loan to Bolivia. Subsequently, the allies concluded a third protocol on 17 June 1879 in which each country agreed to pay 50 percent of the war's expenses (Abecia 1986, II, 72; Novak and Namihas 2013, 76–7).

Even after it had declared war on Bolivia and Peru, Chile persisted in its efforts to detach Bolivia from Peru by exploiting the deep-felt Bolivian need for a Pacific port. In so doing, Chile sought to trade Bolivian incorporation of the Peruvian provinces of Tacna and Arica for Chilean sovereignty over the littoral between latitudes 23° and 24° south, together with the coastal region north of the Loa River. This policy of dismemberment, when it first surfaced in 1866, was a radical change from Chile's general insistence after 1836 on the status quo along the Pacific coast of South America. In April 1879, President Daza received two informal Chilean overtures which urged Bolivia to cooperate with Chile in despoiling the Peruvian littoral, arguing Arica, Ilo, Islay, or Mollendo were natural ports for Bolivia (Escobari 1982, I, 133; Guzmán Escobari 2015b, 31). In late May, Chile proposed an agreement in which Bolivia would grant Chile possession of the littoral to latitude 23° south, and in return, Chile would help Bolivia to seize enough Peruvian territory to readjust its boundary and secure an easy means of communication with the Pacific. In support of this proposal, Chile agreed not to make peace with Peru until the latter had concluded a peace treaty with Bolivia (Querejazu 1983, 111–13). In April 1881, Chile again proposed to Bolivia an exchange of the Bolivian littoral for the Peruvian provinces of Tacna and Arica (Abecia 1986, II, 158).

The War of the Pacific was essentially a maritime conflict which neither side could win without control of the sea, and if Chile gained control of the sea, all Bolivia and Peru could hope to do was to delay the day of reckoning. In the first real test of ironclads at sea, the *Huáscar*, the only Peruvian warship capable of challenging the *Blanco Encalada* and the *Almirante Cochrane*, was captured in October 1879 in the Battle of Angamos, leaving Chile the undisputed master of the sea (Worcester 1963; Novak and Namihas 2013, 77–8). Peruvian forces later won a tactical victory at Tarapacá in November 1879, but the Chileans occupied Tacna in May 1880 and Arica the following month. Although Bolivia refused to sue for peace, the battle of Tacna forced the Bolivian army to retreat to the highlands, taking Bolivia out of the war

(Querejazu 1983, 109; Sater 2007, 20). Short of money, men, and weapons, it was virtually impossible for Bolivia to transport its army any place in Peru where it could be of practical assistance. Consequently, the Bolivian army did not fight again after its defeat at Tacna, and Bolivia was not a factor either in the subsequent fighting or in the peace negotiations that followed.

Struggling to keep their faltering alliance active, representatives of Bolivia and Peru met in Lima on 11 June 1880 and signed two confederation protocols. The first created a federal government with an executive, bicameral legislature, and judicial branch. Under its terms, the departments of each country would become states but retain a large degree of autonomy. The second protocol created a 20-member senate to write a constitution and provide commissions to establish state boundaries and set the public debt. It also provided for a temporary executive with the president of Peru acting as president of the confederation and the president of Bolivia serving as vice president (Escobari 1982, II, 32; Novak and Namihas 2013, 79–80). The Bolivia–Peru Confederation was stillborn. The Peruvian council of state suggested a plebiscite be held to give Peruvians an opportunity to express their opinion on the confederation, but this was as far as the union movement progressed in Peru. In Bolivia, the government of General Narciso Campero (1880–84), which came to power after Hilarión Daza was ousted in April 1879, paid lip service to the idea of confederation but did not actively support it. With the National Assembly split on the confederation issue, the Bolivian national committee also proposed a plebiscite which was never held (Querejazu 1979, 597–603; Abecia 1986, II, 121–3).

As the ill-conceived Bolivia–Peru Confederation floundered on national rivalries, relations between the allies deteriorated in the second half of 1880. After it captured Arica, Chile opened the port to Bolivian commerce, a move strongly criticized by Peru. In response to Peruvian protests, Bolivia temporarily halted commerce through Arica, but faced with a growing scarcity of goods, it was later forced to rescind the interdiction. In retaliation, Peru placed a prohibitive duty on Bolivian goods transiting Peruvian territory and seized some goods for non-payment of duties. When this move threatened to rupture the Bolivia–Peru alliance, a compromise was reached in which Bolivia agreed to pay a 5 percent duty on all goods passing to and from Arica, and at the end of the year, it pledged anew its loyalty to Peru. In June 1881, Bolivia and Peru concluded a commercial treaty which called for free trade between them until they were united in a confederation. The Bolivian government later rejected the agreement, both because it was disadvantageous to Bolivia and because old rivalries between the allies again had manifested themselves (Phillips 1973, 205, 216; Novak and Namihas 2013, 80–1, 83).

## Mediation Efforts

The War of the Pacific attracted a large number of mediation efforts, none of which had a significant impact on the outcome of the dispute. In 1879–80, Argentina, Brazil, Colombia, Ecuador, France, Great Britain, and Italy, separately or collectively, offered to mediate the dispute, but their efforts were unsuccessful in part because the belligerents could not agree on the terms for mediation and in part because Bolivia and Peru hoped the United States would offer its good offices (Burr 1967, 146–8, 150–1; Soder 1970, 65–70). Unfortunately, the allies misread the extent to which President Rutherford B. Hayes was willing to become involved in the dispute in general and to support the cause of Bolivia and Peru in particular. With the exception of an unauthorized and unsuccessful mediation in August 1879 by Newton Pettis, the US envoy to Bolivia, Secretary of State William Maxwell Evarts throughout 1879 insisted on a policy of non-intervention, expressing a willingness to engage in the dispute only if all parties requested US involvement (Gumucio 2005, 104–7; Querejazu 1979, 397–9).

A renewed possibility of European mediation in the spring of 1880 prompted a US initiative which led to a peace conference off Arica in the fall. Meeting on board the US warship *Lackawanna*, the Conference of Arica consisted of three meetings in October 1880. All three belligerents were reluctant participants in the conference. Bolivia and Peru favored arbitration by the United States, but Chile feared US intervention might rob it of the fruits of victory. In this regard, Charles Adams, the newly arrived US envoy to Bolivia, contributed to the failure of the conference by wrongly implying to the Bolivian delegation that Washington would insist on arbitration if the Lackawanna talks failed (Phillips 1973, 228–9; Lehman 1999, 42). In the end, the October 1880 conference was noteworthy only because it accented the divergent, inflexible positions of Bolivia, Chile, and Peru, positions that made a peaceful resolution of the dispute virtually impossible. It should also be noted that Chilean officials during the conference renewed their efforts to detach Bolivia from Peru, assuring their Bolivian counterparts that the May 1879 bases for peace were still available (Novak and Namihas 2013, 82). In the spring of 1881, Ladislao Cabrera, the Bolivian minister to the United States, introduced an innovative peace proposal based on the preservation of territorial integrity. His plan involved the formation of a company with US capital to exploit the nitrate beds in the disputed region with the profits from the endeavor used to pay war reparations to Chile (Gumucio 2005, 112–13; Lehman 1999, 42–3). The outgoing Hayes administration expressed interest in Cabrera's proposal, but the successor Garfield administration refused to commit to it.

With the inauguration of President James A. Garfield in March 1881, US policy in the War of the Pacific changed course. Secretary of State James G. Blaine abandoned the impartial policy of his predecessor, replacing it with one openly favorable to Bolivia and Peru. Motivated in part by a desire to advance the commercial interests of the United States, Blaine sought a solution to the dispute which avoided both European intervention and territorial cession (Espinosa 1965, 222–6; Gumucio 2005, 113–14). While these goals were not radically different from those of Secretary of State Evarts, Chilean military successes by the spring of 1881 had transformed the political situation on the Pacific coast; therefore, Blaine's policy was partisan in the sense that any opposition to the status quo clearly favored Bolivia and Peru. Blaine sent new envoys to Chile and Peru, but retained the US envoy in La Paz, largely because no one else was interested in the post (Tyler 1927, 112–19; Peterson 1969, 9–10).

President Garfield was assassinated in September 1881, and the presidency passed to Vice President Chester A. Arthur who named Frederick T. Frelinghuysen as secretary of state. President Arthur acknowledged Chile's right to annex Tarapacá although he was less enthusiastic when it came to Tacna and Arica. To implement the change in policy, Frelinghuysen instructed the US envoys in Bolivia, Chile, and Peru to confine their activities to impartial mediation attempts, avoiding any attempt to dictate peace terms (Sater 2007, 329). In late 1881, outgoing Secretary of State Blaine had dispatched a special mission to Chile and Peru headed by William Henry Trescot, an experienced diplomat. Upon taking office, Frelinghuysen immediately cabled Trescot, instructing him to extend only friendly, impartial offices to Chile and Peru. Within the week, Frelinghuysen then dispatched detailed written instructions to Trescot, nullifying Blaine's earlier instructions (Dennis 1931, 165–6).

After Trescot received his new instructions, he concluded a protocol with José Manuel Balmaceda, the Chilean minister of foreign affairs, in mid-February 1882. The Viña del Mar protocol provided for the cession to Chile of Peruvian territory south of the Quebrada de Camarones, Chilean occupation of Tacna and Arica for ten years with Peru obliged to pay Chile 20 million pesos at the end of that period, and Chilean occupation of the Lobos islands until their guano deposits were exhausted (Gumucio 2005, 117). Trescot signed the protocol conditionally on the subsequent approval of the Arthur administration, and two days later, he received new instructions obliging him to tell Balmaceda the United States could not tender the good offices provided for in the protocol (Dennis 1931, 169–71). The Viña del Mar protocol was significant only because it highlighted the intransigence of Chile and thus was a harbinger of the final settlement between Chile and Peru. As for the Trescot mission, it accomplished little more than to draw attention to the limited extent to which US diplomacy could restrain the severity of Chilean peace terms.

The negotiation of the Viña del Mar protocol highlighted Bolivia's isolation from the peace process as Trescot reportedly mentioned Bolivia only once in his conversations with Balmaceda, and Bolivia was not mentioned at all in the protocol (Phillips 1973, 284–5). When the Bolivian minister of foreign affairs, Pedro José Zilvetti, protested his country's exclusion from the Viña del Mar talks and demanded to know the contents of the protocol, Trescot sent an envoy to La Paz to discuss the negotiations which led to the protocol. When Trescot's representative met with Zilvetti and other Bolivian officials, he gave them an overview of the Trescot–Balmaceda negotiations and general information on the Protocol of Viña del Mar but refused to disclose its details. When the US envoy reported to Trescot on his meetings in La Paz, he noted Bolivian concerns that the Trescot–Balmaceda talks and the contents of the Protocol of Viña del Mar could leave Bolivia landlocked

(Gumucio 2005, 118–19). As the Trescot mission unraveled, Foreign Minister Zilvetti dispatched a circular to Bolivian diplomats abroad, charging the United States had failed to protect Bolivia from Chile (Lehman 1999, 44).

In the second half of 1882, Secretary Frelinghuysen launched a new peace initiative, instructing Cornelius A. Logan, the newly appointed minister to Chile, to secure for Peru as large a part of the occupied territories as possible with the maximum monetary indemnity for whatever territory Chile retained (Crosby 1949, 269–70). Although the Logan mission failed, the talks Logan held with representatives of Chile and Peru once again demonstrated how unimportant Bolivia had become to a resolution of the dispute. The US minister to Bolivia, George Maney, was not involved in Logan's peace mission, and the only mention of Bolivia during the talks was an indication in the bases for peace proposed by Logan that Bolivia would be invited to participate in the peace treaty (Gumucio 2005, 119–23). Consequently, it was hardly surprising that much of the Bolivian press by the end of 1882 was increasingly hostile to the idea of US intervention (Phillips 1973, 290–1).

By 1882, diplomatic relations between Bolivia and Peru had begun to show the effects of a war in its third year. Bolivia continued to assure Peru of its loyalty to the alliance; however, President Campero delayed recognition first of the Francisco García Calderón government formed in early 1881 and then the administration of Admiral Lizardo Montero Flores formed later in the year. In the belief a truce was an absolute necessity, Bolivia instructed Juan Crisóstomo Carrillo, Bolivian minister to Peru, to meet with Mariano Alvarez, the foreign minister in the Montero government in Arequipa, in the spring of 1882 (Querejazu 1979, 666–8; Novak and Namihas 2013, 85–6). When Carrillo pressed for a truce, Alvarez stressed that the war involved all of the Americas, not just the belligerents, and emphasized Peru would never cede territory to Chile. When Alvarez indicated that Peru had negotiations pending with the United States, Carrillo responded that Bolivia had no confidence in Washington (Peñaloza 1984, 328). The failure of the Carrillo mission frayed bilateral relations between Bolivia and Peru, and in an effort to prop up the alliance, President Campero invited Admiral Montero to La Paz in September 1882. During his visit, Bolivia promised to dispatch 2,000 troops to Arequipa; however, the promised troops never advanced beyond the outskirts of La Paz (Phillips 1973, 270–1; Novak and Namihas 2013, 86–7).

## Final Settlements

On 18 October 1883, representatives of Chile and Peru concluded the Treaty of Ancón, reestablishing peace between the two states. In the agreement, Peru ceded to Chile the littoral province of Tarapacá whose boundaries were described in the treaty as the Camarones River on the north, the Loa River on the south, and the Republic of Bolivia on the east. This proviso effectively precluded Bolivia from regaining its littoral since Chile could not be expected to give Bolivia territory which would separate Tarapacá from the remainder of Chile. The treaty also provided for Chile to occupy Tacna and Arica for ten years from the date of ratification of the treaty after which a plebiscite would determine whether the area would remain a part of Chile or revert to Peru (Dennis 1931, 297–300; Abecia 1986, II, 159–60). Unfortunately, the agreement did not detail the terms of the plebiscite and the failure to do so contributed to abortive efforts over 40 years to hold it. If the plebiscite was conducted, the winner was to pay the loser 10 million Chilean pesos or the equivalent in Peruvian soles. Seven of the remaining 11 articles of the agreement dealt with guano or nitrates, highlighting the underlying issues of the War of the Pacific. According to the treaty, the Lobos Islands were to remain in Chilean hands until one million tons of guano had been extracted after which they would be returned to Peru. The net proceeds of the guano extracted during this period was to be divided equally between the Chilean government and Peruvian creditors whose claims were guaranteed by a lien on the guano. The treaty also stipulated that commercial relations between Chile and Peru would continue on the same footing as before the war. A supplementary protocol addressed details of the Chilean army of occupation (Perú 1936, I, 165–8).

The Treaty of Ancón was a punitive pact with heavy indemnities which poisoned hemispheric relations for decades to come. The victor took as spoils the mineral-rich Atacama Desert, the single greatest source of Bolivian and Peruvian wealth. Over time, this desert wealth would become an important factor in the socioeconomic and political development of Chile (Monteón 1982; Sater 1986, 224–9; Loveman 2001, 145–61; Francaviglia 2018, 216). A study of the fiscal impact of the war indicated that the export tax on nitrates imposed by Chile later accounted for at least half of all government revenues. In the same study, the results of a counterfactual scenario in which Chile did not occupy the nitrate-rich provinces suggested that Bolivian and Peruvian government revenues would have been at least double their historical levels. In turn, Chilean revenues from nitrates over the remainder of the nineteenth century would have fallen by 80 percent (Sicotte, Vizcarra, and Wandschneider 2009). The provisions related to the final disposition of Tacna and Arica were especially unfortunate as they constituted an open sore hampering the development of regional relations and blocking Bolivia's quest for a Pacific port. The ratification of the Treaty of Ancón was secured with some difficulty with the major obstacle being the attitude of foreign governments whose citizens feared they might lose the money they had invested in Peruvian guano and nitrate loans. The issue of bondholder loans, which took years to resolve, was not enough to block ratification of the treaty. Chile and Peru exchanged ratifications of the Treaty of Ancón on 28 March 1884 (St John 1999, 118).

When Bolivia opened formal peace talks with Chile in December 1883, its approach to the negotiations revealed a new strategy for obtaining a Pacific port. During the 1883–84 talks, Bolivia pressured Chile to grant it access to the ocean in the form of a corridor through Chilean territory or by modifying the Treaty of Ancón and ceding it Tacna and Arica. Chile refused to sacrifice

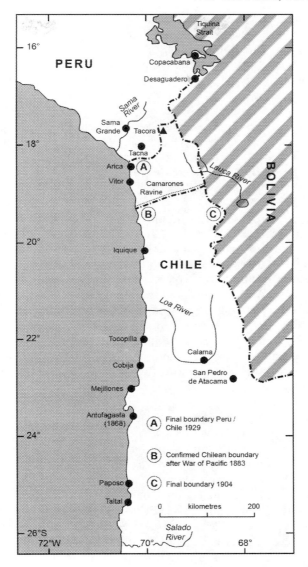

*Figure 4.1* Atacama Littoral, 1883–1929
Source: IBRU, Durham University, UK.

its territorial continuity by granting Bolivia a corridor through its territory and rightly pointed out that it could hardly cede Tacna and Arica to Bolivia before the plebiscite called for in the Treaty of Ancón had determined their ownership. In any case, Chilean President Domingo Santa María saw no need to be so generous to Bolivia (Sater 2007, 344; Ríos 1963, 137–40). The

Chilean negotiators also noted that sentiment in Peru was strongly attached to Tacna and Arica; therefore, it was highly unlikely that Peru would ever agree to cede them to Bolivia (Burr 1967, 162–3; Abecia 1986, II, 164–5). With Chile making plans to renew hostilities, Bolivia eventually signed a truce agreement on 4 April 1884. The Campero government refused to sign a formal peace treaty with Chile until it had secured compensation for its territorial losses in the form of a sovereign outlet to the Pacific Ocean. In turn, Chile refused to address Bolivian demands for a seaport until the plebiscite on Tacna and Arica had been held (Querejazu 1983, 132–5; Roca 2004, 17–18). For decades to come, the interplay of these two separate but related issues, the Bolivian quest for a Pacific port and Peruvian insistence on regaining Tacna and Arica, exacerbated regional tensions.

The terms of the April 1884 truce were extremely favorable to Chile. The agreement provided for Chilean occupation of the Bolivian littoral, specifically the territory between latitude 23° south and the mouth of the Loa River, and for Bolivia to pay Chile an indemnity for war-related damages. The truce also provided for the mutual return of sequestered Bolivian and Chilean property and the restoration of commercial relations on a free trade, most-favored-nation basis. Chile attempted to accommodate Bolivian demands for access to the sea by establishing several ports, including the former Bolivian port of Antofagasta, through which Bolivian-bound goods would pass duty-free, but the port of Arica was not granted this designation. At Arica, goods bound for Bolivia were charged standard Chilean duties with 75 percent of the customs duties collected going to Bolivia and 25 percent going to Chile. Of the custom duties going to Bolivia, 40 percent would go to Chile to pay the indemnity and to repay a Chilean loan to Bolivia and 60 percent would be used to cover normal government costs of operation. Arica would become a free port providing Bolivia with a source of revenue in terms of the duties it could charge on goods in transit to Bolivia only after Bolivia's financial obligations to Chile had been completely satisfied (Salazar 2000, 567–72; Téllez 1989, 227–9). Bolivian critics of the 1884 truce rightly argued that its net effect was to stifle economic growth in general and industrial development and foreign trade in particular (Becerra de la Roca 2002, 62; Oblitas 2001, 415). A protocol, added in May 1885, addressed related topics, including the distribution of customs revenues at Arica and the operation of the arbitration commission. The conclusion of a formal peace treaty between Bolivia and Chile would take another 20 years.

## Postwar Politics

The War of the Pacific discredited the Bolivian military, ended the era of *caudillo* rule, and began a period of republican government dominated by civilians. President Campero refused to sue for peace even after the allied defeat at Tacna signaled the end of Bolivian resistance. His decision to prolong the war produced a major schism in Bolivian political life. On the issue of whether to continue the war effort or come to terms with Chile, opposing factions of the white ruling class coalesced into the two political parties which dominated Bolivian politics for most of the next half-century (Mesa Gisbert 2001a, 485–92; Klein 1969, 14–16). In theory if not always in practice, the Liberal party, centered in La Paz and both anti-Chilean and anti-peace, stood for the classic liberal doctrines of the nineteenth century, including liberty and secular, federalist rule. In contrast, the Conservative party, which represented southern mining interests with Sucre its major center of strength, recognized Catholicism as the official state religion and supported a unitary form of government. On other doctrinal issues, Conservatives and Liberals evidenced few differences, and when it came to economic policy, the Conservatives often were more progressive than the Liberals (Pike 1977, 134–6).

The highland silver mining elite opposed the continuation of a war which had disrupted their traditionally close links with Chilean capital, interrupted their exports, and led them to conclude that their long-term interests lay with the establishment of stable, financially sound government (Klein 2011, 143; Pérez del Castillo 1980, 372–5). In the 1884 election, Eliodoro Camacho and Mariano Baptista, the respective heads of the Liberal and Conservative parties, were expected to be the presidential candidates; however, Baptista was edged out by two silver millionaires, Gregorio Pacheco and Aniceto Arce, sympathetic to the Conservative party. When no candidate received an absolute majority, the National Assembly elected Pacheco president and Arce vice-president with the understanding that Arce would be elected president in 1888 (Mesa Gisbert 2001a, 493). Under Pacheco, Bolivia finally concluded the long-delayed truce with Chile. The Liberals strongly contested the 1888 election and the subsequent election of Mariano Baptista in 1892 and Severo Fernández Alonso in 1896; nevertheless, the Conservative party monopolized the office of the presidency until the end of the century (Guzmán 1998, 216–18).

The era of the conservative oligarchy was a fruitful one for Bolivia. Achievements included a major expansion of the economy, road and railway construction, and the first prolonged period of civilian rule in Bolivian history. It also witnessed the creation of a modern political party system and the foundation of a constitutional form of government (Klein 1969, 29–30; Mesa Gisbert 2001a, 493–504). The adoption of party government also reduced but did not eliminate the instability and violence that had long characterized government in Bolivia. Between 1888 and 1930, Bolivia experienced only two significant civil wars, one marking the transition from Conservative to Liberal rule in 1888–89 and the second ousting the Liberals and bringing the Republicans to office in 1920 (Henderson 2013, 211).

By 1898, the influence of the traditional power bases of the Conservative party, the silver mining interests in the southern altiplano, the aristocrats of Sucre and Potosí, and the landed elite of central and southern Bolivia, had diminished due to steep drops in the output and price of silver and weakness in the southern agricultural sector (Roca 1980, 133–4). As the economic and political clout of the traditional ruling classes declined, the relative strength of new power brokers, namely the wealthy tin barons of the northern altiplano, urban professionals, and export-importers of the Liberal party, increased. In the face of this power shift, a dispute in the National Assembly over Conservative party support for the retention of Sucre as the legal capital of Bolivia precipitated a brief but bloody civil war between Conservatives and Liberals known as the Federal Revolution (Mesa Gisbert 2001a, 510–14; Morales 2010, 87–8; Rodríguez Ostia 1994, 78–86).

As a result, the twentieth century opened with a new Liberal oligarchy in charge. In late 1899, José Manuel Pando (1899–1904), a popular war hero and architect of Liberal uprisings, became the first Liberal president of the modern era, and Ismael Montes (1904–09, 1913–17) further consolidated Liberal party rule, serving two terms as president (Mesa Gisbert 2001a, 515–20, 525–9, 531–3, 535–6; Guzmán 1998, 218–20). After initiating several abortive military campaigns in an effort to crush Brazilian filibusters in the rubber-rich Acre territory, the Pando administration in 1903 sold the vast rubber-rich territory to Brazil for £2 million. The Montes administration completed the Antogagasta to La Paz railway and embarked on new road and railway construction. In the process, it created the infrastructure unity that Bolivia historically lacked, together with the transportation system necessary for the tin industry to reach its full potential (Hillman 1984). The Montes administration also negotiated a definitive peace treaty with Chile in 1904 in which it ceded its occupied littoral. The Acre and Chilean treaties gave the Liberals relative peace on the international front together with the economic resources necessary to continue railroad construction (Pike 1977, 154–6).

## Conflicted Allies

With the conclusion of the 1884 truce with Chile, a sovereign outlet to the Pacific remained Bolivia's primary concern; however, other regional issues were also on its foreign policy agenda. In the case of Peru, war debts, commerce, and the perennial issue of boundaries clouded bilateral relations for the next two decades. In April 1886, the Peruvian minister to Bolivia, Manuel María del Valle, raised the issue of war debts, reminding the Pacheco government that Bolivia had agreed in the mid-June 1879 protocol to pay 50 percent of the war's expenses. To the surprise of its wartime ally, the Bolivian foreign minister, Juan Crisóstomo Carrillo, responded that his government no longer recognized the obligation because both Bolivia and Peru had assumed equal risks and made similar sacrifices during the war. Taken aback, the Peruvian envoy responded that his government considered the debt to be a binding obligation with liquation both practical and possible. Shortly thereafter, a compromise was reached in which Bolivia agreed to pay Peru a total of one million bolivianos in twice yearly installments over a ten year period. In October 1886, the Valle–Carrillo agreement was replaced by a new one negotiated by the Bolivian minister to

Peru, Eleodoro Camacho, and the Peruvian foreign minister, Ramón Ribeyro, in which Peru agreed to forgive the Bolivian debt and abandon any thought of Bolivian compensation for war debts (Novak and Namihas 2013, 88–9; Basadre 1968, IX, 283–4).

Having resolved the post-war debt issue, Bolivia and Peru turned their attention to the resolution of outstanding border questions (Novak and Namihas 2013, 89). Over 60 years after independence, complex border issues remained unresolved both because they were located in remote, ill-defined areas of Amazonia and because Brazil claimed portions of the contested territory. On 20 April 1886, Bolivia and Peru concluded a preliminary treaty of limits which provided for a mixed commission to fix the frontier (Basadre 1968, IX, 284). After border incidents occurred in 1892 and again in 1894–95, Bolivia and Peru agreed in the Candamo–Terrazas protocol to Brazilian arbitration of the dispute. The protocol also outlined an alternate method to resolve the dispute without proceeding to arbitration, but a settlement by either method proved impossible. The dispute intensified in 1896 after Bolivia created customs zones in the Purús, Aquiri, Manú, and Madre de Dios regions, territories claimed by Peru. In the first half of 1897, the failure to find a diplomatic solution to the dispute threatened to lead to war before protocols concluded in May and June 1897 defused the crisis (St John 1999, 138–9).

Four years later, Bolivia and Peru in November 1901 inked a general arbitration treaty which provided for the resolution of current and future territorial disputes on the basis of *uti possidetis de jure de 1810*. In September 1902, they concluded an additional treaty in which they agreed to demarcate their common frontier from the Chilean border in the west, defined in accordance with article three of the Treaty of Ancón, to the Nevados de Palomani in the east, an end point which was later changed to read where the eastern limit meets the Suches River. In the treaty, the signatories also agreed to mark the frontier between the Peruvian provinces of Tacna and Arica and the Bolivian province of Carangas once the former were returned to Peru (Salazar 2000, 581–4). Finally, Bolivia and Peru in December 1902 agreed to submit their dispute in the Madre de Dios region to arbitration by the president of Argentina. The agreed upon bases for arbitration were the colonial boundaries of the Audiencia de Charcas within the Viceroyalty of Buenos Aires and the Viceroyalty of Peru as both existed in 1810, excluding the section of the boundary defined in the September 1902 treaty (Salazar 2000, 585–6).

As Bolivia and Peru worked to resolve their outstanding border issues, they addressed nagging commercial issues which had been subject to repeated modification and nonfulfillment, resulting in occasional tensions between the two neighbors. In August 1885, Bolivia and Peru concluded a protocol providing for Peru to name a customs agent at or near the Bolivian port on Lake Titicaca and for Bolivia to name a customs agent at the Peruvian port of Mollendo with the goal of facilitating the free transit of goods between Bolivia and Peru. After the 1885 protocol was amended in 1887, Bolivia and Peru concluded a new agreement in November 1888 related to the movement of certain alcoholic beverages from Peru to Bolivia. Additional bilateral agreements were concluded in 1893 and 1900 in an ongoing effort to regularize commerce between the two states (Basadre 1968, IX, 284–5; Novak and Namihas 2013, 56–8).

## Acre Dispute

The growing demand for rubber in the late nineteenth century, driven by the bicycle craze of the 1890s and the popularization of the automobile after 1900, drew citizens from Bolivia, Brazil, and Peru into the Acre region of the Upper Amazon, activating territorial disputes which had been dormant for many years (Weinstein 1983, 8–9). In earlier efforts to resolve these disputes, Brazil and Peru concluded a treaty in October 1851, and Bolivia and Brazil signed a separate pact in March 1867. In theory, these treaties delimited the borders between Bolivia, Brazil, and Peru in the Upper Amazon, and all that remained was for joint commissions to demarcate the frontier. In practice, the inability of Bolivia and Brazil to locate the source of the Javary River prevented any demarcation of the frontier outlined in the 1867 treaty beyond the placement of boundary monuments at both ends (Abecia 1986, II, 313–15; Fifer 1972, 121–2). In the interim, Peru continued to claim large tracts of land in the Upper Amazon, arguing Bolivia ceded land to Brazil in the 1867 agreement over which it lacked legal title.

In 1896, Bolivia and Brazil reached a degree of agreement on the source of the Javary River which enabled them to determine the position of the oblique line in the 1867 treaty running from the confluence of the Mamoré and Beni rivers to the source of the Javary River. Boundary pillars were erected at the places on the river banks where the 1867 oblique line was believed to cross the Purus, Yaco, and Acre rivers. At the end of the decade, Bolivia moved to exercise jurisdiction over the territory south of the oblique line because possession of this part of the Acre would give it egress to the Atlantic Ocean by way of the Aquiry and Purús rivers. In January 1899, Bolivia established a custom house at Puerto Alonso on the left bank of the Acre River on the Bolivian side of the oblique line, and in 1899–1900, the newly installed Pando government dispatched three costly military expeditions to the Acre in an unsuccessful attempt to exert Bolivian control over the area (Guzmán 1998, 227–8; Abecia 1986, II, 315–18). Over time, the arbitrary conduct of the Bolivian customs officers at Puerto Alonso, which included the imposition of taxes and other restrictions on rubber moving down the river, provoked the 60,000 Brazilians living in the region who were largely ignorant of or indifferent to the terms of the 1896 agreement (Fifer 1972 122–3; Garay 2008, 361).

Bilateral relations between Bolivia and Brazil deteriorated further when Bolivia in December 1901 leased thousands of square miles of the disputed region to an Anglo-American company, the Bolivian Syndicate of New York, a concession which included both economic control and civil authority over the area (Weinstein 1983, 176–7). Brazil viewed this move as a flagrant disregard for its interests in the Acre as well as an attempt to introduce into the Americas the system of chartered companies which European governments employed in Africa (Garay 2008, 347–51). In response, Brazil closed the Amazon to Bolivian commerce in August 1902, arguing the free navigation of the river by adjacent riparian states was a privilege which could be revoked at any time absent a reciprocal agreement. In the spring of 1899, discontented Brazilian colonists had temporarily occupied the Bolivian custom house at Puerto Alonso, and the closure of the Amazon provoked the Brazilians resident in the Acre to rise up again in August 1902, eventually occupying the entire territory. When the insurgents proclaimed their independence and sought annexation by Brazil, troops were sent from Rio de Janeiro to protect Brazilian interests in what was the richest rubber growing region in the world at the time (Abecia 1986, II, 321–6; Fifer 1972, 126–7).

At this point, the newly appointed foreign minister of Brazil, Baron do Rio Branco, engaged in creative diplomacy, lifting the embargo against Bolivia and paying the Bolivian Syndicate £110,000 to renounce their concession. Bolivia and Brazil then negotiated a *modus vivendi* in March 1903 which led to a final settlement in November, ending the Bolivia–Brazil territorial dispute and fixing the boundary between them (Ganzert 1934, 436–8; Weinstein 1983, 177). In the Treaty of Petrópolis, Bolivia ceded an estimated 73,726 square miles of land south of latitude 10° 20′ south, an area larger than Belgium, Holland, and Portugal combined, in return for some 2,000 square miles of territory between the Madeira and Abuná rivers which provided Bolivia access to the Madeira River. Additionally, Bolivia received four tracts of swampy land which provided windows toward the Paraguay River. Recognizing the inequity of the land transfers, Brazil agreed to pay Bolivia an indemnity of £2 million and to build a railroad around the Madeira-Mamoré Falls which would give Bolivia access to the lower Madeira River, thus providing Bolivia with a tenuous outlet to the Atlantic Ocean via the Amazon River system (Salazar 2000, 587–93; Abecia 1986, II, 333–4).

The loss of the Acre rubber district was the largest single territorial concession to date in the long and troubled history of Bolivian boundary disputes. Therefore, it was surprising that the terms of the Treaty of Petrópolis excited little interest and limited reaction from the majority of Bolivians, especially those in La Paz and the mining regions, as few of them were involved in, affected by, or even aware of what had transpired. In this regard, the Acre settlement was unique among Bolivia's territorial disputes in that it did not generate a sense of grievance or result in a long-standing impairment of bilateral relations like the loss of the Atacama or the later loss of the Chaco (Fifer 1972, 129–30; Abecia 1986, II, 334–7). Peru on the other hand loudly protested the terms of the 1903 treaty, arguing Peruvian rights were jeopardized because the area acquired by Brazil included territory that Bolivia and Peru had agreed in 1902 to submit to Argentine arbitration.

Eventually, Brazil and Peru in July 1904 concluded two agreements which restored the peace, albeit largely on Brazilian terms (Calderón 2000, 70–2; Moore 1904, 29–32).

## Postwar Relations with Chile

From 1884 to 1887, Chilean policy towards Bolivia and Peru underwent a major change. The Chilean government of Domingo Santa María sought to buy Tacna and Arica from Peru and turn them over to Bolivia with the dual objective of satisfying the latter's demand for a sovereign outlet to the Pacific and solidifying Chilean hegemony on the west coast of South America. This Chilean initiative failed when Peru refused to sell Tacna and Arica and Bolivia rebuffed Chilean efforts to attract Bolivia into its geopolitical orbit (Burr 1967, 171). In response, the Chilean government of José Manuel Balmeceda altered course, hoping to buy Tacna and Arica, not for the benefit of Bolivia, but rather to become an integral part of Chile, serving as a buffer zone for Tarapacá in the event Peru later tried to reassert itself there. President Balmeceda argued that it was unreasonable for Bolivia to expect to receive an improved outlet to the sea from a war which he felt Bolivia had provoked (Guzmán Escobari 2015b, 27). Consequently, he pursued a peace treaty with Bolivia in which the latter would cede its littoral to Chile without receiving Tacna and Arica as compensation (Ríos 1959, 11–16; Espinosa 1965, 272–3). As part of this policy, the Chilean president hoped to include economic and political agreements in a final settlement which would firmly fix Bolivia within the Chilean orbit (Burr 1967, 178; Peñaloza 1984, 351).

In 1888 and again in 1890, Peru rejected Chilean offers to buy Tacna and Arica, insisting on no modification to the plebiscite provision in the Treaty of Ancón. Frustrated, President Balmeceda told the Peruvian minister in Santiago that Peruvian inflexibility was forcing Chile to undertake the Chileanization of Tacna and Arica to ensure a victory in the plebiscite (Palacios 1974, 53–8). President Balmeceda also failed in his early attempts to get Bolivia to relinquish its demands for a Pacific port as part of any final settlement; however, when his administration in October 1890 again proposed a permanent peace with Bolivia based on Chilean possession of Tacna and Arica, the response of the Arce government was positive. According to the revised Chilean proposal, Bolivia would be compensated for the loss of its littoral and port by a Chilean-built railroad, linking La Paz to Tacna and Arica. The October 1890 proposal also called for the partial incorporation of Bolivia into the commercial and political sphere of Chile through a binational common market and a mutual guarantee of territorial integrity in the event of Peruvian aggression (Encina 1963, 195–7; Bórquez and Sáez 2016, 35–7). The October 1890 proposals, which made Bolivia dependent on a Chilean-controlled railway through Chilean-owned Tacna and Arica, resurrected earlier Chilean efforts to turn Bolivia from an independent state into a Chilean satellite (Burr 1967, 191; Miguel 2011, 87–8).

Hard pressed on several fronts, including a Liberal party uprising, a political crisis with Peru, and the failure of Argentina to ratify a bilateral boundary agreement signed 18 months earlier, President Arce accepted the October 1890 Chilean proposal (Klein 1969, 26–7). Throughout this period, Bolivia had hoped to reach an agreement with Argentina which would provide it access to the Atlantic Ocean via the Río de la Plata system as an alternative to a Pacific port as well as to create a counterpoise to Chilean influence on Bolivian foreign policy. In May 1889, Bolivia in the secret Vaca Guzmán–Quirino Costa treaty had ceded to Argentina part of the Chilean-occupied Puna de Atacama in return for Argentine recognition of Bolivian sovereignty over Tarija and other disputed areas in the central Chaco (Salazar 2000, 573–7; Burr 1967, 183–4; Miguel 2011, 89–90). With President Balmeceda's policy toward Bolivia and Peru tantalizingly close to fruition, a constitutional crisis plunged Chile into civil war. The issue was resolved by the end of 1891, but the series of congressional coalitions which followed reduced government efficiency and frustrated policy continuity (Loveman 2001, 158–9).

In the midst of the civil war in Chile, Serapio Reyes Ortiz, the foreign minister of Bolivia, and Juan Gonzalo Matta, an agent of the Congressional Junta of Iquique opposed to the Balmeceda administration, concluded a protocol in May 1891 (Ríos 1963, 144–5). In this agreement, Bolivia recognized Chilean sovereignty over all lands presently occupied by Chile in return for the latter forgiving the Bolivian wartime obligations detailed in the 1884 truce agreement which with interest totaled 6,604,000 pesos. In addition, Bolivia confirmed Chilean sovereignty over the Puna de Atacama which Bolivia had ceded to Argentina two years earlier, and Chile promised to convert Arica and Antofagasta into free ports for the transit of Bolivian commerce (Miguel 2011, 92). The Matta–Reyes Ortiz protocol did not mention the railroad issue nor did it require Bolivia to renounce its pretensions to Tacna and Arica. The Bolivian National Assembly, afraid the protocol with Chile compromised its earlier agreement with Argentina which confirmed Bolivian sovereignty over Tarija in return for Argentinian sovereignty over the Puna de Atacama, rejected the May 1891 pact (Bórquez and Sáez 2016, 37–9; Burr 1967, 192–4).

In August 1892, Peruvian Foreign Minister Eugenio Larrabure y Unánue proposed a creative new solution in which Peru would retain control of Tacna and Arica in return for extending commercial privileges highly beneficial to Chilean commerce. The Peruvian initiative included an offer to assist in resolving the Bolivian question by allocating two-thirds of customs receipts to Bolivia and constructing railroads in Bolivia to improve its access to the outside world. Chile quickly rejected the Peruvian proposal on the grounds it was not interested in any solution which eliminated the possibility of it acquiring Tacna and Arica. A serious offer in itself, the 1892 Peruvian proposal was only one facet of a broader Peruvian strategy aimed at regaining control of both provinces. Peru was convinced it could win a fair plebiscite; therefore, it focused its diplomatic efforts on conducting the plebiscite provided for in the Treaty of Ancón. In January 1894, Peru and Chile reached an agreement, known as the Jiménez–Vial Solar accord, which provided for a plebiscite under the conditions of reciprocity which both governments deemed necessary to conduct an honest election (Ríos 1959, 17, 19–23; Calderón 2000, 54–5).

Domestic politics in Chile and Peru intruded at this point to frustrate what might have been a workable solution. A change in the Chilean government was followed by the sudden death of Peruvian President Remigio Morales Bermúdez, and these two events combined to delay negotiations until the ten-year occupation period had passed and a different diplomatic climate had developed in Chile. In March 1894, Peru learned that the new Chilean government of Jorge Montt had disavowed the January 1894 agreement and was requesting new talks. Chile proposed a four year postponement of the plebiscite or cession of Tacna and Arica, and Peru rejected both proposals outright. Chile then proposed to divide the two provinces into three zones with only the middle zone subject to a plebiscite, but Peru also rejected what Chile considered to be a compromise because Peru still hoped to regain all of Tacna and Arica through the plebiscite provision (McNicoll 1937, 205–6; Calderón 2000, 61).

Negotiations between the Bolivian government of Mariano Baptista and the Chilean government of Jorge Montt reopened in early 1895. After several months of talks, Bolivia and Chile on 18 May 1895 signed three treaties and two protocols relevant to Bolivia's quest for a Pacific port (Abecia 1986, II, 247–8, 269–70; Bórquez and Sáez 2016, 135–9). A treaty of peace and friendship officially ended the state of war between the signatories, and Chile assumed certain Bolivian financial obligations in return for Bolivian recognition of Chilean sovereignty over both the Bolivian littoral and the territory in the Puna de Atacama which Bolivia ceded to Argentina in 1889 (Miguel 2011, 99–100, 171–3; Concha and Garay 2013, 323–5). The second agreement was a commercial treaty which included a reciprocal trade agreement, guarantees of mutual protection for the nationals of either country doing business in the other, and provisions for railroad construction. The third and most important treaty was a secret agreement in which Chile agreed to transfer Tacna and Arica to Bolivia if it acquired them through a plebiscite or direct negotiations. In return, Bolivia agreed to pay Chile 5 million pesos. If Chile failed to acquire the two Peruvian provinces, it pledged to provide Bolivia with a port at Vitor Bay in the southern part of Arica province, a territory occupied but not yet owned by Chile, and to pay Bolivia 5 million pesos. If Bolivia and Chile agreed instead upon a bay similar to Vitor elsewhere on the Chilean coast, Chile agreed to pay Bolivia 5 million pesos for its development (Miguel 2011, 101–2, 174–6; Concha and Garay 2013, 326–7). Finally, the two protocols regulated credits and commercial obligations (Barros 1924, 75–7; Peñaloza 1984, 354–6). With the conclusion of the May 1895 agreements, Bolivia obtained a promise of a Pacific port as long as the plebiscite provided for in the Treaty of Ancón resulted in Chile obtaining at least Arica province. In return, Bolivia agreed to support Chile's policy of hegemony on the west coast of South America because only in this manner could Bolivia achieve its primary foreign policy objective, a sovereign outlet to the Pacific (Burr 1967, 208–9).

The May 1895 treaties provoked a bitter debate in Bolivia, especially among members of the Liberal party; consequently, the Baptista government did not submit them to the National Assembly for approval until the end of October. Bolivia was on the eve of national elections, and with many Bolivians preferring a policy of cooperation with Argentina as opposed to Chile, foreign policy was a major issue in the election campaign. Bolivians opposed to the agreements argued Bolivian recognition of Chilean sovereignty over the Bolivian littoral in the treaty of peace should have been tied more closely to the promise of a seaport in the secret treaty. If Chile failed to secure Tacna and Arica, Bolivians feared they would have sacrificed their littoral in vein. If Chile did secure Tacna and Arica and deliver them to Bolivia, critics expressed concern that Peru would respond by attacking Bolivia; therefore, they argued the May 1895 treaties also should have included a promise of Chilean assistance in the case of Peruvian aggression (Burr 1967, 212–15; Abecia 1986, II, 269–70; Miguel 2011, 102–16).

Facing strong criticism, the Bolivian National Assembly delayed ratification of the May 1895 pacts until Chile agreed in a December 1895 protocol that the cession of the Bolivian littoral would be voided if Chile did not deliver within two years the port on the Pacific coast mentioned in the secret treaty. In addition, the protocol stated that the obligations of Chile to Bolivia would not be fully satisfied until the latter received a port and zone satisfactory for both its current and future commercial and industrial needs (Abecia 1986, II, 270–3; Bórquez and Sáez 2016, 140). With the addition of the December 1895 protocol to the May 1895 treaties, the Bolivian National Assembly approved the three treaties and one of the two protocols. Chile on the other hand remained concerned about the wording of its commitment to provide Bolivia a port in Vitor Bay or elsewhere, and yet another protocol clarifying this point was concluded at the end of April 1896 (Barros 1924, 78–9; Concha and Garay 2013, 96–102). Bolivia had long sought to tie cession of its littoral to the procurement of a seaport; therefore, the terms of the 1895 agreements represented a major albeit pyrrhic diplomatic victory. When Peru learned of the May 1895 agreements, it issued a strong protest on the grounds that it intended to recover Tacna and Arica and would never cede them to Bolivia, Chile, or any other state (Novak and Namihas 2013, 93; Becerra de la Roca 2002, 66).

After 1895, Chilean policy toward Bolivia underwent a gradual change in part due to a Chilean *rapprochement* with both Argentina and Peru and in part due to Bolivian intransigence over the seaport issue. The shift in Chilean policy also was influenced by the refusal of Peru to abandon its policy of seeking the full reincorporation of Tacna and Arica, despite the failure in 1893 to hold the plebiscite provided for in the Treaty of Ancón (Ulloa 1941, 302–4; Concha and Garay 2013, 133). Faced with the unwillingness of Peru to cede the territory desired by Bolivia and concerned that Peru might support Argentina in a widening conflict with Chile, the Chilean government of Federico Errázuriz Echaurren reached an understanding with the Peruvian government of Nicolás de Piérola. In the Billinghurst–Latorre protocol, dated 16 April 1898, Chile and Peru agreed that voter eligibility in the plebiscite to decide the future of Tacna and Arica would be decided by the queen regent of Spain with the plebiscite conducted by a board comprised of a Chilean, a Peruvian, and a neutral member designated by the Spanish arbitrator (Wagner de Reyna 1964, I, 90; Ríos 1959, 28–32). The terms of the 1898 protocol were the best Peru could have negotiated at the time in that only natives of Tacna and Arica could vote in the plebiscite, and Peruvians celebrated the agreement as a diplomatic victory.

The Peruvian Congress approved the Billinghurst–Latorre protocol by a wide margin, and the Chilean Senate also approved it. But once the Argentine crisis passed, the Chilean House pigeonholed it, pending assurances that the Chilean nitrate monopoly would be protected and perpetuated (Miguel 2011, 141–5). The Billinghurst–Latorre protocol was the only serious Chilean effort to hold the plebiscite from 1894 to 1925, and Chilean rejection of it was notable in that it reaffirmed Chile's determination to retain Tacna and Arica (Bello 1919, 25–42; Bákula 2002, II, 975–8). The Billinghurst–Latorre protocol did not constitute a technical violation of the May 1895 pacts because Bolivia could still have Tacna and Arica if Chile won the plebiscite. At the same time, it represented a major albeit temporary shift in Chilean policy as it set the stage for a fair plebiscite, and Bolivia, Chile, and Peru all recognized it was unlikely that Chile could win a fair plebiscite.

## A Peace to End All Peace

As Peru savored its diplomatic victory, the Chilean government of Germán Riesco Errázuriz opened talks with the Pando government regarding a definitive peace settlement which recognized Chilean sovereignty over the Bolivian littoral but did not include a provision for a sovereign Bolivian seaport. As compensation, Chile offered to assume certain Bolivian debts and to construct a railroad from Bolivia to a Chilean seaport through which Bolivian goods would pass duty free (Bello 1919, 189–90). The ensuing negotiations, which stretched from 1902 to 1904, highlighted the extent to which Bolivian foreign policy had been undermined by events in Argentina, Chile, and Peru. The Billinghurst–Latorre protocol reduced the possibility of an anti-Chilean alliance between Argentina and Peru, and it did so without promoting closer Bolivian ties with Argentina. Bolivia's subdued response to the Billinghurst–Latorre protocol reflected the false hope that the plebiscite would result in a Chilean victory in Tacna and Arica. The Pando government also failed to challenge Chile's aggressive pursuit of a boundary settlement with Argentina, and in September 1898, Argentina and Chile agreed to submit their dispute to British arbitration with the result that the war threat subsided (Gumucio 2005, 143–8; Abecia 1986, II, 277–9). After 1898, domestic economic and political problems in Bolivia, together with the boundary dispute with Brazil over the rubber-rich Acre district further weakened the negotiating position of the Pando administration. In contrast, the negotiating position of Chile improved with the resolution of its dispute with Argentina in the 1902 Pactos de Mayo (Bello 1919, 175–85; Encina 1963, 245–50). Where Chile had once faced with the threat of encirclement and war with Argentina, the 1902 agreements created a new equilibrium in its favor (Burr 1967, 252–6).

After Chile had resolved its boundary dispute with Argentina and appeared willing to negotiate a settlement with Peru, the Pando government was driven by a heightened sense of urgency as it could no longer use the threat of an alliance with Argentina or Peru as a lever in its negotiations with Chile (Guzmán Escobari 2015b, 29–30). At the same time, Chile was less and less interested in Bolivian demands as exemplified by the infamous König memorandum (Carrasco 1920, 112–13; Albarracín 2005, 121–32). In January 1900, the Errázuriz government nominated Abraham König Velásquez to be the Chilean minister to Bolivia. Upon arriving in La Paz, König spent much of the summer proposing different bases for negotiation, all of which were rejected by the Pando administration. Impatient with the lack of progress, König delivered an ultimatum in August 1900 in the form of a long memorandum to the Bolivian government in which he stated that Chile owned the Bolivian littoral as a right of conquest, and if it decided to give Bolivia compensation for it in the form of a port or otherwise, it would be an act of charity (Abecia 1986, II, 305–9; Prudencio Lizón 1975, 110–22; Miguel 2011, 145–51, 177–88).

Shocked by the arrogant, uncompromising tone of the König memorandum, Bolivia instructed its envoy in Washington, Fernando Guachalla, to seek US mediation of the dispute. The Bolivian request for mediation was based in part on the interest the United States had shown in promoting the Pan-American movement. Washington used the Bolivian request to encourage Chile to participate in the upcoming Pan-America Congress; however, when Chile opposed the proposed mediation, the United States declined to move forward on the grounds that any mediation should be requested and approved by both parties to a dispute. In September 1900, only five weeks after König delivered his memorandum to the Bolivian government, the Chilean envoy in Lima proposed to the Peruvian government of Eduardo López de Romaña that Tacna and Arica remain under Chilean sovereignty in exchange for the division of the Bolivian nation between Chile and Peru in a joint military action (Maldonado 2005, 17). When Peru protested to the US Department of State what it termed the Chilean proposal to "polonize" Bolivia, the State Department received the protest but took no action (Gumucio 2005, 157–60; Abecia 1986, II, 280–6). With its options increasingly limited, the Pando government in early 1902 dispatched an unofficial agent to Chile with instructions to seek a peace treaty to replace the 1884 truce (Ríos 1963, 161–7). Bilateral talks proceeded slowly in the wake of the May 1902 pacts between Argentina and Chile; however, in August 1903, the Bolivian minister of foreign affairs, Eliodoro Villazón, reported to the National Assembly that progress was being made. In so doing, he admitted that Bolivia's position vis-à-vis Chile had deteriorated to the point that Bolivia must be prepared to relinquish its hope for a Pacific port. Attempting to soften the blow, he added that Bolivia could expect other forms of compensation for the loss of its littoral (Bello 1919, 191–4; Burr 1967, 257; Querejazu 1979, 754–6).

A Treaty of Peace, Friendship, and Commerce, known as the Bello Codesido–Gutiérrez treaty, was signed on 20 October 1904, ending the war between Bolivia and Chile which had begun 25 years earlier. In the agreement, Bolivia ceded to Chile in perpetuity the Bolivian littoral, including the ports of Antofagasta, Cobija, Mejillones, and Tocopilla. In return, Chile guaranteed Bolivia commercial transit rights through Chile together with facilities at certain Chilean ports, notably Antofagasta and Arica. In so doing, the terms of the treaty continued the free transit regime through Arica which Bolivia had enjoyed since the November 1847 treaty as ratified in the October 1848 and November 1863 treaties. Chile also agreed to pay Bolivia £300,000 to relieve some of its pressing financial problems and to build a railroad from the port of Arica to La Paz with ownership of the Bolivian section of the railroad passing to Bolivia 15 years after the railroad had been constructed. The agreement also provided for the free transit in perpetuity of Bolivian goods across Chilean territory and granted Bolivia the right to establish customs houses in certain Chilean ports. Other provisions included a Chilean guarantee of the interest on investment capital required by Bolivia to construct five domestic railroads in return for which Chile was granted reduced freight rates on those railroads (Salazar 2000, 595–601; Téllez 1989, 231–5). Finally, the 1904 treaty paid an important, unspecified dividend to Chile. In addition to the commitment to construct a railroad between Arica and La Paz, the agreement provided for the demarcation of the boundaries for Tacna and Arica. Chile would later cite these two provisions as evidence it was exercising effective sovereignty over Tacna and Arica (Bello 1919, 196–7; Burr 1967, 257–9).

With much of the Bolivian public shocked by the terms of the 1904 treaty, the newly installed Liberal government of Ismael Montes (1904–09) tried to justify the agreement on the grounds that Bolivian commerce was threatened by the old treaties which gave Chile control over Bolivian tariffs, and it was time for Bolivia to restore control over its economy (Maldonado 2005, 16; Albarracín 2005, 12–13, 17–20; Galindo 1977, 77–8). Given the deep connections of the Liberal party to export-importers in general and to the mining industry in particular, the terms of the 1904 treaty meant Bolivia would soon have a railroad to export ore and other products to the world (Guzmán Escobari 2015b, 29; Mesa Gisbert 2016, 133–4). In addition to the 1904 treaty, Bolivia and Chile also concluded a confidential protocol which committed Bolivia to assist Chile to win the plebiscite to decide the future of Tacna and Arica by encouraging Bolivian residents in the disputed territories to vote for Chile (Carrasco 1920, 115–17; Barros 1924, 100–1). Predictably, Peru rejected the 1904 treaty in the strongest terms, especially article three pertaining to the Arica–La Paz railroad. The Peruvian government denied Chilean sovereignty over Arica or any obligation the railroad might enjoy in what remained legally Peruvian territory (Novak and Namihas 2013, 93–4; Oblitas 2001, 448–9; Concha and Garay 2013, 237–41).

Once the Bolivian Congress approved the 1904 treaty, the intense initial criticism of the pact abated, and some portion of the body politic appeared to accept the result. Debate over the terms of the agreement was soon replaced by argument over how best to spend the large sums of money now available to Bolivia. In 1905, congressional debate centered on how best to spend the £2 million which Brazil had recently deposited to Bolivia's account in London for the Acre, together with the monies forthcoming from Chile. With Bolivia now in a position to bring to reality long-standing railroad dreams, provincial congressmen were soon engaged in contentious talks aimed at justifying a new rail line for their district (Klein 1969, 42). At the same time, some Bolivians rightly viewed the 1904 treaty as an imposed peace and continued to criticize it (Escobari 1982, I, 261–6).

## Conclusion

The 1904 Treaty of Peace, Friendship, and Commerce was a treaty of peace but not of friendship or commerce as more than a century of acrimonious bilateral relations which followed made clear. The agreement ratified the failure of Bolivian foreign policy toward Chile and Peru after 1879 as the heart of that policy had been a sovereign outlet to the Pacific Ocean. In a wider sense, it also marked the failure of core tenets of Bolivian foreign policy since 1825. Bolivian leaders at independence set out to guarantee Bolivia's economic future by securing a port facility which would encourage investment and trade and by concluding alliances which would guarantee the nation's sovereignty, economic independence, national security, and territorial integrity. The 1904 treaty ratified a significant violation of the territorial integrity of Bolivia, and it left the nation landlocked, compromising economic independence, sovereignty, and national security by leaving its lifelines to the Pacific in the control of a neighboring state. While the agreement did not end Bolivian aspirations for a sovereign port on the Pacific, it rendered irrelevant the legal arguments Bolivia had assiduously developed after 1825. The legal evidence supporting the applicability of *uti possidetis de jure* never had a day in court, and after Bolivia signed the 1904 treaty, it no longer applied.

# 5 Landlocked, Dependent, Challenged, 1904–30

Having signed the 1904 peace treaty, Bolivia spent much of the next three decades trying to escape the landlocked condition ratified by the agreement. At the same time, it addressed boundary issues with Argentina, Brazil, and Peru; free transit on the Upper Amazon; and related navigation issues on the Bermejo, Paraguay, and Pilcomayo rivers, among other questions. After Chile and Peru concluded the 1929 Treaty of Lima, dividing Tacna and Arica between them, Bolivia protested the agreement, especially article one of the additional protocol which stipulated that neither Chile nor Peru could cede to a third state any of the territories over which they were granted sovereignty in the treaty without the prior agreement of the other signatory. With no obvious strategy to regain sovereign access to the Pacific, Bolivia turned its attention south to the Chaco Boreal in search of an outlet to the Atlantic via the Paraguay River.

## Economic Consequences of the Peace

The 1903 Treaty of Petrópolis with Brazil and the 1904 Treaty of Peace, Friendship, and Commerce with Chile gave the Liberal oligarchy which came to power in 1899 both relative peace on the international scene and the financial wherewithal to continue railroad construction. With the temporary elimination of the most divisive international issues, the Liberal movement proved so strong there were no coup attempts from 1899 to 1920, a record in the history of Bolivia (Lehman 1999, 56; Klein 2011, 161–2). During the first administration of President Ismael Montes (1904–9), rising tin exports, which made up more than half the country's exports from the early 1900s to the 1980s, led to an economic boom which the government used to expand the state bureaucracy and buy out potential opposition. The intimate relationship of the government with the tin oligarchy fostered *la rosca*, "a tightly interwoven clique of political and economic elites that served and answered to the tin barons" (Morales 2010, 95). The Montes administration committed to a massive expansion of public works, and with a sizeable surplus in the balance of trade, it successfully secured private international funding for government loans. In 1906, private US bank loans enabled the government to complete its international rail connections with spurs to Cochabamba and Sucre and additional links to the mining centers of Potosí and Oruro (Siekmeier 2011, 15). Completed in 1904, a railroad from La Paz to Guaqui on Lake Titicaca linked the Bolivian rail network to that of Peru, enabling goods to go by steamer to Puno and on by train to Mollendo by 1908. In 1906, work began on the Arica to La Paz railroad which was completed in 1913, and the final leg in the railway linking La Paz and Antofagasta was completed in 1908 (Guzmán 1998, 243–6; Jordán 1999, 221–2).

By World War I, Bolivia had three railway routes to the Pacific, namely Antofagasta, Arica, and Mollendo; unfortunately, unprecedented railroad construction had decidedly mixed results for a landlocked nation aspiring to a sovereign Pacific port. The feeder lines which the US-based Speyer and Company constructed to connect Bolivia's major cities and mining centers were leased for 99 years to the British-owned Antofagasta and Bolivia Railway Company, giving it a monopoly on the lines constructed by Speyer as well as most of Bolivia's other railway facilities (Marsh 1928, 73–4; Pike 1977, 164). The rail links through Chile, Chilean-occupied territory, and Peru largely robbed Bolivia of its claim to be without access to the sea because its plea for access was being answered by transit concessions. The Antofagasta and Bolivia Railway Company employed differential rates on these feeder routes to channel a significant amount of mineral exports through the port of Antofagasta even after the railroad to Arica was completed. At the same time, when the emptied rail cars returned from the coast to the highlands, they often carried foreign goods, from raw materials to manufactured products, which had a crippling effect on the development of domestic manufacturers and suppliers who could not compete with the price and quality of imported goods (Fifer 1972, 71–2). With the transport of goods from Bolivia east of the Andes still by mule, Santa Cruz sugar sold for more than twice the price of the imported Peruvian product, and a similar situation was true of Cochabamba wheat when compared to North American and Chilean imports (Lehman 1999, 54).

At the outset of the second Montes administration (1913–17), attempts to establish a national bank resulted in bitter pressure from a key segment of the Bolivian elite (Carrasco 1920, 118). At the same time, a crisis in international trade caused tin production and exports to plunge by one-third in 1913–14. Adverse weather conditions in the same period led to a severe agricultural crisis. With money tight and government revenues shrinking, President Montes was unable to placate the opposition with public works and national welfare. In 1914, the Liberal party splintered into two groups with the newly formed Republican party, a carbon copy of its predecessor. The Republican party drew its support from the same socioeconomic groups, supported the demands of the mining oligarchy and the *rosca*, and was as racist and oligarchic as the Liberal party (Henderson 2013, 213; Mesa Gisbert 2001a, 537, 548). "The final result of the return of effective two-party politics was a return to the politics of closed and fraudulent presidential elections and an ultimate resort to violence and coups on the part of the opposition" (Klein 2011, 163). When the last Liberal president, José Gutiérrez Guerra (1917–20), attempted to control the 1920 elections, the Republican party rose in revolt and ended Liberal party rule.

The advent of Republican rule was accompanied by a short but intense depression in 1920–22. Once mine production resumed, labor agitation subsided, and President Bautista Saavedra (1921–25) turned to private capital markets to promote large development projects, the source of public support for earlier governments. In 1922, Bolivia negotiated a $33 million New York bank loan for railroad, public works, and Banco de Nación financing (Marsh 1928, 98–120, 137–78). The terms of the loan included external control over Bolivian taxation services. With debt servicing already high, this provision was highly unpopular with most Bolivians. Despite its excellent credit rating, Bolivia also accepted high interest rates. As a result, opposition to the so-called Nicolaus loan, floated in part by the Stifel-Nicolaus Investment Company of St. Louis, was widespread and intense (Galarza 1971, 105; Abecia 1986, II, 420–1).

Attempts to resolve the great debate over petroleum concessions in the eastern lowlands compounded the problems of the Saavedra administration. Bolivia first granted petroleum concessions in 1865, but nothing came of them. At the turn of the century, new concessions were granted to Bolivian-financed companies; however, they proved incapable of attracting sufficient capital and opening productive wells (Abecia 1986, II, 477–80; Mesa Gisbert 2001a, 540). Instead of the active exploitation of their deposits, the primary aim of these national firms became speculation in the petroleum concessions themselves. After 1912, a Royal Dutch Shell subsidiary explored the potential for developing Bolivian oil deposits but was unable to make arrangements to export the oil through Argentina. This setback went largely unnoticed at the time; however, the question of exporting oil through Argentina would become a critical issue, contributing to the Chaco War in the 1930s. In 1916–20, local Chilean and Anglo-Bolivian capital also invested in the Bolivian concessions, reorganizing earlier grants into larger holdings, but without any concessionaire actually beginning production (Cote 2016b, 17–18). In 1920, Bolivia opened its reserve areas to foreign companies, and several North American entrepreneurs secured concessions. These seemingly small companies proved mostly to be fronts for the Standard Oil Company (New Jersey), and in 1921, the Saavedra administration allowed it to purchase the concessions of the smaller companies and create the Standard Oil Company of Bolivia. In November 1921, Standard Oil requested changes to its original contract, and the Saavedra government in July 1922 agreed to several modifications highly favorable to it. Among other changes, the 1922 contract removed a clause allowing Bolivia to confiscate properties for fraud and lowered state royalties from 15 to 11 percent. By 1925, Standard Oil had established 11 work camps in Bolivia, and by 1927, it was producing an average of 71 barrels of crude oil daily (Marsh 1928, 56–63; Klein and Peres-Cajías 2014, 146–7; Cote 2016a, 160).

The Saavedra government was unpopular, and its special treatment of Standard Oil led to a public outcry (Mesa Gisbert 2001a, 564–5). To the familiar issues of corruption, favoritism, and executive domination, an entirely new force was added to Bolivian politics, economic or resource nationalism (Siekmeier 2011, 17–18; Cote 2016a, 158–61).

> Natural resource wealth – particularly tin and oil – occupied the central position in the popular nationalist imaginary that developed starting in the 1920s ... resource nationalism, the idea that resource wealth should be used for the benefit of the nation – would be the key factor uniting mine workers, urban workers, students, war veterans, middle-class professionals, and other urban sectors.
>
> (Young 2017, 1)

US companies had long provided investment in infrastructure, mining, and other sectors of the economy, but petroleum was a unique case from the day the first concession was granted to a foreign company (Miranda 1999, 244–5). From the start, petroleum was treated as a special subject, and intense criticism of Standard Oil quickly became a standard component of the rhetoric of the traditional right and the nascent left movements in Bolivia (Klein 2011, 166–7).

In addition to the development of a potent new form of nationalism, the expansion of the petroleum sector in the 1920s had other long-term consequences for Bolivia. As the eastern lowlands developed, Santa Cruz grew from a small frontier town on the eastern edge of the Andes to the largest city in contemporary Bolivia. Concomitant with this growth, a cultural dissonance developed between eastern lowland Bolivians and their western highland compatriots even as the development of the petroleum sector helped integrate the country. Long-standing elements of regionalism and racism manifested themselves in this dichotomy. "It is an opposition of east and west, *collas* (from the Altiplano) and *cambas* (from the lowlands), indigenous peoples, whites and mestizos, tradition and modernity, collectivism and private initiative, peoples and oligarchs" (Barragán 2008, 83). The operation of the Standard Oil Company of Bolivia in the 1920s contributed to the east–west division which developed in Bolivia. Easterners identified more closely with the concepts of global capitalist integration prevalent at the time while highland Bolivians were more focused on protecting the nation's natural resources from foreign exploitation (Cote 2016b, xii–xv, 31, 33, 60–1; Roca 1980, 199–201).

During the presidency of Hernando Siles Reyes (1926–30), the Bolivian economy continued to decline. The Siles Reyes administration faced mounting budget deficits and an increased difficulty in meeting its international debt obligations. The foreign debt, which was practically zero in 1908, approximated $3,842,000 in 1920 and mushroomed to $60,384,000 by June 1930. At the same time, the market price of tin peaked and began its steady decline into the Great Depression. In 1929, Bolivia achieved a record output of 47,000 tons of tin exports but at a price well below that earlier in the decade. Tin quoted at $917 a ton in 1927 dropped to $794 a ton in 1929 and $385 a ton in 1932. Government revenues tracked the downward spiral of tin prices. In 1929, 37 percent of the government budget was devoted to servicing the foreign debt with another 20 percent funding the armed forces. Most of the remainder covered basic government necessities, leaving next to nothing for public works and national welfare (Klein 2011, 168–9; Morales and Pacheco 1999, 157).

To meet the growing crisis, the Siles Reyes administration pursued a mix of orthodox and unorthodox economic policies. With the backing of newly created taxes, it secured a new loan in 1927, primarily through the banking house of Stifel-Nicolaus with the Equitable Trust Company and Spencer, Trask, and Company playing a subsidiary role. Under the terms of the 1927 loan, which was strongly criticized by the opposition, customs receipts, the source of 45 percent of the national revenues of Bolivia, were pledged to secure the debt. In 1928, Bolivia arranged another loan, this time with Dillon, Read, and Company (Pike 1977, 197). Collectively, the loans secured by the Saavedra and Siles Reyes governments constituted the majority of the debt contracted by Bolivia in the first half of the twentieth century (Mesa Gisbert 2001a, 557). The Siles Reyes government adopted some of the fiscal reforms proposed by the Kemmerer Mission, headed by Professor Edwin W. Kemmerer of Princeton University, and it established a Central Bank to oversee the national money supply (Galarza 1971, 103–8; Siekmeier 2011, 16). It also continued many of the irresponsible economic policies and bad financial practices of the past, like exaggerated revenues and recurrent deficits, with the result that Bolivia was in a weakened condition when the Great Depression came in 1929 (Jordán 1999, 224–7; Klein 2011, 168).

## Early Pan-American Conferences

In 1888, the US government invited the Latin American states to attend an inter-American conference in Washington, D.C. Bolivia, Chile, and Peru were among the 18 states which accepted the invitation. Juan Francisco Velarde represented Bolivia at the conference. Peru eventually accepted the invitation; however, it delayed its response in an abortive attempt to get the Tacna and Arica issue on the agenda. The conference invitation called on the delegates to discuss various concerns, most of which involved trade and customs issues (Peñaloza 1984, 345–6). To this extent, the conference reflected the interests of US commercial bodies which had begun to recognize investment and trade opportunities in Latin America. The conference invitation also called for the adoption of an arbitration procedure, an initiative which highlighted US interest in using the inter-American system as an instrument to promote international stability through improved peacekeeping procedures. At the same time, Washington increasingly viewed the inter-American system as a convenient structure to gather the Latin American states under its leadership. In this sense, the First Pan-American Conference marked a shift in the underlying rationale for the inter-American system. Where it previously enjoyed a largely idealistic foundation, the inter-American system now began to move toward a more pragmatic, utilitarian base, increasingly dominated by the United States (Inman 1965, 33–4).

In the end, the delegates to the First Pan-American Conference discussed a wide variety of issues, including a customs union and an International Union of American Republics, a forerunner to the Organization of American States (OAS) (Abecia 1986, II, 296). That said, the subject which elicited the most debate was the arbitration question because it touched on a variety of national rivalries and interests. Secretary of State James G. Blaine was a leading proponent of arbitration, and the United States informally submitted a draft arbitration treaty early in the conference. Several Latin American governments questioned the US proposal with Chile at the forefront of opposition to the principal of obligatory arbitration. The Chilean delegation willingly accepted the principle of arbitration; however, with the Tacna and Arica dispute in mind, it refused to accept the principle as obligatory and unconditional, especially in the case of pending disputes. In turn, Peru in concert with Argentina and other supporters sought to use the arbitration issue as a means to bring the question of Tacna and Arica before the conference. When the conferees addressed a related report which recommended the adoption of a resolution condemning the right of conquest, Chile found itself in a delicate position; however, widespread delegate concern with the report minimized Chilean embarrassment. In the end, the anti-conquest resolution was tied to the arbitration agreement, and while both were adopted, neither was ratified. Bolivia joined ten other states in signing the arbitration treaty, but Chile and Peru refused to sign (Scott 1931, 44; Cuevas 1976, 284–93; Peñaloza 1984, 345–9).

The Second Pan-American Conference convened in Mexico City in October 1901. Once again, the arbitration issue was at the forefront of talks before and during the conference. After the contentious negotiations in Washington in 1889, Chile was reluctant to attend a second conference, and its reservations were confirmed when the executive commission of the International Union of American Republics decided the Mexico City conference should formulate an arbitration plan applicable to both pending and future disagreements. For months, the Chilean envoy in Washington, Carlos Morla Vicuña, worked to persuade the executive commission to exclude compulsory arbitration from the Mexico City agenda (Bello 1919, 50–8, 89–93). His task was made easier when Argentina's term on the executive commission ended, and the more tractable Ecuador replaced Chile's bitter rival. Subsequently, the Chilean delegation to the conference was both surprised and angered when Mexico, two weeks after the conference opened, introduced a resolution favoring compulsory arbitration, including issues pending at the time. The US delegation spoke against this broad arbitration proposal; nevertheless, by December 1901, ten countries led by Argentina, Bolivia, and Peru were urging compulsory arbitration of pending and future disputes. For a time, it appeared as though the conference might break down over the issue (Abecia 1986, II, 296–7; Pike 1963 126–31). Eventually, a compromise was reached in which the 19 participating states agreed to subscribe to the arbitration provisions of the 1899 Hague Convention, and on a voluntary basis, submit disputes to the Permanent Court of Arbitration (Bello 1919, 63–4, 109–75; Wilgus 1931).

The issue of compulsory arbitration was again center stage in discussions leading to the Third Pan-American Conference in Rio de Janeiro in 1906. Peru supported by Bolivia pressed for unrestricted discussion of the issue, but Chile supported by Brazil and Ecuador opposed passage of an obligatory arbitration resolution in any form. Chile wanted the subject of compulsory arbitration left off the official agenda, arguing it was unnecessary to include it because the Second Pan-American Conference had agreed to the principle of voluntary arbitration embodied in the 1899 Hague Convention. In the end, Chile achieved a significant diplomatic victory as the subject of obligatory arbitration was not on the agenda when the Third Pan-American Conference opened in Rio de Janeiro. Instead, the program called for an agreement affirming the application of the principle of arbitration as a means to settle disputes in the Americas (Pike 1963 131–2). At the end of the Rio Conference, the delegates in attendance approved a resolution calling for the upcoming Second Conference at The Hague to approve a General Convention of Arbitration, temporarily removing the question from Pan-American jurisdiction (Bello 1919, 185–6; Wilgus 1932)

When the Fourth Pan-American Conference convened in Buenos Aires in 1910, the subject of arbitration was not on the agenda. Prior to its opening, Peru had argued before the executive commission of the International Union of American Republics that the topic of compulsory arbitration should be on the agenda, but no other country supported the Peruvian position (Pike 1963, 134). Moreover, the question of Tacna and Arica was not discussed at either the Rio de Janeiro or Buenos Aires conferences (Bello 1919, 186). Disappointed with a 1909 Argentine arbitral award in its boundary dispute with Peru, Bolivia broke diplomatic relations with Argentina in mid-1909; consequently, it did not attend the Fourth Pan American Conference in Buenos Aires in 1910. The Fifth Pan-American Conference, originally scheduled for late 1914 or early 1915 did not convene until 1923 due to World War I. After Chile in early 1923 refused to consider a revision to the 1904 treaty, Bolivia also declined to attend the Fifth Pan-American Conference when it convened in Santiago in March 1923 (Querejazu 1979, 779; Abecia 1986, II, 425). Bolivia tried to win support for the seaport issue at an International Law Conference which convened in Buenos Aires in 1925 but again was unsuccessful (Glassner 1964, 41).

The Sixth Pan-American Conference opened in Havana in early 1928. Chile was a reluctant participant in part because of the controversies its 1883 treaty with Peru and its 1904 treaty with Bolivia had raised at earlier Pan-American Conferences and in part because it was concerned the United

States would intervene in the Tacna and Arica dispute. To prevent this from happening, Chile sought the support of Argentina and Brazil, which they extended, agreeing that Bolivia and Peru should not be allowed to bring their respective cases before the conference. In the face of this support, the United States agreed with Chile that its difficulties with Bolivia and Peru would not be discussed in Havana. The Chilean and Peruvian delegations maintained cordial relations throughout the Sixth Pan-American Conference, and in the course of the meeting, both delegations opposed a Bolivian proposal favoring the revision of international treaties (Ríos 1959, 178–84; Gumucio 2005, 325–6)

## Landlocked

From 1904 to 1918, the Liberal governments in power in Bolivia emphasized railroad construction at the expense of a sovereign outlet to the sea; however, when they discussed the seaport issue, they pressed for a Pacific outlet through Arica. "No attempt was made to conceal the fact that Bolivia's acquisition of Arica was the basis of the country's entire foreign policy. All external relations were measured against the yardstick of how far the actions might assist or impede this realization" (Fifer 1972, 72–3). In 1901, Peru severed diplomatic relations with Chile over its *chilenización* of Tacna and Arica, and it did so again in 1910 after Chile expelled all Peruvian priests active in the occupied provinces (Ríos 1959, 33–8, 52–6; Palacios 1974, 69–104). In the interim, Chile in 1906 again offered to purchase Tacna and Arica, and Peru again refused to sell (Maldonado 2005, 18).

In April 1910, the minister of foreign affairs of Bolivia, Daniel Sánchez Bustamante Vásquez, approached the governments of Chile and Peru, asking if they would consider resolving the Tacna and Arica issue by having both states renounce their claims in favor of Bolivia (Escobari 1988, 102; Abecia 1986, II, 398–9). The Peruvian government rejected the Bolivian proposal, emphasizing that Peru could never consider giving Tacna to Bolivia. The response of the Chilean government was ambiguous in that it expressed interest in a Bolivia–Chile confederation, an initiative outside the scope of the Bolivian proposal (Novak and Namihas 2013, 94; Bustos 2003, 105–8; Gumucio 2005, 213–37). Three years later, former President Ismael Montes made a similar proposal in an informal meeting of prominent Chileans in Santiago where he had stopped on his way from Paris to La Paz to begin a second term (Becerra de la Roca 2002, 132; Abecia 1986, II, 400–1). The Chileans present also rejected the idea of a tripartite settlement in which Arica would pass to Bolivia. Later, Abraham König Velásquez, author of the infamous König memorandum, noted in his diary: "What is Montes trying to do?...Does he think Chile is a land of fools?" (*¿Qué es lo que pretende Montes?...¿Cree que Chile is una tierra de tontos?*) (Querejazu 1979, 766–9, quoted on 768; Denegri 1988, 110–11).

As Chile and Peru continued to reject Bolivian proposals for a sovereign port on the Pacific, the completion of rail links from the altiplano through

Chilean territory to the Pacific undermined Bolivia's claim to be without outlets to the ocean. In the 1904 treaty, Chile granted Bolivia free transit in perpetuity through the ports of Antofagasta, Arica, Iquique, Mejillones, Pisagua, and Tocopilla, and in 1913, the La Paz to Arica railway provided for in the treaty was completed (Ríos 1963, 181–5; Encina 1963, 265–7). In the end, transit concessions and railway construction appeared to Chilean observers, if not to their Bolivian counterparts, to be answering Bolivian demands for improved access to the sea (Escobari 1988, 119–33; Ross 2016, 202).

As improved rail links undermined a part of its argument for a Pacific port, Bolivia increasingly emphasized what it described as the inherent right of any state to a sovereign outlet to the sea. Proponents of this line of thinking were heartened by the idealistic proclamations of President Woodrow Wilson in his Fourteen Points and elsewhere, notably his January 1917 statement to the US Senate in which he argued every country had a right to a direct outlet to the sea (Querejazu 1979, 769–70; Dennis 1931, 201). In the apparent belief that deference to the United States was of paramount importance to the success of Bolivia's seaport policy, Wilson's statements were the determining factor in the Bolivian decision to break diplomatic relations with Germany in April 1917, a highly unpopular move with the influential German community in Bolivia (Fifer 1972, 72; Bieber 1984, 97–8). Bolivia was the first South American country to break diplomatic relations with Germany, and because it did so, it was invited to the Paris Peace Conference which opened in Versailles in January 1919 (Carrasco 1920, 118–19).

Motivated in part by the belief that Japan would play an important role in Pacific issues, a region where Chile already enjoyed first class diplomatic representation, President José Gutiérrez Guerra dispatched a diplomatic mission to Asia in 1918. Where earlier missions in 1908 and 1914 had produced limited results, the 1918 mission under the leadership of Víctor Muñoz Reyes brought order to Bolivian diplomacy throughout the region. Existing consulates were placed under the control of the Bolivian embassy in Tokyo, and new consulates were established in China and the Dutch East Indies (Republic of Indonesia today). The Muñoz Reyes mission also concluded a treaty of friendship with China in December 1919 (Abecia 1986, II, 402–3).

On 14 January 1919, former President Montes in his role as Bolivian envoy to France sent a note to the French Foreign Office asking the League of Nations to give Tacna and Arica to Bolivia because a sovereign outlet to the sea was essential for its economic development and commercial expansion (Escobari 1988, 102–3; Bákula 2002, I, 532). The following month, the Bolivian government dispatched a circular to Bolivian legations abroad in which it repeated the essence of the Montes note without expressly referring to Tacna and Arica (Perú 1919, 95–114; Carrasco 1920, 141–2, 152; Gumucio 2005, 245). Peru responded to the Bolivian arguments in an April 1919 circular which stated that Tacna and Arica were and always had been an integral part of Peru. The Peruvian circular also warned that it could be dangerous for the Bolivian government to use the doctrine of superior rights to justify claiming territory which happened to lie adjacent to Bolivia (Perú 1919, 115–23; Ross 2016, 193–4). If the Bolivian circular had hoped to generate a sympathetic response in Peru, the timing of its issuance could not have been worse. Peru was in the midst of a heated presidential campaign in which former President Leguía was campaigning for reelection on a platform which emphasized the Tacna and Arica issue, promising to regain not only those two provinces but also Tarapacá.

In November 1919, South American newspapers published reports that Bolivia and Chile had concluded or were about to conclude an agreement related to the occupied Peruvian provinces of Tacna and Arica (Carrasco 1920, 120–1; Novak and Namihas 2013, 94–5). In response to a Peruvian inquiry, the foreign minister of Bolivia, Carlos Gutiérrez, denied the newspaper reports, but at the same time, Bolivia continued to argue that neither Chile nor Peru had any definitive rights to the port of Arica and the surrounding territory (Escobari 1988, 103–5; Becerra de la Roca 2002, 134–6). On 10 January 1920, Foreign Minister Gutiérrez and a Chilean envoy, Emilio Bello Codesido, concluded a protocol in which Chile expressed its desire to incorporate Tacna and Arica in order to guarantee the security of its northern frontier (Guzmán Escobari 2015a, 116–18, 523–9). Bello offered Bolivia a sovereign outlet to the sea through a corridor north of the port of Arica and the Arica–La Paz railway in return for Bolivian support in the pending plebiscite. In response to the Chilean request, Foreign Minister Gutiérrez reiterated the necessity of his country to have a sovereign port at Arica (Querejazu 1979, 768; Abecia 1986, II, 407–8). The Chilean envoy also suggested that Arica might become a free port under joint Bolivian–Chilean control, but in return, Chile expected to be granted trade preferences which Bolivia complained would end any hope of it ever being more than a commercial annex of Chile (Fifer 1972, 73; Bustos 2003, 111–13). Less than two weeks later, the Bolivian National Assembly on 22 January 1920 passed a resolution calling for the reincorporation of the port of Arica and surrounding territories (Escobari 1982, I, 153). The resolution failed to address how Bolivia could reincorporate land it had never owned and had occupied only once in its entire history. In response, the Peruvian government expressed surprise at Bolivian pretensions, emphasizing it would never negotiate the future of the provinces of Tacna and Arica because they were an integral part of Peru (Bákula 2002, I, 532–3).

By March 1920, tensions between Bolivia and Peru had escalated to the point that both countries began moving troops to the frontier (Denegri 1988, 113–15; Escobari 1982, I, 153–5). With war clouds on the horizon, the US government intervened with the stated purpose of maintaining peace in Latin America. The Wilson administration asked Bolivia and Peru to refrain from warlike activities, told Bolivia it was damaging its interests related to an outlet to the sea by pressing the issue before Chile and Peru had reached a settlement, and chastised Chile for aiding and abetting Bolivia. Tensions were relieved in mid-July 1920 when the government of President José Gutiérrez

Guerra was ousted in a *golpe de estado* (Mesa Gisbert 2001a, 545). The incoming Republican administration of President Bautista Saavedra opposed the policy of seeking a solution through Arica, advocating instead the return of the entire Bolivian littoral (Escobari 1988, 105; Abecia 1986, II, 408–12).

## League of Nations

At the beginning of November 1920, the delegates of Bolivia and Peru presented separate petitions to the first Assembly of the League of Nations requesting the revision of the peace treaties Bolivia and Peru had signed with Chile. Bolivia based its petition on article 19 of the Covenant of the League of Nations which empowered League members to reconsider treaties which were no longer applicable or whose continuance might endanger world peace (Denegri 1988, 116–19; Gumucio 2005, 265–70). In invoking article 19, Bolivia argued: 1) the 1904 treaty was "imposed" on Bolivia, 2) Chile failed to fulfill "fundamental" clauses of the treaty, 3) the current situation constitutes a "permanent threat" to peace, and 4) the 1904 treaty left Bolivia completely enclosed and deprived of access to the sea (Andaluz 2002, 145–7, quotes 146–7; Baptista 1978, 19–20). The Bolivian and Peruvian petitions were presented independently, but the Peruvian note acknowledged and supported the Bolivian proposal (St John 1999, 154; Guzmán Escobari 2015a, 128–9). According to some sources, Peru wanted Bolivia as an ally but could not abide with its demands for Arica; therefore, it agreed to support Bolivia's claim for the restitution of all territory lost to Chile in the War of the Pacific if Bolivia would stop agitating for Arica (Barros 1924, 161). Chile responded immediately to both petitions, arguing the Assembly of the League of Nations had no authority to act on such matters (Abecia 1986, II, 415; Gumucio 2005, 269–70). Shortly thereafter, the secretary-general of the League informed Bolivia and Peru that their petitions had been submitted too late for consideration by the 1920 Assembly.

Peru withdrew its petition in early December 1920, reserving the right to bring the issue of Tacna and Arica before the League of Nations at a later date which it failed to do. Bolivia took a different tack, asking the League Assembly to place its petition on the agenda of its 1921 session (Guzmán Escobari 2015a, 130–5). The separate requests of Bolivia and Peru to annul their respective peace treaties with Chile on the grounds they were concluded under duress generated considerable debate at the League. Several members of the League were party to treaties which one or more of the signatories considered inequitable and unjust. Therefore, the adoption of a principle that a unilateral declaration on the part of one party to a treaty of limits was sufficient to invalidate the treaty and free that state from its obligations appeared to some to threaten chaos in the world community (Ríos 1963, 193–7). In response to Bolivia's intent to resubmit its petition in 1921, a committee of three jurists appointed by the League Assembly concluded on 22 September 1921 that the petition of Bolivia was "inadmissible" because the League

Assembly "cannot modify by itself any treaty," seeing "the modification of treaties is the exclusive competence of the contracting parties" (Andaluz 2002, 151–3, quote 151). At this point, Bolivia withdrew its demand for League of Nations action, reserving the right to bring the seaport issue up at a later date (Barros 1924, 136; Baptista 1978, 57).

The Saavedra government in December 1921 invited the governments of Chile and Peru to participate in a tripartite conference composed of countries vitally interested in the grave questions of the Pacific. The invitation outlined the essence of the Bolivian position for the next eight years when it stated that the nationality of the occupied provinces was not the only issue outstanding from the War of the Pacific and an international conference was necessary to address and resolve all of them. The Chilean government declined the Bolivian invitation, noting that Chile was currently involved in negotiations with Peru which concerned a treaty signed by those two states in which Bolivia had no direct interests. After recognizing that Bolivia's desires were legitimate, Peru also declined due to the position taken by the Chilean government (Querejazu 1979, 776–9; Abecia 1986, II, 421–3; Guzmán Escobari 2015a, 137–9).

In January 1923, the Bolivian envoy to Chile, Ricardo Jaime Freyre, in a renewed effort to secure for Bolivia sovereign access to the Pacific proposed a revision of the 1904 treaty (Espinosa 1965, 346–50; Abecia 1986, II, 423–5). Chile rejected the Bolivian proposal, refusing to consider a modification either to the 1904 treaty or to its territorial continuity (Glassner 1964, 41–2; Becerra de la Roca 2002, 138–9; Guzmán Escobari 2015a, 143–9). Throughout this period, no Bolivian government pursued with any real conviction the return of the entire Bolivian littoral, focusing instead on a window to the Pacific at Arica (Araya 2017, 85–6). After a *golpe de estado* brought the Republicans to power in July 1920, their short-lived policy of advocating for the return of Antofagasta was interesting only because it showed how little effort was made after 1884 to retrieve the panhandle. The lack of Bolivian interest in Antofagasta was due in part to its inconvenient location compared to Arica, a concern widely recognized since independence, and in part because of the extraordinary amount of Chilean development in the Bolivian littoral since the War of the Pacific (Fifer 1972, 73).

## On the Outside

Even as Bolivia continued efforts to involve itself in the ongoing bilateral negotiations between Chile and Peru, it pursued a dual track, hoping to persuade the US government to use its good offices to assist it in obtaining a sovereign port on the Pacific. In early January 1922, President Warren G. Harding invited Chile and Peru to send representatives to Washington to discuss the issues dividing them. Once Chile and Peru had accepted the invitation, President Saavedra petitioned President Harding, requesting the inclusion of Bolivia in the upcoming conference. The Harding administration denied Bolivia's request on the grounds the Washington talks were relevant only to problems related to the Treaty of Ancón of which Chile and Peru were the only signatories (Gumucio 2005, 271–81; Encina 1963, 274–5). The Washington Conference convened in May 1922 and led to President Harding accepting the position of arbitrator in the Tacna–Arica dispute (Ríos 1959, 73–6; Pike 1963, 215–16). In early March 1925, President Calvin Coolidge, who succeeded Harding after his untimely death in the fall of 1923, announced his opinion and award, declaring Chile and Peru were still obliged to hold the plebiscite called for in the Treaty of Ancón. Over the next year, the plebiscitary committee appointed by Coolidge labored to conduct a free and fair plebiscite in an increasingly charged atmosphere. Eventually, efforts to hold a plebiscite were abandoned and Chile and Peru agreed to conduct bilateral negotiations under the good offices of the United States (Ríos 1959, 448–61; Yepes 1999).

When the abortive plebiscitary proceedings in Tacna and Arica ended in the spring of 1926, the dual track strategy of Bolivia appeared set to bear fruit. With the failure of the plebiscite formula, Secretary of State Frank B. Kellogg called on 30 November 1926 for the cession of Tacna and Arica to Bolivia (Maldonado 2005, 23–4; Guzmán Escobari 2015a, 158–64). When Bolivia learned of the Kellogg proposal, it immediately accepted it. The Siles Reyes administration also asked to be allowed to send a delegation to Washington to participate in the negotiations between Chile and Peru but again was rebuffed (Glassner 1964, 44). On 4 December 1926, the Chilean government in the so-called Matte Memorandum conditionally accepted the Kellogg proposal on the grounds that any such agreement would have to stipulate that Bolivia could never transfer all or part of Tacna and Arica to another state (Guzmán Escobari 2015a, 160–1). The Chilean response highlighted the extent to which the crux of the Tacna and Arica issue for Chile was "a question of a safe and fixed northern border" (Dennis 1931, 273). The Peruvian government rejected the US proposal outright in mid-January 1927 on the grounds it could never abandon the Peruvian citizens living in the two provinces. Noting Chile had sabotaged the plebiscite provided for in the Treaty of Ancón, Peru argued that it now was entitled to possession of both Tacna and Arica. At the same time, the Peruvian response expressed a willingness to consider the internationalization of the provinces, granting Bolivia a corridor to the Pacific, or any other proposal which included the return of the port of Arica to Peru (Bákula 2002, I, 537–42; Escobari 1988, 110–11). Much to the dismay of Bolivia, Secretary of State Kellogg considered the Peruvian response a rejection of his proposal and refused to make additional suggestions (Gumucio 2005, 289–324). Thereafter, the Kellogg proposal would be cited by Bolivians as an indication of US support for their cause (*La Razón*, 8 March 2015).

After 1926, the Siles Reyes government continued its efforts to involve Bolivia in the Chile–Peru talks but to no avail. Despite ongoing efforts by the Bolivian minister in Washington, Eduardo Diez de Medina, Bolivia was excluded from the bilateral talks between Chile and Peru which took place in 1928–29 under the auspices of the US government (Gumucio 2005, 325–45).

In June 1929, representatives of Chile and Peru signed the Treaty of Lima, also known as the Tacna and Arica Treaty and Additional Protocol. The treaty assigned Tacna to Peru and Arica to Chile. In article one of the additional protocol, the signatories agreed that neither Chile nor Peru could cede to a third party any of the territories over which they were awarded sovereignty in the treaty without first obtaining the agreement of the other signatory. In the same article, they also agreed that neither signatory could build a new international railroad across Tacna or Arica without the agreement of the other signatory (Perú 1936, I, 183–7; Salazar 2000, 617–21). Concerned a settlement involving the division of Tacna and Arica between Peru and Chile could lead to the construction of railways and a port in Tacna which would seriously erode the financial viability of the Chilean port at Arica, the minister of foreign affairs of Chile, Conrado Ríos Gallardo, pressed for the inclusion of the first article of the additional protocol (Querejazu 1979, 787–8; Ríos 1959, 278–87, 295–301, 347–52). Nevertheless, the Chilean government for decades after 1929 insisted the Peruvian government authored the additional protocol. It was not until 1977 that Ríos admitted it had originated with himself (Escobari 1988, 112–14). In early August 1929, the Siles Reyes administration directed a circular to all Bolivian legations protesting the terms of the Treaty of Lima and in particular the contents of the first article of the additional protocol. In so doing, the Bolivian government recognized, 104 years after the creation of an independent Upper Peru, that the terms of article one of the additional protocol finally and unalterably confirmed the failure of the Arica for Bolivia movement.

The inability of the Bolivian government in 1921–22 to insert itself into bilateral negotiations between Chile and Peru over the future of Tacna and Arica marked the failure of its policy of regaining a sovereign Pacific port through a tripartite settlement. Excluded from the preliminary talks between Chile and Peru, it also was barred from the 1922 Washington Conference, the US arbitration of the Tacna–Arica controversy, and the bilateral talks under the good offices of the United States which resulted in the Treaty of Lima. Bolivia's self-proclaimed rights were not considered at any point after 1921 in the prolonged bilateral negotiations between Chile and Peru which eventually led to a resolution of the Tacna and Arica dispute. The terms of the Treaty of Lima became known in Bolivia as double lock (*doble cerradura*) because in the agreements Chile succeeded in involving Peru in any likely future solution to Bolivia's landlocked status. Where Bolivians had lionized the United States in the wake of the 1926 Kellogg proposal, they were deeply disappointed with Washington's role in facilitating the 1929 settlement between Chile and Peru (Gumucio 2005, 341–8).

## Outstanding Border Issues

The Treaty of Lima fixed the Bolivia–Chile–Peru border at a tripoint in the Cordillera Occidental; however, the Bolivia–Peru boundary around Lake Titicaca and further north remained to be defined. In September 1902, representatives of Bolivia and Peru had agreed to divide the southern section of their boundary into three parts: 1) from the snowy peaks of Palomani in the Cordillera de Apolobamba as far as the Bay of Coccahui, 2) from the Bay of Coccahui across Lake Titicaca as far as the opening of the Desaguadero River, and 3) from the opening of the Desaguadero River as far as the confluence of the Mauri and Ancomarca rivers (Salazar 2000, 581–2; Wagner de Reyna 1964, I, 74–5). Demarcation of the first and third sections to the north and south of Lake Titicaca was fairly straightforward, but land ownership patterns on the Copacabana Peninsula were more complex. Following the conclusion of a treaty in June 1925, detailed plans and maps were drawn extending three or four miles on each side of contested villages, and the results were incorporated into a January 1932 protocol. In an October 1941 protocol, Bolivia and Peru considered properties left on the wrong side of the 1932 boundary and recognized rights of ownership established before 2 December 1939 in the exchanged areas. The people in the exchanged areas retained their former nationality unless they recorded a desire to change it within three months of the announcement of the 1941 protocol (Fifer 1972, 78–82).

Further north in the remote, largely unknown region of the Madre de Dios headwaters, Bolivia and Peru agreed in December 1902 to an arbitration by the president of Argentina with the request that the former boundaries of the Viceroyalties of Peru and Río de la Plata, together with the extent of the Audiencias of Charcas, Cuzco, and Lima, be defined as the solution (Salazar 2000, 585–6; Wagner de Reyna 1964, I, 74–5, 77–80). Following nearly seven years of study of documents, maps, and orders, the arbitrator in July 1909 announced his award. After elaborating on the complexities of the task, the Argentine president rejected the recent claims of both Bolivia and Peru and instead attempted to draw an equitable line between the extreme claims of both parties. In Bolivia, the award was greeted with great disappointment, and following mob attacks on the Argentine legation in La Paz, Bolivia rejected the decision of the arbitrator and severed diplomatic relations with Argentina (Guzmán 1998, 230–1; Abecia 1986, II, 361–75). With armed conflict between Bolivia and Peru a distinct possibility, Brazil attempted to mediate the dispute, asking the British and US governments in a July 1909 circular to suggest to Argentina that it advise Peru to agree to a modification of the proposed boundary. Both Great Britain and the United States declined to intervene unless requested by both parties; nevertheless, adjustments to the proposed boundary were agreed in the Polo–Sánchez Bustamante Protocol in September 1909. Those adjustments favored Bolivia in that they moved the boundary some 30 miles west for approximately 125 miles between the Madre de Dios and Acre rivers (Fifer 1972, 140–5; Wagner de Reyna 1964, I, 80).

At the request of Peru, the Royal Geographical Society in London nominated officers to survey and demarcate the new boundary. During their survey, they discovered the confluence of the Lanza, Suches, and Tambopata rivers lay south of latitude 14° south which necessitated a rewording of the 1909 protocol and a new agreement was sanctioned in May 1912 (Wagner de

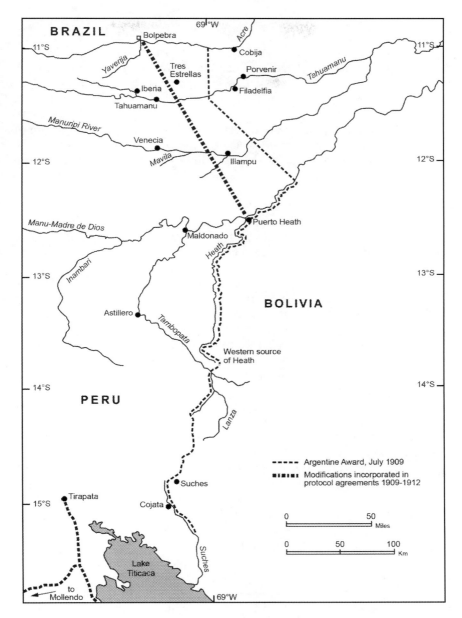

*Figure 5.1* Northern Sector, 1909–12
Source: Nathan Bailey St John.

Reyna 1964, I, 135–6). Otherwise, demarcation of the Bolivia–Peru boundary in the northern sector proceeded without major problems. The final boundary followed the Suches, Lanza, and Heath rivers north from Lake Titicaca to Puerto Heath where a diagonal line was drawn from Puerto Heath to Bolpebra, a small Bolivian village at the tripoint of Bolivia, Brazil, and Peru. Bolpebra is a portmanteau of those three countries (Fifer 1972, 145–50; Abecia 1986, II, 377–80).

Further south, the 1903 Treaty of Petrópolis had revived the old dream of the Madeira–Mamoré railway as a key to improved Bolivian access to the Amazon River (Escobari 1982, II, 310). Within four years of the conclusion of the treaty, Brazil had begun construction of the railway from San Antonio to Guayaramerín, with a branch through Villa Murtinho to Villa Bella, as called for in article seven of the 1903 agreement (Salazar 2000, 591). Both countries were to enjoy equal rights on the railway, and with rubber prices strong in the early 1900s, enthusiasm for the project was high on both sides of the border. Unfortunately, an ambiguity in the wording of article seven soon clouded completion of the railroad. The Portuguese version of the treaty called for the railway to run as far as Guajará Mirim (Brazil) whereas the Spanish version called for it to run to Guayaramerín (Bolivia). Guajará Mirim and Guayaramerín were twin towns on opposite sides of the Mamoré River, and a dispute developed over whether Brazil was obliged to build a bridge to carry the railway over the river instead of leaving the railhead on the Brazilian side. Bolivia intended to continue the railway from Guayaramerín westwards to Riberalta and at one stage on to La Paz; therefore, construction of a bridge across the Mamoré River was necessary to eliminate any break in the load. By July 1912, the 228-mile railroad was completed as far as Guajará Mirim, but neither the bridge connecting Guajará Mirim and Guayaramerín nor the promised branch line between Villa Murtinho and Villa Bella were ever built (Marsh 1928, 72–3). The South America rubber boom ended in 1912 resulting in abandoned dreams and a retreating commercial frontier. In lieu of further railway construction, Brazil agreed in a December 1928 treaty to make available to Bolivia £1 million for railway extensions elsewhere in Bolivia. As for the proposed extension from Guayaramerín to Riberalta, the collapse of the rubber boom put an end to the project (Fifer 1972, 132–40; Escobari 1982, II, 324).

## Prelude to War

After the Treaty of Lima scuttled for the foreseeable future any possibility of a sovereign outlet to the Pacific, Bolivia turned with renewed enthusiasm to the Paraguay River as its most feasible outlet to the ocean. At independence, almost one-third of the approximately 850,000 square miles claimed by Bolivia, lay within the Paraguay Basin (Fifer 1972, 161–3). After independence, the importance of the Paraguay River led Bolivia, Brazil, and Paraguay to establish settlements along its banks in an effort to secure control of its navigation. These competing claims raised questions as to the ownership of the adjacent Gran Chaco, a sparsely populated, grassy and wooded savanna which crossed the borders of Argentina, Bolivia, and Paraguay (Wood 1966, 19; Chesterton 2016, 2–5).

Historically, the Gran Chaco, which approximated 250,000 square miles in size and was located west of the Paraguay River and east of the Andes, was divided into three sections. The Chaco Boreal (northern Chaco) lay north of the Pilcomayo River and west of the Paraguay River and divided Bolivia and Paraguay. The Chaco Central was the section in Argentina south of the Pilcomayo River and north of the Bermejo River. The Chaco Austral (southern Chaco) lay south of the Bermejo River and merged with the Pampa region of Argentina in the south. In 1852, Argentina and Paraguay concluded a Treaty of Limits, Commerce, and Navigation in which they agreed that the Paraguay River, south of unspecified Brazilian claims and as far south as its confluence with the Paraná River, belonged from bank to bank to Paraguay (Abecia 1986, II, 176–82). Within a month, Bolivia issued an official protest in which it reiterated its rights as a riverine state on the west bank of the Paraguay River at least as far as latitude 22° south. Argentina's reply to the Bolivian protest was non-committal which Bolivia chose to interpret as favorable. Brazil also made known its reservations with the Argentina–Paraguay pact, disapproving of the reference in the treaty to Brazilian claims when Brazil was not a party to it. After receiving a copy of Bolivia's protest note, Brazil stated it could not accept Bolivia's status as a riverine state between latitudes 20° and 22° south unless and until it had ceded that right to Bolivia in a formal agreement (Fifer 1972, 176–8).

Bolivia again found itself on the outside when Argentina, Brazil, and Uruguay in May 1865 responded to a Paraguayan declaration of war with a treaty of offensive and defensive alliance. Assuming the successful conclusion of hostilities in the Chaco Boreal, the treaty confirmed the west bank of the Paraguay River as far north as Bahía Negra would belong to Argentina. At the time, the Argentine foreign minister reportedly told a British diplomat that his government would be willing to acknowledge some Bolivian rights on the Paraguay River; nevertheless, Bolivia remained uncertain of Argentina's intentions at a time when Bolivia itself was encountering difficulties with both Brazil and Chile (Fifer 1972, 178–80). Two years later, Bolivia and Brazil signed a treaty of amity, limits, navigation, commerce, and extradition, known as the Muñoz–Netto convention. In the second article of this agreement, Bolivia signed away its claims to the west bank of the Paraguay River as far as latitude 20° 10′ south (Bahía Negra); consequently, there was little wonder that Bolivia remained concerned with the terms of the May 1865 treaty (Salazar 2000, 541–8).

The 1876 peace treaty which followed the defeat of Paraguay in the War of the Triple Alliance (1864–70), together with an 1878 arbitration award by US President Rutherford B. Hayes in a dispute over the southeastern Chaco, confirmed the Pilcomayo River as the boundary between Argentina and Paraguay.

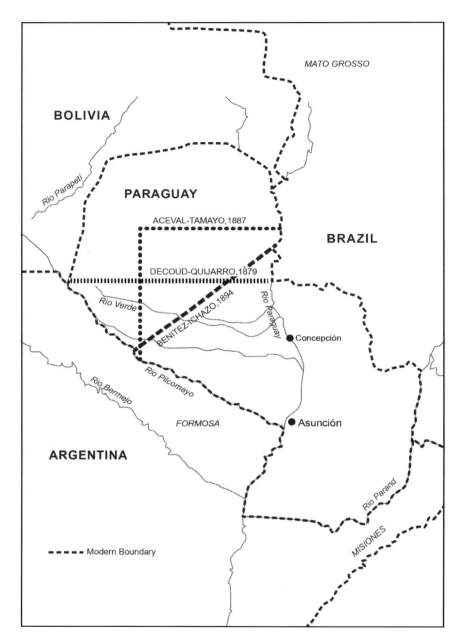

*Figure 5.2* Failed Treaties, 1879–94
Source: Nathan Bailey St John.

It also confirmed Paraguay's ownership of the Chaco between the Verde, Paraguay, and Pilcomayo rivers. At the same time, Argentina relinquished its claims to the Chaco Boreal (Abecia 1986, II, 182–4; Rout 1970, 7–8). With Bolivia determined to hold on to its claims to the Paraguay River between latitudes 20° and 22° south, Bolivia and Paraguay in 1879 began a series of protracted negotiations over the future of the Paraguay River and ownership of the Chaco Boreal, including the three failed treaties of Decoud–Quijarro (1879), Aceval–Tamayo (1887), and Benítez–Ichazo (1894), which continued inconclusively for years (Abecia 1986, II, 186, 193–5, 200–2; Chesterton 2016, 4, 6; Querejazu 1992, 14–19). At the beginning of the twentieth century, Bolivia had failed to establish a foothold anywhere on the west bank of the Paraguay River, and its penetration into the Chaco Boreal was minimal. The few Bolivian settlements which had been established clung to the western fringe of the region near the junction of mountain and plain (Fifer 1972, 178–85; Rout 1970, 9–11).

As Bolivian attempts to acquire footage on the Paraguay River produced an ever-more-complicated series of boundary lines across the Chaco Boreal, the Bolivian government turned its attention to the western portion of its southern lands where a long period of silence had followed the incorporation of Tarija in 1826 (Escobari 1982, II, 267–9). For almost four decades, little attempt was made to delimit the Argentina–Bolivia frontier. Even then, it came in the form of a Bolivian protest to the clause in the May 1865 treaty of offensive and defensive alliance which confirmed the west bank of the Paraguay River as far north as Bahía Negra would belong to Argentina. Desultory discussions took place over the next 23 years as to the former limits of the Viceroyalty of Río de la Plata, which included the Audiencia of Charcas, and the Viceroyalty of Peru. In June 1888, representatives of Argentina and Bolivia agreed latitude 22° south as far as its intersection with the Pilcomayo River would be the provisional boundary in the remote and little-known Chaco Boreal (Fifer 1972, 185–7; Abecia 1986, II, 214).

Further west, no delimitation was agreed; however, it was understood that neither country would advance beyond its actual possessions. In May 1889, a boundary through the foothill and mountain country was outlined, and in 1892–93, Bolivia yielded to Argentina a corner of the inter-montane plateau known as the Puna de Atacama (Abecia 1986, II, 216–24; Escobari 1982, II, 270–1). Originally Bolivian territory, the Puna de Atacama was occupied by Chile during the War of the Pacific and incorporated into Antofagasta in 1888. Consequently, Chile disputed the right of Bolivia to pass its ownership to Argentina, and an arbitration by the US government in 1899 divided the disputed territory between Argentina and Chile in a Solomon-like judgment. Subsequent attempts to delimit the remainder of the boundary between Bolivia and Argentina were frustrated by rough terrain and inaccurate maps, and an additional protocol was signed in January 1904 in an effort to rectify the anomalies (Fifer 1972, 186–8). Before the protocol was ratified, bilateral relations suffered a sharp setback after a July 1909 arbitral award by the president of Argentina in the Bolivia–Peru boundary dispute led to widespread Bolivian demonstrations against Argentina. After Bolivia broke diplomatic relations with Argentina and refused to attend the 1910 Pan-American Conference in Buenos Aires, Argentina refused to ratify the 1904 protocol (Escobari 1982, II, 272–4). Diplomatic relations were restored in December 1910, and Bolivia and Argentina eventually concluded a definitive treaty of limits in July 1925 (Salazar 2000, 609–11; Abecia 1986, II, 224–6).

In the 1903 Treaty of Petrópolis, Bolivia received four small tracts of swampy land which provided windows onto or towards the upper Paraguay River. None of these areas provided Bolivia with satisfactory port facilities on the river; nevertheless, these concessions by Brazil provoked extreme displeasure in Paraguay. As Bolivia investigated the future possibilities of the four windows, it continued to probe southeast down the Pilcomayo River, establishing small forts at Guachalla and Ballivián in 1906 (Querejazu 1992, 20). In January 1907, the minister of foreign affairs of Bolivia, Claudio Pinilla, and the interim minister of foreign affairs of Paraguay, Adolfo Soler, concluded a protocol in which they agreed to submit the zone between latitude 20° 30′ south, the northern line claimed by Paraguay, and the zone between longitudes 61° 30′ and 62° west to arbitration by the president of Argentina (Salazar 2000, 603–4). When the 1907 protocol was not ratified by the Bolivian National Assembly, Bolivia and Paraguay in 1913 agreed to abide by the 1907 status quo and negotiate a final boundary agreement within two years (Abecia 1986, II, 463–7; Rout 1970, 11–12). When this proved impossible, Bolivia continued to construct roads and forts down the east bank of the Pilcomayo River and across the plain of the Chaco Boreal in an effort to exert de facto sovereignty over the area. Viewing the Bolivian advances as a serious threat to its existence, Paraguay also continued to build forts in the area (Querejazu 1992, 23–6). In 1925, Argentina agreed to mediate the dispute, but events on the ground compromised the process. By 1928, Bolivia had completed outposts on a north–south line from approximately 120 miles northwest of Asunción on the Pilcomayo River northward for some 300 miles to a point northwest of Bahía Negra, the head of barge navigation on the Paraguay River. Both countries also promoted foreign investment and settlement in the areas under their influence. In addition to Franciscan missions established to convert Indians to Christianity and Mennonites from Canada who settled in the eastern Chaco in the mid-1920s, there were scattered ranches and lumber camps in an otherwise mostly uninhabited area (Wood 1966, 19–20; Chesterton 2016, 4).

As the number and strength of military installations in the Chaco Boreal increased, incidents between Bolivian and Paraguayan military units multiplied. In early December 1928, Paraguayan troops attacked and destroyed the Bolivian outpost at Fort Vanguardia at the northern end of the line of Bolivian outposts on the Paraguay River. Bolivia responded by occupying the Paraguayan outpost at Fort Boquerón, located in the Chaco Boreal at the southern end of the line. The Paraguayan attack occurred five days before a scheduled meeting of the International Conference of American States on Conciliation and Arbitration in Washington, DC. Under the auspices of the conference, arrangements were made in early January 1929 for a suspension of hostilities and the appointment of a five-member Commission of Inquiry and Conciliation, consisting of representatives from Colombia, Cuba, Mexico, Uruguay, and the United States. Members of the Commission later concluded that the incident at Fort Vanguardia was planned by Paraguay, probably in an effort to draw attention to the escalating conflict and bring about a solution by outside forces (Wood 1966, 21; Rout 1970, 30–1). Bolivia and Paraguay signed an Act of Conciliation in September 1929, but it did little to slow the inexorable march to war (Salazar 2000, 623–4; Mesa Gisbert 2001a, 558–9). In July 1930, the combatants restored the frontier situation to where it was before December 1928, including the return of Fort Vanguardia and Fort Boquerón; however, efforts to arrange a permanent settlement through arbitration or direct negotiations met with no success (Querejazu 1992, 26–30).

The earlier discovery of oil in the Standard Oil Company of Bolivia concessions in the eastern Andes, coupled with the prospect of significant oil deposits in the disputed territory, added to the complexity of the Chaco dispute at the end of the decade. The only way for Bolivian oil to reach international markets was through the construction of roads or railroads and pipelines over the Andes, through the Amazon Basin, across Argentina, or through the Chaco Boreal to the Paraguay River. The first two options were deemed impractical, leaving Argentina and the Paraguay River as the most feasible outlets (Cote 2016a, 158). In 1929, the Salamanca government approached Argentina with a proposal to build an oil pipeline across its territory to the Atlantic Ocean. Aligned with Royal Dutch Shell (which held Paraguayan holdings), the Argentine government concluded Standard Oil was behind the Bolivian proposal and rejected it on the grounds it did not want to introduce competition to the Argentine state oil company (*Yacimientos Petrolíferos Fiscales*, YPF) or become involved in a geopolitical dispute involving Standard Oil (Abecia 1986, II, 480–3; Cote 2016b, 79). With a pipeline through Argentina no longer an option, the Salamanca government viewed control of the Chaco Boreal as necessary for the construction of a pipeline to the Paraguay River (Fifer 1972, 192–212; Klein and Peres-Cajías 2014, 147–8). Open hostilities began in June 1932, but a peace treaty giving Paraguay the bulk of the disputed territory would not be signed for another six years.

## Conclusions

In an ongoing pursuit of sovereignty, national security, territorial integrity, and economic independence, Bolivian foreign policy in the first three decades of the twentieth century focused on the attainment of a sovereign outlet to the Pacific Ocean. Treatment of long-standing external concerns like the resolution of boundary questions with Argentina, Brazil, and Peru; improved diplomatic representation in Asia; free transit on the Upper Amazon; and related issues on the Bermejo, Paraguay, and Pilcomayo rivers reflected its concentration on the seaport issue. Other foreign policy opportunities, like its sporadic and largely inconsequential participation in the Pan-American movement, were subordinate to this goal. The Treaty of Lima between Chile and Peru marked the failure of Bolivian efforts to secure a sovereign Pacific port through a tripartite settlement and effectively ended the Arica for Bolivia movement. The treaty left Bolivia landlocked with no immediate strategy to regain sovereign access to the Pacific. Consequently, Bolivia turned south to the Chaco Boreal in search of an outlet to the Atlantic through the Paraguay River. Meanwhile, Bolivia's growing economic dependence, the product of market and trade policies which benefitted the ruling elite but disadvantaged domestic manufacturers and suppliers, together with the impact of a soaring public debt and the Great Depression, left Bolivia in a weakened economic state, undermining its ability as the century progressed to pursue an aggressive, effective foreign policy.

# 6  War, Revolution, Water, 1930–70

In the four decades after 1930, a traumatic war with Paraguay was followed by a socioeconomic and political revolution, leading to major changes in the scope and direction of Bolivian foreign policy. The Chaco War was a catalyst for the development of Bolivian nationalism and a leading cause of the 1952 National Revolution. Anti-imperialist sentiment also grew in this period. In the first seizure of a US company in Latin America, Bolivia nationalized the Standard Oil Company of Bolivia. Bolivia resolved long-standing disputes with Argentina, Brazil, Paraguay, and Peru; however, the Lauca, Silala, and Maurí watershed disputes opened new conflicts with Chile and Peru. Throughout the period, Bolivia continued to devote an enormous amount of energy, talent, and goodwill to its quest for a sovereign outlet to the Pacific. Meanwhile, the United States involved itself in the domestic and foreign affairs of Bolivia to an ever-growing extent.

## Chaco War, 1932–35

After 1929, successive Bolivian governments were preoccupied with the impact of the Great Depression and the dispute with Paraguay in the Chaco Boreal. Bolivia was in a deep economic and political crisis by 1930, and when President Siles Reyes attempted to modify the constitution and remain in office, he was ousted in a *golpe de estado* (Ugarteche 1986, 85–7). After a short period of military government, Daniel Salamanca Urey (1931–34) was elected president. His domestic policies were repressive and unproductive, and his foreign policy was disastrous (Mesa Gisbert 2001a, 568–70). Despite the fragile state of the Bolivian economy, Salamanca poured millions of pesos which Bolivia did not have into armaments, aggressively expanded Bolivian control over the Chaco Boreal, and escalated a small border clash with Paraguay into a catastrophic war (Abecia 1986, II, 522–4, 526–9; Klein 2011, 172–3).

The Chaco War began in July 1932 with a series of attacks and counter-attacks around the Paraguayan Fort of Carlos Antonio López (Fort Mariscal Santa Cruz to Bolivia), located near Lake Pitiantuta (Lake Chuquisaca to Bolivia) on the north-central front. Both sides viewed the lake as a strategic location because it offered a year-round water supply, a rarity in the Chaco

Boreal (Macías 1936, 9–15; Querejazu 1992, 40–50). At the time, Bolivia had three times the population of Paraguay, seven times as many soldiers, and outgunned Paraguay by as much as ten to one. The Bolivian war machine appeared strong, and most observers assumed the Paraguayan army would be no match for it. In drawing this conclusion, they overestimated the importance of Bolivia's apparent superiority in manpower and weapons and underestimated the logistical challenges involved in training, transporting, and supplying troops "in an environment so foreign as to be another world" (Malloy 1970, 72–3, quote 73). Internal political and social divisions in Bolivia compounded these difficulties. In contrast, Paraguayan soldiers enjoyed shorter supply lines, superior logistics, and help from Argentina. Argentina continued to import goods from Paraguay, and it supplied the latter with oil and weapons, openly at first and covertly after it declared neutrality in the war (Chesterton 2016, 4–5; Cote 2016b, 74–5). At the same time, Argentina closed its borders and markets to Bolivia, and while the latter could still import goods through Peru and off and on through Chile, it took more time and was more expensive (Mesa Gisbert 2016, 167–8). Honoring existing treaties, Brazil joined Peru in declining to impede the free transit of goods with either Bolivia or Paraguay (Wood 1966, 89–90; Fifer 1972, 214–15).

Despite the widespread belief that Bolivia would defeat Paraguay, the prospect of war was unpopular in Bolivia, and the general staff warned the Salamanca administration that the country was not ready for war. To make their point, the general staff refused to endorse President Salamanca's war plans until he took full responsibility in a written document for all decisions related to the initiation of the war (Klein 2011, 178). In three years of fighting, there were four Bolivian army commanders, and three Bolivian armies were destroyed in the field. In the process, the military's warnings proved prescient as the war became a litany of Bolivian defeats (Abecia 1986, II, 530–3, 537–43, 546–52, 577–80; Guzmán 1998, 234–8). By early 1935, the Paraguayans were within striking distance of the Bolivian oil centers in Santa Cruz and Tarija and the Bolivian command center at Villamontes (Villa Montes). Although Bolivia was able to contain the Paraguayan advance and retain control of the oil region, both sides were spent, and a cease-fire was signed on 12 June 1935 (Macías 1936, 180–200; Querejazu 1992, 411–36, 464–71; Salazar 2000, 637–42).

Bolivia and Paraguay agreed to a cease fire in 1935, but it would take more than three years for a peace treaty to be signed. When the disputants could not agree on a boundary line, they concluded a treaty of peace, friendship, and limits in July 1938 in which they renewed an earlier non-aggression pledge and agreed to allow an arbitral college, consisting of representatives of Argentina, Brazil, Chile, Peru, Uruguay, and the United States, to confirm a border agreed to in advance by Bolivian and Paraguayan negotiators. In the agreement, Paraguay also guaranteed the free transit across its territory of goods from abroad destined for Bolivia as well as goods proceeding from

War, Revolution, Water, 1930–70   99

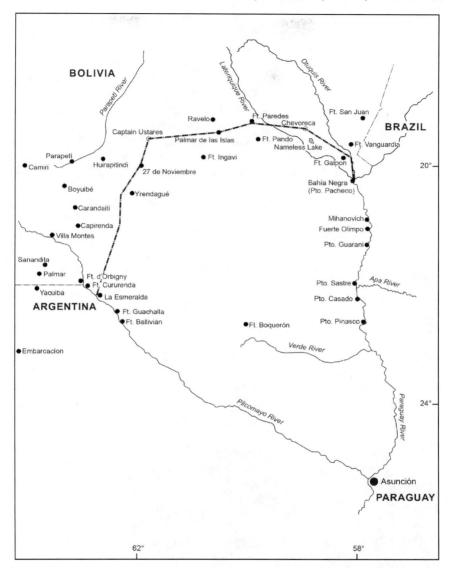

*Figure 6.1* Bolivia–Paraguay Boundary, 1938
Source: Nathan Bailey St John.

Bolivia for shipment abroad through Puerto Casado on the Paraguay River (Rout 1970, 243–6; Salazar 2000, 659–64). In October 1938, the Chaco Arbitral College announced a frontier that began in the west at La Esmeralda on the Pilcomayo River, moved north to Captain Ustares, turned east to Fort Paredes, and concluded at Bahía Negra on the Paraguay River. Bolivia and

## 100  *War, Revolution, Water, 1930–70*

Paraguay renewed diplomatic relations in late November 1938, and one month later, both sides verified the arbitral award had been executed (Rout 1970, 206–7; Abecia 1986, II, 589–97, 602–5).

The end of the Chaco War was greeted with relief in both Bolivia and Paraguay albeit the mood in Bolivia was one of resignation and that in Paraguay was one of jubilation (Querejazu 1992, 470–1). Bolivia could take some satisfaction in the retention of its oil fields in Santa Cruz and Tarija, and Paraguay could point with pride to confirmation of its ownership of the Paraguay River and most of the Chaco Boreal. The three-year war which ended a century-old dispute resulted in the death of approximately 60,000 Bolivian and 40,000 Paraguayan soldiers. With a total population of around 2 million, Bolivian losses were in a ratio equal to the losses of European nations in World War I (Guzmán 1998, 238; Klein 2011, 182–3). Not only had the Paraguayans achieved a great military victory, they had saved their country from a defeat that could well have meant the end of Paraguay as an

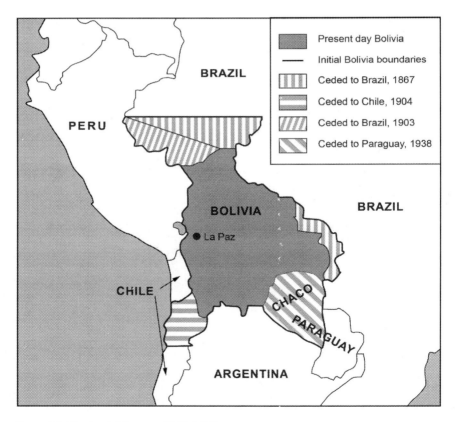

*Figure 6.2* Territorial Losses, 1867–1938
Source: Nathan Bailey St John.

independent state (Wood 1966, 95–6). In turn, Bolivia sacrificed its claim to approximately 455,600 square miles of territory, its single largest loss of territory since independence. Bolivia's borders were now complete but reduced to approximately 50 percent of its theoretical holdings in 1825. In addition, Bolivia found itself excluded from the Paraguay River with the exception of those small windows bordering the extreme northeast corner of the Chaco Boreal where Brazil in the 1903 Treaty of Petropolis had given Bolivia 25 miles of river bank in an area where the river was useless for navigation (Fifer 1972, 218). Sixty years later, Bolivia would open a canal through one of those windows to the Paraguay River, reportedly reducing the transportation cost of goods to the Atlantic Ocean by as much as 50 percent (*Los Tiempos*: 20 November 1998). In his memoirs, Víctor Andrade, a veteran of the Chaco War and a future Bolivian ambassador to the United States, captured the psychological and political impact of the war on his generation:

> The Chaco War presented violent, Dantesque contrasts between the most holy examples of self-renunciation and the most abominable acts of cowardice. The anonymous populace ... silently suffered the tragedy and burdens of incompetence in the direction of the war. ... The war was the culmination of an epoch of total falsity, one in which a defective social order had devalued and neglected an entire nation. ... The seed of the [1952] revolution germinated from the common experience of the civilian and military youth in the war: a national consciousness was formed.
> (1976, 5)

## Competing Narratives

Throughout the 1920s, the Standard Oil Company of Bolivia pursued a dual strategy based on retaining control over the country's best oil reserves while deliberately limiting production. Standard Oil had no incentive to increase production when the costs of shipping were high and the world market price was low. Therefore, it supplied Bolivia's oil needs through its Mexican and Peruvian subsidiaries as it strived to retain legal control over Bolivian reserves. At the end of the decade, Standard Oil officials worried they would become involved in a war that could cost them control of Bolivia's oil reserves or result in the confiscation of trucks, animals, and other assets. To avoid these problems, Standard Oil declared itself neutral in the Chaco War, transferred assets from its oil camps in Bolivia to its operations in Argentina, and refused to increase production or refine aviation gasoline in its refineries at Camiri and Sanandita (Miranda 1999, 245–6; Cote 2016b, 54, 60, 66, 78–9).

The strategy of the Standard Oil Company of Bolivia before and during the Chaco War helped explain the competing narratives that developed later to explain the origins, conduct, and outcome of the fighting. One Bolivian narrative argued that Standard Oil did not do enough to help Bolivia win the war. Proponents of this viewpoint cited Standard Oil's declaration of neutrality, transfer of assets to Argentina, and refusal to increase production or refine aviation gasoline (Miranda 1999, 245–6; Klein and Peres-Cajías 2014, 147–8). A competing narrative argued that Standard Oil, in league with the Salamanca government, was responsible for starting the war in order to gain access to what proved to be nonexistent oil deposits in the Chaco Boreal and to build a pipeline to the Paraguay River (Young 2017, 20–2). After the Treaty of Lima in 1929 blocked Bolivian efforts to secure a Pacific port and Argentina rejected a Bolivian proposal to build an oil pipeline across Argentina, frontage on the Paraguay River offered Standard Oil its only viable avenue to export oil to world markets. The Toro administration later undermined this argument when it cited the intransigence of Standard Oil during the war as a reason for the nationalization of its holdings in 1937 (Fifer 1972, 219–20; Cote 2016b, 69).

A third narrative argued Standard Oil and Royal Dutch Shell directly or indirectly through Argentina aggravated tensions between Bolivia and Paraguay or supported Paraguay in the war to the detriment of Bolivia (Blasier 1971, 57; Seiferheld 1983; Guzmán 1998, 260). While Argentina clearly favored Paraguay in the war, no credible evidence emerged to suggest its policies before or during the war resulted in Bolivia's defeat. At the same time, "the ability of Argentina to prevent peace moves until the end, along with continued Paraguayan successes, meant that once the war began Bolivia had little ability to stop its onslaught" (Klein 2011, 176). Argentina and Bolivia later concluded an agreement in November 1937 which allowed the Bolivian state oil company, YPFB (*Yacimientos Petrolíferos Fiscales Bolivianos*), to export oil through Argentina. In February 1938, Bolivia and Brazil also concluded an agreement covering the supply and export of Bolivian petroleum through Brazil. In February 1941, Bolivia and Argentina agreed to build railways and a pipeline connecting the two states with loans from Argentina to be repaid in Bolivian oil (Fifer 1972, 222–3, 227–8; Abecia 1986, III, 100–2, 113–14). Bolivia and Argentina concluded new pacts related to trade in 1947, 1954, and 1957 (UN 1958a, 315–16, 328–9). In 1958, Bolivia and Brazil concluded multiple new treaties, known as the Roboré Agreements (*Acuerdos de Roboré*), which built on the February 1938 pacts (Escobari 1982, II, 285–6, 323–9, 331–41, 359–81). Collectively, the Bolivian treaties with Argentina and Brazil initiated a process of regional energy integration that has continued to the present day (Abecia 1986, II, 226–8; Cote 2016b, 106).

At various times during the war, Paraguay claimed the Standard Oil Company (New Jersey) was assisting the Bolivian war effort. In making these charges, Paraguayans did not always distinguish between Standard Oil and the US government. Consequently, a widespread belief developed in Paraguay that the United States was providing financial aid to Bolivia to continue the war. Paraguayan prejudices in this regard were reinforced by three speeches Senator Huey Long of Louisiana made between 30 May and 8 June 1934 in which he described the Standard Oil Company as a traditional promoter of interstate conflict in Latin America, claiming it was aiding Bolivia in the

Chaco War in order to obtain a port to export petroleum. Senator Long had a long-standing grudge against Standard Oil stemming from the company's support of an abortive effort in April 1929 to impeach Long, then the governor of Louisiana, after he tried to impose a tax on in-state oil production (Wood 1966, 65–7; Querejazu 1992, 437–8). Following the nationalization of the Standard Oil Company of Bolivia in 1937, Paraguay in 1939 granted Bolivia permission to build a pipeline across the Chaco Boreal to the Paraguay River. Additional agreements in 1943 and 1956 afforded Bolivian oil the fullest possible freedom of transit through Paraguayan territory, including the construction by Bolivia of warehouses, refineries, and other facilities in a free trade zone on the western bank of the Paraguay River; however, the pipeline was never built (UN 1958a, 330). If Paraguay had agreed to a similar Bolivian request in 1932, the Chaco War might have been prevented (Abecia 1986, II. 605–6; Cote 2016b, 79–80, 106–7).

Contemporary historians have found little evidence to support the above narratives; nevertheless, the mythology surrounding Standard Oil's involvement in the Chaco War influenced Bolivian foreign policy for decades to come. As for the military historiography of the war, it has remained until recently nationalistic in perspective. Roberto Querejazu Calvo's *Masamaclay: Historia, política, diplomática y militar de la Guerra del Chaco* (1992) exemplifies the war told from the Bolivian perspective, and Silvio Macías's *La Guerra del Chaco: Paraguay versus Bolivia, 1932–1935* (1936) illustrates the war told from the Paraguayan viewpoint. English-language studies of the war, such as Bruce W. Farcau's *The Chaco War: Bolivia and Paraguay, 1932–1935* (1996) and David H. Zook's *The Conduct of the Chaco War* (1960) tend to favor Bolivia over Paraguay (Chesterton 2016, 12–13). Some English-language scholars also have overemphasized the impact the Treaty of Lima had on the war. Arthur P. Whitaker said the Tacna-Arica controversy caused Bolivia to commence a *Drang nach Osten* (push eastward) which embroiled it in the controversy with Paraguay (1948, 180), and Bryce Wood expressed a similar viewpoint (1966, 19). In the end, all of the single factor narratives of the Chaco War remain incomplete with most of them failing to acknowledge the controversy dated from the colonial period. While the issue was largely dormant until the end of the nineteenth century, the growing pressure after 1926 on the southeastern frontier of Bolivia would have likely reached an exploding point sooner or later regardless of the Treaty of Lima or the influence of outside interests (Alexander 1982, 65; Arze 1991, 416–21).

## Post-war Politics

The Great Depression precipitated a crash in global tin prices, undermining the economic and political power of the tin oligarchy, and the Chaco War increased the vulnerability of Bolivia to a nationalist, populist backlash. The war also turned the Bolivian military against the entrenched economic and political control of the tin oligarchy and associated establishment interests known as the *rosca*. In November 1934, President Salamanca was overthrown and replaced by Vice President José Luis Tejada Sorzano (1934–36). The Tejada government ended the war but failed to appease the multiple political movements which surfaced at its end (Klein 2011, 186–7). Believing the country's problems could not be resolved within the existing political system, the military in May 1936 preempted scheduled elections with a *golpe de estado*, initiating a period of government led by younger Chaco War officers. Colonel Germán Busch (1936, 1937–39) and then Colonel David Toro (1936–37) served as the chairman of a civilian–military government (Alexander 1982, 66–7; Mesa Gisbert 2001a, 582–3). Above all else, these military reformers were nationalists who stood for social justice, economic development, and popular participation. Declaring itself to be a government of "military socialism," the Toro administration in December 1936 created the Bolivian state oil company, and in March 1937, it cancelled the contract of the Standard Oil Company of Bolivia and turned over its properties and operations to YPFB (Young 2017, 24–5). This was the first seizure of a US company in Latin America, an expropriation without offer of indemnification, predating by a year the Mexican nationalization which did offer indemnity (Miranda 1999, 246–7; Klein and Peres-Cajías 2014, 148). The move was popular with nationalists, on the left and on the right, because it was aimed at the United States, a country associated with unfair loans, repeated meddling, and threats to Bolivian national sovereignty. It also was popular because it targeted Standard Oil, the bane of Bolivian nationalists since the early 1920s (Klein 1969, 260–3; Navia 1984, 42–5).

As Toro and Busch struggled to control the political turmoil unleashed in the wake of the Chaco War, anti-establishment nationalist and Marxist parties emerged to replace the traditional political parties of Bolivia (Arze 1991, 485–91). The Revolutionary Workers' Party (*Partido Obrero Revolucionario*, POR), was established in 1934 and was part of Trotsky's Fourth International from its inception. The Bolivian Socialist Falange (*Falange Socialista Boliviana*, FSB) was established in 1937 and was a Fascist-oriented party patterned more or less after the Spanish Falange. The Party of the Revolutionary Left (*Partido de la Izquierda Revolucionaria*, PIR), was established in 1940 and was a truly national Marxist–Leninist party throughout the decade. Founded in 1941, the Nationalist Revolutionary Movement (*Movimiento Nacionalista Revolucionario*, MNR), led by Víctor Paz Estenssoro, emphasized a program with a patriotic, socialist, revolutionary, and nationalist character (Klein 1969, 195–6, 334–43, 351–2; Mesa Gisbert 2001a, 591–2, 600–2). The emergence of radical, revolutionary parties after the Chaco War set the stage for dramatic political developments throughout the 1940s (Malloy 1970, 95–119; Morales 2010, 119–21).

In July 1937, Busch unseated Toro as chairman of the government junta, and in April 1939, he assumed dictatorial powers. Under enormous strain, President Busch committed suicide in August 1939, and with his death, the myth of Busch as a martyr to the revolutionary left was born (Mesa Gisbert

2001a, 592–4, 597; Klein 2011, 194). In an effort to contain the radical tide, the *rosca* formed the Concordance (*La Concordancia*), an alliance of traditional parties intent on maintaining the status quo. The Concordance supported the governments of two distinguished Chaco War veterans, General Carlos Quintanilla Quiroga (1939–40) and General Enrique Peñaranda del Castillo (1940–43). The policies of the Peñaranda administration were liberal on political questions and conservative on economic and labor issues (Morales 2010, 121–3; Klein 2011, 198–9). In December 1943, a secret military lodge, the Reason of the Fatherland (*Razón de Patria*, RADEPA) made up of young, nationalist reformers, allied with the MNR to overthrow the Peñaranda government (Ostria 1958, 7–9, 14–17; Mesa Gisbert 2001a, 604). Led by Major Gualberto Villarroel (1943–46), the MNR/RADEPA alliance was short-lived. Within six months, MNR had left the cabinet, and in August 1944, Villarroel was elected president. The MNR later rejoined the Villarroel administration, but after President Villarroel returned to exclusive military rule, he was ousted from office and his body hung from a lamppost in July 1946 (Klein 1969, 369–82; Alexander 1982, 71–5).

The death of Villarroel was followed by six years of social struggle and repression known as the *sexenio* in which the *rosca* enlisted military and political reactionaries to roll back the reforms implemented in the decade after the Chaco War (Malloy 1970, 127). In January 1947, Enrique Hertzog (1947–49), the oligarchy's candidate, was elected president, and when he resigned in October 1949, he was succeeded by Vice President Mamerto Urriolagoitía (1949–51). By 1951, Bolivia was polarized between the forces of reform and reaction (Ostria 1958, 77–90; Klein 1969, 388–9). When Víctor Paz Estenssoro, the MNR candidate for president, won a plurality in the 1951 elections, President Urriolagoitía resigned and turned the government over to the head of the army, General Ovidio Quiroga, who appointed General Hugo Ballivián Rojas (1951–52) as interim president. The military junta appeared to offer hope for the old order, but a prostrate economy and deep political polarization quickly undermined its support (Malloy 1970, 149–58; Mesa Gisbert 2001a, 611–19).

## 1952 Revolution

The Bolivian Revolution began on 9 April 1952 with the Battle of La Paz. It was led by a broad coalition consisting of the MNR, workers, peasants, miners, and students. After three days of fighting, the rebels triumphed and Víctor Paz Estenssoro was sworn in as president. Despite charges of communist influence, the revolution was primarily nationalist in orientation (Eckstein 1976, 8, 31). Like the Mexican Revolution in 1911, the Bolivian Revolution initiated radical socioeconomic and political change albeit not as much as early observers believed (Lehman 2016, 7–11). Universal suffrage, land reform, nationalization of the mines, universal education, and the integration of the indigenous majority into national life were some of the reforms implemented. Where only 5 percent of the population voted in 1951, the number had increased to 26 percent by 1960 (Malloy 1970, 73–7, 167–87; Mesa Gisbert 2001b, 650–2).

The decision to nationalize the largest tin mines and create the state Mining Corporation of Bolivia (*Corporación Minera de Bolivia*, COMIBOL) resulted in unanticipated economic and political challenges. In order to gain both diplomatic recognition and foreign aid from the US government, Bolivia was forced to compensate the tin barons at a considerable loss to the treasury. With limited capitalization and production, nationalization of the aging mines also brought unexpected expenses and liabilities. Drastic cuts in the US tin quota compounded the economic crisis in Bolivia, and a new petroleum code drawn up with US assistance favored US interests over YPFB. Reflecting the high priority the Eisenhower administration placed on the new petroleum law, US officials hinted to the Bolivian government that a failure to implement the law could jeopardize future US aid (Young 2017, 63). Washington linked US assistance to the imposition in 1956–57 of a stern austerity/stabilization program, the first time the International Monetary Fund (IMF) executed an austerity/stabilization program in the developing world (Mitchell 1977, 55–6; Ugarteche 1986, 89–95; Morales and Pacheco 1999, 174–5). US economic aid to Bolivia was among the most generous in the region; nevertheless, it was conditional and served to control and moderate the revolution. "Starting in 1953 [the US government] used foreign aid and tin purchase agreements as means of restraining resource nationalism, progressive fiscal policy, and the power of labor" (Young 2017, 11, 37–8, 53–8, quote 11). As a result, the policies of the MNR government, despite its rhetoric to the contrary, failed to achieve the country's independence. In order to win increased national autonomy, the revolutionary nationalists had to concede their dependency (Lehman 2003, 91–113).

The ideological and class diversity of the MNR proved an asset in making the revolution but a liability once in power. The original program of the MNR, which focused on national autonomy and economic development, was moderate in tone and direction; however, its alliance with miners, peasants, and workers radicalized the party, dividing it into competing factions (Mesa Gisbert 2001b, 654–65). In the 1956 election, the MNR successfully appealed to the middle class vote, distancing itself from its labor allies. Over the next four years, the Hernán Siles Zuazo government enacted an economic stabilization plan which benefitted the middle class but directly attacked labor (Pike 1977, 290–1; Crespo 1997, 197–229). By 1960, the MNR had begun to unravel. Its three factions, Paz Estenssoro and the pragmatic reformers, Siles Zuazo and the conservative nationalists, and the proletarian left of Juan Lechín, split off to form independent parties. By 1964, only the Paz wing of the original MNR remained, and the failure of the movement to unite Bolivian society and institutionalize the revolution invited a military counterrevolution (Mitchell 1977, 92–6; Klein 2011, 222).

In November 1964, a military junta ousted the Paz Estenssoro government, initiating a long period of military rule interspersed with brief periods of civilian government which lasted until the end of 1982 (Prado 1984, 143–52; Morales and Pacheco 1999, 175). General René Barrientos Ortuño, a charismatic, populist leader who cultivated the indigenous leadership of his native Cochabamba, justified the *golpe de estado* as a restoration of the revolution. Over the next 19 months, Barrientos and General Alfredo Ovando Candía, commander-in-chief of the Bolivian army, ruled Bolivia, and in 1966, Barrientos was elected president (Prado 1984, 153–87; Mesa Gisbert 2001b, 680–2). President Barrientos preserved major reforms but also pursued conservative, repressive policies, labeling any political opposition as communist in origin. A new investment code and pro-business policies which favored US corporations led to increased private investment. The US military presence in Bolivia also increased (Mitchell 1977, 97–102; Dunkerley 1984, 128–9; Field 2014, 190, 194).

In November 1966, Ernesto "Che" Guevara launched his guerrilla *foco* experiment in Bolivia. Departing from traditional Marxist–Leninist views, Guevara argued that a guerrilla force could serve as a nucleus of armed insurrection – a *foco insurreccional* – creating a revolutionary situation by its own momentum. In so doing, he insisted that the political element of the revolutionary forces, the Communist party of Bolivia and other leftist groups, should be subordinate to the military element, an approach diametrically opposed to that successfully pursued by Marxist–Leninists in Vietnam (Lamberg 1970, 27–30; St John 1980, 812–28). On the surface, Bolivia appeared the ideal country in which to launch a continent-wide revolution. There were vast jungle areas in which a guerrilla army could incubate and grow, and the Bolivian army, which had never won a war, consisted mainly of one-year recruits. Moreover, the *golpe de estado* that overthrew the Paz regime in 1964 appeared to leave Bolivia on the edge of chaos. Guevara planned to establish a secure base of operations in Bolivia and then expand the revolution into neighboring Argentina, Brazil, Chile, Paraguay, and Peru (Mallin 1968, 74–84).

"A new stage begins today" (James 1968, 80). With those simple words, Ché Guevara in the first entry in his diary (7 November 1966) announced the beginning of the Cuban-inspired insurgency in Bolivia. Optimistic at the start, Guevara failed to understand Bolivian reality, including the state of the nation, and he miscalculated the level of opposition to Barrientos. The clandestine guerrilla front he established in the jungles of Santa Cruz generated few recruits and almost no local support. The peasants in this remote part of Bolivia expressed a limited sense of nationalism, but they also exhibited that narrower sense of regional parochialism often found in Bolivia (James 1968, 60). A counterinsurgency effort led by the Bolivian military and aided by the US government ended with Guevara's death in October 1967 (Ryan 1998, 126–54).

Barrientos survived the armed opposition of the left and retained considerable popular support among the peasantry only to die unexpectedly in an April 1969 helicopter crash. Vice President Luis Adolfo Siles Salinas occupied the presidency briefly before being ousted in September 1969 by General Ovando (Prado 1984, 232–49; Mesa Gisbert 2001b, 686–8). A nationalist reformer enamored with General Juan Velasco Alvarado's military government in Peru, President Ovando in a highly popular move abrogated the petroleum law and nationalized the facilities of Bolivian Gulf Oil in October 1969 (Guzmán 1998, 370–4; Young 2017, 162–3). At the time, the calculation of the company's tax liability was disputed as were its rights to the natural gas deposits found with the oil but not mentioned in the original concession. Bolivian Gulf Oil and other major producers retaliated with a boycott of Bolivian crude, costing the Bolivian government some $14 million in revenues. After the US government responded with a sharp reduction in economic assistance, the besieged Ovando government in September 1970 promised Bolivian Gulf Oil $78 million in compensation (Mitchell 1977, 107–14; Ugarteche 1986, 98–100). In pursuit of a more independent foreign policy, President Ovando opened ambassador-level contacts with the Soviet Union and expanded diplomatic and trade relations with Czechoslovakia, Romania, and Hungary (Dunkerley 1984, 166; Morales 1992b, 183). In October 1970, General Juan José Torres seized power, and in short order, "Torres would prove to be the most radical and left-leaning general ever to have governed Bolivia" (Klein 2011, 226–8, quote 226; Prado 1984, 296–324). In August 1971, the Bolivian military under the leadership of General Hugo Banzer Suárez and in alliance with business interests in Santa Cruz ended Torres's radical experiment.

**Trilateral Issues**

Focused first on the Chaco War and then on the fallout from the Bolivian Revolution, the Bolivian government also faced associated diplomatic challenges with Peru and Chile. In January 1932, Bolivia and Peru signed a protocol which fixed their respective limits on the Copacabana Peninsula (Abecia 1986, III, 128–9). Thereafter, bilateral relations between them revolved around the Chaco War for the remainder of the decade. With the outbreak of fighting in June 1932, Peru agreed to work with its neighbors for peace in the hemisphere. Having declared itself neutral in the war, Peru continued to honor the terms of a November 1905 treaty of commerce and customs with Bolivia which provided for the free movement of goods, including armaments, between them. Peru was not alone in this regard as Argentina and Chile also permitted the shipment of arms and munitions through their territories to Paraguay and Bolivia, respectively, during the war (Wood 1966, 89, 100–1; Novak and Namihas 2013, 112–13, 124–6). Peru supported the search for peace in the Chaco but played a minor role in the peace treaty concluded in July 1938 (Perú 1937–39, vii–viii). In the interim, a delegation from an opposition party in Peru, the American Popular Revolutionary Alliance (*Alianza Popular Revolucionaria Americana*, APRA), approached the short-lived Toro government with an offer to support Bolivian efforts to obtain the port of Arica in return for assistance in overthrowing the Peruvian government of Óscar R. Benavides. Motivated by ideological compatibility and a belief that an Aprista government would help Bolivia obtain Arica from Chile, President Toro in August 1936 offered APRA arms and ammunition (Perú 1934–36, iv–viii).

Aware of the plot, the Benavides government moved quickly to forestall Bolivian support. In September 1936, Bolivia and Peru concluded a non-aggression pact, known as the Ulloa–Ostria treaty, which prohibited intervention in the internal or external affairs of the signatories. In the pact, Bolivia traded a guarantee of free transit of goods for a declaration that it had no political or territorial problems with Peru (Gumucio 1997, 98; Salazar 2000, 649–54). Peruvians considered the treaty a major diplomatic victory as it eliminated Bolivian aspirations for a Pacific port at the expense of Peru (Bákula 2002, I, 548). Bolivia and Peru also concluded additional agreements in June 1948 aimed at regularizing the movement of goods and people across their common border (Escobari 1982, II, 57–8; Novak and Namihas 2013, 127–8, 137–8).

In late 1946, the Bolivian ambassador to Chile, Alberto Ostria Gutiérrez, opened informal talks with the Chilean government which led the Urriolagoitía administration in La Paz to propose direct negotiations in June 1950 aimed at granting Bolivia a sovereign exit to the Pacific Ocean. Chile agreed to discuss the question; however, its response raised the issue of compensation and emphasized its obligation under the Treaty of Lima to consult with Peru (Fellmann 1967, 104, 146–8; Salazar 2000, 689–92; Bustos 2003, 138–40). After this initial exchange, the 1950 negotiations made little progress (Mesa Gisbert 2016, 161–2; Guzmán Escobari 2015a, 210–13). Among other concerns, Bolivia opposed a Chilean proposal in which compensation for a Pacific port would take the form of the diversion of water from the Bolivian altiplano for use in the economic development of Tacna and Arica (Escobari 1988, 141–2; Andaluz 2002, 202–5). Widespread opposition to an agreement also developed in Chile, especially in the northern part of the country, the presumed location of a Bolivian corridor to the sea (Prudencio Lizón 2004, 35, 40; De Cossío Klüver 2011, 26–37). Peru opposed any negotiations which might cede to Bolivia territory that had once been Peruvian (Novak and Namihas 2013, 129). Peru also opposed the Chilean suggestion that the waters of Lake Titicaca be used to compensate Chile for a Bolivian port as Peru had long considered those waters held in condominium by Bolivia and Peru for their exclusive use (Becerra de la Roca 2002, 146; De Cossío Klüver 2011, 53–6). In July 1955, Bolivia and Peru signed an agreement declaring they held the waters of Lake Titicaca in indivisible condominium, and in February 1957, they initiated planning for the common use of those waters (Escobari 1982, II, 99–113).

In 1953, Chile agreed to renew a 1937 convention covering the transit of Bolivian goods through Chilean ports, and in 1957, Bolivia and Chile also agreed to build an oil pipeline from Sica Sica in Bolivia to a Chilean port on the Pacific. This agreement led to the subsequent construction of the Sica Sica–Arica oil pipeline which runs through northern Chile's Lluta Valley (Ostria 1958, 175–6; Escobari 1982, II, 56–7; Abecia 1986, III, 85, 88–9). Upon learning of Bolivia's intent to raise the issue of sovereign access to the Pacific at the upcoming Inter-American Conference in Quito, Ecuador, the Chilean ambassador to Bolivia, Manuel Trucco, in July 1961 handed the minister of foreign affairs of Bolivia a note, known as the Trucco Memorandum, in which Chile said it was open or willing (*llano*), consistent with the de jure situation established in the 1904 treaty, to study with Bolivia the possibility of satisfying both Bolivian aspirations and Chilean interests. Referencing the June 1950 negotiations, the memorandum added that Chile was open to direct negotiations aimed at giving Bolivia sovereign access to the Pacific Ocean in return for compensation of a non-territorial nature. The Chilean proposal elicited a positive Bolivian response; however, talks failed to advance after it became clear that the non-territorial compensation referred to in the proposal concerned the disputed waters of the Lauca River. In March 1963, the Chilean government denied that the Trucco Memorandum constituted an official note, arguing it was simply a statement of views at a given point in time (Guzmán Escobari 2015a, 223–34, 237–40).

Although the mid-century talks between Bolivia, Chile, and Peru produced no conclusive results, they highlighted aspects of the seaport issue which would influence Bolivian foreign policy for the remainder of the century. The issue of compensation was first raised by Bolivia in 1910, and at that time, there was some acceptance in Bolivia that it should expect to pay compensation to Chile in exchange for a Pacific port. Later, the Bolivian position hardened, and the question of compensation became a major issue in negotiations with Chile (Fellmann 1967, 116–17; Escobari 1988, 197–207). In addition, the talks after 1950 highlighted the tripartite nature of the seaport issue. Throughout the nineteenth and twentieth centuries, any sovereign Pacific port acceptable to Bolivia involved the interests and rights of both Chile and Peru. After 1936, Bolivia was not seeking access to the sea through Peruvian territory; however, it was seeking access to the Pacific through territory formerly a part of Peru before it was ceded to Chile in the 1929 treaty (Escobari 1982, II, 41–2). When Chile appeared willing to exchange a corridor on the Chilean side of the Chile–Peru frontier for Bolivian compensation elsewhere, Peru used the terms of the Treaty of Lima to veto the move on the grounds it could not accept the transfer to Bolivia of land that was formerly a part of Peru. In return, Peru proposed the creation of an international corridor under international governance terminating at Arica. As early as 1825, Bolivia expressed interest in substituting Arica for Cobija as its principal port on the Pacific, and after that time, it repeatedly emphasized that it would not be satisfied with anything less. The Bolivian policy of attachment to Peru, ratified in the 1936 treaty, proved notably unsuccessful in this regard because Peru never, with the exception of the treaty of 1826, accepted the principle of Arica for Bolivia. Finally, the diplomatic initiative launched by Bolivia in 1950 reflected both the popularity of the issue in Bolivia and the recognition by Bolivian politicians of the political value of emphasizing it from time to time (St John 1977, 70–2).

In July 1955, Bolivia and Peru signed a joint declaration covering the construction of a railway between Puno and La Paz; the building of roads between Ilo, Moquegua, Desaguadero, and La Paz as well as between Tacna, Charaña, and La Paz; the joint utilization of Lake Titicaca; and the negotiation of an agreement facilitating transit between the two countries. In recognizing that Bolivia and Peru enjoyed joint sovereignty over the waters of Lake Titicaca, which could be exploited only with the direct consent of both states, the 1955 declaration effectively checkmated Chilean ambitions in this area. In February 1957, Bolivia and Peru concluded another convention related to Lake Titicaca in which they agreed to develop a plan for the common use of its waters for fishing, irrigation, and the generation of electrical energy. In so doing, they once again confirmed the indivisible condominium and exclusive use of the waters of Lake Titicaca for Bolivia and Peru. Four years later, Bolivian and Peruvian officials met in Arequipa to adopt measures to improve the services of the Peruvian port of Matarani and to increase commerce between Bolivia and Peru (Escobari 1982, II, 55–113; Novak and Namihas 2013, 130–1).

## The Silala, Lauca, and Maurí Rivers

The Silala Basin, known in Chile as the Siloli Basin, is located in the Atacama Desert approximately 185 miles northeast of Antofagasta and is shared upstream by Bolivia and downstream by Chile. Prior to the War of the Pacific, the basin was located entirely within Bolivian territory, but with the Chilean occupation of the Bolivian littoral, it became a shared resource (Martínez 2002, 74). The Silala waters originate in high altitude wetlands formed by a large number of small-volume groundwater springs that discharge in the Bolivian province of Sur Lípez, department of Potosí. Small, manmade channels drain most of the springs, directing the flow to two central drainage canals which join into a principal canal. The principal canal flows for a short distance before crossing the international border into Chile. Near the border, the mean discharge of the principal canal is relatively small, but even this limited flow rate is important because the Silala Basin is located in the Atacama Desert, the second driest place on Earth (Urquidi 2005, 56–70; Rossi 2017, 56–7). After 1908, the principal canal directed the waters of the Silala into the San Pedro de Inacaliri River in Chile and from there into the Loa River before emptying into the Pacific Ocean. While some Bolivians have suggested the Silala River never existed and was a myth created by Chile (Bazoberry 2003; *La Razón*: 13 April 2018), credible geographical,

112  War, Revolution, Water, 1930–70

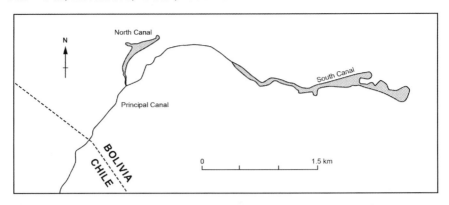

*Figure 6.3* Silala River Dispute
Source: Nathan Bailey St John.

topographical, and historical evidence exists to suggest the Silala springs flowed overland from Bolivia to Chile prior to canalization (Mulligan and Eckstein 2011, 597; Rossi 2017, 61; Kriener 2017; Vucíc 2017).

As Chile expanded its mining operations in the Atacama Desert, rail was the only reliable way to get the nitrates and other minerals to market, and the steam locomotives of the day required a regular supply of water, a scarce commodity in the desert. In 1908, the Antofagasta (Chili) and Bolivia Railway Co. Ltd., which operated the railroad from Antofagasta in Chile to Oruro in Bolivia, applied for a concession to use the waters of the Silala springs to power its steam engines (Bazoberry 2003, 72–3, 131–40). In response, the prefecture of the Bolivian department of Potosí granted the company a concession to build canals in Bolivian territory and to use the waters of the Silala for its locomotives (Martínez 2002, 78–9). In 1961, the railroad replaced the steam engines with diesel engines, and the Silala waters were no longer used for the purpose for which the concession was granted (Mulligan and Eckstein 2011, 597–8). In the interim, Chile put the commingled waters of the Loa River to other uses, including process water for the Chuquicamata copper mine located approximately 55 miles west-southwest of the basin. Located in what was once part of Bolivia, the Chuquicamata mine, one of the largest open pit mines in the world, is run by the state-owned National Copper Corporation (*Corporación Nacional del Cobre*, CODELCO) and generates approximately one-third of the Chilean government's income (Rossi 2017, 63; Francaviglia 2018, 272–3, 308–9).

The Lauca River rises in the Ciénaga de Parinacota, a marsh fed by Cotacontani Lake in Chile approximately 75 miles east of the port of Arica, and flows along an s-shaped course for approximately 140 miles before emptying into Coipasa Lake, a salty closed basin in Bolivia (Urquidi 2005, 40–56). In 1939, Chile announced its intention to irrigate the Azapa Valley,

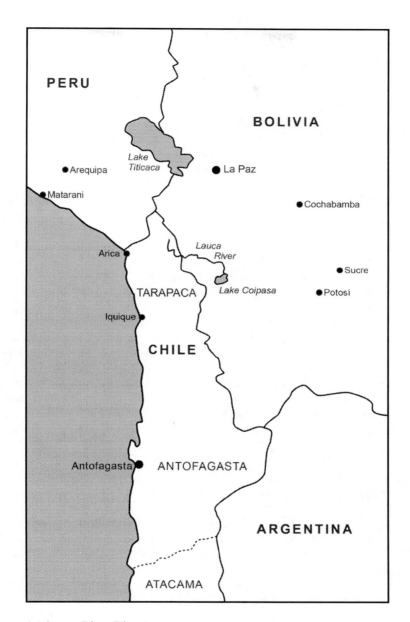

*Figure 6.4* Lauca River Dispute
Source: Nathan Bailey St John.

also known as the Apaza Valley, with water diverted from the Lauca River through a public works project involving the construction of a tunnel and canal (Encina 1963, 279–80; Espinosa 1964, 8–11; Guzmán Escobari 2015a, 225). The initial response of Bolivia was a relatively mild protest which noted that under international law the upper riparian, Chile in this case, had the right to use the water of an international river only as long as it did nothing to modify the hydrologic conditions or the natural regime of the river (Moya 1962, 81–3; Iturralde 1963, 32–4). In support of this position, Bolivia cited article two of the Declaration of Montevideo on the Industrial and Agricultural Use of International Rivers which states this principle of international law. The Bolivian response also noted that the proposed diversion of the waters of the Lauca River could impact on the use of the river for irrigation and industrial purposes (Escobari 1988, 159; Martínez 2002, 17–19, 96–9). When Chile in August 1939 allocated money for a preliminary study of the proposed project, Bolivia again issued a protest to which Chile responded that the contemplated works would in no way prejudice Bolivian interests as the lower riparian of the Lauca River (Espinosa 1964, 15–16; Lagos Carmona 1981, 117–18).

Throughout the long history of the dispute, Bolivia and Chile developed voluminous arguments in support of their respective cases; however, the core positions taken by the two countries in this initial exchange of notes remained largely unchanged. Bolivia viewed the diversion of waters from the Lauca River to irrigate farmland in the Azapa Valley both as a transgression of its rights as a lower riparian state and as the most recent example of a Chilean policy of economic, military, and political aggression dating back to the 1830s (Moya 1962, 5–7). Chile viewed the Lauca project as simply one of many development projects being carried out throughout the country. If it was in any way unique, it was its location in a part of Chile not as Chilean as the government in Santiago would have desired because it had only been part of Chile since 1929 (Lagos Carmona 1981, 118–19; Glassner 1970b, 193–4, 198). In Chilean eyes, the international dimension of the dispute was a minor consideration as Chile exercised complete sovereignty over its part of the Lauca drainage basin. Consequently, Chile considered it well within its rights under international law to use part of the waters, without provoking damages to Bolivia, for the purposes of the Lauca project (Melo 1963, 144; Tomasek 1967, 356–63).

International dialogue over the proposed project resumed in December 1947 when the Chilean Congress approved funds for the scheme. Following an exchange of notes between Bolivia and Chile, a mixed commission of technicians was appointed to study the Chilean scheme and submit its findings (Moya 1962, 36–7, 88–94; Martínez 2002, 22–4). In August 1949, the commission issued its report which found the engineering works underway conformed to the original plans insofar as Bolivia was concerned, and Chile felt free to begin work on the project (Encina 1963, 280; Melo 1963, 145–6). When Chile in 1951 notified Bolivia that it had started work on the project,

Bolivia failed to protest the move probably because it feared a protest might jeopardize the seaport talks in progress with Chile and Peru (Fellmann 1967, 93–4). Two years later, the Paz Estenssoro government in December 1953 raised the diversion issue and also protested a Chilean hydroelectric plant at Chapiquiña (Moya 1962, 42–4, 121–31). Chile responded in March 1954, citing its interpretation of the 1933 Declaration of Montevideo as well as the report of the mixed commission (Iturralde 1963, 42–9; Escobari 1988, 163–4). Five years later, Bolivia again raised the issue, and after an exchange of notes, Chile in November 1959 agreed to the creation of a second mixed commission. In September 1960, the new mixed commission issued its report which in essence approved the project, disavowing Bolivia's objections (Espinosa 1964, 34–5; Glassner 1970b, 196; Guzmán Escobari 2015a, 226–9).

When Bolivia in October 1961 learned Chile would soon begin running water through a tunnel at Chapiquiña as part of the Lauca project, it raised a new issue, arguing the use of international waters for agricultural or industrial purposes was only legitimate when carried out within the same drainage basin or when compensation was received for the flow from another drainage basin (Espinosa 1964, 39–41). After Chile rejected this argument, Bolivia threatened to take the issue to an international body. Following a further exchange of notes, Foreign Minister Fellmann in February 1962 hinted for the first time that Bolivia considered the Lauca River issue to be related to its quest for a sovereign Pacific port. As a basis for negotiations, Fellmann on 13 April 1962 proposed to Chile turning the clock back to 1939 and following the procedures outlined in the Declaration of Montevideo (Melo 1963, 148; Iturralde 1963, 86–91). On the same day, he sent a note to the Permanent Council of the Organization of American States (OAS), charging Chile with a threat to the territorial integrity of Bolivia as well as "imminent aggression" (Salazar 2000, 719–21, quote 719). On the following day, the Chilean president ordered the floodgates to be opened and the diversion of the waters of the Lauca River began. In bringing its case before the Permanent Council of the OAS, Bolivia argued the diversion of the waters constituted a disturbance of the peace under article six of the Rio Treaty of Reciprocal Defense (1947) and thus should prompt collective security provisions against Chile (Salazar 2000, 723–9; Mesa Gisbert 2016, 170–2). As the Permanent Council of the OAS deliberated the issue in an informal, unsuccessful attempt to find a peaceful solution, Bolivia in April 1962 broke diplomatic relations with Chile (Moya 1962, 63; Mulligan and Eckstein 2011, 601). When the Permanent Council of the OAS failed to support Bolivian demands, Bolivia withdrew from the OAS from September to October 1962 and again from June 1963 to February 1965 (Tomasek 1967, 363; Escobari 1988, 168–79; Guzmán Escobari 2015a, 231–4).

In late 1962 and early 1963, two attempts were made to resolve the Lauca dispute. The first involved an exchange of draft acts by Bolivia and Chile which attempted to resolve the issue by placing it within the framework of coordinated economic development along the northern border. This attempt failed when Bolivia rejected the Chilean draft on the grounds it was not clearly concerned with the dispute. The second attempt involved an unofficial and unsuccessful initiative on the part of the president of the Permanent Council of the OAS to reestablish diplomatic relations (Tomasek 1967, 355–6; Escobari 1988, 175–7). By March 1963, the diplomatic situation had deteriorated to the point that the Chilean foreign minister, Carlos Martínez Sotomayor, was compelled to give a rare radio address to the Chilean people, explaining the Chilean position on both the Lauca and seaport issues. Foreign Minister Fellmann responded in early April in a long address which reiterated the Bolivian position in rather less restrained terms than those used by his Chilean counterpart (Fellmann 1967, 151–77). In addition to exposing information and opinions that had not before been aired publicly, the two speeches were important because they highlighted the full extent to which the Lauca River and seaport issues had become intertwined (Glassner 1970b, 200).

In an October 1963 press interview, Foreign Minister Fellmann made one of the most specific statements to date of Bolivian aims. He suggested the cession of the port of Mejillones, together with the creation of an enclave around the port and the use of the railroad connecting Mejillones to the port of Antofagasta, would satisfy his government. In return, Bolivia would agree to divert water from five small rivers high in the Andes to help irrigate the deserts of northern Chile (*NYT*: 13 October 1963; Tomasek 1967, 360). Around the same time, Teodoro Moscoso, the US Alliance for Progress administrator, introduced a development proposal based on the use of Lake Titicaca waters for irrigation and hydroelectric power to develop the triangle formed by southern Peru, northern Chile, and the Bolivian altiplano. In return, Bolivia would receive a sovereign corridor to the Pacific Ocean where it could construct a modern port and other works financed by the Inter-American Development Bank (IDB). Billed as a fresh approach, the Moscoso proposition generated opposition in Bolivia, Chile, and Peru similar to earlier condominium proposals (Fellmann 1967, 116–17; Gumucio 2005, 374–5).

In July 1966, President-elect Barrientos held informal talks with the Chilean ambassador to the United States. When nothing came of this initiative, Bolivia reverted to a hardline position on the seaport issue. President Barrientos refused to attend an April 1967 meeting of hemispheric presidents in Punta del Este, Uruguay, whose official purpose was to discuss the socioeconomic problems affecting development throughout the hemisphere. Barrientos considered Bolivia's landlocked status to be its major obstacle to socioeconomic development, and when the meeting organizers refused to include the seaport issue on the summit agenda, he dismissed the meeting as farcical (Gumucio 2005, 376–81). While his publicly declared reason for not attending was the failure to include the seaport issue on the agenda, his stance also diverted public attention from critical domestic issues, including the guerrilla war launched by Ché Guevara in the fall of 1966. Five decades ago, Martin Glassner observed with good reason that "the Lauca had become essentially a tool with which the Bolivian government could unite its people on the less dramatic, but much more basic, question of an outlet to the sea," adding "the dispute was also an internal political football in Bolivia" (1970b, 199). His observations on the Lauca River dispute remain accurate today, and a similar observation is applicable to the Silala watershed dispute.

The Maurí River controversy is a third watershed dispute which must be considered briefly within the context of the Silala and Lauca issues. The Maurí River flows eastwards into the Desaguadero River, the outlet for Lake Titicaca. Similar to the Lauca case, the boundary with Bolivia cuts across the watershed of the Desaguadero River, leaving the headwaters of the Maurí River in Peru (Escobari 1969, 14–16). With Chile occupying the area after the War of the Pacific, Chilean capitalists in 1921 began construction of a canal to carry water from Laguna Blanca and the Maurí River to the Tacna Valley for agricultural and industrial uses (Lagos Carmona 1981, 116). Bolivia immediately protested the scheme, arguing any diversion of water from the Maurí drainage basin to another hydrographic basin was illicit and would hamper navigation on the Desaguadero River (Iturralde 1963, 101–15). A Bolivian commission later confirmed that construction of the canal would hamper navigation on the Desaguadero River and endanger the water supply of the village of Charaña. In 1929, Chile ceded to Peru in the Treaty of Lima all rights to the Maurí Canal, including the section crossing Chilean territory (Dennis 1931, 317; Martínez 2002, 12–13).

In December 1961, Peru informed Bolivia that it planned to construct irrigation and hydroelectric works in the department of Tacna which would utilize water from the Maurí River. In response, Bolivia reiterated its position that the use of the waters of international rivers should not injure a downstream state, and in what Bolivians came to refer to as the "Thesis of 1921" that the waters of one hydrographic basin should not be transferred to another (Escobari 1969, 17). In October 1966, Bolivia and Peru issued a joint presidential declaration in which they recognized the importance of working together to ensure the legitimate, rational use of waters held in condominium in accordance with the terms of the Declaration of Montevideo. Three years later, Bolivia and Peru established a joint technical commission to monitor use of the Maurí River (Novak and Namihas 2013, 133–4). The commission recommended the completion of a study of how Bolivia and Peru could best use the waters of the Maurí River followed by the development of a plan for the equal use of the Maurí based on the joint study. In so doing, the work of the joint technical commission appeared to embody the spirit and letter of the "Thesis of 1921" (Escobari 1969, 31–2).

## Evolving Relations with the United States

In the 1930s, Bolivians were critical of what they saw as the limited role played by the United States both in the Chaco dispute and in resolving the seaport issue; however, events in 1939–40 led to an improvement in bilateral relations. World War II endangered traditional US tin supplies and drove up global prices. In response, the US Congress in 1940 authorized the establishment of a tin smelter in Texas City, Texas designed specifically for Bolivian ores, and later in the year, the United States concluded a five-year agreement with Bolivian producers to buy 18,000 tons annually at 48.5 cents per pound. From that time until the mid-1950s, the United States purchased approximately half of all Bolivian tin concentrates. The United States also concluded a three-year agreement covering the purchase of the entire production of Bolivian tungsten in May 1941 (Navia 1984, 35–8; Heilman 2017, 25–6). In July 1941, the US ambassador exposed the so-called Nazi Putsch, a pro-Axis plot that allegedly involved direct German encouragement. In response, the Peñaranda administration declared the German ambassador *persona non grata*, declared a state of siege, imprisoned opposition leaders, and censored the media. The Nazi Putsch greatly benefited Bolivia, Great Britain, and the United States, and most historians agree it was fabricated by British and US authorities working with the Peñaranda regime and the Bolivian oligarchy to discredit fascist sympathizers (Bieber 2004, 122–8; Morales 2010, 124; Siekmeier 2011, 25). For Britain, it linked Bolivia and the United States more closely to the Allied cause; for the United States, it reduced Axis influence in the hemisphere and further guaranteed Bolivian tin supplies; and for Bolivia, it provided both an opportunity to crack down on the opposition and political cover to resolve the Standard Oil issue (Lehman 1999, 77–8; Klein 2011, 199). In the second half of 1941, the United States agreed to provide development assistance to Bolivia, and the two countries concluded their first military assistance pact together with a lend–lease agreement. In January 1942, Bolivia and the United States signed agreements ending the Standard Oil dispute, and the US Export–Import Bank (EXIM) immediately allocated loans for Bolivian development projects.

> The economic aid granted to Bolivia constituted the first time Washington granted a significant amount of economic aid, or aid for economic development, to a nation in the developing world. From this point forward, Bolivian requests of assistance, and US assistance projects, would be an integral (if not the most important) part of the US-Bolivian relationship.
> (Siekmeier 2011, 20–1, quote 21; Cote 2016b, 113–14)

The tin contract, Standard Oil settlement, and associated agreements signaled a major shift in the breadth and depth of relations between Bolivia and the United States. After Bolivia declared war on the Axis powers, President Peñaranda visited the United States in May 1943, meeting with President Roosevelt and soliciting US assistance in helping Bolivia to obtain a sovereign outlet to the Pacific Ocean (Salazar 2000, 669–71). During the visit, the Bolivian minister of foreign affairs, Tomás Manuel Elío Bustillos, delivered a memorandum to Secretary of State Cordell Hull which outlined the maritime aspirations of Bolivia (Guzmán Escobari 2015a, 201–2). The memorandum noted Bolivian aspirations for a sovereign exit to the Pacific Ocean, expressing the hope that Chile would help it to achieve that goal through direct negotiations. The Roosevelt administration expressed sympathy for the Bolivian position, but faced with the challenges of World War II, it characterized the seaport question as a regional as opposed to a global issue (Escobari 1988, 137; Becerra de la Roca 2002, 144). Secretary of State Hull forwarded a copy of the Bolivian memorandum to the Chilean government. In response, Joaquín Fernández y Fernández, the foreign minister of Chile, noted there was no pending territorial issue between Bolivia and Chile nor was there any possibility of Chile ceding territory to Bolivia, emphasizing the free transit agreements in place provided Bolivia with satisfactory access to the Pacific (Escobari 1988, 137–9, 148; Orias 2004, 55–6; Gumucio 2005, 354–5).

In a March 1951 address to the foreign ministers of the Americas, President Harry S. Truman departed from prepared remarks to reference an April 1950 conversation he had with the president of Chile in which the latter suggested giving Bolivia a port on the Pacific in return for Bolivia allowing Chile and Peru to use the waters from Bolivia's high mountain lakes to develop the coastal areas of Chile and Peru (Espinosa 1965, 395–7; Escobari 1988, 142–3; Mesa Gisbert 2016, 162–3). The Chilean press later reported that the idea was for Chile to give Bolivia a corridor to the Pacific ten kilometers wide whose terminal would be located 32 kilometers from the port of Arica in return for Bolivia giving Chile access to the waters of lakes Titicaca, Coipasa, and Poopó to irrigate northern Chile and southern Peru (Becerra de la Roca 2002, 145). The Gonzalez–Truman project was soon shelved in the face of widespread opposition in Bolivia, Chile, and Peru (Glassner 1970b, 200; Escobari 1988, 143–5; Martínez 2002, 7–9; Bustos 2003, 39–53, 144–50). In March 1951, the Urriolagoitía administration also concluded a Technical Cooperation Agreement with the US government as part of the Truman administration's Point IV Program. In Bolivia, the program provided for initiatives in agriculture, health, and education as well as road construction and hydrocarbon development. After the MNR took power in the April 1952 National Revolution, US economic assistance to Bolivia escalated as did US involvement in Bolivian politics (Krueger 2017–18, 155; Zambrana 2017–18).

When Víctor Andrade, the Bolivian ambassador to the United States in 1944–46, 1952–58, and 1960–62, presented his credentials to President Truman in August 1952, the latter again expressed his support for a sovereign Bolivian outlet to the Pacific, reiterating his belief that a compromise solution involving the use of the waters of Lake Titicaca to irrigate northern Chile seemed to be the best option. After thanking Truman for his support, Ambassador Andrade emphasized the seemingly insurmountable physical and political obstacles involved in a compensation solution of this sort (Andrade 1976, 127–9). In the interim, the Department of State in 1951 approved a basic policy document which sympathized with Bolivian aspirations for access to the sea but emphasized that the US government was not committed to any scheme which involved compensation to Chile and Peru in the form of access to the waters of Lake Titicaca (Gumucio 2005, 368–70). A detailed study of the Truman administration and Bolivia published six decades later concluded rather harshly that US policy toward Bolivia in this period was "a failure on almost every level" (Dorn 2011, quote 185; Heilman 2017, 39–51).

Although the Bolivian Revolution initiated a process of radical socioeconomic and political change, President Dwight D. Eisenhower and Secretary of State John Foster Dulles, both fervent anti-communists, agreed that any possible communist infiltration of the MNR government did not necessitate the kind of US intervention that occurred in Guatemala in 1954 (Navia 1984, 89–95; Dorn 2011, 186–90). Important to the United States, Bolivia at the time remained low on Washington priority lists in part because it was a small, poor country and in part because the United States was awash with tin. Consequently, policy recommendations on Bolivia generally emanated from the lower echelons of the State Department where the tendency was to promote diplomatic solutions to foreign policy issues. Moreover, the tin companies in Bolivia did not enjoy the high level of political connections and media interest as did the United Fruit Company in Guatemala. The popularity of the MNR government, combined with the absence of viable alternatives once the army was dismantled, traditional political parties undermined, and conservative forces in retreat, also played a role. Finally, Washington perceived the communist threat in Bolivia to be declining while it held the opposite viewpoint on the situation in Guatemala (Lehman 1999, 106–13; Heilman 2017, 55–8, 63–4). With these thoughts in mind, the 1952 revolution became "the only genuine social revolution to which the United States provided early and sustained support" (Blasier 1971, 53; Krueger 2017–18, 156).

In 1955–56, the United States contributed almost three times as much to Bolivian government revenues as did Bolivian taxpayers, and once the Siles Zuazo government had accepted the IMF austerity/stabilization program, US aid continued to increase. By the end of the decade, Bolivia had received $100 million in US aid, making it the largest single recipient in Latin America and the highest per capita recipient in the world (Mesa Gisbert 2001b, 673; Klein 2011, 217–18). Relatively small amounts of economic assistance to Bolivia gave US officials considerable leverage over a poor country; however, US aid also gave Bolivian officials a newfound capacity to influence US policy.

> Once the economic assistance began to flow, Bolivian leaders realized they could use this assistance to assert a degree of agency over their relationship with the United States. Bolivian leaders discovered that they could increase the flow of assistance either by claiming outright that more assistance would prevent the nation from falling under communism or by quietly reaching out to the East bloc.
> (Siekmeier 2011, 5, 41, quote 5; Young 2017, 6)

When Vice President Richard M. Nixon visited Bolivia in May 1958, the surface cordiality which marked his visit hid an erosion in bilateral relations which was readily apparent one year later. In March 1959, Bolivia erupted in violent anti-US protests resulting from a growing recognition of the reality of US power and the fact of Bolivian dependency (Lehman 1999, 114–42).

By 1961, relations between Bolivia and the United States were again running smoothly, and Bolivia was beginning to receive substantial military aid in addition to becoming a showcase for the Alliance for Progress (Field 2014; Heilman 2017, 87–91). At the same time, the second Paz Estenssoro administration (1960–64) continued to manipulate US concerns that a *golpe de estado* could lead to a military dictatorship to bolster its demands for US assistance. Similarly, it made overtures to and accepted approaches from the East bloc as an additional means to compel Washington to increase the amount of aid (Siekmeier 2011, 96–7). In August 1963, the Kennedy administration offered to mediate the Bolivia–Chile dispute in an effort to restore diplomatic relations and resolve all outstanding issues (Fellmann 1967, 105). Bolivia accepted the offer of US mediation with the stipulation that any talks would include the seaport issue, but Chile rejected it outright. Unwilling to pressure Chile, the United States ended its mediation efforts and returned to the passive role in the seaport dispute it had played for most of the previous three years. After Bolivia supported the United States during the September 1963 Cuban missile crisis, President Paz Estenssoro was rewarded with an official visit to Washington. He met with President Kennedy in October 1963, Kennedy's last official guest before his assassination one month later. During their conversation, President Paz Estenssoro took the opportunity to emphasize the problems raised by Bolivia's landlocked status. Kennedy sympathized with Bolivia's problem, but the Department of State maintained its policy of non-intervention in the dispute with Chile. The Kennedy administration also informed Bolivian officials that in the future they would have to depend more on internal capital formation and private funds from abroad, an ominous development for a country largely dependent on Washington's supply of public funds. In 1952–64, the United States provided more per capita economic aid to Bolivia than to any other Latin American country (Blasier 1971, 53; Pike 1977, 310; Gumucio 2005, 372–4).

When a *golpe de estado* ousted the Paz Estenssoro government in November 1964, US support for the moderate wing of the MNR easily transferred to General René Barrientos Ortuño. The US government quickly offered diplomatic recognition to the military junta headed by Barrientos as well as significant amounts of economic assistance (Heilman 2017, 100; Krueger 2017–18, 158). Washington also supported Bolivian efforts to eliminate the guerrilla column led by Che Guevara, support it erroneously assumed would be rewarded with improved bilateral relations. Instead, Guevara's defeat in October 1967 led to a resurgence in Bolivian nationalism and a deterioration is US–Bolivian relations (Siekmeier 2011, 100–1, 118–21). Exacerbating anti-US sentiment, Minister of the Interior Antonio Arguedas, a trusted member of the Barrientos administration, charged the government with widespread graft and corruption, disrupting the US security apparatus in the country. At the same time, the appearance of a radical military regime in Peru transformed the geopolitical situation in the region. The ongoing controversy surrounding the operations of Bolivian Gulf Oil offered another flashpoint. The death of President Barrientos in April 1969 exposed widespread nationalist and anti-imperialist sentiment in Bolivia, leading to a temporary crisis in bilateral relations with the United States. Under Barrientos, nationalization was not a viable political option; however, his successor, General Alfredo Ovando Candia, took that step in October 1969 (Klein and Peres-Cajías 2014, 149–50; Cote 2016b, 143–6). In May 1971, the short-lived Torres government, in a concession to the Bolivian Left, also expelled the Peace Corps (Heilman 2017, 132–3. The nationalization of Bolivian Gulf Oil and the expulsion of the Peace Corps demonstrated that Bolivian leaders, while desirous of US assistance, did not slavishly adhere to US policy. The expulsion of the Peace Corps also suggested US officials did not understand Bolivian society and culture. With few options available, the US government passively accepted the expulsion of the Peace Corps and began the decade of the 1970s with its influence diminished but intact (Whitehead 1970; Gumucio 2005, 376–81; Siekmeier 2011, 10–11, 126–9, 131–2, 137–51).

## Conclusions

Between 1930 and 1970, Bolivia suffered through the Great Depression, lost a catastrophic war with Paraguay, and conducted a far-reaching socioeconomic and political revolution. These events set the stage for a major reorientation of Bolivian foreign policy. After more than a century, Bolivia resolved long-standing disputes with neighboring Argentina, Brazil, Paraguay, and Peru, and it established important new commercial ties with all four countries. On the other hand, Bolivia was unable to expand commercial or political ties with Chile, and its quest for a sovereign outlet to the Pacific remained unfulfilled. The Silala, Lauca, and Maurí watershed disputes came to a head in this period, and in the case of the Silala and Lauca disputes, Bolivia for the first time joined those issues to the seaport issue. Tying the watershed and seaport issues together produced little in the way of positive results, and Chile would later institute legal proceedings against Bolivia regarding the use of the waters of the Silala. Bolivia's relationship with the United States underwent dramatic change in this period. Before 1930, the bilateral relationship largely centered on Bolivia occasionally looking for US assistance in resolving first territorial issues and later the seaport issue. Beginning with World War II, the scope of the bilateral relationship expanded to a remarkable extent with the United States ever more deeply involved in the internal and external affairs of Bolivia. The increased involvement of the United States in Bolivian affairs contributed to the development of Bolivian nationalism, especially economic resource nationalism, as well as an increasingly virulent strain of anti-imperialism. In the coming decades, virtually all Bolivian governments at one time or another would manipulate the watershed issues, seaport question, and latent anti-US feeling to generate domestic support for their regime.

# 7 New Horizons, Old Constraints, 1971–90

In the final decades of the twentieth century, Bolivian foreign policy continued to expand in scope and purpose. Bolivia was an early participant in the movement for regional cooperation and integration that led to the Cartagena Agreement in 1969 and in additional subregional and regional pacts over the next two decades. In addition, it increased its participation in a variety of international organizations and established or widened existing commercial and diplomatic ties with many states. On two occasions, Bolivia engaged in unsuccessful negotiations with Chile in an effort to improve its access to the sea. In a related effort, Bolivia joined landlocked, transit, and nontransit states in multiple international forums largely focused on improved transit rights. After a period of military rule, Bolivia returned to democratic governance in the 1980s. In the process, the United States was increasingly involved in the domestic and foreign policies of Bolivia, highlighting Bolivian dependence on other governments and bodies.

## Landlocked States

Stepping back, Bolivia in 1914 was one of only four independent landlocked states outside Europe. The other three were Afghanistan, Ethiopia, and Paraguay. In Europe, landlocked and transit states had devised a workable system of international rivers, special transit rights, duty free zones, and other arrangements to ensure a relatively free flow of goods and people between landlocked states and the sea. Outside Europe, the number of landlocked states continued to grow, almost quadrupling by 1974. When Europe was included, there were 47 landlocked states by 2018. As the number of landlocked states increased, efforts to address their unique problems also expanded. The Covenant of the League of Nations did not speak directly to the question of access to the sea but instead focused on the broader question of freedom of transit. Article 23(e) of the Covenant was significant in this regard as it was the first attempt to deal with the issue of freedom of transit on a global basis. Two years later, the Convention and Statute on Freedom of Transit, adopted in Barcelona in April 1921, obligated the contracting parties to "facilitate free transit by rail or waterway on routes in use convenient for international transit" through their territory (Glassner 1970a, 247–53, quote

249; Uprety 2006, 48–50). Chile ratified both the Convention and Statute on Freedom of Transit and the Convention and Statute on the Regime of Navigable Waterways of International Concern, a second document concluded in Barcelona in 1921, but Bolivia and Peru did not ratify either document (Glassner 1970a, 1–2, 17–23).

In February 1957, the UN General Assembly passed a resolution asking the upcoming UN Conference on the Law of the Sea to "study the question of free access to the sea of landlocked countries as established by international practice or treaties" (Boas 1959, 22). Shortly before the conference opened in February 1958, 14 landlocked countries, including Bolivia, drew up a list of seven general principles to guide the committee charged with preparing recommendations for the conference. Two of the seven principles were germane to Bolivia's quest for a sovereign outlet to the Pacific Ocean. According to the first principle, "the right of each land-locked State of free access to the sea derives from the fundamental principle of freedom of the seas." In turn, the fifth principle read in part, "The transit of persons and goods from a land-locked country towards the sea and vice versa by all means of transportation and communication must be freely accorded, subject to existing special agreements and conventions" (UN 1958b, 78–9; Tredinnick 1998, 341–8). The Bolivian delegation played an active role in the work of the Preliminary Conference which developed and presented the seven principles and in the work of the Fifth Committee responsible for recommendations regarding the question of free access to the sea of landlocked countries (UN 1958a).

The Bolivian representative to the 1958 Conference on the Law of the Sea, Walter Guevara Arze, served as vice president of the Fifth Committee, and during its meetings, the Bolivian delegation worked diligently albeit unsuccessfully for the inclusion in UN conventions of a firm guarantee of the rights of landlocked states to access to the sea (Glassner 1970a, 133–4). The Fifth Committee was comprised of landlocked, transit, and non-transit states, with the landlocked states in the minority. In the end, the committee reached an impasse over the issue of whether landlocked states enjoyed the right to free access to the sea based on the principle of freedom of the high seas or whether the right of free access could only be the product of treaties between the interested parties (UN 1958b, 60–3; Boas 1959, 23–7). After 25 meetings, the Fifth Committee adopted recommendations that reflected the unwillingness of transit states to recognize a real right of access to the sea for landlocked states (Uprety 2006, 60–5). Bolivia was a sponsor of the final recommendations despite its support throughout the discussions for the right to free access to the sea based on the principle of freedom of the high seas (UN 1958c, 18–19). The recommendations of the Fifth Committee were embodied in both the Convention on the Territorial Sea and Contiguous Zone and the Convention on the High Seas (Milic 1981, 501–3, 508; Tredinnick 1998, 349–52). Article three of the Convention on the High Seas read in part, "in order to enjoy the freedom of the seas on equal terms with coastal States, States having no sea coast should have free access to the sea" (UN 1963). On the surface, this article seemed to favor landlocked states, but in the end, access to the sea remained dependent on the mutual agreement and goodwill of coastal states. Moreover, the issue of access to the sea continued to be discussed in the context of transit rights as opposed to the sovereign access to the sea claimed by Bolivia.

In the modern world, economic progress necessitates rapid, reliable and cost-effective international trade; consequently, freedom of transit is vital for landlocked states trying to diversify trade and promote development. With access to the sea a major obstacle to economic development, it is not surprising that landlocked countries have some of the lowest growth rates in the world. The obstacles to development and trade commonly experienced by landlocked states include but are not limited to higher transportation costs; unexpected expenses arising from warehousing stocks and port delays; increased risks of loss, damage, pilferage, or spoilage; and the interruption of free transit by the actions of private citizens (Glassner 1970a, 5; Guillermo 1986, 10–11; Uprety 2006, 13–22). By 1960, the difficulties Bolivia experienced in executing development programs and sustaining economic growth increasingly appeared to reflect its dependence on Chilean ports, together with an inadequate free transit system. In September 1962, José Fellmann Velarde, the minister of foreign affairs of Bolivia, raised the seaport issue at the seventeenth session of the UN General Assembly. The brief presentations made by Fellmann and his Chilean counterpart added no new information and made no immediate contribution to a resolution of the seaport issue; however, their dialogue encouraged discussion of the special development challenges faced by landlocked states. As a result, the UN General Assembly set in motion the machinery required for the United Nations to consider the transit rights of all landlocked states (Fellmann 1967, 81–7; Glassner 1970a, 105–6).

In June 1965, the UN Conference on Trade and Development (UNCTAD) opened the UN Conference on Transit Trade of Land-locked Countries in New York. At the time, UNCTAD comprised 120 countries, 25 of which were landlocked. During the conference, which surfaced considerable disagreement among landlocked countries, Bolivia was a leader of those landlocked states demanding firm guarantees of their right to unlimited access to the sea. When that goal appeared unreachable, the Bolivian delegate on 11 June 1965 made a statement emphasizing that "Bolivia considered its right to the restoration of the Pacific coastline to be inalienable, and the fact that it had entered into bilateral agreements in order to reduce the disadvantages caused by its temporary lack of that coastline must not be taken as indicating any intention on its part of relinquishing its claim to territory on the Pacific." He concluded his statement with an acknowledgement that Bolivia "had always received helpful and considerate treatment from Argentina, Brazil, Paraguay and Peru" in connection with its transit issues, refusing to acknowledge the transit facilities Chile had provided Bolivia (Glassner 1970a, 135–6, quote 135; Gutiérrez Moscoso 2000, 70–1).

In July 1965, the UN Conference on Transit Trade of Land-locked Countries produced a document, the Convention on Transit Trade of Land-Locked States. Bolivia signed the convention in December 1965 but did not ratify it, and in signing it, the Bolivian delegate to the conference expressed the following reservations:

> I have been instructed by my Government to place on record the Bolivian view, which is already to be found in the records of the Conference, that "Bolivia is not a land-locked State but a nation which is deprived by temporary circumstances of access to the sea across its own coast" and that "unrestricted and unconditional freedom of transit must be recognized in international law as an inherent right of enclosed territories and countries for reasons of justice and because of the need to facilitate such transit as a contribution to the general progress on a basis of equality".
>
> (UN 1968, 3–138, quote 104)

The Third UN Conference on the Law of the Sea (UNCLOS III) convened in New York in December 1973. The conference was mandated to adopt a convention dealing with all questions relating to the law of the sea, including questions related to landlocked states. The Bolivian delegation took advantage of the conference to publicize its demand for sovereign access to the sea (Medeiros 1975, 83–4). During the seventh session, the Second Committee of which Bolivia was a member was tasked with negotiating the rights of landlocked states to access to the sea. The main issue in the Second Committee was recognition of the right of access of landlocked states as a principle of international law. Some transit states were in favor of access but many opposed it, arguing it should be the subject of negotiation between landlocked and transit states (Milic 1981, 510–12). On the defensive, the landlocked states in alliance with a group of geographically disadvantaged states agreed to nine principles known as the Kamapala Declaration that represented their rights. The principles in the Kampala Declaration of greatest interest to Bolivia were principle one, which stated the right of landlocked states to free and unrestricted access to and from the sea; principle three, the right of landlocked states to transit rights and facilities from transit states; and principle five, the right of landlocked states to use, on an equal basis, facilities, equipment, and all other installations in ports. Seventeen landlocked states, including Bolivia, endorsed the principles found in the Kampala Declaration (Tredinnick 1998, 271–5; Uprety 2006, 82–5).

Bolivia played a minor role in the formulation of the Convention on the Law of the Sea eventually adopted by UNCLOS III, and it made no real progress in its demand for a sovereign outlet to the Pacific (Traverso 1986, 122; Tredinnick 1998, 367–76). Article 69 of the convention addressed the rights of landlocked states to participate in the exploitation of the living resources of the exclusive economic zones of coastal states but only as those rights were established by the parties concerned through bilateral, subregional, or regional agreements. Bolivia had expressed interest in this issue as early as July 1963 when it joined Afghanistan, Austria, Belgium, Nepal, and Singapore in presenting a proposal calling for landlocked states to share in the exploitation of the living resources found in the economic zones of coastal states (Abecia 1986, III, 93). Articles 124–132 of the convention addressed the right of access to and from the sea and freedom of transit of landlocked states. Article 125 stated that "land-locked states shall have the right of access to and from the sea" and "enjoy freedom of transit through the territory of transit states," but once again, those rights had to be "agreed between the land-locked States and transit States concerned through bilateral, subregional or regional agreements" (Uprety 2006, 190–2, quote 190–1). The UN Convention on the Law of the Sea was adopted on 30 April 1982 with 130 votes in favor, four against (Israel, Turkey, United States, and Venezuela), and 17 abstentions. Bolivia signed the convention on 27 November 1984 and deposited its ratification on 28 April 1995. In signing the convention, the Bolivian delegate noted that the agreement of his government to the convention did not signify in any way acceptance of its landlocked status (Traverso 1986, 120). Thereafter, Bolivia continued to pursue a sovereign outlet to the Pacific even as it worked in multilateral forums to improve its transit rights to the sea (Gutiérrez Moscoso 2000, 71).

## Debt, Democracy, Drugs, and Development

In August 1971, Bolivia began a decade of authoritarian government and recurrent political crisis that helped define its foreign policy for the remainder of the century. After masterminding a *golpe de estado*, Colonel Hugo Banzer Suárez became president and then dictator of Bolivia from 1971 to 1978, a period known as the *banzerato* (Prado 1984, 325–7; Sivak 2002, 121–217). At the time, Latin American countries were heavily influenced by the modernizing military models of Brazil and Peru. Where former presidents Ovando and Torres had favored the Peruvian model, Banzer based his rule on the more authoritarian approach of the Brazilian military, a model more directly aligned with US interests and free-market policies. Over the next seven years, the Banzer regime received unequivocal support from the United States for several years, from a politically ambitious Brazil, and from agro-industrial interests in the Santa Cruz region (Lehman 1999, 165–6; Morales 2010, 191). In the case of the United States, the Banzer government's conservative politics and capitalist development model encouraged Washington to double and then triple military and other aid to Bolivia (Nash 1979, 37–9).

Under President Banzer, a combination of repressive stability and generous offshore borrowing, rising oil prices, growing natural gas exports, and strong tin prices for a time generated strong economic growth. The middle and upper classes in particular experienced increasing prosperity, aggravating existing socioeconomic inequalities with factory workers, miners, and the peasantry (Mitchell 1977, 121–32; Malloy 1982, 6–8; Mesa Gisbert 2001b,

702–4). Enjoying favorable terms of trade, the Banzer administration welcomed foreign direct investment, encouraging US oil companies to increase exploration in eastern Bolivia, and in 1974, it awarded Brazil a generous natural gas contract (Sachs 1987, 279; Klein and Peres-Cajías 2014, 152–3; Cote 2016b, 148–9). Unfortunately, outward signs of prosperity did not translate into sustained economic development. "By the late 1970s the economy had little more to show than exhausted mines, depleted petroleum reserves, declining agricultural outputs, stalled construction projects, and a massive foreign debt" (Malloy and Gamarra 1988, quote 72; Heilman 2017, 144–50). Originating in Santa Cruz, the 1971 coup returned regionalism to the forefront of the political agenda in Bolivia. Over the next decade, the eastern lowlands emerged as an increasing important economic and political center, rekindling the regional tensions in national politics present since the independence era (Malloy 1982, 6; Klein 2011, 228–9).

When President James Earl "Jimmy" Carter took office in January 1977, his government emphasized human rights in Latin America, criticizing the authoritarian approach of the Banzer regime (Morales 2010, 194; Siekmeier 2011, 154). This new focus on human rights loomed large in Bolivia, a country long more vulnerable to external pressure than its larger, more developed neighbors, especially pressure from the United States (Malloy and Gamarra 1988, 95; 155–7, 159–60). As the economy worsened in the second half of the decade, President Banzer also lost the support of middle-class nationalists when he admitted the failure of the Charaña talks with Chile (Klein 2011, 233). After the July 1978 presidential elections were nullified, Bolivia over the next four years lurched from elections to coups d'état to elections, experiencing nine governments, only two of which were constitutional (Alvarez 1995, 128, 130; Mesa Gisbert 2001b, 713–34; Cajías 2014, 7). Conservative military commanders opposed constitutional elections and a return to democratic governance in part because they feared civilian rule would lead to charges of army corruption and involvement in the drug trade. Due to human rights abuses and blatant drug ties, the short-lived government of General Luis García Meza Tejada (1980–81), one of the most corrupt regimes in Bolivian history, became an international pariah. It enjoyed the support of the military regimes in Argentina and Brazil but was denied recognition by the United States and other countries (Lehman 1999, 174–8; Hylton and Thomson 2007, 89). When international aid dried up, senior Bolivian military officers, embarrassed by the nation's tattered reputation and shattered economy, combined with regional forces in Santa Cruz to force García Meza out of office (Malloy 1982, 1–3, 8–9; Prado 1984, 500–15). President García Meza was later convicted of crimes committed during his government. While serving a 30-year prison sentence in Bolivia, an Italian court in 2017 convicted him in absentia for involvement in the murder of Italian citizens during Operation Condor, a US-backed campaign of political repression and state terror, officially implemented in 1975 by right-wing regimes in the Southern Cone of South America. García Meza died in prison in April 2018 (*Reuters*: 17.01.17; *AP*: 29.04.18). Following a period of political uncertainty, the Congress elected in 1980 met and elected president former chief executive Hernán Siles Zuazo (1956–60, 1982–85).

According to Morales, three related problems faced President Siles Zuazo and the civilian governments that followed (2010, 201–2). First, the military governments, especially those of Banzer and García Meza, contracted massive external loans, saddling their successors with a legacy of unsustainable public debt. Inheriting $5 billion in foreign debt, falling commodity prices, an annual inflation rate of around 300 percent, and an economy declining in real terms, the Siles Zuazo administration lacked the resources to make even the interest payments on the national debt. In 1984, a draconian IMF stabilization program, together with neoliberal policies intended to control rampant inflation, imposed such hardships that as many as 2 million Bolivians faced starvation (Sachs 1987, 280; Mann and Pastor 1989, 170–1). Second, the political and economic order in the hemisphere and the wider world had undergone significant change by the 1980s. Globalization and related market forces created new challenges and opportunities for developing states like Bolivia (Sachs 1999, 40–2; Morales and Pacheco 1999, 187–9). Third, Bolivia in the 1980s faced an enormous drug problem. The illicit drug trade dated back to the 1960s when Bolivia joined the United States and other countries in signing the Single Convention on Narcotic Drugs (1961). President Ronald Reagan declared a so-called war on drugs in October 1982; however, Bolivian military officers, as individuals and as groups, had been involved in the drug trade since the *banzerato* (Healy 1988, 105–26; Morales 2001, 113; Heilman 2017, 177–83). A fourth problem, corruption, must be added to the three highlighted by Morales. Largely due to the increase in drug trafficking, corruption in the 1970s far exceeded levels in the previous two decades (Malloy and Gamarra 1988, 119; Cajías 2014, 13).

From the start, the foreign policy of the Siles Zuazo administration was a challenge for the Reagan administration. While it was a democratic government that promised a vigorous anti-drug program, it also promoted the independent, neutralist type of foreign policy long opposed by Washington. The Siles Zuazo government sought closer relations with Nicaragua and Cuba, favored the Contadora process in El Salvador, and supported Argentina in the Falklands War. It recognized liberation movements like the Polisario Liberation Front, the Palestine Liberation Organization, and the Salvadoran revolutionary struggle, and it forged closer relations with the Soviet Union and Eastern bloc nations and established diplomatic relations with the People's Republic of China. Bolivia also cultivated ties with Western nations, like Belgium, France, Germany, Spain, and Switzerland, all of which extended economic aid. Enjoying some success abroad, the populist Siles Zuazo government was unable to overcome the domestic challenges inherent in reconciling debt, democracy, drugs, and development, opting in the end for early presidential elections (Morales 1992b, 178, 185–6; Mesa Gisbert 2001b, 737–45).

When no candidate received a majority in the 1985 presidential elections, the Congress turned to former President Víctor Paz Estenssoro to lead the country (Sanders 1986, 1–8; Mesa Gisbert 2003, 167–70). Pragmatism rather than populism or ideology motivated Paz Estenssoro, and his government resorted to authoritarian measures to implement orthodox economic policies (*WSJ*: 29.8.1986). In late August 1985, Paz Estenssoro implemented Decree 21060, known as the New Economic Policy (*Nueva Política Económica*). Decree 21060 went beyond macroeconomic stabilization to include fiscal reform, trade liberalization, decentralization of public enterprises, and decontrolled prices (Sachs 1987, 281; Mann and Pastor 1989, 171–6; Morales and Pacheco 1999, 184–6). In so doing, President Paz Estenssoro reversed the economic nationalism he had championed in the 1952 revolution and dismantled the state bureaucracy his earlier revolution had helped create (Mayorga 2007, 109–18, 137–53; Young 2017, 176–8). Bolivia became the first Latin America nation with a democratically elected government to embrace the neoliberal policy prescriptions which came to be known as the "Washington Consensus." Central tenets of this approach included fiscal discipline, tax reform, unified exchange rates, financial and trade liberalization, privatization, deregulation, and respect for private property. In the late 1980s and early 1990s, much of the rest of South America followed Bolivia's lead in adopting the Washington Consensus (Klein 2011, 244; Siekmeier 2011, 152, 155–6).

Decree 21060 later dominated popular memory of the 1985–89 government, but it was not the sole issue of consequence. In October 1985, the international tin price collapsed with prices falling 70 percent, leading to the closure of state mines. In response, many unemployed miners turned to coca production to survive. Thereafter, the cocaine trade increasingly impacted on economic and political life (Kohl and Farthing 2006, 60–1, 66; Dunkerley 2007, 147–82). As the cultivation of coca leaf expanded, the Paz Estenssoro government accepted a further militarization of the drug war, including the active intervention of US military advisers and troops (Malamud-Goti 1990, 41–3; Lehman 1999, 200). At the same time, the parallel coca economy lessened the impact of the orthodox economic policies implemented by Paz Estenssoro with approximately $500 million of an estimated $3 billion in annual drug trade profits returned yearly to the domestic economy (Kohl and Farthing 2006, 74).

## Charaña Talks

In 1969, Bolivia and Chile elevated the status of their consulates in La Paz and Santiago to empower their respective consul generals to resolve the many day-to-day problems resulting from the lack of diplomatic relations since 1962. Appointed consul general in Santiago by the Siles Salinas government, Ambassador Franz Ruck Uriburu made no progress on the maritime issue with the outgoing Chilean government of Eduardo Frei, but the new government of President Salvador Allende was more receptive to his proposals. The

Bolivian envoy soon reached a preliminary agreement with the Allende administration which contemplated a territorial corridor, port, enclave, and exclusive use of a dock at Arica. In a May 1971 meeting in Costa Rica, the foreign ministers of Bolivia and Chile confirmed these arrangements. A few days later, President Allende in his first address to Congress stated his desire to normalize relations with Bolivia (Gordon 1979, 324; Gumucio 2005, 383–6; Guzmán Escobari 2015a, 267–70).

The installation of the Banzer government in August 1971 was followed by a series of meetings over the next two years aimed at resolving the maritime issue (Guzmán Escobari 2015a, 270–2). In June 1973, the foreign minister of Chile noted that his country alone could not address Bolivian needs because the issue was a tripartite problem which involved Peruvian interests. The foreign minister of Peru responded to the Chilean statement later in the month, expressing sympathy for Bolivian aspirations. This was the first official statement of Peruvian support for Bolivia's quest for a sovereign Pacific port since 1929 (Escobari 1982, II, 40–4; Novak and Namihas 2013, 102). Unfortunately, the September 1973 *golpe de estado* in Chile against the democratically elected government of President Allende prevented an agreement from being reached (Holland 1975, 352–3).

In March 1974, President Banzer met with General Augusto Pinochet, president of the ruling government junta in Chile, during the inauguration ceremonies for President Ernesto Beckmann Geisel of Brazil. This was the first meeting in 12 years of the heads of state of Bolivia and Chile. Orchestrated by President Geisel, the meeting was facilitated in part by the violent overthrow of the Allende government. In the wake of the *golpe de estado* which ousted President Allende, the Chilean junta had few allies in the hemisphere; therefore, it focused on diplomatic ties with military regimes of similar ideological proclivities. In the course of the meeting, President Geisel suggested that a Bolivian land corridor to Arica might be a workable solution to a persistent source of instability in the Andes (Shumavon 1981, 184; St John 1994b, 20). Peru reacted immediately to the Brazilian proposal, reminding all parties of its right to be consulted on any and all questions pertaining to the Chile–Peru border region (Guachalla 1982, 78–9). At the time, the general feeling in Peru, most especially in the patriotic ranks of the armed forces, was that any transfer of territory in or around Arica should return it to Peru, its rightful owner, and not to a third party (Gordon 1979, 324–5).

Upon his return to La Paz, President Banzer organized a conference of Bolivian leaders to review and discuss outstanding issues with Chile. The product of this meeting was the Act of Cochabamba which identified the question of a sovereign Pacific seaport as the national issue of greatest importance to all Bolivians. In an effort to develop a national consensus on the issue, Banzer established a Maritime Commission to study the question of improved access to the Pacific (Galindo 1977, 89–90; Prudencio Lizón 2011, 22–5). One of the first decisions of the commission was that any proposed solution should be tripartite, involving Bolivia, Chile, and Peru. If that proved impossible, Peru should be informed of any pending proposal simultaneously with its presentation to Chile. The commission also agreed that any proposed solution to the issue of a seaport for Bolivia should take into account the regional interests and desires of southern Peru, western Bolivia, and northern Chile. This decision was a harbinger of a sustained effort at the end of the century, *El Proyecto Trinacional*, to develop a three-state development focus in the Atacama Desert at the intersection of Bolivia, Chile and Peru (Araníbar 2001). The Maritime Commission also took the fateful position that any solution should not involve territorial compensation on the part of Bolivia. Finally, it recognized that a seaport for Bolivia was only one aspect of broader issues, including tariff and transit regimes, which had to be discussed to resolve Bolivia's maritime question (Salazar, et al. 2001, 51–62; Guzmán Escobari 2015a, 276–7).

As the Maritime Commission continued its work, Presidents Banzer and Pinochet met on 8 February 1975 in a railway car northeast of Arica on the Bolivia–Chile border. To the surprise of most observers, the Act of Charaña issued at the end of these talks declared an immediate resumption of diplomatic relations, ties severed in 1962 when Chile moved unilaterally to divert the headwaters of the Lauca River (Botelho 1980, 91–2; Salazar et al. 2001, 278–9; Andaluz 2002, 353–4). The two heads of state also reaffirmed their adhesion to the 1974 Declaration of Ayacucho, a statement of unity and solidarity in the Americas which mentioned the legitimacy of Bolivia's desire to secure an outlet to the sea. Finally, Banzer and Pinochet pledged to continue talks in pursuit of a resolution to the many issues separating them (Bolivia 1976, 11–12).

Based on the work of the Maritime Commission, Ambassador Guillermo Gutiérrez Vea Murguía, Bolivian envoy to Chile, presented an *aide-mémoire* (*ayuda memoria*) to the Chilean government on 26 August 1975 (Lagos Carmona 1981, 127; Prudencio Lizón 2011, 56–62). The central element of the Bolivian proposal was the cession of a sovereign coastline between the Chile–Peru border, the so-called Line of Concordance or Concordia Line (*Línea de la Concordia*), and the city of Arica with a strip of sovereign land connecting the coastline and the Bolivia–Chile frontier and including the transfer of the Arica–La Paz railway. In addition, the proposal called for the cession to Bolivia of a sovereign enclave 50 kilometers long and 15 kilometers wide further south in the area of Pisagua, Iquique, or Antofagasta where Bolivia could build a port. The proposal also referred to infrastructure development in the ceded area and to Bolivia's willingness to consider the reciprocal interests of both parties (Chile 1975, 72–3; Bolivia 1976, 69–70; Salazar 2000, 747–50). Significantly, the Bolivian proposal did not mention compensation (*compensación*) or refer to a need or desire to compensate Chile for a Bolivian seaport on the Pacific. Instead, it referenced the contributions (*aportes*) that the Bolivian proposal would make to trinational development in the region (Guzmán Escobari 2015a, 291–4).

On 19 December 1975, the Chilean foreign minister, Patricio Carvajal Prado, responded to the Bolivian proposal in a formal diplomatic note in

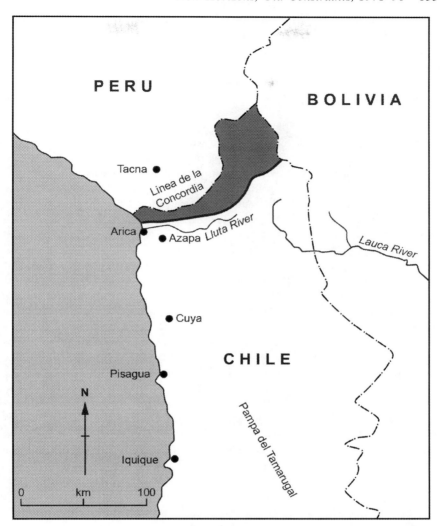

*Figure 7.1* Chilean Proposal 1975
Source: IBRU, Durham University, UK.

which Chile offered to exchange a sovereign land-sea corridor along the Chilean border with Peru in return for roughly equivalent compensation in the Bolivian altiplano (Guzmán Escobari 2015a, 299–303, 544–6). In regards to the proposed transfer, the Chilean proposal suggested the territory exchanged in the Bolivian altiplano could be either a single contiguous tract or several discontinuous tracts along the Bolivia–Chile frontier. The sovereign land-sea corridor outlined by Chile was narrower than that proposed by Bolivia and would be declared a demilitarized zone. Moreover, it lacked a road as the Arica to Tambo Quemado highway remained in Chilean territory, and the corridor had no water source as the Lluta River also remained in Chile. Furthermore, the Chilean response called for Bolivia to authorize Chile to take advantage of "the totality of the waters of the Lauca River" (*la totalidad de las aguas del río Lauca*) but rejected the cession to Bolivia of an enclave further south (Chile 1975, 74–6, quote 75; Bolivia 1976, 70–3; Salazar 2000, 753–6).

Incorporating the principle of territorial exchange, the 1975 Chilean proposal marked a partial throwback to the solution proposed by Chile in 1950. At the same time, the land-sea corridor in the 1975 proposal extended 200 miles into the sea at a point where the shoreline waters were not deep enough to accommodate most oceangoing vessels. In demanding territorial compensation equal in area to both the land corridor and the 200 mile extension into territorial waters, the Chilean proposal appeared to establish or at least seek to establish a new precedent in international law, the concept that land and sea space were comparable in value (Pittman 1984, 133). The Chilean proposal also called for Bolivia to renounce all claims to territory lost in the War of the Pacific and to grant Chile exclusive rights to the headwaters of the Lauca River. In addition, Chile sought up to $200 million in compensation for the cession of the Arica–La Paz railway as well as the demilitarization of the proposed corridor along the Chile–Peru border. Since the proposed corridor included the shallow waters of the territorial sea, the Chilean proposal would have left the Bolivian navy without a military function in the Pacific. Finally, the Chilean proposal echoed the terms of the Treaty of Lima as it called for both Bolivia and Chile to agree not to cede any of the territories exchanged to a third party (Salazar et al. 2001, 75–7).

In January 1976, the Banzer administration created the National Maritime Council (*Consejo Nacional Marítimo*, CONAMAR) to develop a counterproposal. Inside and outside this official body, all aspects of the Chilean proposal were questioned and criticized with the issues of territorial compensation, demilitarization, and the Lauca River receiving the greatest attention (Salazar et al. 2001, 114–17; Prudencio Lizón 2011, 118–21, 132, 143–6). Most Bolivians rightly concluded that meaningful sovereignty would necessitate the right to exercise military control over the proposed corridor. Bolivians also agreed that Bolivia should not have to make territorial concessions elsewhere or cede control of the headwaters of the Lauca River in order to obtain territory seized in an aggressive war (Guachalla 1982, 86–92; Escobari 1988, 276–8). Left with few options, the Banzer government on 10 March 1976 officially rejected those aspects of the Chilean proposal relating to demilitarization, territorial compensation, and control of the Lauca River. At the same time, President Banzer stressed there were many areas of general agreement, suggesting a firm basis for future negotiations had been established (Gordon 1979, 325; Shumavon 1981, 186–8; Lagos Carmona 1981, 129).

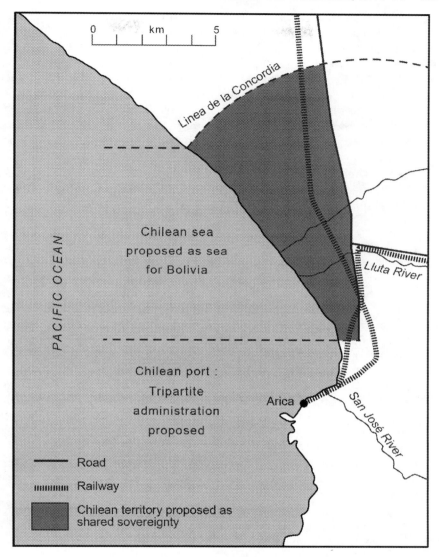

*Figure 7.2* Peruvian Proposal, 1976
Source: IBRU, University of Durham, UK.

Following an extensive but largely fruitless series of talks between Bolivia, Chile, and Peru in the summer and fall of 1976, Peru on 19 November 1976 launched a new initiative based on a tripartite formula (Prudencio Lizón 2011, 215–77; Guzmán Escobari 2015a, 311–16). Peruvian officials called for creation of a zone of joint Bolivia–Chile–Peru sovereignty between the city of Arica and the Peruvian border with Bolivia granted a sovereign corridor feeding into this zone. Trapezoidal in shape and approximating 66 square kilometers, the tripartite zone proposed by Peru included both a sovereign port for Bolivia and trinational administration of the port of Arica (Chile 1976, 168–70; Puente 1989, 45–53). In a masterstroke of diplomacy, the Peruvian initiative offered Bolivia almost as much as the Chilean proposal without calling for territorial exchange, and it reintroduced the issue of Peruvian rights in the disputed zone. In so doing, the Peruvian proposal reflected the concerns of Peruvian nationalists opposed to any bilateral agreement between Bolivia and Chile which ceded all or part of the former Peruvian province of Arica to Bolivia. In calling for trinational development of the disputed territory, the Peruvian initiative also highlighted the tripartite character of the dispute. Peruvian officials packaged their proposal as a reflection of the renewed emphasis in the region on Andean cooperation and development (St John 1994b, 21; Novak and Namihas 2013, 105–6).

Chile immediately rejected the Peruvian initiative on the grounds it introduced issues unrelated to the questions at hand, infringed on Chilean sovereignty, especially in regards to the city of Arica, and threatened modifications to the Treaty of Lima (Chile 1976, 170–3; Lagos Carmona 1981, 131–2). Privately, Chileans viewed the Peruvian proposal as a direct attack on the 1929 agreement (Guzmán Escobari 2015b, 34–6). In recognizing the Peruvian right to consultation over the disputed zone, Chile argued Peru was entitled to approve or disapprove any bilateral arrangements between Bolivia and Chile but not to offer independent initiatives. In a formal response to Peru, dated 26 November 1976, Chile emphasized its respect for the sanctity of treaties and its intention to guard its national sovereignty. The Chilean response concluded with a call for Bolivia to respond with a counterproposal to its December 1975 initiative (Chile 1976, 173; Lagos Carmona 1981, 131–2; Prudencio Lizón 2011, 288–9).

With negotiations seemingly stalemated, the Banzer administration in December 1976 rejected in principle Chilean demands for territorial compensation together with the Peruvian proposal for trilateral occupation. Emphasizing Bolivia's commitment to the principles of peace, development, and integration, President Banzer proposed instead a tripartite development zone in a sovereign Bolivian space (Chile 1977, 90–2; Salazar et al. 2001, 263). In a major address on 23 March 1977, the Day of the Sea (*Día del Mar*), an annual event commemorating the seaport issue, Banzer described access to the sea as a vital necessity, a basic right, and an economic imperative for Bolivia. Decrying the geographical encirclement of Bolivia, he stressed that sovereign access to the Pacific Ocean remained a fundamental objective of Bolivian foreign policy (Bolivia 1977).

For years, the US government had shown little interest in Bolivia's maritime issue; however, the Gerald Ford administration in its closing days finally took notice of the dispute. When newly appointed Ambassador Alberto Crespo Gutiérrez presented his credentials to President Ford in May 1976, he called attention to the problems which Bolivia's landlocked condition created for Bolivia and its neighbors. President Ford expressed sympathy with Bolivian aspirations, and Secretary of State Henry Kissinger and his Bolivian counterpart, Foreign Minister Óscar Adriázola Valda, later issued a joint statement which said in part: "a negotiated solution to this centennial problem would constitute a substantial contribution to the peace and development of the South Cone of Latin America" (*una solución negociada a este centenario problema constituía una sustancial contribución a la paz y el desarrollo del Cono Sur de Latinoamérica*) (Gumucio 2005, 395). The Carter administration took an even more active role in encouraging a solution to Bolivia's landlocked status. In early September 1977, President Carter raised Bolivia's maritime issue with the presidents of Chile and Peru. A few days later, during an official visit by President Banzer, President Carter told the press corps that he hoped Bolivia, Chile, and Peru could reach an agreement which would provide Bolivia with direct access to the sea. In so doing, he identified the issue as tripartite in nature and supported direct talks between the interested parties as the best path to resolution. President Carter again referred to the issue in June 1978 during the opening session of the Eighth OAS General Assembly. With the resolution of the Panama Canal issue as an example that disputes in the hemisphere could be resolved peacefully, he urged the interested parties to find a solution to Bolivia's landlocked status (Lehman 1999, 169–70; Lavaud 2003, 48–51; Gumucio 2005, 393–405).

After another year of inconclusive talks, Bolivia severed diplomatic relations with Chile in March 1978 (Prudencio Lizón 2011, 305–32, 350–5; Guzmán Escobari 2015a, 323–5). Describing the resumption of diplomatic relations in 1975 as a promising opportunity to reach an historic settlement, Foreign Minister Adriázola in a short note to his Chilean counterpart was harshly critical of Chilean diplomacy, accusing Chile of inflexibility and an inability or unwillingness to compromise (Botelho 1980, 143–4; Guachalla 1982, 74). In a communiqué issued the same day, the Banzer administration referenced the related issue of the Lauca River, reasserted Bolivia's right to sovereign access to the Pacific, and promised to continue to pursue the seaport issue in international forums (Chile 1978, 33–8; Salazar et al. 2001, 291–4). Meanwhile, domestic political turmoil in 1978–82 diverted the attention and energy of successive Bolivian governments, diluting or undermining Bolivian diplomatic initiatives. This period of political instability and failed national consensus illustrated once again the interdependence of foreign and domestic policies in Bolivia (Mesa Gisbert 2003, 158–66; Dunkerley 2007, 249–91).

## Regional Cooperation and Integration

In 1948, Bolivia was a founding member of the Economic Commission for Latin America (*Comisión Económica para la América Latina*, CEPAL). In 1963, Bolivia, Paraguay, and Uruguay, under the auspices of the Inter-American

Development Bank (IDB), formed the URUPABOL Group (*Grupo URU-PABOL*), a portmanteau of the member states, in an effort to promote economic development and integration. In 1967, Bolivia joined the Latin American Free Trade Association (*Asociación Latinoamericana de Libre Comercio*, ALALC), and it was a founding member of the Latin American Integration Association (*Asociación Latinoamericana de Integración*, ALADI) in 1980 (Escobari 1982, II, 148–54, 159; Abecia 1986, III, 257–60; Glassner 1988, 162–3). Bolivia was also a founding member in 1964 of the Group of 77 (*Grupo de los 77*, G-77), a coalition of developing states (Camacho 1981, 105–20, 143–50).

In Andean America, the formal movement toward enhanced subregional cooperation began in August 1966 with the Declaration of Bogotá which committed Chile, Colombia, Ecuador, Peru, and Venezuela to negotiate a formal agreement for economic integration. Chile successfully opposed Bolivian participation in the Bogotá meeting, arguing the seaport issue would detract from the proceedings. Bolivia later adhered to the Declaration of Bogotá in August 1967, and in May 1969, Bolivia, Chile, Colombia, Ecuador, and Peru concluded the Cartagena Agreement. It established a customs union known as the Andean Pact (*Pacto Andino*) or Andean Group (*Group Andino*). The objective of the Andean Pact was to promote economic integration, and its members developed a number of collective policies, including the common treatment of foreign capital, industrial programming, and a common external tariff (Camacho 1981, 305–70; Escobari 1982, II, 159–60; Abecia 1986, III, 265).

The Andean Pact enjoyed some early success but soon experienced problems (Seoane 2000b, 294–5, 298–300). Approved in December 1970, Decision 24 created a common regime for the treatment of foreign capital. It also required the transformation of foreign firms to mixed or local companies before they could take advantage of tariff reductions (Tironi 1978). Following the September 1973 overthrow of the Allende regime, the ruling military junta in Chile insisted on revisions to the investment code. When the other members opposed the proposed revisions, Chile withdrew from the Cartagena Agreement in October 1976. According to Fontaine, the Banzer administration supported Chile in revising Decision 24, at least behind closed doors, but voted against Chile when final positions were recorded (Fontaine 1977, 40; Escobari 1982, II, 169–70). Because of its strategic location and higher level of economic development, the departure of Chile represented a major setback for Andean economic integration (Avery 1983, 159–61; Rivera 2014, 182). The controversy over the treatment of foreign investment also retarded progress toward integration in other areas. The agenda for industrial programming, designed to promote industrial development throughout the region, enjoyed some success, but the allocation of industrial activities among member states proved controversial. As for trade liberalization, various problems hampered early initiatives, including underdeveloped regional infrastructures. In the end, the withdrawal of Chile resulted in the postponement for several years of the adoption of a common external tariff and the complete liberalization of intraregional trade (Aninat 1978; Ferris 1979, 54; Vargas-Hidalgo 1979, 219–23).

With the member states of the Andean Group in very different stages of economic development, one of their immediate challenges was to ensure an equitable distribution of benefits, notably to lesser developed countries like Bolivia and Ecuador (Avery 1983, 156–7). While both states were granted significant exceptions in trade liberalization and tariff reduction, the export economy of Bolivia in the 1970s continued to be based on tin, and with no market for tin in Latin America, Bolivia had little to export to its neighbors (Morales and Machicado 1978, 31–9, 47–52; Ugarteche 1986, 120–6). Bolivia also lacked a consistent trade policy with several ministries involved in policy formulation. Underdeveloped communication and transportation systems, aggravated by the lack of a sovereign port on the Pacific, further undermined its export prospects. With the exception of a few small, antiquated factories, Bolivia also had a limited industrial base, a critical shortcoming when it came to industrial programming (Morales and Machicado 1978, 22–31). Finally, Bolivia continued to be wracked by chronic political instability at a time when political certainty was an important ingredient in the negotiation of long-term economic agreements.

In Bolivia, disenchantment with the implementation of the Andean Pact stemmed from three factors: 1) concern over modest regional trade increases, 2) complaints regarding sectoral allocations, and 3) the alleged failure of other members to meet their obligations to Bolivia. Regarding the first complaint, Bolivia argued its trade benefits were unfairly limited because other members employed nontariff barriers to limit its regional exports. The validity of this complaint was questionable. In 1970–74, Bolivian exports to the region rose from $6 million to $64 million. After 1975, exports dropped off sharply with Bolivia garnering a bare 2 percent of the regional export market; however, much of the decline was due to the withdrawal of Chile, a traditional trading partner of Bolivia. In any case, Bolivian exports to the region, even before the withdrawal of Chile, were only a small part of Bolivia's total trade. The other Bolivian complaints could not be so easily dismissed. Members of the Andean Group clearly failed to honor some of the special concessions granted Bolivia, especially in sectoral allocations, because it was not in their immediate interest to do so (Avery 1983, 161, 167–70; Escobari 1986a, 28).

In part because of the above, Bolivian support for the Andean Pact was decidedly mixed. With a few exceptions, private business opposed many of its policies, rightly fearing they would make Bolivian products less competitive. In turn, organized labor was ambivalent. On the one hand, labor organizers expressed concern the policies of the Andean Group would increase the power of multinational corporations and lead to monopolies within the region. On the other, they hoped regional integration would improve the negotiating strength of the labor movement and increase the ability of Bolivia to protect its national resources. Some politicians also argued the enhanced economic and political interdependence resulting from subregional integration would generate sympathy for a sovereign port on the Pacific. Decision 141, which obliged all member states to adopt the means necessary to facilitate the access of Bolivian goods to Pacific ports, appeared to validate this position. With public support for the Cartagena Agreement limited, the short-lived García Meza government pushed for more liberal investment and trade policies, withdrawing temporarily from active participation in Andean Group activities in December 1980 (Camacho 1981, 207–10; Avery 1983, 161–2; Rivera 2014, 182). Meeting in Santa Cruz and then in Lima in the first half of 1983, representatives of Bolivia, Colombia, Ecuador, Peru, and Venezuela addressed the concerns of Bolivia and other members, calling for more balanced and harmonious development under more equitable conditions (Abecia 1986, III, 268–70).

As Bolivia worked to maximize the benefits of its participation in the Andean Group, it concluded other agreements aimed at increased subregional, regional, and international cooperation. In April 1969, Bolivia joined Argentina, Brazil, Paraguay, and Uruguay in signing the Treaty of the Rio de la Plata Basin (*Tratado de la Cuenca del Plata*), a Brazilian initiative intended to promote the harmonious development and physical integration of the Plata River Basin. In June 1976, it joined the Latin American and Caribbean Economic System (*Sistema Económico Latinoamericano y del Caribe*, SELA) which was founded in 1975 to promote regional economic cooperation and social development (Escobari 1982, II, 154–6). In July 1978, Bolivia and seven other Amazonian states formed the Amazon Cooperation Treaty Organization (*Organización del Tratado de Cooperación Amazónica*, OTCA), a body created to encourage sustainable development and social inclusion in the region (Abecia 1986, III, 260–4, 73; Glassner 1988, 163–4). In 1979, it joined the Non-Aligned Movement (NAM), a group of states not formally aligned with a major power bloc (Escobari 1986a, 30; Salazar 2000, 781–7, 797). Bolivia was a founding member in December 1986 of the Rio Group (*Grupo Río*, G-Río), an association of Latin American countries seeking a common foreign policy on a variety of issues. Bolivia's accession to the General Agreement on Tariffs and Trade (GATT) was ratified in September 1990 with ratification of its membership in the World Trade Organization (WTO) following in 1995. Bolivia concluded a Complementary Economic Agreement (*Acuerdo de Complementación Económica*, ACE), known as ACE 22, with Chile in April 1993 and a similar agreement with Mexico (ACE 66) in May 2010. Both agreements reduced or eliminated tariffs on specific products. In November 2011, the creation of the Community of Latin American and Caribbean States (*Comunidad de Estados Latinoamericanos y Caribeños*, CELAC) supplanted the activities of the Rio Group (Camacho 1981, 152–68, 209).

## Bilateral and Multilateral Initiatives

As the scope of Bolivian foreign policy expanded, it turned more and more to regional and international forums to promote the seaport issue (Morales

2002, 27–8). On 14 February 1979, the 100$^{th}$ anniversary of the Chilean occupation of the port of Antofagasta, the Bolivian representative to the Organization of American States launched a detailed and passionate defense of the Bolivian position in an effort to gain moral and political support within the organization for Bolivia's claim to a sovereign Pacific outlet. In the most comprehensive statement of the official Bolivian position in many years, Ambassador Gonzalo Romero began by denouncing wars of aggression and strongly criticizing postwar Chilean attempts to depict Bolivia as the aggressor in the War of the Pacific. In so doing, he conducted a thorough review of the early years of the conflict, highlighting the increasingly desperate attempts of Bolivia to challenge effectively Chilean penetration of the Atacama Desert. Depicting the 1904 treaty as a pact imposed on a weak state by an aggressor at a time when the former was under diplomatic pressure from neighboring states, he argued Chile later failed to comply with the terms of the treaty. Regarding the Charaña talks, Ambassador Romero placed the blame for their failure squarely on the shoulders of Chile. Rejecting Chilean claims for territorial compensation, he argued the prolonged Chilean exploitation of the riches of the Atacama Desert, when combined with the disastrous economic consequences for Bolivia of landlocked status, meant it was Chile that owed Bolivia compensation not the other way around. In an attempt to frame the issue as one of hemispheric importance, Ambassador Romero concluded by emphasizing the natural rights of all nations (Bolivia 1979a; Romero 1986, 38–9).

In response, the Chilean representative to the Organization of American States opened with a spirited defense of Chilean policy before and after the War of the Pacific. He challenged directly and in detail Bolivian claims that Chile initiated hostile activities, lacked legitimate claims in the Atacama Desert, imposed the 1904 treaty, and failed to fulfill the obligations of the treaty, specifically its agreement to provide free transit rights to Bolivia. Although he added nothing in the way of new information or interpretation, his rebuttal of Bolivian allegations constituted a thorough and professional summation of the Chilean case. Referring to the Charaña talks, the Chilean envoy argued that Bolivian officials had accepted at the outset the general principle of territorial exchange, a concept he described as the essence of negotiation. He ended his remarks with a strong statement in support of the sanctity of international treaties, concluding the 1904 treaty had been freely arrived at by both signatories. Consequently, "Chile owes Bolivia nothing" (*Chile nada debe a Bolivia*) (Chile 1979, 510–22, quote 522).

When the ninth session of the OAS General Assembly met in La Paz in late October 1979, Bolivia capitalized on the meeting to showcase the maritime issue (Bolivia 1979b; Bolivia 1979c; González 1986, 25). In so doing, Bolivia drew widespread sympathy and support from several Latin American states for its efforts to reclaim free and sovereign access to the Pacific. Although most of Bolivia's neighbors agreed it had a right to a seaport, there was little support for active OAS intervention on Bolivia's part. In the end, the meeting adopted Resolution 426 which declared that it was in the permanent interest of the members to find a just and equitable solution to Bolivia's demand for sovereign access to the Pacific. Recommending the involved parties initiate bilateral negotiations aimed at providing Bolivia with a sovereign land corridor to the ocean, the resolution also called for any negotiations to take into account the interests of the other parties to the dispute. Finally, it suggested any agreement reached include a multinational development zone and take into account Bolivia's refusal to consider territorial compensation (Romero 1986, 39; Salazar 2000, 769–70). The OAS General Assembly approved Resolution 426 with 21 votes in favor, one abstention (Paraguay) and one vote opposed (Chile) (Mesa Gisbert 2016, 188–9; Guzmán Escobari 2015a, 343–5). The issue of Bolivian access to the sea appeared on the agenda of the tenth session of the OAS General Assembly, which met in Washington in November 1980; however, the perfunctory OAS resolutions passed at that meeting and later in the decade failed to include a strong multilateral commitment to resolve the issue (Montenegro 1987, 177–82; Orias 2000, 390–7; Mesa Gisbert 2016, 191–2).

Bolivia also raised the seaport issue in December 1982 at the Foreign Ministers of the La Plata Basin Group meeting in Brasilia. Six months later, representatives of Bolivia, Chile, and Peru joined delegates from the other Bolivarian states in Caracas to celebrate the bicentennial birth of Simón Bolívar. Bolivia used the forum to articulate a policy of unity and solidarity aimed at generating hemispheric support for economic development, together with a multilateral approach to the seaport issue. Bolivia also presented its case for a seaport in other international forums, including President Siles Zuazo's visit to the United Nations in early 1983, a meeting of the Andean Pact Parliament in March 1983, the Non-aligned Movement summit in New Delhi in March 1983, and the Group of 77 meeting in Buenos Aires in April 1983 (Morales 1984, 186–7, 191; Abecia 1986, III, 356; Salazar 2000, 770–1, 781–7).

Bilateral relations with several Latin American states also boosted Bolivian foreign policy in this period. For example, the Colombian government of President Belisario Betancur in late 1983 offered to serve as a venue for talks between Bolivia and Chile aimed at resolving the maritime problem (Orias 2000, 392; Guzmán Escobari 2015a, 349–50). This promising initiative eventually came to naught when Chile in January 1985 rejected third party intervention on the grounds the scope of the issue was bilateral, not multilateral. In any case, Chile argued, Colombian mediation could not occur before Bolivia and Chile had reestablished diplomatic relations. The Siles Zuazo government responded that its maritime issue clearly included a multilateral dimension, arguing Colombian mediation could serve to resolve the landlocked status of Bolivia (Morales 1984, 187; Orias 2000, 392–4). After 1985, the newly installed Peruvian government of Alan García Pérez explored a variety of different paths to improved diplomatic relations with its neighbors in general and Bolivia in particular. Foreign Minister Allan Wagner Tizón traveled to La Paz in early June 1986, the first official visit by a Peruvian foreign minister in four decades, to discuss improved commercial relations together with joint efforts to control narcotics traffic. Bolivian Foreign Minister Guillermo Bedregal Gutiérrez later made an official visit to Lima in February 1987 to exchange ratifications of the 1957 convention which confirmed the indivisible condominium and exclusive use of Lake Titicaca for Bolivia and Peru (Novak and Namihas 2013, 152–7). President García later suggested to President Paz Estenssoro that Peru was prepared to accept the Chilean cession to Bolivia of land occupied by Chile during the War of the Pacific (Ferrero 1987, 63–6; Maldonado 2005, 27–8). Unfortunately, Bolivia was unable to take advantage of this apparent shift in Peruvian policy before the García government was replaced by that of Alberto Fujimori in July 1990 (St John 1992b, 28–9).

Departing from the multilateral strategy Bolivia had pursued for almost a decade, the Paz Estenssoro administration moved to reopened bilateral talks with Chile in February 1986. In what came to be known in Bolivia as the "Fresh Approach" (*Enfoque Fresco*), Foreign Minister Bedregal on 18 April 1987 presented his Chilean counterpart with two memorandums containing alternate proposals to resolve the seaport issue (Camacho 2000, 351–2; Andaluz 2002, 227–35, 377–82). In the first memorandum, Bolivia proposed that Chile grant it a sovereign corridor to the sea located between the Chile–Peru border and the city of Arica and connected to Bolivian territory. The proposal stipulated that Bolivia should enjoy full sovereign rights both in the ceded land corridor and in the adjacent territorial sea. While the first memorandum did not mention compensation or offer territorial exchange, it proposed the creation of a binational commission to study the joint use of the waters of the Bolivian altiplano for development of the Arica region. The memorandum also suggested a trinational development zone at the junction of Bolivia, Chile, and Peru similar to that proposed by Peru in 1976. In the second memorandum, Bolivia proposed that Chile cede it a land and maritime enclave in northern Chile which would be connected to Bolivia with roads, railroads, and a pipeline but not affect the territorial continuity of Chile (Bolivia 1987, 99–107; Guzmán Escobari 2015a, 351–62). The talks sparked a wave of popular opposition in Chile, and the ruling *Junta de Gobierno* rejected the Bolivian initiative outright on 9 June 1987 without making a counterproposal (Bolivia 1988, 155–7; Salazar 2000, 809–10; Araya 2017, 88). Admiral José Toribio Merino, president of the junta, was later quoted as saying, "To Bolivia, nothing, ever" (Morales 1992b, 178–9, quote 179; Becerra de la Roca 2002, 155–7; Novak and Namihas 2013, 110–11).

In the 1970s, authoritarian governments in Bolivia and Brazil, regimes that shared a common world view and national security doctrine, increased their bilateral and multilateral cooperation. In the process, Bolivia shifted from its traditional alliance with Argentina to a closer relationship with Brazil. Acknowledging long-standing Santa Cruz interests in opening their economy to Brazilian markets, the Banzer regime concluded a number of economic agreements which favored Brazil over Argentina in the development of

Bolivian natural resources, especially the iron ore and natural gas reserves in the eastern part of the country (Klein 2011, 231). Both states signed the Treaty of the Rio de la Plata Basin (1969) and the Treaty of Amazon Cooperation (1978), and in 1974, Bolivia and Brazil concluded an agreement covering the sale of Bolivian natural gas to Brazil, a project later put on hold (Torres 2000b, 315, 325). Overall, the decade of the 1970s was an active and fruitful one for Bolivian–Brazilian relations with frequent diplomatic missions, cultural delegations, and military exchanges taking place. The economic crisis in Bolivia in the early 1980s reduced bilateral interaction with Brazil for a time; however, a meeting in 1988 between the presidents of Bolivia and Brazil reinvigorated the relationship, leading to fresh talks regarding the construction of a gas pipeline and the sale of Bolivian natural gas to Brazil (Seoane 2001, 114–15).

Bolivia and Argentina defined their border in a 1925 treaty of limits as amended by protocols in 1939 and 1941 and an exchange of notes in 1959 (Torres 2000a, 184–5). In addition, Bolivia was actively involved in the multilateral talks leading to the Treaty of the Rio de la Plata Basin in 1969. Bolivia and Argentina concluded few bilateral agreements of any real importance in 1950–70, and during the *banzerato*, Bolivia favored Brazil over Argentina in commercial affairs. At the same time, the ideological compatibility of the military governments in Argentina and Bolivia from the mid-1960s to the early 1980s led to collaboration on other fronts, including the political conspiracy known as Operation Condor (*NYT*: 10.8.1980). Energy issues also were increasingly important, notably the construction of a natural gas pipeline connecting Argentina with Bolivia (Cote 2016b, 146–7; Klein 2011, 232). Brazilian support for the *golpe de estado* which brought General Banzer to power in 1971 set a precedent for Argentine involvement in the 1980 *golpe* which brought General García Meza to power. Argentine officials contributed to the well-planned and executed *golpe* after which the short-lived García Meza administration turned to the murky world of international neofascism for help in retaining power (Malloy and Gamarra 1988, 144, 146). The newly installed Siles Zuazo administration later moved quickly to dismantle the paramilitary apparatus its predecessors had created with the support of Argentine officials and foreign fascists (Klein 2011, 240). In the 1980s, Bolivia and Argentina faced common challenges and opportunities, including nascent democracies, debt disputes, migratory issues, and commercial questions. The migratory issue intensified in the second half of the 1980s when the orthodox economic policies of the Paz Estenssoro government resulted in large numbers of Bolivians migrating to Argentina in search of work. In an attempt to resolve the issue, Bolivia and Argentina concluded a migratory convention and two additional protocols; nevertheless, the migration issue continued to bedevil relations into the 1990s. Efforts to improve commercial relations with Argentina led to the conclusion of a Complementary Economic Agreement (ACE 19) in December 1989 (Torres 2001a, 57–64).

## Conclusions

The two decades after 1971 were a period in which Bolivian foreign policy expanded its horizons even as its policy options remained constrained. Active engagement with other landlocked and geographically disadvantaged states in a multitude of international venues produced limited results. Invariably, the dialogue in those conferences focused on improved transit rights, a dialogue in which Bolivia was the odd man out when it came to generating support for its quest for a sovereign outlet to the Pacific. Most often, the Bolivian diplomatic corps did a professional job of presenting the Bolivian case; however, their efforts failed to generate meaningful support for the central issue in Bolivian foreign policy. This failure was due in large part to the unique nature of the Bolivian case as Bolivia was virtually the only country in the world which aimed to go beyond improved transit rights to regain sovereign access to the sea.

In retrospect, most Bolivians considered the Charaña talks to have been their best opportunity in the twentieth century to regain a seaport. Although they produced no concrete results, the Charaña talks were noteworthy because all three parties to the dispute recognized its tripartite nature, even if they were unable to agree on trinational control of the political space around Arica. In addition, Bolivia received formal recognition from both Chile and Peru of its right both to coastal territory and a sovereign port on the Pacific although the proposals of its neighbors differed widely in approach and content. Chile offered Bolivia sovereignty over a corridor to the sea, together with a maritime zone, and Peru agreed to the cession to Bolivia of most of this territory, land which had been part of Peru before the War of the Pacific. Bolivia's consideration of compensation as early as 1910, followed by Chilean insistence on territorial compensation after 1950, suggested Bolivia eventually would have to reconsider its opposition to the principle of compensation if it hoped to improve its access to the Pacific. In the second round of talks with Chile in 1986–87, Bolivia appeared to apply a lesson learned in its offer to trade a corridor to the sea for Chilean access to waters in the Bolivian highlands. Unfortunately, the military junta ruling Chile at the time was in no mood to negotiate.

As Bolivia dealt with old and new concerns, familiar constraints hampered its ability to achieve desired results. On more than one occasion, domestic turmoil undermined foreign policy initiatives, highlighting once again the interrelationship of foreign and domestic policy. Similarly, regionalism continued to influence foreign policy, especially in regards to Bolivia's neighbors. The growing economic and political influence of the Santa Cruz region in particular impacted both on presidential politics and on diplomatic and commercial relations with Argentina and Brazil. Bolivia made some progress in the area of subregional, regional, and international cooperation; unfortunately, the structure and state of the Bolivian economy often limited its success in these areas. Finally, the US government throughout the period was increasingly involved in the domestic and foreign policies of Bolivia in a dependent relationship with serious long-term consequences.

# 8 Bilateral Issues, Multilateral Initiatives, Trilateral Solutions, 1990–2005

At the turn of the century, socioeconomic and political turmoil inside Bolivia increasingly undermined the ability of the central government to conduct an effective foreign policy. The influence of the US government in Bolivia, a major contributor to domestic discontent, peaked in this period, suffering a sharp decline after 2005. Although the maritime issue remained the central concern of Bolivian foreign policy, no progress was achieved in the nation's search for a sovereign outlet to the Pacific Ocean. Bolivia continued to discuss the seaport question with Chile and to raise it in multilateral forums to little effect, and it found nothing beyond rhetorical support from the community of landlocked states. On a more positive note, Bolivia increased its participation in subregional, regional, and international organizations, and it forged stronger ties with Argentina, Brazil, and Paraguay. Relations with Peru, which included the lease to Bolivia of a facility at the Peruvian port of Ilo, remained strong.

## Presidential Politics

In the 1989 presidential election, Gonzalo ("Goni") Sánchez de Lozada, Minister of Planning in the Paz Estenssoro government, was the first place finisher with 23 percent of the popular vote; nevertheless, Congress elected Jaime Paz Zamora, the third place finisher, after he agreed to share government with the second place finisher, Hugo Banzer Suárez (Sanders 1989–90, 9–10; Mesa Gisbert 2003, 170–3). The policies of President Paz Zamora (1989–93) were similar to those of his uncle, Paz Estenssoro, in that he imposed a state of siege soon after taking office and held firm on the neoliberal austerity program instituted by his predecessor (Guzmán 1998, 479–81, 496–9; Hylton and Thomson 2007, 98). Pressure for decentralization increased during the Paz Zamora government with the focus on whether Bolivia should retain its unitary nature and transfer responsibilities to the municipalities or opt for a federalist structure (Kohl and Farthing 2006, 80). The push for greater regional autonomy, which was centered on Santa Cruz, an area of strong economic growth, increased over the next decade (*El Diario*: 23.02.05). While no region seriously contemplated political independence, regional tensions complicated central government efforts to conduct an effective foreign policy.

In February 1990, the presidents of Bolivia, Colombia, Peru, and the United States met in Cartagena, Colombia, and agreed to implement a comprehensive anti-narcotics program aimed at reducing both supply and demand for illegal drugs (*IHT*: 05.03.91). In early May 1990, Bolivia and the United States concluded a bilateral agreement committing the Bolivian armed forces to fight the drug war (Morales 1992a). Prodded by the United States, the Paz Zamora government enacted anti-narcotics policies. At the same time, it forged tacit pacts with coca growers and refused to implement forced eradication policies (Hylton and Thomson 2007, 98). Despite a temporary suspension in 1991, Bolivia received record amounts of anti-narcotics-related assistance in 1990–93. Nevertheless, most Bolivians continued to view the drug war as largely a US problem and primarily one of demand not supply (Lehman 1999, 188–90; Gironda 2001, 251–2, 278–9). Democratic and economic continuity were the major contributions of the Paz Zamora regime, a government widely considered one of the most corrupt since the return to civilian rule due to its links to drug trafficking (Mesa Gisbert 2001b, 756, 758; Morales 2010, 123, 218–19).

In the 1993 presidential election, Goni again led all candidates with almost 36 percent of the vote, and Congress confirmed him as president (Mesa Gisbert 2003, 174–6). The first Sánchez de Lozada government (1993–97) pushed constitutional and economic reforms that rolled backed the last remaining vestiges of the 1952 revolution (*WSJ*: 11.11.94; *FT*: 16.04.96). "As a wealthy mine owner, Sánchez de Lozada favored the power of private enterprise and market capitalism, and his extensive privatization program eliminated many of the remaining vestiges of state capitalism, reversing to an even greater degree the legacy of the National Revolution" (Morales 2010, 222–4, quote, 222–3; Cote 2016b, 150–1). Of all the privatizations, the one with the state oil company, YPFB, in 1996 had the most sustained impact. The contracts signed with foreign companies, together with a drastic reduction in the royalties paid for new discoveries of oil and gas, generated enormous political conflict in coming years (Klein 2011, 259). When the Sánchez de Lozada administration in 1994 implemented a strategy of widespread socioeconomic and political reform, the IMF and World Bank held Bolivia up as a model for developing countries (Mesa Gisbert 2001b, 761–73; Hylton and Thomson 2007, 99).

In the 1997 presidential election, Hugo Banzer Suárez won a plurality with almost 23 percent of the vote, and after a congressional runoff election, he was named president (Mesa Gisbert 2003, 176–9; Dunkerley 2007, 92–7). The second Banzer administration (1997–2001) continued many of the policies of the Sánchez de Lozada government, pursuing economic austerity and forced coca eradication. Banzer's "Zero Coca" campaign, known as the Dignity Plan (*Plan Dignidad*) reduced the traditional crop to its lowest level in decades (*FT*: 06.01.98; *El Diario*: 16.02.00). At the same time, underfunded crop substitution and alternative development programs faltered (*FT*: 02.04.98), increasing the desperation and militancy of former coca growers (Morales 2002, 13–14, 16–19). In October 1998, the arrest of General Augusto Pinochet, the former Chilean dictator, on charges of human rights violations caused angst in the Banzer government because of Bolivia's ties to Operation Condor during the first Banzer administration (*Bolivian Times*: 05.11.98; Sivak 2002, 324–32). While the United States and allied international aid agencies hailed Bolivia as a model of economic stabilization and coca eradication, coca growers and worker-peasant unions responded to the policies of the Banzer government with mounting demonstrations and strikes (Gironda 2001, 284–9, 299–316; Morales 2010, 224–8).

After the Bolivian government in September 1999 leased the state-owned Cochabamba water company to Aguas del Tunari, an international consortium owned in part by the Bechtel Corporation of the United States, a violent protest against water privatization shook the Banzer government in 2000 (*El Diario*: 11.04.00). Political resistance in support of protecting national resources had a long history in Bolivia; consequently, the popular response to the privatization of public and communal waterworks in Cochabamba was predictable (St John 2005a, 3; Kohl and Farthing 2006, 162–7). Terminally ill with cancer, President Banzer stepped down in August 2001, a year before the end of his term, transferring his mandate and the Water War to his vice president, Jorge Quiroga Ramírez (Sivak 2002, 333–45). When Cochabamba erupted in a new wave of protests against water privatization and the protests of coca farmers also increased, President Quiroga was forced to suspend the water privatization contract and the anti-coca efforts he had inherited (Mesa Gisbert 2001b, 775–81; Morales 2010, 228–9). The Water War in Cochabamba did not end until January 2006 when the multinational corporations involved abandoned a legal demand for $50 million in compensation and accepted a token payment of two bolivianos (30 cents) (Dangl 2007, 57–69; Shultz 2008a, 30–2). Meanwhile, corruption continued to be a major problem in Bolivia with Transparency International in 2001 labelling Bolivia the most corrupt country in Latin America (*El Diario*: 28.06.01).

In the 2002 presidential election, Goni won a plurality with more than 22 percent of the vote, and the resulting parliamentary second round voting gave him the presidency (*El Diario*: 05.08.02). The big surprise was the second-place finish of the pro-coca candidate, Juan Evo Morales Ayma, a direct result of the US war on drugs policy (*NYT*: 02.07.02). Despite US meddling in the election, Morales won almost 21 percent of the vote, a harbinger of things to come (Mesa Gisbert 2003, 179–83; Pinto and Navia 2007, 174–8; Crandall 2008, 103–4). Following the inauguration of President Sánchez de Lozada, the Peruvian government in August 2002 proposed to route Bolivian natural gas to the Peruvian port of Ilo through a pipeline parallel to the La Paz–Desaguadero–Ilo road. After Bolivia rejected the Peruvian proposal because it did not include a sovereign outlet to the Pacific, the Sánchez de Lozada government proposed to export Bolivian gas via Chile. The government's gas plans sparked widespread opposition to the liberal economic policies favored by Sánchez de Lozada and many other Latin American leaders over the previous decade (*El Diario*: 12.10.03; *MH*: 20.10.03). Up and down the west coast of South America, the free market policies pursued in the 1990s attracted foreign investment and generated new tax revenues, but the economic benefits did not trickle down to the poor in Bolivia and elsewhere (*NYT*: 17.10.03). Nationalist antipathy, fears of external interference, and opposition to the privatization of natural resources forced President Sánchez de Lozada to flee the country in October 2003 (St John 2003; Olivera 2004, 177–82).

Vice President Carlos Diego Mesa Gisbert, a noted historian and journalist, replaced President Sánchez de Lozada and formed an emergency government (*WP*: 19.10.03; *La Razón*: 20.10.03). Initially, President Mesa enjoyed the country's support, and he was able to restore order temporarily by promising a national referendum on hydrocarbon policy followed by presidential elections in 2007 (*WP*: 18.10.03; *La Razón*: 21.10.03). President Mesa campaigned heavily in support of the referendum on the future of Bolivia's natural gas reserves, which was held in July 2004, arguing Bolivian should choose polls over protests. With more than half of eligible voters going to the polls, the Bolivian electorate responded by giving Mesa over 90 percent support for five separate but related proposals. The results of the referendum suggested a majority of voters favored the nationalization of gas and oil resources and a repeal of the hydrocarbons law enacted by the Sánchez de Lozada government (*La Razón*: 19.07.04). Unfortunately, the referendum sidestepped the issue of outright nationalization; consequently, it failed to diffuse the Gas War (St John 2004; Hylton and Thomson 2007, 119). When Bolivia and Peru in August 2004 signed a letter of intent for Bolivian natural gas to be exported to Mexico and the United States through a Peruvian port, the agreement led to widespread protests in Bolivia (*La Razón*: 05.08.04; *El Diario*: 12.01.05). Tarija, located in southeastern Bolivia close to Chile and home to the bulk of Bolivian natural gas deposits, was the only department to oppose holding the referendum and to show significant support for the export of Bolivian natural gas through Chile (*Los Tiempos*: 23.09.03; *La Razón*: 21.10.03). Public opinion in Tarija on this issue reflected growing support in the east for greater regional autonomy (*La Razón*: 16.06.05; *El Diario*: 03.07.05). After the department of Santa Cruz threatened to secede, President Mesa agreed to grant Santa Cruz and other departments greater autonomy, including the right to select their own prefect (governor) (*La Razón: 03.02.05*).

In March 2005, President Mesa offered to resign, and after Congress refused his offer, the Gas War spilled over into a Second Water War. Civil strife in the city of El Alto eventually forced President Mesa to cancel a contract with Aguas del Illimani, the second multinational water company to have a contract annulled in Bolivia. Meanwhile, nationwide protests led by Evo Morales continued against a government decree that instituted price increases for gasoline and diesel fuel (*WP*: 09.03.05; *MH*: 09.05.95). In May 2005, Congress approved a new hydrocarbons law which increased the state's share of oil and gas revenues but stopped short of nationalization. When the new legislation failed to quell popular unrest, President Mesa resigned in early June (*La Razón*: 07.06.05). After opposition groups rejected the first two officials in the constitutional line of succession, the Senate President and House Speaker, Chief Justice of the Supreme Court Eduardo Rodríguez Veltzé, third in the line of succession, was sworn in as an interim president with the task of conducting general elections before the end of 2005 (St John 2005a). As Bolivians prepared for general elections, the enormous impact domestic events in 1990–2005 would have on the nation's foreign policy was not yet clear, but it soon would be.

## Ilo and After

On 24 January 1992, President Paz Zamora and President Fujimori of Peru concluded a 50-year renewable agreement in which Peru agreed to provide Bolivia with a duty-free port and industrial park at Ilo in return for similar facilities for Peru at Puerto Suarez on the Paraguay River. Peru also granted Bolivia a tourist zone for 99 years, together with five kilometers of Ilo coastline. Bolivians immediately baptized the coastal strip "Boliviamar." The agreement provided for an Inter-American Development Bank (IDB) loan for infrastructure development at Ilo, together with new and improved road construction on the highways linking the port to Bolivian territory (Salazar 2000, 841–4; Ergueta 2000, 93–9, 104–8).

Over the next decade, Bolivia and Peru expanded the original Ilo agreement in a series of pacts designed to promote the development of the duty-free Bolivian port at Ilo. Separate agreements formed a new organization, the Lake Titicaca Binational Agency, to promote the rational management and joint development of the Lake Titicaca Basin, including the Desaguadero River, Lake Popoó, and the Salar de Coipasa (St John 1994b, 24). In 1998, Bolivia and Peru also signed a memorandum of understanding which provided for private entities to construct a gas pipeline from La Paz to Ilo (Novak and Namihas 2013, 169–73). While Bolivia and Peru hailed the Ilo and subsequent agreements as historic pacts which would promote regional economic development, President Banzer was quick to add that they simply marked a new step in Bolivia's determination to recover full rights to the Pacific Ocean (Orias 1998, 54–7). The Ilo agreements implied no transfer of sovereignty to Bolivia; nevertheless, they still received strong support across the Bolivian political spectrum (Deustua 1999, 27–37).

In November 1999, Chile and Peru signed a package of documents which executed the Treaty of Lima, ending 70 years of controversy. The Act of Execution (*Acta de Ejecución*) addressed the requirement in article five of the 1929 treaty for Chile to construct for Peru a wharf, customs office, and railway terminal station at Arica as well as the requirement in article two of the additional protocol which called for absolute free transit of persons, merchandise, and armaments to and from Peruvian territory (St John 2000;

Novak 2000, 57–178). The 1999 agreements were a good result for Chile and Peru, but they did not address the aspirations of Bolivia which continued to demand a sovereign port on the Pacific. After congratulating Chile and Peru for reaching a settlement, the Banzer government expressed the hope that attention could now turn to satisfying Bolivian desires for a sovereign exit to sea. Public reaction in Chile and Peru to the 1999 agreements suggested a growing skepticism in the Tacna–Arica region as to the practicality of a broader, trilateral settlement involving a sovereign port for Bolivia (*El Mercurio*: 12.11.99; *El Comercio*: 13.11.99; *El Diario*: 13.11.99).

In a January 2002 visit to Bolivia, Peruvian President Alejandro Toledo joined President Quiroga in inaugurating both a new international bridge at Desaguadero on the La Paz–Desaguadero–Ilo road and floodgates constructed to regulate the waters of Lake Titicaca (Novak and Namihas 2013, 196–200). In the course of this visit, President Toledo reiterated his country's interest in becoming the exit port for Bolivian natural gas, proposing a strategic alliance between Bolivia and Peru which would include the construction of a petrochemical plant at Ilo (*El Peruano*: 25.01.02; *La Tercera*: 25.01.02). President Toledo's enthusiasm in seeking to resolve the Bolivian gas issue drew criticism in Peruvian diplomatic circles after he appeared to offer Bolivia a sovereign port on Peruvian territory, an initiative which would have marked a major shift in Peruvian foreign policy (*El Comercio*: 28.01.02; *El Diario*: 29.01.02). Peruvian Foreign Minister Diego García Sayán moved quickly to correct Toledo's miscue, stating there was no change in Peruvian policy; nevertheless, the Bolivian media seized on the verbal slip, implying it was a missed opportunity to obtain a sovereign port on the Pacific (*Los Tiempos*: 30.01.02; *La Razón*: 30.01.02). During the visit, the two presidents also signed an agreement intended to regularize labor migration between Bolivia and Peru, a long-standing issue, and they participated in the first session of a newly created binational cabinet scheduled to meet regularly to discuss issues of common interest (Novak and Namihas 2013, 213–14).

Following the inauguration of President Sánchez de Lozada, the Toledo government in late August 2002 again raised the issue of Ilo as a port of exit for Bolivian natural gas, proposing to Bolivia what Peruvian officials described as an integrated strategy. In an interview with the author, Allan Wagner, the foreign minister of Peru, later characterized the competing Chilean approach as wholly commercial in nature in that it involved simply pumping natural gas from Tarija to the Chilean port of Mejillones (09.05.03). In contrast, Wagner outlined an approach which routed the pipeline near several Bolivian cities, including Oruro, Sucre, and La Paz, where natural gas could be drawn off for domestic and industrial use. Wagner argued the Peruvian approach, which called for the pipeline to parallel the La Paz–Desaguadero–Ilo road, would contribute to the economic integration of southern Peru and western Bolivia with gas liquefaction facilities at Ilo being a possible next step (*El Peruano*: 27.08.02). In a related proposal, Peru suggested the formation of a joint venture with Bolivia to transport liquefied natural gas to the United

States with the possible inclusion downstream of natural gas from the Camisea field in central Peru (*El Diario*: 28.08.02; Novak and Namihas 2013, 164–70).

Peruvian observers generally viewed the Toledo administration's proposal as reasonable, even audacious, emphasizing that it offered Bolivia a long-sought maritime quality. At the same time, Foreign Minister Wagner felt it necessary to stress that the Peruvian strategy offered Bolivia an autonomous economic zone with an exit to the sea, but it did not include the cession to Bolivia of sovereignty over Peruvian territory on the Pacific coast (*El Comercio*: 30.08.02). This clarification of the terms of the Peruvian proposal proved a deal breaker. Following additional bilateral talks, the Sánchez de Lozada government emphasized in mid-October 2002 that the only way Bolivia would be inclined to accept the Peruvian proposal was if it included the cession to Bolivia of sovereign access to the Pacific Ocean (*El Comercio*: 15.10.02).

Over the next year, Peru made several attempts to restart the port talks, but little progress was made on the natural gas issue. In mid-November 2002, President Sánchez de Lozado stated publicly for the first time that the export of gas through Peru was not feasible. At the same time, he acknowledged that it would be difficult to persuade the Bolivian people that Chile was an acceptable alternative (*El Peruano*: 13.11.02; *El Diario*: 14.11.02). In August 2003, Foreign Minister Wagner and his Bolivian counterpart, Carlos Armando Saavedra Bruno, agreed to initiate formal negotiations for a free trade agreement, and by mid-September, officials in Bolivia and Peru were pledging to move beyond the gas issue which both sides agreed was in limbo (*El Comercio*: 16.09.03). At the end of the year, the Toledo government once again felt the need to stress that Peru viewed Bolivia's quest for a sovereign port on the Pacific as a bilateral issue between Bolivia and Chile (*El Comercio*: 12.12.03).

During an official visit to Peru in early August 2004, Presidents Mesa and Toledo signed a letter of intent for natural gas from Tarija to be exported to North America through Peru with the latter agreeing to establish a special economic zone at the port (*El Comercio*: 05.08.04; *El Diario*: 05.08.04). After a special mixed Bolivia–Peru commission met in Cuzco to discuss details of the letter of intent, the Toledo administration announced that Peru expected to save $800–$900 million if Bolivian gas was exited through southern Peru because it meant a special pipeline for the Camisea gas field was no longer required (*El Peruano*: 06.09.04). While the Toledo administration and the Peruvian public were delighted with the terms of the letter of intent, the same was not true in Bolivia where the disposition of Bolivian natural gas reserves remained a highly controversial issue (*El Diario*: 11.06.05).

## Point Zero

In his August 1989 inaugural address, President Paz Zamora had stressed that only a sovereign coastline could mitigate the enormous economic and geographical obstacles Bolivia faced as a landlocked country undergoing what he termed a "constrictive geopolitical encirclement" (Morales 1992b, 179–81, quote 179). Shortly thereafter, he launched a broad diplomatic initiative to familiarize the international community with Bolivian aims. Addressing the UN General Assembly in March 1990, for example, President Paz Zamora reaffirmed the basic Bolivian position that it could not and would not renounce its intent to recover its former maritime condition (*Presencia*: 24.03.90). Bolivian diplomacy in 1989–92 communicated Bolivia's maritime policy to a wider audience but left relations with Chile unchanged (St John 2001, 9).

In early 1993, the Chilean government announced President Patricio Aylwin had told Foreign Minister Enrique Silva Cimma to resolve all outstanding border disputes before the end of the year. Bolivian hopes that the Chilean announcement foretold a breakthrough in bilateral talks were soon dashed when the latter clarified its position, stating it had no outstanding border disputes with Bolivia or Peru. One week later, Chile suspended ongoing commercial negotiations with Bolivia after high-ranking Bolivian military officers criticized the talks on the grounds that Bolivia should not have to subordinate its lofty national maritime interests to the conclusion of a commercial agreement with Chile (St John 1994b, 25; Seoane et al. 1997, 27–47). In July 1993, the Bolivian press trumpeted a joint Bolivia–Chile communiqué issued by their respective foreign ministers which referenced pending issues between the two states. According to Bolivian national television, this was the first time since the conclusion of the 1904 peace treaty that Chile had acknowledged in a public statement that it had pending issues with Bolivia. Any hope for sustained progress on the maritime issue was soon dampened by intemperate remarks by outgoing President Paz Zamora. In a speech to high-ranking Bolivian military officers, he described Chile as an "indolent neighbor" and a "retrograde country." Adding Chile remained "in the stone age" concerning Bolivia's maritime situation, he urged Chile to assist Bolivia in resolving its landlocked status (St John 1994a, 67–8, quote 67). Paz Zamora's inflammatory comments were widely criticized in and out of Bolivia as inaccurate and counterproductive since they did nothing to promote dialogue with Chile (St John 1994a, 68).

Over the next few years, Bolivia explored a wide variety of policy options internally and in confidential talks with Chilean officials. Given the reluctance of Chile to discuss a sovereign Bolivian outlet to the Pacific, dialogue centered on the challenges of globalization to Bolivia and Chile, the reestablishment of diplomatic relations within the context of a strategic relationship, and the negotiation of a bilateral treaty which approached the maritime issue from a new direction. In regards to the latter, a consensus developed in some Bolivian circles that any new treaty should include concessions at Arica and elsewhere similar to those obtained by Bolivia at Ilo, albeit not at the sacrifice of a sovereign port on the Pacific. There was also much discussion about the need for a free trade agreement which liberalized bilateral trade as well as a more liberal transit regime (Salazar 2000, 287, 355–6, 371; Orias et al. 2001, 183, 193–4).

Concurrent with these activities, Bolivian diplomats continued to raise the maritime issue in regional and international forums. When Foreign Minister Antonio Aranibar Quiroga raised the subject at an OAS General Assembly in June 1994, his Chilean counterpart responded with an uncompromising statement emphasizing that the question of a Bolivian seaport on the Pacific died with the negotiation of the 1904 treaty. He added that the position of the Chilean government rested on the principle of non-intervention and the sanctity of treaties (Orias 2000, 402–3; St John 2001, 11). Foreign Minister Aranibar continued to raise the issue over the next few years, but there was no movement in the Chilean position. At a meeting of the OAS General Assembly in June 1997, for example, Aranibar expressed frustration with what he termed the inflexible position of the Chilean government. The Foreign Minister of Chile, José Miguel Insulza, responded in part that there were no pending issues of territorial limits between Bolivia and Chile. In the end, little was accomplished in this period because neither party could find a way to bridge Bolivia's demand for sovereign access to the Pacific with Chile's refusal to concede sovereignty (Orias 2000, 405–6).

At the end of the first Sánchez de Lozada administration, the Ministry of Foreign Affairs completed a thorough analysis of its strategic relationship with Chile designed in part as a guide for the incoming second Banzer administration. The report envisioned a future partnership with Chile which would overcome past conflicts yet assure Bolivia a sovereign presence on the Pacific. To achieve this vision, the report called for joint action which moved bilateral relations with Chile from a pattern of conflict and confrontation to one of cooperation and friendship. To remake its relationship with Chile, the report outlined four separate but related strategic imperatives. First, Bolivia must reestablish its maritime presence, defined in the report as sovereign participation on the Pacific coast. Associated elements of this first initiative included freedom of transit, highway and railway improvement, interoceanic corridors, port development, and duty-free zones. Second, recognizing the Bolivia–Chile borderland offered opportunities for cooperation and development, Bolivia must expand the existing border regime with Chile in areas like migration, contraband control, and water resource utilization. Third, Bolivia targeted greater economic complementarity with its neighbor by promoting economic integration, facilitating and diversifying commercial exchange, and encouraging investment. The fourth initiative focused on the need to promote peace and friendship on the border. Throughout the report, the Ministry of Foreign Affairs emphasized that Bolivia's maritime issue remained essentially trilateral in nature with Peru an important player in any comprehensive settlement (Bolivia 1997; Seoane et al. 1997, 27–47).

In the coming year, the Banzer administration discussed the maritime position of Bolivia in a variety of forums. Speaking in Caracas in June 1998, Foreign Minister Javier Murillo de la Rocha described Bolivia's landlocked status as an unjust reality and an obstacle to national and regional economic development. Expanding on these themes in a speech before the UN General

Assembly in September 1998, Murillo stressed the enormous economic costs to Bolivia of being landlocked. After alluding to the negotiations with Chile which had occurred over the years, he concluded his presentation with an emphatic declaration that Bolivia would never relinquish its demand for a sovereign outlet to the Pacific (Bolivia 1998, 27–9; Murillo 1999, 1–19). Although the Banzer government continued to promote the seaport issue throughout 1999, the accomplished Bolivian diplomat and historian, Jorge Escobari Cusicanqui, summed up the lack of progress when he concluded in mid-November 1999 that "we continue at point zero on the maritime theme" (*seguimos en punto cero sobre el tema marítimo*) (*El Diario*: 17.11.99).

As successive Bolivian governments wrestled with the maritime issue, Chile passed a law in 1997 which led to the privatization of its port facilities at Antofagasta, Arica, and elsewhere. With its ports in need of expensive modernizations, Chile turned to the private sector, granting different consortiums multi-year contracts to administer port operations and to upgrade facilities and infrastructure. Where Bolivia for almost 100 years had dealt directly with the Chilean government on port issues, it now had to deal with different private consortiums at Antofagasta and Arica. Long-standing rules and regulations were modified, and the private operators increased tariffs to help pay for improvements to port facilities. At the same time, strong economic growth in Bolivia from 2000 to 2014 led to a progressive increase in Bolivian traffic through the ports, compounding problems of capacity and efficiency. Thereafter, issues arising from the privatization of Chilean ports frequently played an important role in bilateral talks on the maritime issue (Agramont Lechín and Peres-Cajías 2016, 82–4; Mesa Gisbert 2016, 226–9).

## Trilateral Initiatives

At the turn of the century, several official and unofficial initiatives focused on the economic benefits of increased regional integration and economic development in southern Peru, western Bolivia, and northern Chile. On the unofficial level, a group of diplomats, journalists, and scholars, many of whom had prior government experience in Bolivia, Chile, or Peru, launched a creative initiative in 1999 known as the Trinational Project (*Proyecto Trinacional*). As former Bolivian Foreign Minister Aranibar explained in an interview with the author in March 2001, the objective of the project was the removal of obstacles to trinational development together with the creation of a new agenda for the economic integration of the Bolivia–Chile–Peru tripoint (13.03.01). In calling for Bolivia, Chile, and Peru to increase cooperation and integration, former Peruvian Foreign Minister Allan Wagner, an active participant in the project, argued that trinational cooperation could become a motor for regional economic development and in the process facilitate a solution to Bolivia's maritime problem (Wagner 1999, 135–7). Focused on interrelated themes, with complementarity and mutual benefit at the center, the Proyecto Trinacional organized forums and workshops to promote theoretical and practical approaches to trinational development (*La Razón*: 03.04.01). It also published a book which highlighted trade and development opportunities in the region (Araníbar et al. 2001).

On the official level, a new round of bilateral talks began in early 2000 when Foreign Minister Murillo of Bolivia and Foreign Minister Juan Gabriel Valdés Soublette of Chile met during the EU–Río Group summit in Algarve, Portugal. In the Declaration of Algarve, they agreed to open a dialogue centered on six topics: 1) Bolivia's maritime problem, 2) transit facilities, 3) frontier commissions, 4) port modernization, 5) port privatization, and 6) the integration process (*El Diario*: 22.02.00). The joint agenda called for the creation of a regional development zone (*polo de desarrollo*) consisting of southwest Bolivia, northern Chile, and southern Peru. Murillo and Valdés also agreed to propose to Peru a tripartite formula which could lead to a resolution of Bolivia's maritime problem (*El Diario*: 24.02.00). Bolivian President Banzer and Chilean President Ricardo Lagos met in Brasilia in September 2000 and in Panama later in the year (*El Mercurio*: 02.09.00; *El Diario*: 17.11.00). The Panama talks included Bolivia's maritime aspirations together with a trinational perspective for economic development. To facilitate the export of Bolivian minerals, Chile agreed to upgrade the road running from the San Cristóbal Mine in Bolivia to the Chilean port of Tocopilla, and the parties also agreed to open frontier, duty, and police stations on the border 12 hours daily to maximize vehicular traffic (*El Diario*: 17.11.00; *Los Tiempos*: 18.11.00). At year-end, Foreign Minister Murillo admitted that little real progress had been made on the maritime issue but stressed the important thing was to maintain a dialogue with Chile (*El Diario*: 22.12.00).

In late January 2001, the economic development ministers of Bolivia and Chile met in Santa Cruz and reaffirmed their commitment to advance economic integration between northern Chile and western Bolivia (*Los Tiempos*: 30.01.01). Thereafter, bilateral commissions worked toward this broad objective; however, few concrete projects were announced. At the same time, Bolivia continued to express concern over the pending sale of F-16 fighter jets to Chile on the grounds the deal could encourage a regional arms race (*El Diario*: 03.01.01). Presidents Banzer and Lagos met in Quebec in April 2001 during the Third Summit of the Americas. Their statements to the press after the meeting reaffirmed their commitment to free trade and regional integration but also suggested the long road to be traveled before a comprehensive settlement including improved Bolivian access to the Pacific could be reached (*El Diario*: 22.04.01). When compared to the six-point agenda agreed to in the Declaration of the Algarve, the Quebec statements implied some progress had been made in areas like infrastructure development and subregional integration, but there was little indication of movement on core questions like the Silala watershed and maritime issues. Speaking at ceremonies marking the anniversary of the birth of the Bolivian Navy, Admiral Jorge Badani Lenz accurately summarized the situation in late April 2001 when he described as "latent" (*latente*) the Bolivian desire to return to the sea (*El Diario*: 24.04.01).

## "Gas por Mar"

In June 2002, Bolivia and Chile signed a protocol which included a Chilean commitment to grant Bolivia a 50-year renewable lease on 600–1,000 hectares at or near Mejillones where Bolivia could construct a special economic zone to export natural gas to Mexico and the United States (*La Razón*: 13.04.02; *La Tercera*: 13.04.02). Peru immediately responded with a counterproposal which first offered to lease 1,000 hectares at Ilo for 99 years and later increased the offer to 1,500 hectares (*El Diario*: 12.06.02; *El Diario*: 29.07.02). In the interim, a public opinion poll conducted by *Apoyo Opinión* indicated that Bolivians favored a Peruvian port over a Chilean one by a ratio of four to one (*El Diario*: 05.05.02). Thereafter, debate in Bolivia over the construction of a pipeline to carry natural gas to the Pacific coast for export to Mexico and the United States increasingly dominated bilateral relations with Chile. After President Sánchez de Lozado was forced to resign, President Mesa broke protocol by raising the issue at the January 2004 Summit of the Americas (Mesa Gisbert 2016, 206–8). When Mesa called for Chile to negotiate a definitive solution to the maritime issue, a plainly angered President Lagos responded that his government had already made an offer to Bolivia that satisfied all of its conditions and provided enough land for exports (*La Razón*: 14.01.04; *La Tercera*: 14.01.04). Bolivian nationalists, including the Bolivian armed forces, remained adamantly opposed to the Chilean route, and President Sánchez de Lozada in a September 2003 interview with the author later agreed that a major factor in his overthrow was widespread concern in Bolivia that he would agree to export Bolivian gas via Chile (09.09.03).

Following the July 2004 referendum, President Mesa repeated an earlier offer to Chile to export Bolivian gas through a Chilean port in return for a sovereign Bolivian outlet to the Pacific Ocean. When Chile rejected the offer, as Mesa knew it would, he proclaimed a Peruvian port was the only viable option for Bolivia (*El Comercio*: 20.07.04). The June 2005 resignation of President Mesa signaled the end of the Bolivian strategy, known as "gas por mar," of using the gas issue as a bargaining chip in negotiations with Chile for a sovereign port on the Pacific (Guzmán Escobari 2015a, 397–8). After President Rodríguez in August 2005 emphasized that "gas por mar" was no longer the only option available to Bolivia, Chile no longer figured in any Bolivian strategy for the development and export of its natural gas (*La Razón*: 04.07.05; *El Diario*: 19.08.05). Bilateral talks continued on other issues, including a free trade agreement and a mining accord, but there was no progress on the maritime issue (*La Razón*: 10.12.05).

As Bolivia and Chile wrestled over the maritime issue, the Silala watershed dispute once again complicated bilateral relations. In 1997, the Prefect of Potosí, Omar Manzono, had revoked the 1908 concession of the Antofagasta (Chili) and Bolivia Railway Co. Ltd. (FCAB), arguing the Silala waters had long been used for purposes other than those in the original agreement (Mesa Gisbert 2016, 200–1). In 1999, the Banzer administration put the Silala waters out to public tender, and in 2000, it awarded a 40-year concession to a Bolivian company called DUCTEC SRL for the sum of $46.8 million (*El Diario*: 11.08.99; *El Diario*: 14.01.00). DUCTEC SRL attempted to charge FCAB and CODELCO, the Chilean copper producing company, for their use of the Silala waters but no payments were made (*El Diario*: 29.01.03). In 2002, the Quiroga government stated that one possible course of action would be to halt the flow of the waters of the Silala to Chile, a second would be to resume bilateral talks with Chile, and a third would involve arbitration proceedings before an ad hoc court or the International Court of Justice (*El Diario*: 29.06.02). In 2003, the Sánchez de Lozada government rescinded the contract with DUCTEC SRL on the grounds it was unable to fulfill its goal of charging FCAB and CODELCO. In 2004, the foreign ministries of Bolivia and Chile established a working group on the Silala. It met several times in the coming years but failed to resolve the issue (Bazoberry 2003, 110–15; Mulligan and Eckstein 2011, 597–8). In an age in which climate change was impacting on hydrographic basins around the world, the dispute over the tiny, remote Silala watershed was a testament to the importance of fresh water, especially in desert areas of the world (Rossi 2017, 57–8). The "underlying issues of politics, economics, sovereignty, and history" led the UN Environmental Programme in 2007 to describe the Silala as "one of the most hydropolitically vulnerable basins in the world" (UN 2007, 64–5, quote 65).

## Good Neighbors

With natural gas reserves in Tarija and elsewhere in Bolivia estimated at 49.82 billion cubic feet, the second largest in South America, Bolivia at the end of the century became a center for the supply and distribution of energy to the Southern Cone of South America (Torres 2000b, 317–21; Cote 2016b, 151). The Barrientos government signed a 20-year contract to export natural gas to Argentina in 1968, and the subsequent export of gas through a pipeline constructed in 1972 helped to consolidate bilateral relations between the two neighbors (Torres 2001a, 61–63; Klein 2011, 249). In the second half of the 1980s, natural gas exports to Argentina represented 40 percent of total Bolivian exports, highlighting the economic and political importance of Argentina to Bolivia. In the 1990s, the importance of natural gas to Bolivian exports decreased due to a surge in nontraditional exports and a dramatic decline in the price paid by Argentina (Torres 2000b, 322–4). In a new spirit of regionalism, Argentina, Bolivia, and Paraguay in September 2001 signed a trilateral agreement to promote the sustainable development of the Chaco region (*El Diario*: 13.09.01). In addition to energy, policy items on the Bolivia–Argentina agenda at the dawn of the new millennium included the use of the waters of the Bermejo–Grande de Tarija and Pilcomayo river basins, migratory labor, the Southern Common Market (*Mercado Común del Sur*,

MERCOSUR), and contraband (Torres 2001a, 74–97; Tini 2008, 207–7). Shortly after the July 2004 referendum, President Mesa concluded a 20-year supply agreement with President Néstor Kirchner which included construction of a liquefied natural gas plant in Bolivia and a 932-mile, $1 billion pipeline in Argentina, further advancing energy integration in the region (*El Mercurio*: 18.08.04; *La Razón*: 15.10.04).

In 1974, Bolivia concluded an agreement for the sale of natural gas to Brazil, but it would be another quarter century before the terms of the agreement became a reality. In 1996, Bolivia and Brazil concluded the La Paz Treaty enabling the construction of the Gasbol pipeline. In response, foreign direct investment in Bolivia more than doubled in 1996–99 with more than half of it going to the hydrocarbon sector (Morales 2002, 19). The La Paz Treaty granted Petrobrás, the semi-public Brazilian oil company, special conditions in Bolivian gas fields, and it soon became the largest company in Bolivia, accounting for more than 60 percent of gas production in 2005. In addition, it owned the Gasbol pipeline and two petroleum refineries in Bolivia (Delgado and Cunha 2016, 135–6). Brazil also acquired other economic interests in Bolivia including control of upwards of 40 percent of the agricultural and livestock industries in Santa Cruz (Zibechi 2005, 2). With the completion of the Gasbol pipeline, Brazil replaced Argentina as the primary market for Bolivian natural gas (Torres 2000b, 325–7; Klein 2011, 249). In the course of a June 2001 meeting with Brazilian President Fernando Henrique Cardoso, President Banzer described Bolivia as the "nucleus and energy axis" (*núcleo y eje energético*) of the southern cone of South America (*El Diario*: 27.06.01). In addition to natural gas, items on the Bolivia–Brazil agenda include transoceanic corridors, MERCOSUR, contraband, drug trafficking, and the Paraguay–Paraná waterway (Torres 2000a, 217; Seoane 2001, 131–54). Immediately following the July 2004 referendum in Bolivia, President Mesa and President Lula signed agreements providing for the construction of a petrochemical complex and a thermoelectric plant near the Bolivian town of Puerto Suárez (*El Diario*: 09.07.04). In August 2004, President Mesa met with President Toledo of Peru and President Lula of Brazil in Pando to inaugurate a Friendship Bridge (*Puente de la Amistad*) linking the populations of Cobija and Brasilia. The bridge was part of the Southern Inter-oceanic Hub (*Eje Interoceánico del Sur*) of the Initiative for Integration of Regional Infrastructure in South America (*Iniciativa para la Integración de la Infraestructura Regional Suramericana*, IIRSA), a 12-state initiative to develop the region's infrastructure (Rivera 2014, 250). In the "Declaración Presidential del Acre," released at the end of the meeting, the three heads of state pledged to work together to promote regional economic development (*La Razón*: 12.08.04).

After the Chaco War, Bolivia's commercial and diplomatic relations with Paraguay were correct but restrained with "indifference" (*indiferencia*) being the word often used by Bolivians to characterize the bilateral relationship. At the same time, Bolivia and Paraguay remained at the core of the traditional balance of power struggle between Argentina and Brazil (Torres 2001b, 229–32). The death in 1989 of the Paraguayan dictator Alfredo Stroessner and the subsequent democratic transition in Paraguay later combined with an emphasis on regional integration in the 1990s to open new opportunities for Bolivia and Paraguay to expand their relationship. President Sánchez de Lozado hosted Paraguayan President Juan Carlos Wasmosy on an official visit to La Paz in September 1993, and Wasmosy returned the favor, hosting Sánchez de Lozado on an official visit to Asunción in March 1994 (Tini 2008, 210–11). At the end of the century, Paraguay looked to Bolivia to champion a special relationship with the Andean Community, and Bolivia looked to Paraguay to help it establish a special relationship with MERCOSUR (*El Diario*: 12.07.00). Bolivia and Paraguay looked to each other to improve their respective access to the Atlantic and Pacific oceans (*El Diario*: 10.12.02). In addition to CAN and MERCOSUR, other initiatives on the Bolivia–Paraguay agenda include the Transchaco road, the Paraguay–Paraná waterway, the Pilcomayo River basin, contraband, drug trafficking, and the energy sales (Barrios 1995; Torres 2001b, 242–64). The publication in 2000 of *Twelve Stories of the Chaco War* (*Doce cuentos de la guerra del Chaco*), a book consisting of six stories by Bolivians and six by Paraguayans, followed by a third year of joint Bolivian–Paraguayan–United States military exercises symbolized the desire of Bolivia and Paraguay to move beyond the Chaco War (*El Diario*: 09.07.01). Before the turn of the century, Bolivia began exporting liquefied natural gas via tanker truck to Paraguay, and while the small Paraguayan market made construction of a dedicated pipeline economically unfeasible, talks continued regarding a regional conduit connecting Argentina, Bolivia, Brazil, and Paraguay (*El Diario*: 13.03.02; *La Razón*: 19.08.18).

## Regional Cooperation and Integration

At the Andean Pact Summit in La Paz in 1990, the member states took several decisions which together constituted real progress toward the common goal of enhanced Andean integration. With the dismantlement of trade and other barriers, commerce among the member states would become increasingly free, the airlines of member states would operate freely on routes linking them, and modifications to the Andean Code on foreign capital would reduce the concentration of capital in selected countries (St John 2012, 185–6). Meeting in Caracas in May 1991, the members committed to establishing a free trade zone by January 1992 and a common market by 1995. These plans were put on hold after the Fujimori government suspended constitutional rule in August 1992, precipitating a domestic political crisis and Peru's withdrawal from the Andean Group (Rivera 2014, 182). The retirement of Peru was a temporary setback for Group objectives to unify trade and customs regimes as it threatened to inhibit future Andean integration efforts. Undeterred, the remaining members of the Andean Group created a free trade zone in 1993 and began negotiations to harmonize customs policy, reaching agreement in 1994 on a common external tariff that covered 90 percent of imports (St John 1996, 131–3; Bákula 2002, 1548).

In April 1994, Andean Pact Decision 353 detailed the terms of Peru's return to the Andean Group. Peru was to begin immediately to harmonize its macroeconomic policies and external trade negotiations with those of the Group. At the same time, it was to implement a zero tariff rate on intra-regional trade products currently assessed at 5 percent and later to expand this rate to all items, assuming there was progress in the harmonization of trade mechanisms and policies. Peru planned for full reintegration into the Andean Group by June 1995; however, the January 1995 Ecuador–Peru war delayed plans for full reentry into the Group until 1997 (Chan-Sánchez 1995, 4–5). In 1996, the Protocol of Trujillo renamed the Andean Group the Andean Community of Nations (*Comunidad Andina de Naciones*, CAN) and created a General Secretariat based in Lima. The charter of the General Secretariat included both technical and political functions, giving an enhanced political direction to the integration process (Salazar 2000, 881–906). In June 1996, Bolivia joined the Southern Common Market as an associate member. Five years earlier, Argentina, Brazil, Paraguay, and Uruguay had created MERCOSUR with a goal to expand trade through economic integration (Rivera 2014, 226–8). Bolivia's Complementary Economic Agreement (ACE36) with MERCOSUR included it in the organization's free trade zone but not in its customs union (*FT*: 17.12.96). Associate membership in MERCOSUR complemented Bolivia's participation in the Andean Community, its energy partnerships with Argentina and Brazil, and to a lesser degree, increasingly controversial talks for membership in the Free Trade Area of the Americas (*Área de Libre Comerico de las Américas*, ALCA) (Seoane 2000c; Quiroga 2003). ALCA was a US initiative which called for the establishment of a free-trade zone throughout the Americas. It provoked widespread opposition in Bolivia and elsewhere in the region, failed to meet the end-2005 deadline for implementation, and was never finalized (Rivera 2014, 247–9).

In 1998, the Andean Community and MERCOSUR signed an accord committing them to the creation of a free trade area by January 2000, and in 1999, they concluded a Complementary Economic Agreement (ACE39) (*El Diario*: 30.08.00). In 2001, an Andean Passport came into being, enabling citizens to travel within the Andean Community without a visa (*El Diario*: 26.06.01). In January 2002, the CAN heads of state met in Santa Cruz where they discussed changes to the free trade area and the common external tariff (*El Peruano*: 31.01.02; *El Diario*: 15.02.02). Later in the year, the Andean Community and MERCOSUR signed a Complementary Economic Agreement (ACE56) calling for the establishment of a free trade area. In December 2003, the Andean Community and MERCOSUR signed a free trade agreement (*El Diario*: 17.12.03), and in October 2004, they concluded a new Complementary Economic Agreement (ACE 59) which called for the phasing out of all import tariffs over 15 years. In the interim, the secretary general of the Andean Community, Alan Wagner, highlighted Bolivia's landlocked condition as a concern for all CAN members because it presented special problems for regional integration (*La Razón*: 29.01.04). In September 2004, a UN resolution recognized the creation within the Andean Community of an Andean Zone of Peace (*Zona de Paz Andina*) free of biological, chemical, and nuclear weapons. It also recognized the intent of CAN members to eradicate anti-personnel mines from the subregion, a long-standing problem on the Bolivia–Chile border which Chile had been addressing (St John 2010, 165).

The nineteenth session of the OAS General Assembly met in Washington, D.C. in November 1989. Over the previous decade, OAS interest in and support for the maritime issue had declined. In response, the Paz Zamora administration successfully pushed in this session for a continuing resolution on the issue. Resolution 989 reaffirmed the importance of finding a solution to Bolivia's maritime issue and called for it to be on the agenda of future meetings. At the twenty-second OAS General Assembly meeting in the Bahamas in 1992, the foreign minister of Bolivia, Ronald MacLean Abaroa, called for Chile to open a dialogue with Bolivia with no limits on what could be discussed. In response, Enrique Silva Cimma, the foreign minister of Chile, reiterated the long-held Chilean position that Chile had no outstanding maritime issue with Bolivia because the terms of the 1904 treaty were irreversible. Throughout the 1990s, there was little change in the respective positions of Bolivia and Chile. At the annual meetings of the OAS General Assembly, Bolivia repeatedly called for bilateral talks with no preconditions aimed at providing it with a sovereign outlet to the Pacific Ocean. Chile invariably responded with offers to discuss ways to improve Bolivian access to the sea but refused to consider a sovereign outlet through Chilean territory. With bilateral talks deadlocked, Bolivia developed an increasingly sophisticated policy statement on the economic costs of being landlocked. At the June 1998 session of the OAS General Assembly in Caracas, for example, Foreign Minister Murillo gave a presentation on the negative impact of being without a seaport, arguing Bolivia's landlocked status had cost it $4 billion over the last decade (Orias 2000, 397–413). Over time, Bolivian officials expanded this argument to include claims that the absence of a sovereign port and merchant navy retarded industrial and technological development and hampered regional cooperation and integration (*FT*: 23.03.04; *El Diario*: 29.06.04).

At the end of an OAS Special Conference on Security in October 2003, Bolivia adhered to the "Declaration on Security in the Americas," and it also approved a side agreement in which OAS members committed to fighting terrorism, organized crime, drug trafficking, and money laundering (*MH*: 29.10.03). At the OAS General Assembly meeting in Quito in June 2004, the Mesa administration introduced *The Blue Book: The Maritime Claim of Bolivia* (*El Libro Azul: La demanda marítima boliviana*), an illustrated summary of the maritime dispute (Bolivia 2004). In a detailed letter to OAS Secretary General César Gaviria and OAS member states, Chile quickly rejected the arguments contained in *The Blue Book* (*Los Tiempos*: 07.06.04; *El Mercurio*: 24.06.04). In May 2005, the OAS elected José Miguel Insulza, the incumbent interior minister of Chile, as its new secretary general. In the final ballot, Bolivia and Peru refused to join a pro-Insulza consensus despite last minute pressure from the United States. Bolivia abstained and Peru cast a blank vote with both countries citing past disputes with Chile as the reason for their actions (*El Diario*: 02.04.05; *MH*: 03.05.05). One month later, the OAS General Assembly met in Fort Lauderdale, Florida. In a bitterly divisive session, the US delegation proposed the OAS create a permanent committee to monitor the state of democracy in member states, including in Bolivia. Widely perceived as a veiled attack on the Venezuelan government of Hugo Chavez, Bolivia joined other OAS members in rejecting the US proposal and adopting a modified version which stressed the need to attack poverty in the region (*La Razón*: 04.06.05).

In addition to the Organization of American States, Bolivia continued to participate in a growing number of other regional and international organizations. In 1996 alone, the Sánchez de Lozada administration hosted the Río Group (*Grupo de Río*, G-Río), the Summit of the Americas for Sustainable Development (*Cumbre de las Américas para el Desarrollo Sostenible*), and the sixth reunion of the First Ladies of the Americas (*Primeras Damas de las Américas*). One year later, Bolivia hosted a summit of CAN heads of state in Sucre (Mesa Gisbert 2001b, 773–4). In September 2001, the Quiroga administration adhered to the Inter-American Democratic Charter, a Peruvian initiative which identified representative democracy as indispensable for the stability, peace, and development of the region. In May 2003, the Sánchez de Lozada administration signed the Cuzco Consensus, a joint statement issued at the end of a Río Group summit which tied strengthening democratic governance to poverty alleviation and called for reform of the UN system. In December 2004, the Mesa administration joined neighboring states in creating the South American Community of Nations (*Comunidad Sudamericana de Naciones*, CSN), a union of two trade groups, CAN and MERCOSUR, both of which continued to exist in their own right. At the time, the newly created CSN had a population of more than 360 million people, a GDP of some $800 million, and exports approaching $190 billion (*La Razón*: 08.12.04).

In November 2003, UN Secretary General Kofi Annan offered his good offices in resolving the maritime dispute, a proposal Chile immediately rejected (*El Diario*: 15.11.03). Addressing the UN General Assembly in September 2004, President Mesa compared Bolivia's landlocked status to "a rock in the shoe" (*una piedra en el zapato*) that makes it difficult for Bolivia to walk the talk to regional integration (*El Diario*: 23.09.04). From time to time, the United Nations expressed interest in finding a solution to the maritime issue; however, Bolivia continued to focus its efforts on the Organization of American States (*El Diario*: 18.06.04; *El Diario*: 29.07.05). At the same time, Bolivia continued to advocate for reform of the UN Security Council, including an increase in its permanent and nonpermanent membership, and a reduction in global arms spending (Torres 2000c; *El Diario*: 21.09.04).

Although Bolivia continued to participate in international gatherings of landlocked states, the number and impact of those meetings declined. Moreover, with most landlocked states focused on improved transit rights, there was little support in those meetings for Bolivia's claim to a sovereign port on the Pacific. For example, a 2003 UNCTAD meeting of landlocked and transit developing countries attended by both Bolivia and Chile focused on improving air, rail and road transport; inland waterways and ports; pipelines; and communications. There was no mention in the meeting objectives, final report, or final declaration of Bolivia's quest for a sovereign outlet to the sea (UN 2003). In a June 2004 meeting with UNCTAD officials, President Mesa acknowledged the problem when he noted that Bolivia differed from the other 31 landlocked developing nations in that Bolivia was the only country to have had a sovereign seacoast at independence later losing it in what he described as a war provoked by Chile (*El Diario*: 15.06.04). In the end, these occasional gatherings of landlocked states offered Bolivia little more than encouragement and support in its ongoing documentation of the inherent economic disadvantages of a landlocked state (Faye et al. 2004; Uprety 2006, 13–22).

**Beginning of the End**

The two decades after 1985 marked both the highpoint of US power and influence in Bolivia and the beginning of its end. US policy in the Andean region in general and in Bolivia in particular was known as the "3 Ds" (democracy, development, and drug control). The US government employed three primary instruments in support of these objectives. First, it worked with the IMF and the World Bank to promote neoliberal economic policies (Shultz 2008b, 124–31, 137–40). In the mid-1980s, Bolivia was the first Latin American state to embrace the tenets of neoliberal economic reform, policy prescriptions which became known in the 1990s as the Washington Consensus (Siekmeier 2011, 155–6). Second, it engaged in a form of brokered democracy in which the US embassy was deeply involved in the domestic politics of Bolivia, especially the selection of the country's presidents (Lindsay 2005, 6). Third, the Drug Enforcement Agency (DEA) and related US military and police bodies worked closely with Bolivia's security agencies in support of the war on drugs (*WP*: 23.04.91; *NYT*: 20.09.92). As Lehman noted, "all three policies were pursued in ways that were more in line with US than Bolivian interests, though US officials seemed to assume the two were synonymous" (Lehman 2016, 15–16, quote 16; Morales 2002, 7–9; Heilman 2017, 208–9).

In policy statements, US officials generally discussed the "3 Ds" as democracy, development, and drug control, but in practice, they reversed the order. Drug control always came first with the amount of development assistance conditional on effective drug control measures and the successful implementation of neoliberal policies (Gamarra 2005, 4–6). US policy in this regard was based on the false assumption that there was a positive relationship between neoliberal economic policies and improved narcotics control when the reverse was true. As Andreas emphasized, drug production in Bolivia "both facilitates and is fueled by neo liberal reforms and orthodox austerity measures" (1995, 76). Consequently, US foreign policy goals in Bolivia often were in direct conflict with US drug enforcement initiatives (Morales 2001, 126–8). The promotion of democracy was third on the US priority list and mostly focused on technical matters like holding elections (Siekmeier 2011, 162; Lehman 2016, 18–19). Washington appeared "to favor a limited concept of representative democracy," an approach which supported "elections and government institutions while stamping out any grassroots challenge to the underpinnings" of the existing economic and political system (Lindsay 2005, 5–6, quote 6; Morales 2002, 24–7). During the 2002 presidential race, US Ambassador Manuel Rocha actively intervened in the election, stating that US development aid would be at risk if Evo Morales was elected president (Dangl 2007, 51–2; Siekmeier 2011, 170–1). After President Mesa was forced to step down in June 2005, Washington blamed the chaos in Bolivia on Venezuelan President Hugo Chávez and his mentor, Fidel Castro, instead of recognizing it for what it was, the product of a complex mix of socioeconomic and political issues (St John 2005a, 3–4).

In pursuit of its "3 Ds" policy, several aspects of US conduct were particularly galling to Bolivians. The US embassy insisted on an extradition agreement, and it refused to grant visas to Bolivians it suspected of being involved in the drug trade. It also demanded immunity for US personnel working in Bolivia, arguing immunity agreements were needed to protect US citizens from politically biased prosecutions (*El Diario*: 22.01.04; *MH*: 23.10.05). When Bolivia and other Latin American states balked at signing immunity agreements, Washington threatened to cut off development assistance (*El Diario*: 31.08.03; *La Razón*: 20.12.03). Presidential Certification, a process through which the US president scored Bolivia each year on its compliance with US drug policies, was another bone of contention (*El Diario*: 03.02.00). The process was far from transparent and often seemed to Bolivians to be based more on political concerns than on factual data (Morales 2002, 14–15). With the United States ever far from winning the war on drugs, the US policy of rewarding the Bolivian security forces with favors, resources, and invitations to training schools also was criticized. To many Bolivians, this policy appeared to be aimed more at controlling Bolivia than controlling drugs (Lehman 2016, 18).

In December 2003, former President Jimmy Carter visited Bolivia (*La Razón*: 17.12.03). In a short, three-page trip report, he captured most of the contradictions long present in US policy toward Bolivia. His first briefing was with US Ambassador David Greenlee and his staff who noted that the top US priorities in Bolivia were the promotion of democracy and the conduct of an extensive coca eradication program. Later, Carter met with the leaders of the major political parties in the country (*El Diario*: 18.12.03). In the course of those discussions, he found it "interesting that everyone took for granted the deep involvement of the United States in the internal political affairs of

Bolivia. Two of the party leaders expressed resentment at having been forced by the United States during previous elections to join coalitions against their will, claiming threats that they would be denied visas and 'blackballed' re their political futures." Finally, Carter met with media executives, civil society, indigenous groups, union leaders, and church leaders. He found agreement here that "the present harsh [coca] eradication program often violates human rights and encourages violence, results in the deaths of many coca growers and police," does not provide reasonable compensation for crop substitution programs, and divides Bolivia socially and politically (Carter 2003, 1–3, quotes 2).

The election of Evo Morales in December 2005 signaled the failure of US policy in Bolivia since the end of World War II. In a May 2006 cable entitled "Economic Roots of Bolivia's Social Revolution," the US embassy in La Paz belatedly recognized the bankruptcy of neoliberal policies in Bolivia.

> Economic factors, which have fed the growing political disaffection of Bolivia's majority poor, have helped fuel the country's rolling "social revolution." Take persistent poverty. The percentage of Bolivia's population living below the poverty line has remained virtually unchanged (over 60%) through the past decades' "neo-liberal" reforms, and even increased during the economic crisis of 1999–2003. Unemployment, too, spiked during the crisis and remains untenably high. Marked social and economic inequality – which has a rural-urban, a regional and also a distinctly racial dimension – is another decisive factor, and has spurred significant migration to cities.... In combination, these factors have undermined the faith of many Bolivians in the old economic and political order and reinforced public support for the Morales administration and its "new" economic experiment.
>
> (WikiLeaks Cablegate 2006)

## Concluding observations

Bolivian foreign policy has long contained a heavy economic component, and this was increasingly the case at the turn of the millennium. Bolivia was an active participant in the Andean Community of Nations, and it expanded its relationship with MERCOSUR. Moreover, the development of the second largest natural gas reserves in South America enabled Bolivia to expand bilateral relations with Argentina, Brazil, and Paraguay. Taking advantage of a new spirit of regionalism, Bolivia worked to expand and diversify trade with its neighbors as it became the energy center for the southern cone of South America. Economic considerations also dominated bilateral relations with Peru. The Peruvian government worked tirelessly to make Ilo the port of exit for Bolivian natural gas in part because it meant a special pipeline for the Peruvian gas field at Camisea would not have to be built.

Bolivia participated in a growing number of regional and international organizations, and in the process, it sustained an impressive informational campaign in support of its quest for a sovereign outlet to the Pacific. Bolivian efforts in multinational forums generated considerable sympathy and repeated pledges of moral support but no fruitful initiatives and little in the way of practical support. The same was true of Bolivian participation in the occasional gatherings of landlocked and transit states. Bolivia was often the odd man out in such meetings in that its quest for a sovereign exit to the sea was at odds with the focus of other participants on improved transit rights. The Peruvian government provided strong moral support to Bolivia but distanced itself from any consideration of Peru as a potential site for a sovereign Bolivian port. In the wake of the Charaña talks, Chile showed no interest in considering a sovereign port for Bolivia at or near Arica. Often pressured in regional and international forums, Chile retreated to an intransigent policy based on the sanctity of international agreements, non-intervention, and the inviolability of the 1904 treaty. At the end of the day, Bolivia was left alone to negotiate with Chile but the latter showed little interest in negotiating, at least not on terms acceptable to Bolivia.

The water and gas wars bedeviled the Banzer, Quiroga, Sánchez de Lozada, and Mesa administrations, exposing the link between tumultuous government and compromised diplomacy. The movement for greater regional autonomy in the eastern departments of Bolivia also impacted the nation's foreign policy, notably with Argentina, Brazil, and Chile. While no one expected departments like Santa Cruz and Tarija to become independent, movements for regional autonomy raised concerns in neighboring states eager to consummate stable long-term agreements. The dominant US role in Bolivia for much of the last half century also fell victim to domestic politics. For decades, the US embassy articulated a policy of democracy, development, and drug control with drug control as the primary US interest. US intervention in the presidential politics of Bolivia, largely in support of the war on drugs, came to an abrupt end with the election of Evo Morales.

# 9 Evo Morales, 2006–

The pursuit of neoliberal economic policies and hardline anti-drug programs from the Paz Estenssoro to the Bánzer governments shattered any existing consensus within the body politic, setting the stage for the election of Evo Morales in December 2005. President Morales quickly abandoned the neoliberal policies that had prevailed in Bolivia since 1985, implementing dramatic changes to the direction, content, and tone of Bolivian foreign policy. The Morales government played a more prominent role in international forums, pursuing goals of greater social justice, national sovereignty, and democracy in global affairs. It also expanded ties with Europe and Asia and participated in a growing number of regional blocs and organizations. On the maritime issue, President Morales pursued legal recourse with Chile at the International Court of Justice, simultaneously working with Peru to improve Bolivian access to the Pacific through the port of Ilo. Finally, the Morales administration revamped Bolivia's long-standing relationship with the United States in pursuit of enhanced sovereignty and greater independence.

## The New History of Bolivia

Narrowly losing in 2002, Juan Evo Morales Ayma and his Movement toward Socialism (*Movimiento al Socialismo*, MAS), a party with direct roots in the coca grower (*cocalero*) movement, won a resounding victory in the 2005 presidential elections (*El Diario*: 19.12.05). After campaigning on a policy of "coca yes, cocaine no" (*coca sí, cocaina no*), President-elect Morales refused to step down from a leadership role in the coca union, raising doubts about the future of Bolivia's long-standing anti-narcotics policy (Crandall 2008, 104, 110–12; Morales 2010, 260). Earning 54 percent of the popular vote, the Morales landslide marked the first time in the post-military era that a Bolivian president was elected outright by an absolute majority. Morales also was the first democratically elected Bolivian president of indigenous heritage (Pinto and Navia 2007, 182–5, 222–3; Klein 2011, 287–8). His elevation to the presidency marked a peaceful, democratic transition of power from the nonindigenous ruling elite to the indigenous majority, symbolizing the integration of indigenous peoples into the Bolivian political system. Morales' election was due in part to corruption and misrule and in part to the failure of the ruling elite to acknowledge the shortcomings of the neoliberal economic model (*NYT*: 20.01.06).

The ability of Morales to galvanize the myriad social movements and organizations demanding change was essential to his victory (Hylton and Thomson 2007, 127–8). Casting himself as a uniting figure, he also drew support from middle class professionals and small entrepreneurs who saw an opportunity for social peace in a country in which the economy in the past was often paralyzed by social unrest (Salman 2007; Gamarra 2007, 15). Morales based his political platform on the "October Agenda," a set of opposition demands which President Mesa had accepted after the Sánchez de Lozada government resigned in October 2003 (Crabtree and Chaplin 2013, 8, 11). Key elements included the nationalization of the oil and gas industry, a constituent assembly to draft a new constitution to increase the power and rights of "original peoples" (*pueblos originarios*), and a national referendum on regional autonomy (Morales 2010, 238–43). In December 2005, President-elect Morales stated that his election marked the onset of "the new history of Bolivia" (*la nueva historia de Bolivia*) (*La Razón*: 26.12.05).

On 1 May 2006, the Morales administration partially renationalized the hydrocarbon industry via Supreme Decree 28701, forcing foreign contractors to sign new contracts which enhanced the role of the state oil company, YPFB, and increased the revenues payable to the state (Hylton and Thomson 2007, 133–4). This was the third time Bolivia had nationalized the energy sector, following earlier occasions involving the Standard Oil Company of Bolivia in 1937 and Bolivian Gulf Oil in 1969 (Crabtree and Chaplin 2013, 112). The Morales government gave the companies operating in Bolivia 180 days to negotiate new contracts with YPFB which ceded majority control to the state (*El Diario*: 02.05.06). In so doing, Bolivia demanded the previous formula for profit sharing be reversed with 82 percent in the form of royalty earnings and taxes now going to the state and the remaining 18 percent left for the foreign companies (*La Razón*: 29.10.06). All of the international companies signed new agreements, including the Brazilian giant Petrobras which controlled 46 percent of Bolivian gas reserves prior to renationalization and the Spanish–Argentine consortium Repsol–YPF which controlled 27 percent of those reserves (Hindery 2013, 150–3).

The partial renationalization process, implemented by the army in a highly publicized military operation in May 2005, was not well received by the foreign oil companies or their governments. In turn, radical elements in Bolivia strongly condemned it as a half measure instead of the total nationalizations accomplished in the past. In mid-January, president-elect Morales had met with President Lula of Brazil and promised to respect foreign investments, especially the Bolivian operations of Petrobras (*El Diario*: 14.01.06). After Morales broke that promise, bilateral relations with Brazil were strained for months over the way Petrobras was treated. Brazil announced a freeze on future investment in Bolivia and refused for a time to pay higher prices for

Bolivian gas (*WSJ*: 10.05.06). When Argentina agreed to pay higher prices for Bolivian gas, its decision exacerbated Brazilian relations with Bolivia (Philip and Panizza 2011, 143–5; Tini 2008, 212–15). Bolivia conditioned future gas sales to Argentina on a prohibition to resell Bolivian gas to Chile which also affected Bolivian relations with Chile (*La Razón*: 23.05.06). Finally, with Total of France and British Gas active in Bolivia, bilateral relations with France and Great Britain as well as Spain also were strained (Gamarra 2007, 20–2, 34; Farthing and Kohl 2014, 38–9).

While the nationalization of the energy sector was expected, what was not anticipated was the Morales administration's rejection of the privatization program which had dominated national policy since the 1990s (*La Razón*: 06.03.06). Slowly but surely, the state took over all electricity and telecommunication companies, recreated a state airlines company, and pushed for state control over all mineral resources (*MH*: 10.05.06; *La Razón*: 26.06.06). The policies of the Morales government increased state revenues to an impressive degree but had a dampening effect on foreign direct investment for a time (Klein 2011, 288–9; Hindery 2013, 153, 162–3).

In July 2006, Bolivia elected a Constituent Assembly dominated by Morales supporters with a charter to draft and approve a new constitution. Although the results of the election clearly demonstrated how established MAS had become, the ruling party failed to achieve the two-thirds majority required to exert absolute control and ease the passage of constitutional changes (Hylton and Thomson 2007, 138–42). Consequently, constitutional reform became a prolonged struggle between the statist model inherited from the 1952 Revolution and the more recent neoliberal model of the last two decades. Approved by voters in January 2009, the new Political Constitution of the State affirmed the unitary, plurinational, and secular character of Bolivia (*El Diario*: 26.01.09). It also expanded the rights of indigenous peoples, granting them more seats in the legislature, land rights, cultural recognition, and community autonomy. The new charter also approved increased local and departmental autonomy; however, implementation was contingent on additional legislation which had to be approved by two-thirds of the legislature. In response to the earlier militarization of the anti-coca campaign which included the placement of US military units in Bolivia, article ten of the constitution prohibited foreign military bases on Bolivian soil. Finally, the 2009 Constitution set a limit of two consecutive five-year terms for the president, a stipulation President Morales would contest in 2014 and 2019. Taken as a whole, the new charter helped to resolve some of the contradictions in Bolivian society, but it also gave rise to new tensions and conflicts (Crabtree and Chaplin 2013, 13, 182; Farthing and Kohl 2014, 39–43).

On the same day as the Constituent Assembly election, Bolivians voted in a national referendum on regional autonomy. The results of the referendum mirrored the long-standing regional and partisan polarization which had surfaced most recently in the 2005 presidential and 2006 assembly elections (St John 2005b, 2). The eastern lowland departments, known as the *media luna* (half moon or crescent moon), voted strongly in favor of autonomy, reflecting sympathies evident for decades, but the western highland departments overwhelmingly opposed it. In the end, some 57 percent of voters opposed granting the departments additional autonomy; nevertheless, demands for more autonomy did not abate after the referendum. Regional support for autonomy was centered in the city and department of Santa Cruz, and antigovernment strikes, widespread instability, and violent confrontations were common in the *media luna* from 2007 to 2009 (Gamarra 2007, 18; Morales 2010, 246–54). The expansion of large-scale agriculture in the department of Santa Cruz had attracted considerable foreign investment, primarily from Brazil but also from Argentina, Paraguay, and Chile (*FT*: 12.05.06). Moreover, Bolivian gas reserves were concentrated in the south, mainly in the department of Tarija. Therefore, the instability in the *media luna* which brought Bolivia to the brink of civil conflict in 2008 was worrisome to Bolivia's neighbors who were heavily invested in the country and dependent on it for natural gas (Crabtree and Chaplin 2013, 115, 139–40, 180; Farthing and Kohl 2014, 45–6).

## Axis of Good

As the Morales administration implemented domestic reforms, it took foreign policy initiatives which signaled a major redirection of Bolivian foreign policy. Immediately after the election, President-elect Morales promised to renegotiate commercial agreements with Chile concluded during the Rodríguez government, emphasizing that all future negotiations with Chile would be conducted through the prism of Bolivia's maritime demands (*El Diario*: 21.12.05). Traveling to Cuba, his first trip abroad as president-elect, Morales was warmly greeted by President Fidel Castro, a mentor since the late 1980s (*La Razón*: 01.01.06). Following Cuban promises of educational and medical assistance, Morales distanced himself from the George W. Bush administration, stating he would not be pressured by Washington (Gamarra 2007, 13–14). Returning to La Paz, Morales met with US Ambassador David Greenlee in a meeting which, according to vice president-elect Alvaro García Linera who also attended the meeting, focused on democracy and drugs (*Los Tiempos*: 03.01.06). The US embassy refused to comment on the content of the meeting; however, a State Department spokesperson later said the United States was willing to work with any democratically elected government that governed democratically, adding a second condition in the Bolivian case would be cooperation in the war on drugs (*El Comercio*: 03.01.06).

A day after the Greenlee meeting, Morales embarked on a seven-nation international tour, designed in part to demonstrate his ability to work with world leaders. Venezuela was the first stop in a tour which included Belgium, Brazil, China, France, South Africa, and Spain. In Caracas, Morales praised Venezuelan President Hugo Chávez, a long-time ally and vocal critic of US-led trade initiatives (Philip and Panizza 2011, 123). In turn, Chávez termed the Castro–Chávez–Morales relationship an "axis of good" (*eje del bien*) after President Bush earlier had described Iran, Iraq, and North Korea as an "axis of evil" (*El Mundo*: 03.01.06; *El Comercio*: 03.01.06). Thereafter, the Chávez government invested heavily in Bolivia, especially in the hydrocarbon sector (*El Comercio*: 26.05.06). PDVSA (*Petróleos de Venezuela, S.A.*), the Venezuelan state petroleum company, and YPFB organized mixed companies to operate service station chains, installed plants for gas liquefaction, and implemented industrialization projects to produce petrochemical products. In contrast to his warm reception in Venezuela, European leaders mostly greeted Morales with caution, maintaining a certain distance from him (*FT*: 04.01.06; *NYT*: 05.01.06). At the European Union, Javier Solana, the High Representative for Common Foreign and Security Policy, stressed how important it was for Bolivia to respect private investment and support the war on drugs (*El Diario*: 06.01.06). Appearing to take the message to heart, Morales emphasized during his visit to France that his government would cooperate in the drug war as long as it was not a pretext for the maintenance of US control over Bolivia (*El Diario*: 08.01.06). After describing international energy companies as "partners," he denounced neoliberalism as the wrong answer to poverty (St John 2006, 3–4). In Beijing, Morales met with President Hu Jintao. One day later, he referred to China as an "ideological ally" and asked for Chinese help in developing Bolivian gas reserves. According to the *New China News Agency*, President Hu promised "strong and prestigious" Chinese companies would invest in Bolivia (*NYT*: 10.01.06).

## America's Worst Nightmare

On the campaign trail, Morales had pledged to become America's worst nightmare, and soon after his election, a State Department official referred to him as "potentially our [America's] worst nightmare" (*NYT*: 21.12.05). Predictably, Bolivia's role in the Andean drug war soon became a major point of disagreement with the United States (Crandall 2008, 104–6). Despite marked differences over coca cultivation, the US government initially sought to avoid outright confrontation with the Morales government but that quickly proved impossible (Gamarra 2007, 4–5, 31–2; Heilman 2017, 252–3). In February 2006, the Bush administration reduced military aid by 96 percent in retaliation for the refusal of the Bolivian Congress to ratify a bilateral agreement exempting US military personnel from the jurisdiction of the International Criminal Court (ICC) (*NYT*: 09.02.06; *La Razón*: 07.03.06). Three months later, President Bush singled out Bolivia in a speech, criticizing the status of its democracy (*El Diario*: 23.05.06). Bolivian demands for the extradition of ex-President Sánchez de Lozada, living comfortably in the United States, to stand trial in Bolivia for the October 2003 massacre of indigenous protesters was another bone of contention (*La Razón*: 27.09.07; *El Diario*: 19.10.06). In October 2007, the Morales government announced Bolivia's gradual withdrawal from the Western Hemisphere Institute for Security Cooperation

(WHINSEC), formerly known as the US Army School of the Americas. Bolivia cited WHINSEC's history of collaboration with repressive regimes and human rights abuses as reasons for its withdrawal. Nine years later, President Morales opened an anti-imperialist military school to train military leaders from Bolivia and like-minded countries like Cuba, Nicaragua, and Venezuela. Officially known as the *Escuela Antiimperialista de los Pueblos del Abya Yala y de las Fuerzas Armadas* (FFAA), the school was named after General Juan José Torres Gonzales whose short-lived government temporarily expelled the US Peace Corps in 1970. Schooled in subjects like the theory of imperialism and the geopolitics of natural resources, the first class of 150 officers graduated from the "Juan José Torres Gonzales" school in December 2016 (*La Razón*: 19.08.16; *La Razón*: 16.12.16).

In February 2008, a US embassy official left Bolivia and did not return after reports surfaced that he had asked Peace Corps volunteers and a Fulbright scholar to report on the activities of Cuban and Venezuelan nationals working in Bolivia (*MH*: 13.02.08). In mid-September 2008, President Morales expelled US Ambassador Philip S. Goldberg on the grounds he had violated Bolivian national sovereignty by interfering in its internal political affairs and supporting rebellious groups in the *media luna* (*NYT*: 11.09.08). The Bush administration responded by expelling Mario Gustavo Guzmán Saldaña, the Bolivian ambassador to the United States, in a tit-for-tat move (Carlsen 2008, 2). Later in September, the United States temporarily suspended Peace Corps operations in Bolivia due to growing political instability, especially in the *media luna*. Having announced earlier that Bolivia was not compliant in its counternarcotics commitments under the Andean Trade Promotion and Drug Enforcement Act, the Bush White House in November 2008 suspended the preferential treatment Bolivian goods had been receiving in US markets under the Andean Trade Promotion and Drug Enforcement Act (Crandall 2008, 115–18). The suspension of duty free access to the United States cost Bolivia an estimated 20,000 jobs and deprived it of $150 million a year in export earnings (*WP*: 19.10.08; *NYT*: 24.10.08). The Morales government responded by suspending the activities of the Drug Enforcement Agency, announcing Bolivia would take control of all activities in the war on drugs. Bolivia also suspended temporarily the activities of the Agency for International Development (USAID) on the grounds it was plotting with opposition groups in eastern Bolivia (*Reuters*: 03.11.08).

## Shifting Alliances

Following almost two decades of a neoliberal model based on free-market principles, regionalism in Latin America underwent a radical transformation in the first decade of the new millennium. Old initiatives were reconsidered, and new schemes emerged. At the same time, new principles which went beyond trade issues to include social and political dimensions changed the norms and processes of regional economic integration (Mouline 2013, 1–2;

Briceño-Ruiz and Morales 2017, 1). In mid-April 2006, President Hugo Chávez announced Venezuela was withdrawing from the Andean Community after two members, Colombia and Peru, signed free trade agreements with the United States (*Perú21*: 22.04.06). Venezuela's departure from CAN came at the same time as the announcement of its fast-track incorporation into MERCOSUR. Ten days later, Bolivia joined the Bolivarian Alliance for the Peoples of Our America (*Alianza Bolivariana para los Pueblos de Nuestra América*, ALBA), established in 2004 by Fidel Castro and Hugo Chávez as a socialist alternative to the Free Trade Area of the Americas (Malamud 2006a; Malamud 2006b). ALBA later evolved into a subregional cooperation and integration project comprising 11 countries (Antigua and Barbuda, Bolivia, Cuba, Dominica, Ecuador, Grenada, Nicaragua, Saint Kitts and Nevis, Saint Lucia, St. Vincent and the Grenadines, and Venezuela). Funded by the Venezuelan government, ALBA was more an ideological body than one with any real potential for future economic or political development (Philip and Panizza 2011, 162, Rivera 2014, 252). In theory, member countries were supposed to give each other preferential treatment in specific economic sectors; in practice, little trade was transacted under the agreement. Instead, ALBA focused on social projects in areas like culture, education, and health as well as controversial political issues, notably the US-led international campaign targeting Nicolás Maduro who assumed the presidency of Venezuela after Hugo Chávez died of cancer in 2013 (*La Razón*: 17.03.15; *LAHT*: 15.12.17).

Venezuela's withdrawal from the Andean Community was regrettable, but it had the positive effect of reducing the conflicted relationships which had dominated member states from the outset of negotiations for a free trade agreement (*La Razón*: 25.04.06). In a hasty act of solidarity, President Morales announced that Bolivia would not take its scheduled turn as president pro tempore of the Andean Community due to Venezuela's withdrawal. Morales then criticized Peru's negotiation of a free trade agreement with the United States, branding Peruvian President Toledo a traitor to the indigenous peoples of Latin America (*El Comercio*: 23.04.06). President Morales also denounced Colombian President Uribe for signing a free trade agreement with the United States. Finally, he accused the Secretary-General of the Andean Community, Allan Wagner, a two-time foreign minister of Peru, of disrespect when he allegedly failed to accommodate a Bolivian delegation during a CAN meeting in Lima (*La Razón*: 24.04.06).

The fourth Summit of Latin America, the Caribbean, and the European Union (*Cumbre de América Latina, el Caribe y la Unión Europea*, ALC-UE) was the largest gathering of heads of state and government since the 1815 Congress of Vienna (Maihold 2006). At the May 2006 meeting, EU leaders insisted the Andean Community arrive at a common position before opening talks for a free trade agreement. Rejecting bilateral pacts with member states, European leaders were especially critical of the investment and trade policies of the Morales and Chávez governments (*NYT*: 13.05.06). During the summit, President Morales reconsidered his earlier position and agreed to support CAN-EU trade talks, and he called on President Chávez to rethink his withdrawal from the Andean Community (*La Razón*: 13.05.06; *Perú21*: 15.05.06). President Morales later assumed the rotating CAN presidency, convening a summit in Quito to boost its revival. In June 2006, the presidents of Bolivia, Colombia, Ecuador, and Peru agreed to relaunch the Andean Community without Venezuela and to work to persuade the United States to extend trade preferences created to counter the narcotics trade (*Reuters*: 13.06.06). Morales acknowledged the right of CAN members to conclude bilateral trade agreements with the United States; however, he billed the decision, a clear policy reversal, as a necessary step in the fight against narcotrafficking as opposed to a concession to Washington (*La Razón*: 14.06.06).

At the South American Energy Summit in April 2007, the South American Community of Nations renamed their organization the Union of South American Nations (*Unión de Naciones Suramericanas*, UNASUR). The organization was formally established in May 2008 when its constitutive treaty was signed by the 12 member states, including Bolivia, and two observer countries, Mexico and Panama (Philip and Panizza 2011, 162–3; Rivera 2014, 252). ALBA, MERCOSUR by the mid-2000s, and UNASUR were substantially different from earlier regional schemes. "The initiatives of regionalism developed in Latin America after the mid-2000s aimed at being more than a defensive mechanism vis-à-vis globalization. Instead, regionalism came to be perceived as a space for contestation and resistance to neoliberalism" (Briceño-Ruiz and Morales 2017, 6–8, quote 8; Artaraz 2012, 161–5). When separatist groups in eastern Bolivia launched violent attacks against the central government in September 2008, UNASUR held an emergency meeting to discuss the situation, expressing in the Declaration of La Moneda its full support for the Morales government (Phillips 2008). On the other hand, when President Morales in 2009 called for UNASUR to reject foreign military bases in Latin America, his argument that the presence of US military bases in Colombia threatened regional security and integration mostly fell on deaf ears (*La República*: 27.08.09; *La Razón*: 10.12.09).

The fifth ALC-UE summit met in Lima in May 2008. The agenda focused on sustainable development and social progress, issues which reflected the asymmetries between the attendees.

> This asymmetry, pivotal in Latin American interventions, not only expresses the interest in a differentiated treatment of Latin America in trade negotiations between the EU and Central America (SICA), the Community of Andean Nations (CAN) and MERCOSUR, but also reflects contradictory political priorities in terms of thematic interests.
> (Maihold 2008, 1)

Asymmetry was clearly evident in pre-summit conflicts within CAN regarding the negotiation of free trade agreements with the European Union (*La República*: 16.05.08; *El Diario*: 14.07.08). Before the meeting opened,

Peruvian President García called for the European Union to hold talks with Colombia and Peru on an individual basis reminiscent of the approach which had led both countries to reach free trade agreements with the United States. President Morales immediately denounced the Peruvian proposal as a breach of the principle of Andean integration. Prior to the summit, Venezuelan President Chávez hurled insults at German Chancellor Angela Merkel, and during the meeting, Chávez and Ecuadorian President Correa clashed with Colombian President Uribe over the ongoing civil conflict in Colombia, undermining efforts at enhanced integration within the Andean Community or between it and the European Union. Given the different interests of the Latin American members, asymmetry threatened to become the new norm in Euro-Latin American relations (Maihold 2008, 2–3).

In the second decade of the new millennium, the Morales administration joined like-minded governments in continuing to push for a new model of regional integration which largely excluded Western powers. Following the creation of ALBA in 2004 and UNASUR in 2008, Bolivia joined 32 other countries in creating the Community of Latin American and Caribbean States (*Comunidad de Estados Latinoamericanos y Caribeños*, CELAC) in February 2010. CELAC offered the countries of the northern and southern hemisphere, with the exception of Canada and the United States, a new forum to deepen the socioeconomic and political development of the region, and as such, was seen by some countries as an alternative to the Organization of American States (Mouline 2013, 6–7). Over time, the OAS had become increasingly plagued by problems which included "disinterested member states, diplomatic deadlock, the re-assertion of the prerogative of national sovereignty, and lack of resources. It also suffered from the tensions inherent in US-Latin American relationships" (Binetti and Raderstorf 2018, 5). In June 2012, the foreign ministers of Bolivia, Ecuador, Nicaragua, and Venezuela announced they were withdrawing from the Inter-American Treaty of Reciprocal Assistance, a pact which called for member states to consider an armed attack against one of them to be an attack against all of them. In announcing their decision, they characterized the treaty as a US initiative which had become irrelevant. At the same time, they called for the reform or elimination of the Inter-American Commission on Human Rights (IACHR), accusing it of acting in concert with the US government to target socialist governments. Not surprisingly, the principal detractors of the IACHR were among the countries whose human rights records had drawn the most scrutiny from the commission in past years (*WP*: 05.06.12). Thereafter, the Morales administration continued to push for major reforms within the Organization of American states (*La Razón*: 24.03.13; *El Diario*: 01.04.17).

In December 2012, the MERCOSUR countries announced they were considering upgrading Bolivia from associate to full membership, and over the next six years, Bolivia progressed slowly but surely in that direction (*Reuters*: 17.07.15; *El Diario*: 22.12.17). In the meantime, the four-nation Pacific Alliance, launched in 2012 by Chile, Colombia, Mexico, and Peru, forged ahead to become a serious economic bloc while trade among MERCOSUR states declined as MERCOSUR moved "from success story to slow motion crisis" (Carranza 2017, 127–34, quote 127). Weakened by internal dissent, MERCOSUR faced serious obstacles to progress toward becoming a full-fledged customs union and common market. The major obstacle being the so-called "implementation gap," the failure of member states to implement the bloc's norms (*AP*: 22.05.13). Despite talk about integrating the Pacific Alliance and MERCOSUR, the division between the open, outward-looking vision of the former and the protectionist stance of the latter remained (Binetti and Raderstorf 2018, 2).

At the G-77+China summit held in Santa Cruz in June 2014, President Morales touted the economic reforms implemented by his administration, including its emphasis on sovereignty over natural resources, emancipation from the existing international financial system, and freedom from foreign interference. He also called for more attention to be paid to climate change and the environment, issues he had raised previously at the United Nations and in other international forums (*El Diario*: 15.06.14; *La Razón*: 01.12.16). At the historic VII Summit of the Americas which opened in Panama in June 2015 and which was attended by President Barack Obama and Cuban leader Fidel Castro, President Morales noted the political change sweeping the region, contending that "Latin America has changed forever" (*La Razón*: 12.04.15). In April 2018, Argentina, Brazil, Chile, Colombia, Paraguay, and Peru announced they were temporarily withdrawing from UNASUR, reflecting deep political divisions in an organization which operated on consensus (*Reuters*: 20.04.18). Although the division of UNASUR could be dismissed as simply another example of the breakdown of Latin America's much touted solidarity, reduced cooperation and integration meant "less coherence on extra-regional trade strategies; less trade and integration of value chains within the region; and fewer multilateral accountability mechanisms on democracy, human rights, anti-corruption measures, and economic openness" (Binetti and Raderstorf 2018, 1–4, quote 3–4). In that regard, the Bolivian government and its leftist or center-left allies, notably Ecuador and Venezuela, enjoyed some success in weakening if not destroying the old order but failed to replace it with a new one. As the second decade of the new millennium drew to a close, the impulse of post-neoliberalism momentum waned, leaving Latin America with overlapping approaches to regionalism.

Throughout the Morales years, Bolivia received the most EU bilateral economic aid of any state in Latin America, and the European Union was the largest aid source. It supported programs to improve access to basic services, promote job creation and poverty reduction, fight drug trafficking, strengthen the justice system, and improve watershed management (Farthing and Kohl 2014, 73). In 2014–20, Bolivia was targeted to be the largest Latin American recipient of EU bilateral aid with a total commitment of €281 million, and in 2018, the European Union increased its assistance to Bolivia, committing an additional €575 million to fight drug trafficking (*La Razón*: 10.06.15;

*LAHT*: 05.05.18). Individual European states, notably France and Germany, also supported the Morales government. The French government was especially active, agreeing to provide both development and security assistance. France financed a solar development project and two wind power sites and supported Bolivian scholarship students. In turn, Bolivia contracted with the French company Thales to install a €191 million radar defense system for military defense and air traffic control to better combat contraband and drug trafficking. Among other projects, Germany pursued participation in the lithium industry and in the proposed Bioceanic Railway Corridor Project, an ambitious undertaking linking the Brazilian port of Santos with the Peruvian port of Ilo and estimated to cost at least $10 billion (*La Razón*: 08.06.15; *Reuters*: 22.03.17). At the end of 2018, the Bolivian state company, YLB, and the German company, ACI Systems, announced a joint venture to extract lithium from the Uyuni salt flats and to build a lithium-hydroxide plant and a factory for electric vehicle batteries in Bolivia (*Reuters*: 12.12.18).

The Morales government also expanded bilateral ties with Russia with both sides viewing the other as both an economic partner and a political ally. In 2008, Bolivia signed a contract with Gazprom, the Russian gas group, for the exploration and exploitation of Bolivian gas reserves. In 2009, President Morales visited Moscow for talks on increased Russian military aid following the cutoff of US military assistance (*FT*: 18.03.08; *La Razón*: 16.02.09). During a 2013 meeting, President Morales and President Putin discussed wider economic cooperation in a number of areas, including energy, nuclear research, security, and trade (*El Diario*: 03.07.13). In July 2014, President

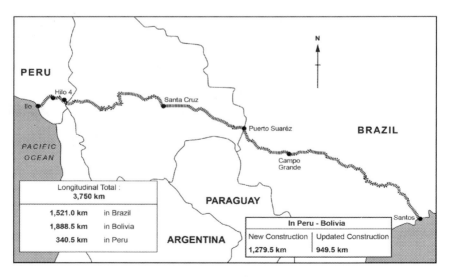

*Figure 9.1* Proposed Bioceanic Railway Corridor Project
Source: Nathan Bailey St John.

Putin offered to assist Bolivia in the development of a peaceful nuclear energy program, and in October 2015, Bolivia announced plans to build a $300 million nuclear research center with Russian technology (*Reuters*: 06.03.16). At the same time, Gazprom expanded its operations in the gas fields of southeastern Bolivia, and Bolivia invited Rosneft, Russia's largest oil company, to work in the country. After concluding a framework for bilateral military cooperation in 2009, Bolivia and Russia expanded the agreement in 2016 (*La Razón*: 24.08.17). In the interim, Bolivia ordered 20 jet fighters from Russia, allegedly for use in intercepting drug trafficking across its borders. As construction of the nuclear research center proceeded, Gazprom in June 2018 announced it would invest $1.2 billion in the Bolivian energy sector with a focus on exploration and production (*La Razón*: 15.07.17; *Reuters*: 14.06.18).

## Asian Openings

Before the turn of the century, Bolivia began to expand its relatively limited commercial and diplomatic relations with Asia. During the Siles Zuazo administration, Bolivia established diplomatic relations with the People's Republic of China (PRC) and suspended ties with the Government of the Republic of China (Taiwan). The Paz Estenssoro government opened embassies in Malaysia and Thailand, established diplomatic relations with Singapore and Vietnam, and strengthened relations with the PRC. President Paz Zamora was the first Bolivian head of state to visit the Pacific Basin when he traveled to the PRC, and President Sánchez de Lozada followed with visits to Japan and the PRC (Torres 1997, 51–4). At the turn of the century, Bolivia had diplomatic relations with 11 Asian states (Australia, China, Indonesia, Japan, Malaysia, New Zealand, the Philippines, Singapore, South Korea, Thailand, and Vietnam). Bolivia was not yet a member of Asia-Pacific Economic Cooperation forum (APEC), Pacific Basin Economic Council (PBEC), or Pacific Economic Cooperation Council (PECC); however, it had expressed interest in joining APEC (Barrios 1997, 2; Torres 1997, 185–99).

The visit of president-elect Morales to Beijing in January 2006 highlighted ongoing Bolivian interest in expanding relations with China (*La Razón*: 09.01.06). During the first Morales administration, commercial relations between Bolivia and the PRC were relatively limited, but political and military relations made significant advances. In December 2007, Foreign Minister Choquehuanca visited the PRC where he signed an agreement expanding economic and technical cooperation (*La Razón*: 20.12.07). A purge of Bolivia's military leadership during the first Morales government set the stage for an ideological reorientation of the military which accompanied the deepening relationship with China (*WP*: 17.01.06). After the Bolivian defense minister traveled to China in August 2006 to meet with his counterpart, the PRC announced the first of several gifts of military equipment. Most of the early Chinese investment in Bolivia was in the primary product sectors, but Chinese companies also began to expand into other areas, including telecommunications (Ellis 2009, 137–47).

Over the next few years, the Bolivia–China relationship continued to grow. President Morales returned to China in August 2011 and in December 2013. During the latter trip, Morales was present when China launched a satellite, the Tupac Katari, built by China for Bolivia (*Xinhua*: 19.12.13). Morales also met with Chinese President Xi Jinping in July 2014 during the first summit between the PRC and CELAC, the organization China chose as its main vehicle for engaging the region (Ellis 2018, 5). By 2014, Chinese trade with Bolivia had expanded six-fold when compared to 2000, and the PRC surpassed Brazil as the number one source of Bolivia's imports. The Bolivia–China trade relationship was heavily skewed in China's favor with the dollar value of Bolivian imports from China four times the value of its exports to the PRC. By 2016, China was Bolivia's largest creditor with Bolivia owing $680 million to Chinese financial institutions (Ellis 2017, 5–10; Agramont and Bonifaz 2018, 10–14, 19–20). Thereafter, Bolivian indebtedness to China continued to grow (*El Diario*: 05.10.16). President Morales boasted that the resultant development model liberated Bolivia from the onerous neoliberalism of the past; however, critics charged that it merely substituted "one imperialism for another" (Achtenberg 2017, 1–7, quote 2; La Marca 2017, 4). Military cooperation with the PRC also increased but not as much as in other areas (*La Razón*: 03.08.16). Institutional ties also expanded with deepening people-to-people ties in the form of visits, exchanges, and training (Ellis 2017, 5, 12). In 2018, President Morales returned to the PRC and concluded a strategic partnership with President Xi Jinping (*Xinhua*: 19.06.18). More than simply a "diplomatic designation," China used strategic partnerships "to facilitate coordination and advance its objectives with respect to trade, investment projects, and sometimes political issues" (Ellis 2018, 5).

The developing bilateral relationship between Bolivia and China carried with it strategic implications for Latin America as a whole. Located in the center of South America, Bolivia was something of a bridge between the Pacific-facing countries, Chile and Peru, and the Atlantic-facing countries, Argentina, Uruguay, and Brazil. Ongoing discussions concerning the Bioceanic Railway Corridor Project highlighted the importance of Bolivia's strategic location (*El Diario*: 03.02.16; *Reuters*: 14.12.17). At the same time, China continued to play a role in the efforts of Bolivia to develop its vast lithium reserves, a strategic resource in the development of mobile phones, electric cars, and more (*Reuters*: 27.12.17; *El Diario*: 19.10.18). In February 2019, the Morales government announced a $2.3 billion joint venture with China's Xinjiang TBEA Group to produce lithium from the Coipasa and Pastos Grandes salt flats (*Reuters*: 06.02.19). Bolivia also occupied a strategic political position. With the collapse of Venezuela, the limited Cuban rapprochement with the United States, and the election of right-of-center governments in Argentina and Brazil, Bolivia stood virtually alone as a proponent of popular socialism in the region. In this regard, its behavior in multilateral bodies, like CAN and the OAS, together with its support for political bodies with limited global support, like Iran and the Palestinians, often perplexed and bedeviled its neighbors (Ellis 2017, 4).

Long active in Bolivia, Japan supported the Morales administration albeit in a much more limited role than the PRC. In February 2004, Japan forgave $503 million in Bolivian debt, and at the outset of the Morales administration, it forgave another $67 million, the totality of Bolivian debt to Japan at the time (*El Diario*: 18.02.06). One year into his first term, President Morales made an official four-day visit to Japan in search of Japanese investment and markets for Bolivian products (*La Razón*: 05.03.07). The major Japanese project involved a reported $613 million loan for a geothermal project at Laguna Colorado (*El Diario*: 28.09.16). Elsewhere, Bolivia reopened its embassy in Seoul after a 15 year hiatus, and South Korea began to provide limited grant aid and technical assistance (*La Razón*: 12.01.15). Finally, the Morales government and the Lao People's Democratic Republic (Laos) established diplomatic relations, a small but symbolic step in terms of Bolivian relations with the Asia-Pacific Basin. Like Bolivia, Laos is a landlocked state with a socialist-style government.

As the Morales government expanded ties in the Far East, it rewrote Bolivia's relationship with the Middle East. The most dramatic change was the establishment of diplomatic relations with Iran (Morales 2016, 183–6). President Mahmoud Ahmadinejad called President-elect Morales in January 2006 to congratulate him on his electoral victory, and during a September 2007 visit to Bolivia, the Iranian president pledged to invest $1.1 billion in Bolivia over five years (*El Diario*: 28.09.07). Ahmadinejad's visit was criticized by the Bolivian opposition, including ex-President Quiroga, and the Bush administration considered it a threat to US national security (*La Razón*: 31.10.07). In August 2008, the Morales government established diplomatic relations with Libya, and a few weeks later, President Morales visited Iran to continue talks to boost bilateral ties (*WP*: 14.08.08; *El Diario*: 02.09.08). President Ahmadinejad returned to Bolivia in 2012, and one year later, Iran agree to cooperate with Bolivia in the energy sector. President Morales returned to Iran in 2015, and in 2016, Bolivia and Iran signed a memorandum of understanding covering cooperation in the development of space technology (*La Razón*: 26.08.16). Subsequent discussions covered bilateral cooperation in a variety of areas, including defense, but little in the way of concrete projects emerged.

In January 2009, the Morales administration broke diplomatic relations with Israel and threatened to take Tel Aviv to the International Criminal Court over its invasion of the Gaza Strip, a prolonged and deadly attack which left more than 1,000 Palestinians killed (*La Razón*: 14.01.09). Five months later, Israel charged that Bolivia and Venezuela were supplying Iran with uranium for its nuclear program. This was the first time Israel had alleged that Bolivia and Venezuela were involved in the development of Iran's nuclear program, and both countries denied the report (*La Razón*: 26.05.09). In December 2010, Bolivia recognized Palestine as an independent state

(*AP*: 22.12.10). Fraught with controversy, the Bolivia–Israel relationship was again in the news in 2014 when President Morales condemned a new Israeli offensive in the Gaza Strip. In addition to labeling Israel a "terrorist state," Bolivia eliminated a visa waver program for Israeli citizens (*WP*: 31.07.14). Bolivia was not alone in taking action as Brazil, Chile, Ecuador, El Salvador, and Peru withdrew their ambassadors from Israel in protest, and MERCOSUR issued a statement calling for a cessation of violence and an end to the Israeli blockade of Gaza (Morales 2016, 186–7). Thereafter, President Morales continued to condemn Israel and to express support for Palestine in international gatherings (*La Razón*: 17. 09.16).

## Partner, not a *Patrón*

Between the election and inauguration of President Barack Obama, President Morales paid an unofficial visit to Washington in November 2008 where he addressed a largely sympathetic audience of academics and students at American University and made a formal speech at the Organization of American States (*WP*: 22.11.08). He also reached out to key US legislators to express his views on the break in relations with the United States and his interest in mending ties. The OAS called a special session to hear Morales speak; however, regional diplomats reportedly gave him a much cooler reception than he received at American University. Returning to Bolivia, Morales in mid-December 2008 proposed that all Latin American states expel US ambassadors until the United States lifted its embargo on Cuba, a recommendation that found little support among regional leaders (*NYT*: 18.12.08).

During Obama's first year in office, his government made an effort to normalize relations with the Morales administration. On multiple occasions, senior Obama administration officials met with their Bolivian counterparts, including a May 2009 visit to La Paz by the US Assistant Secretary of State for Western Hemisphere Affairs, Thomas Shannon (*WP*: 21.05.09; *El Diario*: 08.12.09). A variety of issues were at the core of their discussions. The most obvious one was counternarcotics policy in Bolivia absent US presence. A related area was the suspension of trade preferences following the expulsion of the Drug Enforcement Agency (*La Razón*: 22.05.09; *El Diario*: 01.07.09). A third issue centered on former Bolivian officials, notably ex-President Sánchez de Lozada, who remained in the United States despite Bolivian extradition requests. A fourth issue was the construction of a new pattern of bilateral relations based on mutual trust and respect (*El Diario*: 21.05.09). President Morales captured the essence of this last issue when he affirmed in December 2009 that he sought a "partner, not a *patrón*" (Molina 2011, 86–99, quote 86). In November 2011, Bolivia and the United States agreed to a bilateral framework intended to lead to a normalization of relations (*WP*: 08.11.11). Designed to provide guarantees of mutual respect for each other's sovereignty, this was the first time the United States had agreed to such an arrangement. Significantly, the agreement limited US funded activities in Bolivia which did not have Bolivian government approval. In the past, USAID had refused to accept any Bolivian control over how it spent its money in the country (Gamarra 2016, 193, 201–2).

Although the framework agreement established a joint commission to pursue its implementation, little progress was made in normalizing diplomatic relations. About the only hint of improved relations was a January 2012 agreement between Bolivia, Brazil, and the United States to conduct joint counternarcotics operations. Otherwise, the Morales government continued to insist that the United States was undermining and conspiring to overthrow it (*La Razón*: 12.10.12). In May 2013, President Morales announced the expulsion of USAID, allegedly for supporting lowland indigenous peoples protesting the construction of a major highway through their territory (Gamarra 2016, 204–6). With a presidential election coming in 2014, it appeared that President Morales "calculated that he had more to gain politically than what was lost economically by closing down the USAID Mission" (Heilman 2017: 283). In July 2013, the detention in Vienna of an airplane transporting President Morales from Moscow because Edward Snowden, the US National Security Agency whistleblower, was thought to have been on board, followed by allegations of US spying throughout Latin America, set back prospects for a normalization of relations (*La Razón*: 03.07.13; *Reuters*: 10.07.13).

After the Obama administration in December 2015 announced it would pursue renewed diplomatic relations with Cuba, bilateral relations with Bolivia looked set to improve (*El Diario*: 16.04.15). With the Venezuelan economy in crisis and Cuba increasing its ties with the United States, President Morales appeared to realize that it made sense for Bolivia to normalize relations with Washington (*El Diario*: 12.08.15). Unfortunately, stubborn obstacles stood in the way of any significant thaw in bilateral relations. The most important sticking points remained trade and the drug war. The Andean Trade Promotion and Drug Enforcement Act uncomfortably bundled the two issues, providing preferential trade for Bolivia in exchange for collaboration in the US directed drug war. The extradition of former President Sánchez de Lozada and two former ministers and the past performance of USAID in Bolivia were additional obstacles to improved bilateral relations. In July 2017, Bolivia and the United States concluded a Customs Mutual Assistance Agreement (CMAA), a bilateral agreement which provided the legal framework for the exchange of information related to the enforcement of customs laws, including trafficking, money laundering, and terrorism related activities. In April 2018, a jury in a US federal court found former President Sánchez de Lozada and former Defense Minister Sánchez Berzaín legally responsible for extrajudicial killings in the fall of 2003, a major victory for the Morales government and the families of the victims (Farthing 2018). In a surprise development, a federal judge later overturned the jury decision, finding there was insufficient evidence to support the verdict that included $10 million in damages (*AP*: 30.05.18). Otherwise, the recently installed administration of President Donald J. Trump made little progress in resolving the multiple issues complicating a resumption of diplomatic relations. The Trump administration's role in defunding diplomacy and foreign assistance in particular was of little help.

## ICJ Decides

A public opinion survey conducted in May 2005 reported that 72 percent of Chileans polled were opposed to giving Bolivia an outlet to the sea in the northern part of the country (*Perú21*: 29.05.05). Nevertheless, outgoing Chilean President Ricardo Lagos approached newly elected President Morales in early 2006 in what proved to be an abortive effort to explore once again the export of Bolivian gas through a Chilean port (*La Razón*: 20.01.06; *El Diario*: 28.01.06). A few weeks later, President Morales visited Chile for the installation of President Michelle Bachelet. President Morales hoped a shared ideological affinity with the new Chilean president would lead to a definitive solution to the maritime issue (*El Mercurio*: 11.03.06; *El Diario*: 11.03.06). Unfortunately, the goodwill between Bolivia and Chile which developed around the inauguration of President Bachelet was soon lost when the Morales government conditioned the sale of natural gas to Argentina on a prohibition against reselling the gas to Chile (Gamarra 2007, 22). Following talks at the working level, Bolivia and Chile formed a joint commission in November 2006 to begin regular discussions on a 13-point agenda of outstanding issues (Chile 2007; Correa and García 2012, 90–7). Over the next few years, progress was made on soft subjects like culture and education and even on more difficult subjects like frontier integration and free transit, but no real progress was achieved on the maritime and Silala issues (*La Tercera*: 29.01.15; Araya 2017, 89–90). In the closing days of the first Bachelet government, Chile did offer Bolivia an enclave without sovereignty south of the Quebrada de Camarones and north of Iquique to be used as a port for the export of Bolivian minerals, but nothing came of this proposal (Guzmán Escobari 2015a, 407–8). In early 2011, the Morales government pushed for dedicated talks on the maritime issue, but the Chilean government of President Sebastián Piñera failed to respond with fresh proposals. At that point, President Morales resolved to take the maritime issue to the International Court of Justice at The Hague (Mesa Gilbert 2016, 212–15).

In April 2013, the Morales government instituted proceedings before the Court, calling on it to rule that Chile had an obligation to negotiate in good faith an agreement with Bolivia granting it sovereign access to the sea (ICJ 2013). The decision to turn to the Court for the first time in Bolivian history highlighted both the apparent futility of bilateral talks with Chile and changing economic and political realities in the region. Tensions between the two states had a polarizing effect on the Bolivarian Alliance for the Peoples of Our America (ALBA) and the Pacific Alliance, and it also spilled over into international bodies like the Organization of American States and the United Nations. The maritime dispute also threatened Bolivia's ability to take advantage of new economic opportunities in the region (Alvarado 2013). At the time, the southern leg of the Initiative for Integration of Regional Infrastructure in South America effectively bypassed Bolivia, linking Brazil to the Pacific Ocean through several Peruvian ports. Bolivia also was not yet a part of multilateral discussions to build a bioceanic railway, linking the Atlantic to the Pacific. The Morales administration had tried to insert itself into the railway discussions, but there was little enthusiasm outside Bolivia for its proposal to reroute the railway through Bolivia, terminating at the Peruvian port of Ilo (St John 2015a).

A decade after it published the *The Blue Book*, Bolivia published *The Book of the Sea* (*El libro del mar*), a more extensive treatment of the history and legal arguments of Bolivia in the maritime dispute. The 158 page book detailed the antecedents to the dispute, attempts to resolve it, and the economic and political consequences of being landlocked (Bolivia 2014). Chile attempted to refute the Bolivian arguments in a monograph entitled "Chile and the Bolivian Maritime Aspiration: Myth and Reality" (*Chile y la aspiración marítima boliviana: mito y realidad*) (Chile 2014). Six months later, Chile released a second monograph, "Bolivian Free Transit: The Reality" (*El libre transito de Bolivia: la realidad*), which argued Chile had provided Bolivia with the free transit facilities called for in the 1904 treaty (Chile 2015).

Bolivia and Chile presented oral arguments to the International Court of Justice during the first full week of May 2015. In the first round of arguments, the Chilean representatives to the Court argued that article six of the Pact of Bogotá (American Treaty on Pacific Settlement) excluded the Court's jurisdiction under article 31 of the treaty. Article six read in part that pacific procedures "may not be applied to matters already settled by arrangement between the parties, or by arbitral award or by decision of an international court, or which are governed by agreements or treaties in force on the date of the conclusion of the present Treaty [30 April 1948]" (ICJ 2015e, 19). In a related argument, the Chilean legal team suggested that a Court decision to accept jurisdiction would compromise the authority of article six, resulting in a long "list of historical issues in Latin America that could be reopened" before the Court (2015a, 18). Members of the Chile legal team also argued that the Treaty of Peace, Friendship, and Commerce signed in October 1904 had resolved the issue.

> The 1904 Treaty was a treaty of peace *and* of amity. It did more than simply declare the re-establishment of peace and friendship. It established what was intended by the parties to be enduring arrangements for their future peaceful relations. It settled the territorial limits of the two states vis-à-vis each other by delimiting the boundary. It acted to strengthen the political and commercial relations between the two States through a number of concrete initiatives.
> 
> (ICJ 2015a, 34–5)

In conclusion, members of the Chilean legal team asked the Court to find that Bolivia's claim was not within the Court's jurisdiction (ICJ 2015a). In the second round of oral arguments, the Chilean legal team added nothing of substance to their initial presentation, concluding with a request that the Court "adjudge and declare that the claim brought by Bolivia against Chile is not within the jurisdiction of the Court" (ICJ 2015c, 44).

The Bolivian representatives to the Court in their initial oral arguments contended that Bolivia had jurisdiction in the case based on article 31 of the Pact of Bogotá. They noted that Chile had promised from the April 1884 truce onwards to let Bolivia retain sovereign access to the sea. In the eyes of the Bolivian legal team, this commitment did not end with the 1904 treaty. On the contrary, Chile repeatedly affirmed thereafter that it would negotiate Bolivia's sovereign access. Although Chile argued the 1904 treaty was a definitive treaty of peace, the Bolivian legal team noted that Chile on numerous occasions after 1904 had agreed to discuss the question of sovereign Bolivian access to the Pacific. In support of this assertion, Bolivia cited formal or informal exchanges in 1895, 1918–23, 1926, 1950, 1961–62, 1975–78, 1986–87, and 2006. The Bolivian legal team then focused on the 1950 talks in which Bolivia proposed to Chile direct negotiations aimed at granting Bolivia a sovereign exit to the Pacific Ocean. The Bolivian agents also explained to the Court how Chile in 1975 had offered Bolivia sovereign access to the sea through a corridor running along the Chile–Peru border to the Pacific (St John 2015c). As Payan Akhavan, a member of the Bolivian legal team, noted in his summary of the Bolivian case: "If the 1904 Agreement closed the matter of sovereign access forever, what was the meaning of these [post-1904] negotiations?" (ICJ 2015b, 54). The Bolivian agents also stressed repeatedly that Bolivia had not come before the Court to reject the 1904 treaty or to reopen agreed upon issues. Instead, Bolivia came before the Court because it had rights under international law, including the right for Chile to complete its obligation to negotiate sovereign access to the sea (ICJ 2015b, 11, 50–1). In the second round of arguments, former President Rodríguez concluded that "Bolivia's claim calls only for the fulfillment of Chile's obligation to negotiate a sovereign access to the Pacific Ocean. It is an obligation that is separate and distinct from the 1904 Treaty. It is an obligation arising from a series of commitments, declarations and exchanges over the years" (ICJ 2015d, 37).

As it developed its legal case against Chile, Bolivia was encouraged by the outcome of a related ICJ case in which Peru had asked the Court to delimit its southern maritime boundary with Chile. In January 2014, the Court ruled largely in favor of Peru, encouraging Bolivia to think it could also be successful before the Court (ICJ 2014). At the same time, Bolivia continued to face the constraints imposed by the Treaty of Lima. The 1929 agreement stipulated that neither Chile nor Peru could cede to a third state any of the territories over which they were granted sovereignty without the prior agreement of the other signatory. With Peru enjoying veto power over any Chilean proposal to cede part of Arica to Bolivia, and Chile enjoying veto power over any Peruvian attempt to cede part of Tacna to Bolivia, Peru had to be involved in any conceivable solution to the Bolivian maritime dispute. Moreover, the ICJ judgment in the Chile–Peru case complicated the Bolivia–Chile maritime issue because any solution to the latter which gave Bolivia a sovereign outlet to the Pacific would automatically involve Bolivia in the Chile–Peru dispute over rich fishing waters off the coast (St John 2015b; Rossi 2017, 73–4).

In September 2015, the International Court of Justice ruled that it enjoyed jurisdiction in the maritime issue, finding article six of the Pact of Bogotá did not bar its jurisdiction under article 31 of the same document. Of the 16 judges on the Court, 14 confirmed the admissibility of the case with the remaining two judges arguing a decision should be delayed until its merits were heard (ICJ 2015e). None of the 16 judges held the case was inadmissible, as Chile had affirmed, an apparent measure of the strength of the Bolivian argument. The day after its ruling on jurisdiction, the Court set 25 July 2016 as the time limit for Chile to file a Counter-Memorial to the original Bolivian complaint. In the interim, bilateral talks between Bolivia and Chile were possible but unlikely. A public opinion poll published in Chile on the day of the Court decision found 86 percent of Chileans were opposed to giving Bolivia sovereign access to the sea through Chilean territory. Chile accepted the Court's ruling, but showed no interest in opening talks with Bolivia. In a speech to the UN General Assembly five days later, President Bachelet stressed the need for nations to respect the inviolability of all treaties (*El Mercurio*: 24.09.15).

The Court decision was a major win for Bolivia, and the success of its initiative was due in large part to the approach adopted by the Morales administration. In the past, Bolivian governments often had manipulated the seaport issue to generate popular support. President Morales seemed to take a different approach. He portrayed the issue as a great national cause, beyond ideological differences, and he sought the counsel and support of a wide range of Bolivians, including former presidents and foreign ministers (Mesa Gisbert 2016, 215–16). Former President Rodriguez was appointed Agent before the Court and former President Mesa was made responsible for explaining the Bolivian case to the international community. Both men also were deeply involved in developing as well as presenting the Bolivian case. In a word, the Bolivian initiative before the Court appeared to be a team effort. If Bolivia was successful, President Morales stood to gain politically, but the initiative did not appear to be designed solely to further his political career. In the event the initiative failed, of course, the team approach would provide Morales with political cover for a major foreign policy failure (St John 2015b).

In July 2016, Chile presented a six-volume Counter-Memorial to the Court, consisting of one volume of argument and five volumes of supporting documents. In contending Chile was under no legal obligation to negotiate with Bolivia, the Counter-Memorial offered little in the way of new argument, information, or documentation. In conclusion, the Counter-Memorial of

Chile requested "the Court to DISMISS all of the claims of the Plurinational State of Bolivia" (ICJ 2016b, 204). In March 2017, Bolivia presented the Court with a five-volume Reply to the Counter-Memorial of Chile. In the first volume, Bolivia argued Chile had misinterpreted key aspects of Bolivia's legal argument, notably the obligation to negotiate, the 1895 treaty, and the negotiations in 1950, 1975, and after. The final four volumes of the Reply contained supporting documents familiar to any student of the issue. In conclusion, Bolivia asked the Court to declare that Chile was obliged to negotiate with Bolivia, had breached that obligation, and must now perform it promptly and in good faith (ICJ 2017a). In September 2017, Chile issued a three-volume Rejoinder to the Bolivian Reply in which it characterized the Bolivian position as inconsistent and unsustainable while its own was unchanging. In conclusion, Chile once again requested the Court to dismiss all Bolivian claims (ICJ 2017b).

In March 2018, the Court held two rounds of public hearings. At the end of those hearings, Bolivia asked the Court to adjudge and declare that "a) Chile has the obligation to negotiate with Bolivia in order to reach an agreement granting Bolivia a fully sovereign access to the Pacific Ocean; b) Chile has breached the said obligation; and c) Chile must perform the said obligation in good faith, promptly, formally, within a reasonable time and effectively, to grant Bolivia a fully sovereign access to the Pacific Ocean." In turn, Chile simply asked the Court to "dismiss all of the claims of the Plurinational State of Bolivia" (ICJ 2018a, 2).

The International Court of Justice announced its judgment at the beginning of October 2018. After noting that Bolivia and Chile had a long history of dialogue, exchanges, and negotiations aimed at identifying a solution to the landlocked situation of Bolivia, the Court ruled in favor of Chile. In a judgment based on procedure and protocol, the Court found by 12 votes to three "that the Republic of Chile did not undertake a legal obligation to negotiate a sovereign access to the Pacific Ocean for the Plurinational State of Bolivia" in the course of these talks. At the same time, the Court stated that its "finding should not be understood as precluding the Parties from continuing their dialogue and exchanges, in a spirit of good neighbourliness, to address the issues relating to the landlocked situation of Bolivia, the solution to which both have recognized to be a matter of mutual interest" (ICJ 2018b, 54).

Emerging from the Court, President Morales vowed to continue Bolivian efforts to overcome its landlocked status, taking comfort in the Court's invocation of continued dialogue and negotiation (*La Razón*: 01.10.18). At home, Bolivians watching the Court decision unfold on live television were shocked and dismayed. Subsequently, Bolivian politicians and experts on international law were critical of the Morales administration's treatment of the issue, terming it at best "deficient" (*deficiente*) (*El Diario*: 28.12.18). In Chile, President Piñera celebrated with a cheering crowd, criticizing the Bolivian government for creating false hopes and unnecessary frustration among its people (*El Mercurio*: 01.10.18). In Peru, Foreign Minister Néstor Popolizio reiterated the long-standing Peruvian position that Bolivia's landlocked status was a bilateral issue between Bolivia and Chile (*El Peruano*: 01.10.18). On the day after the judgment, the foreign minister of Chile, Roberto Ampuero, announced four preconditions for future talks with Bolivia, including Bolivian acknowledgement of international law, respect for the 1904 treaty, respect for the Court's decision, and a reconstruction of mutual confidence (*La Razón*: 02.10.18). President Piñera later emphasized that dialogue with Bolivia would only be possible after Bolivia "understands and respects" (*entienda y respete*) the Court's Judgment, suggesting it might be necessary for Bolivians to elect a new president before that could happen (*La Razón*: 03.10.18). The long-term impact of the Court's decision remained unclear, but it appeared to make a resolution to the dispute feasible only if it led both parties to seek a compromise short of sovereign Bolivian access to the sea.

As its legal case before the ICJ proceeded, the Morales government had continued to highlight the negative economic effects of its landlocked status (Mesa Gisbert 2016, 226–9). Prior to the Second UN Conference on Landlocked Developing Countries in November 2014, Bolivia reported average annual GDP growth rates of 4.5 percent in 2002–12. Exports represented 38 percent of Bolivia's GDP, and imports averaged around 69 percent of GDP. At the same time, Bolivia acknowledged transport challenges due to the inadequacy and unreliability of its transport infrastructure and the resulting negative impact on the competitiveness of its exports. Bolivia also reported that excessive bureaucracy at border crossing points and a lack of harmonization with the customs procedures of neighboring states hampered transit (Nalavala 2014, 6). In 2016, Oxfam published a report, "Bolivia, a country without a coast: Notes for a pending debate" (*Bolivia un país privado de Litoral: apuntes para un debate pendiente*), which suggested that Bolivia's landlocked status cost it as much as 1.5 percent annually in GDP growth due to increased transit costs, inadequate infrastructure, and bureaucratic barriers (Agramont and Peres-Cajías 2016, 17). In an address to a European audience six months later, Morales claimed that Bolivia's landlocked status cost it at least 2 percent annually in GDP growth (*La Razón*: 07.06.17). Thereafter, the Morales administration continued to focus on the alleged cost of being without a sovereign outlet to the ocean. Its efforts in this regard made for good public relations at home but did nothing to move Bolivia closer to its goal of a sovereign port on the Pacific.

## Andean Water Wars

During the first Morales administration, the working group on the Silala (Siloli) set up by Bolivia and Chile in 2004 continued to meet but made little progress toward its stated goal of providing elements of common understanding on the utilization of the contested waters. Bolivia maintained the Silala was an exclusively Bolivian watercourse, and Chile contended it was an international river. The Silala issue was included in the 13-point agenda for discussion adopted in July 2006, but no progress was made in reaching a mutually satisfactory solution (*El Diario*: 01.06.06; Chile 2007). In 2006, the Morales administration established a small military base on the banks of the Silala, a move the Chilean government considered provocative (*La Razón*: 28.12.06). Chile responded by increasing its military presence near the border, a move Bolivia labeled a provocation (*El Diario*: 09.05.16). In 2009, the Prefecture of Potosí hired a consulting company to conduct a feasibility study for a hydroelectric plant on the Silala. The study concluded that only 50kW of electricity could be generated on the site which was no more than enough to power the nearby military base and possibly a future tourist facility (Mulligan and Eckstein 2011, 598–9). About the same time, Bolivia provided the media with a draft preliminary agreement on the use of the waters of the Silala allegedly agreed to by both parties in July 2009 (Bolivia 2009, 2). Among other things, the draft agreement attempted to arrive at a pro-rated formula for Bolivia to sell its share of the Silala waters to Chile (*La Razón*: 04.08.09; *El Diario*: 27.08.09). The terms of the agreement were criticized in Bolivia and Chile, and it never advanced beyond the discussion stage (Guzmán Escobari 2015a, 407; Mesa Gisbert 2016, 201). Seeking compensation for the decades in which Chile used the water for other purposes, Bolivia later put a $1 billion price tag on the historical debt which Chile owed in recompense (*La Razón*: 29.03.16).

At this point, it is important to place the Silala watershed dispute within the context of the evolving international law on transboundary water resources. "The dispute highlights the coming crisis of fresh water resources in an age of global climate change, even among the most water-rich countries in the world" (Rossi 2017, 59). The central issues in the Silala dispute are two-fold. Is the Silala an international river or in modern legal parlance an international watercourse, and if it is an international river or international watercourse, does it emanate from groundwater springs fed by an aquifer which straddles the Bolivia–Chile border (UN 2007, 65)? According to article two of the UN Convention on the Law of the Non-Navigational Uses of International Watercourses, an international watercourse differs from an international river in that an international watercourse is "a system of surface waters and groundwaters constituting by virtue of their physical relationship a unitary whole and normally flowing into a common terminus" with parts of the watercourse "situated in different States" (UN 1997, 3). Unfortunately, little is known about the relationship between the surface and ground water of the Silala or about the transboundary aquifer and watershed. Complicating these questions, international water law regarding transboundary groundwater is at an early stage of development (Vucíc 2017, 95–7, 105–7; Kriener 2017, 3–9). As previously indicated, the available geographical, topographical, and historical evidence suggests the Silala springs flowed overland from Bolivia to Chile before canalization; however, even if this is accepted, there remains the question of whether the flow was intermittent or perennial, an issue which adds confusion to the legal status of the waters. In this regard, it should be noted that neither Bolivia nor Chile signed the UN Convention on the Law of the Non-Navigational Uses of International Watercourses when it was adopted in May 1997 (Rossi 2017, 60–1, 74–6).

In March 2016, President Morales vowed to take Bolivia's claim to sovereign ownership over the Silala watershed to the International Court of Justice (*La Razón*: 23.03.16). In a preemptive move, Chile in June 2016 instituted proceedings against Bolivia at The Hague with regard to the status and use of the waters of the Silala River system (*El Mercurio*: 07.06.16). In its application, Chile stated that the Silala River originates from groundwater springs a few kilometers northeast of the Bolivia–Chile boundary. It then flows across the border into Chilean territory where it receives additional waters from various springs before reaching the San Pedro de Inacaliri River. Chile noted in its application that the waters of the Silala River historically have been used in Chile for different purposes, including the provision of water to the city of Antofagasta and other Chilean towns. According to Chile, its dispute with Bolivia concerns the nature of the Silala as an international watercourse and the resulting rights and obligations of Bolivia and Chile under international law. Consequently, Chile requested the Court to adjudge and declare that "the Silala River system, together with the subterranean portions of its system, is an international watercourse" and "Chile is entitled to the equitable and reasonable use of the waters of the Silala River" (ICJ 2016a, quote 22). Chile later expanded on the arguments in its Application in a six-volume Memorial presented to the Court in mid-2017 which developed historical, scientific, and technical arguments in support of its claim that the Silala is an international watercourse (*La Tercera*: 01.07.17; *El Mercurio*: 28.03.18).

In a Counter-Memorial to the Court, the Morales administration in late August 2018 maintained that the Silala was not an international watercourse and thus not an international river. Instead, the Silala was a water channel that originated in the Department of Potosí and crossed over the border in artificial ducts which Chilean companies built in the early twentieth century. Consequently, Bolivia asked the Court to declare that the Silala was not an international watercourse and that Chile had no rights over its waters. Bolivia also asked the Court to find that it enjoyed full sovereignty over the water flowing through the artificial channels and drainage mechanisms built by Chilean firms on Bolivian territory, including the right to decide whether and how to maintain them. Finally, Bolivia argued that any delivery of the waters of the Silala from Bolivia to Chile, including the compensation to be paid for said delivery, was subject to the conclusion of an agreement with Bolivia (ICJ 2018c). Chile replied to the Counter-Memorial of Bolivia in mid-February 2019, reiterating its argument that the Silala was an international watercourse which flowed naturally from Bolivia to Chile through a ravine formed several thousand years ago (*La Tercera*: 15.02.19). President Morales responded immediately to the Chilean reply, repeating the familiar Bolivian argument that the Silala was not an international watercourse because the waters of the springs of the Silala flowed artificially into Chile through canals constructed by Chileans in the last century (*La Razón*: 16.02.19).

The Lauca National Park is located in the far north of Chile and has been a protected area since 1981 when UNESCO declared it a Biosphere Reserve. It is considered one of the most fragile ecosystems in the world (*El Diario*: 27.08.04). The Chungará Lake and the wetlands of the Cotacotani Lagoon are located nearby. At the turn of the century, Chilean development interests exerted strong pressure on local communities to transfer water from Chungará Lake and the Cotacotani wetlands to the coast to support export agriculture in the Azapa Valley and to supply potable water to the coastal zone of Arica. Related Chilean interests challenged the protected status of Lauca National Park in order to begin mining operations and extract water from wells illegally dug by the Ministry of Public Works in the 1990s. In 2004, Chile approved the extraction of groundwater from six wells in the Lauca National Park arguing the source of the water was a confined aquifer. Bolivia protested the Chilean decision in part because it came on the heels of a separate Chilean decision to privatize the ports of Antofagasta and Arica (Guzmán Escobari 2015a, 394–7). Collectively, the two decisions threatened Bolivia's quest for a sovereign port in northern Chile (*La Razón*: 28.01.04; *El Mercurio*: 30.08.04). Public action later stopped the Lauca project (Maldonado 2005, 37–8; Larrain and Schaeffer 2010, 34).

In 2010, Chile decommissioned 31,500 hectares of the Lauca National Park to allow private mining in the area. This decision was immediately protested by local Aymara residents who argued the land was protected as a National Park in the case of the Lauca Basin, as a National Monument in the case of the Salar de Surire, and as a National Reserve in the case of Las Vicuñas. Moreover, a long-standing Indigenous Law included provisions to safeguard the domain of land and wetlands of Aymara ethnicity along with the waters that supplied them (Larrain and Schaeffer 2010, 34). In mid-July 2016, two weeks before Chile was scheduled to present its Counter-Memorial to the International Court of Justice, a Bolivian delegation headed by Foreign Minister David Choquehuanca made a controversial visit to the Lauca River and the ports of Antofagasta and Arica allegedly to verify if Chile was fulfilling the free transit guarantees found in the 1904 treaty. The Bolivian delegation was kept waiting for several hours before being allowed to enter the port of Arica, and once inside, representatives of the private companies running the port restricted their access to key facilities, including the offices of the two Bolivian agencies operating in the terminal. The Morales administration used the visit to denounce what it termed a "violation" (*vulneración*) of the terms of the 1904 treaty (*La Razón*: 19.07.16). The Bachelet administration rejected the accusations of the Bolivian government, protested what it described as a private visit, and threatened to require Bolivian diplomats to apply for a visa prior to future visits to Chile (*El Mercurio*: 17.07.16; *El Mercurio*: 24.07.16).

In an era of increasing concern for fresh water resources, the Mauri River controversy also resurfaced early in the 2000s. After 1970, Peru had initiated several projects to transfer water from the upper basin of the Mauri River to the Pacific Coast with proposals under study to extract and transfer additional amounts of water. By 2002, Bolivians living in the lower part of the Mauri Basin were increasingly concerned that any future Peruvian plans to extract more water from the Mauri Basin take into account the environmental impact of such plans, the rights of downstream users, and the evolving international law on transboundary water resources (*El Diario*: 19.06.02). At that point, the current rates of extraction had already led to a significant loss of aquatic water systems (wetlands) and a deterioration of water quality with increased levels of arsenic and boron reported (*El Diario*: 09.11.02; *El Diario*: 30.05.09). In 2003, Bolivia and Peru formed a bilateral commission to determine the maximum discharge which could be diverted without affecting Bolivia. When the commission failed to reach a consensus decision, the two parties agreed in October 2010 to implement hydrometric binational stations to monitor the water sharing of the Mauri River. In the absence of significant progress since then, the stations have continued to monitor water flows across the border (Alurralde et al. 2011, 4, 6, 14).

## Neighborly Relations

In the early months of the Morales administration, bilateral relations with the Peruvian government of President Alejandro Toledo were on hold. In addition to the leftward tilt in Bolivian politics and the intervention by President Morales and President Chávez in the 2006 presidential campaign in Peru, deep philosophical differences separated the Morales and Toledo administrations (*La República*: 25.04.06; *La Razón*: 23.05.06). Where Toledo promoted orthodox economic policies and free market reforms in Peru, Morales questioned the benefits of globalization, advocating nationalization and statism in Bolivia. Where Toledo signed a free trade agreement with the United States, Morales signed a people's trade agreement with Cuba and Venezuela. Where Toledo expanded multilateral ties with international trade and finance organizations, like APEC and the World Bank, Morales looked for support to the alternative trade and finance structures promoted by President Chávez. Where Toledo cultivated stronger bilateral ties with a wide variety of states, including the United States, Morales allied with a smaller number of mostly left-leaning states, like Cuba, Nicaragua, and Venezuela (St John 2010, 147). Most importantly, as President Toledo emphasized to the author in an April 2006 interview, the Peruvian government rejected the populist appeal of the Morales government, denouncing populism "as a one night party that inevitably will end up in a funeral" (19.04.06).

The July 2006 inauguration of Alan García Pérez as the president of Peru appeared to offer an opportunity for better relations between Bolivia and Peru, but this proved not to be the case (Novak and Namihas 2013, 217–18). During the presidential campaign, candidate García was harshly critical of President Morales as well as President Chávez of Venezuela, and after his election, he cast his administration as the regional antithesis of Bolivia and

Venezuela. A blend of old and new, the foreign policy of the García government most often mirrored the policies of the Toledo administration. Support for market friendly policies and a free trade agreement with the United States, together with a continuation of earlier Peruvian policies in a variety of international bodies, provoked harsh criticism from President Morales (St John 2017, 89–90). On the Peruvian side, an early source of concern was a Bolivian agreement with Venezuela for the latter to fund military bases along the Peruvian border. Bolivia's reluctance to accept modifications to the CAN agreement necessary to implement Peru's free trade agreement with the United States, and its refusal to negotiate a common CAN trade agreement with the European Union also frustrated Peruvian officials (Valdez 2012, 170–4).

Midway through his first term, President Morales expressed concern about the Peruvian decision to take its maritime dispute with Chile to the International Court of Justice, fearing any decision at The Hague could compromise Bolivia's case for a sovereign Pacific port (*El Diario*: 25.03.09). Another source of friction was the Peruvian government's decision to grant political asylum to former officials in the Morales administration (*La República*: 03.08.09; *La Razón*: 11.05.09). In June 2009, President Morales, in a critique of the capitalist system, described presidents Bush and García as the "worst presidents in the world" (*peores presidentes del mundo*) (*La República*: 23.06.09), and in August 2009, the foreign minister of Peru, José Antonio García Belaúnde, described Evo Morales as "a declared enemy of Peru" (*un enemigo declarado del Perú*) (*La República*: 30.08.09). Later in the year, Foreign Minister García Belaúnde, as he explained to the author in a January 2014 interview, saw an opportunity to improve relations with the Morales government (14.01.14). In December 2009, he asked former Foreign Minister Manuel Rodríguez Cuadros to serve as the Peruvian ambassador to Bolivia (*El Diario*: 15.12.09). Upon assuming his new post, Ambassador Rodríguez immediately endorsed Bolivia's demand for an exit to the sea (*El Comercio*: 19.02.10). In mid-October 2010, the first 2+2 meeting of the foreign and defense ministers of Peru and Bolivia took place. One day later, Presidents García and Morales met in Ilo to sign the Declaration of Ilo (*Declaración de Ilo*), a protocol to the 1992 Boliviamar agreement which provided Bolivia with a duty free industrial and economic zone and a tourist zone for 99 years as well as access to Peruvian port facilities at Ilo (Perú 2011, 45–6, 68, 107, 155, 210–211, 230–1; Novak and Namihas 2013, 221–4). Additional meetings related to borderland development, the management of Lake Titicaca, and other issues took place over the coming months as the Morales and García governments worked to improve bilateral relations (St John 2017, 94–5; García-Corrochano 2012, 81–94).

Ollanta Humala Tasso was elected president of Peru in 2011. In a quick visit to La Paz, President-elect Humala invited President Morales to consider bilateral integration in which the two countries would unite into a confederation reminiscent of the ill-fated Peru–Bolivia Confederation (1836–39). Nothing came of this surprising proposal; however, in February 2013, Peru,

Bolivia, and Brazil concluded a tripartite agreement to fight organized crime and drug trafficking in their borderland areas (Perú 2013, 28, 67–8). Thereafter, as the foreign minister of Peru, Rafael Roncagliolo, emphasized in an October 2014 interview with the author, improved bilateral relations with Bolivia continued to be a priority of the Humala government (20.10.14). In September 2013, the Foreign Relations Committee of the Congress of Peru finally approved the 1992 Boliviamar agreement, renewed and expanded in 2010. The Morales government welcomed the committee's decision, which required ratification by the full Congress of Peru before it came into effect, and talked of the construction of a mega port near Ilo, together with a Bolivia–Brazil rail link (*La Razón*: 24.03.13; Perú 2014, 29, 164). In July 2015, Peru and Bolivia concluded a so-called "strategic alliance" consisting of more than 90 separate accords, and in January 2016, they initialed a pact aimed at the environmental restoration of Lake Titicaca (*La Razón*: 12.01.16; St John 2017, 101–2).

The abbreviated Peruvian presidency of Pedro Pablo Kuczynski began in July 2016 and ended in March 2018 when he was forced out and replaced by Martín Alberto Vizcarra. Bilateral relations between Bolivia and Peru mostly remained cordial throughout this period. Presidents Morales and Kuczynski met in Sucre in November 2016 for a second binational cabinet meeting during which they signed the Declaration of Sucre (*Declaración de Sucre*). Among other topics, the document highlighted projects underway or planned in transboundary water resources, security and defense, and cultural exchange. The Declaration of Sucre also reiterated the interest of Bolivia and Peru in the Bioceanic Railway Corridor Project (*La Razón*: 04.11.16; *El Peruano*: 05.11.16). In September 2018, presidents Morales and Vizcarra met in Cobija in a fourth binational cabinet meeting focused on transboundary water resources, notably cleaning up Lake Titicaca; security and defense, especially cross border organized crime and drug trafficking; economic development; and infrastructure integration with the bioceanic railway the core project in this area (*El Peruano*: 03.09.18). In the course of the meeting, President Vizcarra announced that Peru planned to build a new port terminal at Ilo in conjunction with the bioceanic railway project (*La Razón*: 03.09.18). In September 2018, Foreign Minister Popolizio, stated that "important advances" (*avances importantes*) had been made in bilateral relations with Bolivia, highlighting the progress made over the last few years (*El Peruano*: 05.09.18).

As the Morales government worked through difficult issues with Peru, it faced new challenges from its southern neighbors. In the early years of the Morales administration, Argentina and Brazil struggled to find enough energy to avoid supply shortages which would derail their growing economies. At the time, political unrest and the renationalization of the hydrocarbon industry in Bolivia, combined with Venezuela's failure to make needed investments in Bolivian gas fields, resulted in limited new production (*NYT*: 25.02.08). Bolivian relations with Petrobrás were not fully normalized until 2012 when it announced new investments in gas prospecting which had been frozen since the renationalization. In the interim, Bolivia joined Brazil-led regional integration mechanisms, such as UNASUR and CELAC, and applied for full membership in MERCOSUR (Delgado and Cunha 2016, 139–40). Bolivia also continued to cooperate with Argentina and Brazil on border security issues, especially the regional war on drug trafficking (*La Razón*: 31.10.16). In 2018, Argentina experienced an economic crisis which forced it to reduce its purchase of Bolivian gas and fall in arrears on gas payments, straining its relationship with Bolivia. Consequently, Bolivia in early 2019 renegotiated its key gas contract with Argentina, agreeing to greater flexibility in scheduling deliveries in return for a modest price increase (*El Diario*: 16.02.19). In the meantime, border tensions with Argentina increased as the economic crisis in 2018 forced Bolivians working there to return home (*Los Tiempos*: 19.05.18; *La Razón*: 03.09.18). Bilateral relations with Paraguay experienced ups and downs during the Morales government. In the fall of 2009, Paraguay expressed concern after President Morales announced arms purchases from Russia, and in June 2012, Bolivia–Paraguay relations were frozen for 18 months after Paraguay impeached left-leaning President Fernando Lugo (*El Diario*: 10.09.09; *Xinhua*: 06.12.13). By 2015, bilateral relations had improved, and Paraguayan President Horacio Cartes joined President Morales in inaugurating a liquefied petroleum gas (LPG) plant in Tarija which allowed Bolivia to export LPG to Paraguay. In 2018, Bolivia reported that 99 percent of its LPG exports went to Paraguay and Peru (*LAHT*: 26.08.15; *La Razón*: 03.09.18).

**Concluding Observations**

After 2005, the Morales administration implemented a radical reorientation of Bolivian foreign policy. In a series of bold strokes, Bolivia redefined its allies and adversaries in the region and the world. In so doing, President Morales took advantage of strong economic growth and his widespread popularity. In addition, the Morales government often benefitted from auspicious timing. China's growing appetite for raw materials helped to keep global prices for mineral exports high and state revenues increasing. It also encouraged Chinese investment in Bolivia and elsewhere in the region. With both President Lula of Brazil and President Kirchner of Argentina sympathetic to the Morales regime, the renationalization of the oil and gas sector was accomplished with minimal conflict and with both states continuing to import Bolivian gas. Subsequently, bilateral relations with Argentina, Brazil, and Paraguay were driven largely by Bolivia's role as a regional energy supplier.

Aspects of the international political environment also were favorable to Bolivia. Focused on the Middle East, the United States at the turn of the century mostly abandoned the interventionist policy it had pursued in Latin America since the end of World War II. The Bush and Obama administrations avoided outright confrontation with the Morales government despite marked policy differences, especially over coca cultivation. At the same time, much of Latin America was rejecting the neoliberal economic model and electing a new generation of left-leaning presidents. Highly sympathetic governments in Ecuador and Venezuela, together with left-of-center governments in Argentina and Brazil, gave Bolivia for a time unaccustomed space in the international arena. Moreover, the decline in US influence gave rise to other economic powers, like Brazil, China, and India, who contributed an ever-growing share of investment and trade. Finally, Bolivia foreign policy benefitted from certain regional and international partners not overly concerned with its anti-US positions in international forums.

In 2015, President Morales became the longest serving chief executive in Bolivian history, surpassing the tenure of Andrés Santa Cruz (1829–39) and outlasting most of his South American contemporaries. He was the last remaining chief executive of the so-called "Pink Tide" which included Hugo Chávez in Venezuela, Nestor Kirchner and Cristina Fernández de Kirchner in Argentina, Luiz Inácio Lula da Silva in Brazil, and Rafael Correa in Ecuador. Another political ally, Nicolás Maduro, was locked in a better struggle over legitimate authority in economically ravaged Venezuela. After Morales pledged not to run for a fourth term and narrowly lost a referendum abolishing term limits, the Constitutional Court in November 2017 ruled that elected officials could run indefinitely for office. In response, President Morales announced he would seek a fourth term, suggesting opposition from the United States convinced him to run in 2019, an accusation he would repeat throughout the presidential campaign (*Reuters*: 30.11.17; *La Razón*: 17.12.18). The achievements of his first three terms in office were numerous and widely recognized; nevertheless, there was strong opposition to a fourth term (*NYT*: 08.12.18). As natural gas exports and revenues declined and public debt soared, the popularity and approval ratings of Morales dropped. A January 2017 public opinion poll found that 58 percent of Bolivians approved of the Morales presidency, but 63 percent opposed his running for a fourth term (*El Mercurio*: 23.01.17). Foreign policy was not a major issue in the 2005, 2009, and 2014 elections; however, this looked set to change in 2019. If the ruling in the Bolivia–Chile maritime case was followed by a second defeat in the Silala watershed dispute, foreign policy could assume a new significance in the 2019 presidential elections.

# 10  Conclusions

At independence, the socioeconomic and political traditions of Bolivia were an adaptation of Spanish colonialism to the realities of the New World. The prolonged struggle for independence introduced change to the existing system, but it did not produce a meaningful transformation of colonial structures. On the contrary, independence from Spain left intact the core elements of a society which had developed over three centuries of colonial rule. Bolivian society was hierarchical in structure with limited opportunities for political participation, and the economy was grounded in agriculture and mining. Over time, the prevailing characteristics of colonial structures would change, but it would be a very slow and painful evolution. The Bolivian electorate represented as little as 2 percent of the population and never more than 6 percent until as late as 1952 when the National Revolution introduced universal adult suffrage.

The makeup of Bolivian society contributed to the political turmoil which emasculated Bolivia during and after independence with an often devastating impact on its early foreign policy. Bolivia adopted a democratic form of government, but the Spanish colonial system had not prepared the citizenry to participate within the framework of a democratic republic. Moreover, the independence movement lacked a clear political ideology with the central issue in the political debate being the optimum form of government. The monarchy versus republic split was followed by a prolonged debate over centralism versus federalism. The battle of Ingavi confirmed Bolivian independence, but regional interests within Bolivia would continue to challenge central authority to the present day. Regionalism was at the center of the debate over whether Sucre or La Paz should be the official capital and seat of government, a debate which led eventually to the Federal Revolution in 1898–99. After the National Revolution, the main line of division was between the Andean highlands and the eastern lowlands with all departments vying with each other for resources from the central government. Regionalism was rekindled in the 1970s during and after the *banzerato*. More recently, the 2005 election of President Evo Morales challenged lowland economic interests in the *media luna*, inflaming long-standing regional and racial tensions which seemed at times capable of tearing the nation apart.

Bolivia endured decades of capricious, chaotic, and destructive rule by a succession of military chieftains. Militarism surfaced in Bolivia before independence was won, and it remained a prominent feature of Bolivian politics for decades thereafter. *Caudillismo* also was pervasive in Bolivia and had a strong influence on foreign policy in the early years of national life, a period in which foreign policy was closely tied to domestic policy, especially trade and fiscal policy. Bolivia did not experience its first civilian head of state until 1857, and it did not enjoy protracted periods of civilian rule until the final quarter of the nineteenth century. Militarism and *caudillismo* combined to produce a prolonged era of *golpes de estado* and illegal successions which undermined efforts to conduct a rationale, consistent, and transparent foreign policy. Domestic political turmoil continued to impinge on foreign policy in the twentieth century with 1978–82 and 1990–2005 examples of periods in which domestic strife undermined or compromised diplomatic initiatives.

In common with most newly independent Latin American republics, the foreign policy of Bolivia throughout the nineteenth century had a narrow focus which centered on relations with neighboring states. Core concerns included sovereignty, national security, continental solidarity, territorial integrity, and economic independence. Like most small to medium-sized states, Bolivia was highly vulnerable to external penetration and exploitation; therefore, its foreign policy remained closely tied to domestic conditions and issues of economic development. Low levels of national integration and consensus added to the prevailing state of internal instability and exerted a negative influence on Bolivian foreign policy. The interests of Argentina, Chile, Colombia, Ecuador, and Peru were at the forefront during the struggle for Bolivian independence. Once independence was won, the corrosive aspects of regional competition impacted on the domestic and foreign policies of Bolivia, retarding national integration and hampering balanced economic growth. As a political force, regional antagonism and rivalry contained the seeds of international conflict as competition with its neighbors enveloped Bolivia in repeated controversies.

## Continental Solidarity

In common with most Latin American states, enhanced continental solidarity was a central element in Bolivian foreign policy for much of the nineteenth century. Símon Bolívar failed to create a Federation of the Andes; nevertheless, he remained a strong proponent of Pan-Americanism. The Congress of Panama, organized by Bolívar in 1826, produced four conventions, including a treaty of perpetual union, league, and confederation. Although Colombia was the only state to ratify the conventions, the Panama Congress marked the beginning of the inter-American movement. Bolivia dispatched two delegates to the congress, but both failed to arrive. Following the Panama Congress, Bolivian diplomacy drew attention to the bifurcation of interests which characterized its policies in the Andean region. In support of interdependence, Bolivian relations with its sister republics, notably Ecuador and

Peru, evidenced a feeling of kindred spirit and solidarity, including formal union. Supporting independence, bitter rivalries with neighboring Argentina and Chile over economic and territorial issues worked against any centripetal tendency toward unity. A nascent state of Bolivian nationalism, combined with the search for a sense of national unity, preoccupied Bolivians throughout the nineteenth century, further complicating the issue. As late as the War of the Pacific, any sense of national unity was almost completely lacking in the soldiery of Bolivia. In the twentieth century, the activities of the Standard Oil Company, the Chaco War, the National Revolution, and the policies of the United States contributed to the rise of nationalism as a force in Bolivian politics. More recent examples of nationalist expression include the water and gas wars at the beginning of the new millennium.

At the 1847 Lima Conference, Bolivia joined other states in concluding four agreements, including a treaty of union and confederation. When the Lima Conference reconvened in 1848, Bolivia moved to strengthen the treaty of union and confederation with a clause allowing member states to intervene in the internal affairs of another member state if a *golpe de estado* occurred in that state. The Bolivian proposal was rejected by a majority of the delegates present on the grounds any form of intervention in the affairs of a member state would constitute a denial of political sovereignty. The Second Lima Conference convened in the Peruvian capital in late 1864, and once again, Bolivia took a forward position in support of continental solidarity. Prior to the opening of the conference, the foreign minister of Bolivia circulated a proposal which called for greater political union. In the end, the Second Lima Conference drafted a treaty of political union, but it was never implemented. Instead, the participants opted for a voluntary approach to continental union. The 1864 Lima Conference marked a watershed in inter-American relations as it was the last time the American republics seriously pursued greater cooperation on the basis of confederation.

By the turn of the century, Bolivia had joined other Latin American states in foregoing the issue of political union in favor of a stronger emphasis on international law as a means to regulate regional affairs. At the First Pan-American Conference (1889–90), the rationale for the inter-American system shifted from an emphasis on the more idealistic aims of continental union to more practical, utilitarian issues like trade, customs, and peacekeeping procedures. In the end, the conference failed to establish a customs union but concluded commercial and trade pacts and established the International Union of American Republics, a predecessor to the Organization of American States. Arbitration was a controversial issue at the First Pan-American Conference because it touched on national interests and rivalries, including fallout from the War of the Pacific. When the US delegation proposed a draft arbitration treaty, Chile was at the forefront of opposition to any consideration of compulsory arbitration in the pact. With the Tacna and Arica dispute and Bolivia's refusal to sign a peace treaty in mind, Chile refused to accept the principle of arbitration as unconditional and obligatory, especially in the case of pending disputes. After much debate, Bolivia joined ten states in signing the arbitration treaty which was adopted; however, Chile refused and the treaty was never ratified. The arbitration issue was also at the forefront of talks during the Second Pan-American Conference (1901–02). Once again, Bolivia joined ten states in urging the compulsory arbitration of pending and future disputes, a measure Chile adamantly opposed. Eventually, the conference delegates reached a compromise in which they agreed to subscribe to the arbitration provisions of the 1899 Hague Convention and to submit disputes on a voluntary basis to the Permanent Court of Arbitration. In discussions leading to the Third Pan-American Conference (1906), Bolivia joined Peru in pressing once again for unrestricted debate of the arbitration issue; however, Chile succeeded in keeping the subject of obligatory arbitration off the conference agenda.

Elsewhere, Bolivia participated in a growing number of subregional, regional, and international organizations. Bolivia was invited to the Paris Peace Conference in 1919 and was a founding member of the League of Nations. Later, Bolivia joined the United Nations and the Organization of America States. An active participant in UN General Assembly debates and other UN activities like the Law of the Sea Conferences, Bolivia often used its participation in regional and international meetings as a forum to promote the maritime issue. When the United Nations began to host conferences to address the unique problems of landlocked states, Bolivia was an active participant even though its quest for a sovereign outlet to the Pacific separated it from other landlocked states who focused on freedom of transit issues. In the second half of the twentieth century, Bolivian participation in subregional and regional organizations mushroomed. It joined the Economic Commission for Latin America, Latin American Free Trade Association, Group of 77, and Andean Group, to name a few. Later, it joined the Latin American and Caribbean Economic System, Non-Aligned Movement, World Trade Organization, and South American Community of Nations. With the advent of the Morales era, Bolivia continued to participate in most of the above organizations but also joined new ones with radically different visions and goals. Obvious examples include the Bolivarian Alliance for the Peoples of Our America and Community of Latin American and Caribbean States.

Over time, the growing number and increasing frequency of subregional, regional, and international meetings stretched the diplomatic resources of Bolivia. For example, the fourth Summit of Latin America, the Caribbean, and the European Union, a biennial meeting which took place in Vienna in 2006, was the largest gathering of heads of state and government since the Congress of Vienna in 1815. As the number of multilateral groupings and meetings proliferated, Bolivia suffered from "summit overload," a common complaint among small to medium-sized states. With limited resources, Bolivia found it increasingly difficult to staff and participate in the growing number of multilateral groups holding regular meetings. In part for this reason, Bolivian diplomats often focused on the maritime issue at such gatherings.

## National Security and Territorial Integrity

Well into the twentieth century, border conflicts and territorial disputes threatened the national security and territorial integrity of Bolivia. Most of these issues stemmed from the failure of Spain to delineate clearly its territorial possessions, together with the unsatisfactory resolution of local issues. Territorial disputes were complicated by the commercial interests at stake as Bolivia and its neighbors quarreled over trade routes and seaports and later over control of gold, guano and nitrate deposits; rubber wealth; and oil and gas deposits. Ideological differences intensified such conflicts as did concerns over regional hegemony. On the surface, Bolivian emphasis on these questions differed little from that of its neighbors in that all of the newly independent republics put a high priority on the clear delineation of their borders. At the same time, the Bolivian case was unique in that weak governance, limited state institutions, and a focus on the maritime issue frequently combined to weaken an already weak state at critical junctures, undermining Bolivian efforts to protect the national security and territorial integrity of the state.

Based on *uti possidetis de jure de 1810*, Bolivia at independence claimed the Salado River, located below latitude 26° south, as its southern boundary with Chile in the Atacama Desert. In 1866, the Melgarejo administration signed the Treaty of Mutual Benefits, moving the southern boundary with Chile north to latitude 24° south and hastening the War of the Pacific. One year later, the Melgarejo government concluded a treaty with Brazil, ceding to it some 58,000 square miles of territory. Bolivian critics of the treaty charged Brazil took advantage of the ignorance and vanity of President Melgarejo to cede territory rightfully Bolivian. In 1879, Chile occupied the Bolivian littoral, and in 1904, Bolivia ceded in perpetuity its Pacific littoral, including the ports of Antofagasta, Cobija, Mejillones, and Tocopilla. In the interim, the Arce administration ceded to Argentina part of the Chilean-occupied Puna de Atacama in return for Argentine recognition of Bolivian sovereignty over Tarija and other areas in the central Chaco. The Pando administration later sold the rubber-rich Acre territory to Brazil in Bolivia's largest single territorial concession to that time. In the Treaty of Petrópolis (1903), Bolivia ceded to Brazil an estimated 73,726 square miles of contested land. In return, Bolivia received 2,000 square miles of territory which provided access to the Madeira River, four tracts of swampy land which provided windows toward the Paraguay River, and an indemnity of £2 million.

In 1901–02, Bolivia and Peru conducted talks which eventually led to a demarcation of their border around Lake Titicaca and the headwaters of the Madre de Dios River. In the latter case, final adjustments to the border favored Bolivia, a rare victory in the long and troubled history of its territorial disputes. When the Treaty of Lima (1929) eliminated for the foreseeable future any prospect for a sovereign outlet to the Pacific, Bolivia turned its attention to the Paraguay River as its most feasible outlet to the ocean. Once again, bad judgment on the part of a Bolivian chief executive led to a disastrous war in which Bolivia was forced to sacrifice its claim to 455,600 square miles of territory, its largest single loss of land since independence. Even after enormous territorial sacrifices, challenges to the territorial integrity of Bolivia have not ceased. After Bolivia in 1975 proposed to Chile the cession of a sovereign coastline between the Chile–Peru border and the city of Arica, Chile responded with a counterproposal in which it offered to exchange a sovereign land-sea corridor along the Chilean border with Peru in return for roughly equivalent compensation in the Bolivian altiplano. In calling for territorial concessions, the Chilean proposal once again threatened the territorial integrity of Bolivia.

## Sovereignty

Achieving and maintaining sovereignty has been a prolonged challenge for Bolivia. The first 15 years after independence were a period in which the central question was whether Bolivia would join a confederation of states, unite with Peru, or remain an independent, sovereign entity. Once its future as an independent state was confirmed, Bolivia was challenged on a regular basis by more powerful neighbors seeking territorial adjustments at Bolivia's expense. The result was the slow, steady diminution of Bolivian territory summarized above. Bolivia finally stopped the bleeding, literally as well as figuratively, with its acceptance of the 1938 Chaco arbitral award. Nevertheless, challenges to its sovereignty did not abate. The 1975 Chilean proposal called for any land-sea corridor created to be a demilitarized zone, a clear and unacceptable limitation of Bolivian sovereignty. In the wake of the Chaco War, Bolivian sovereignty also was challenged increasingly from an entirely new quarter, the United States of America.

After independence, Bolivian relations with the United States passed through three distinct periods. In the longest period which stretched from 1825 to World War II, bilateral relations were limited and often revolved around Bolivian efforts to secure US support for Bolivia's quest for a sovereign outlet to the Pacific. The Peru–Bolivia Confederation concluded a general convention of peace, friendship, commerce, and navigation with the United States as early as 1836, but the US government did not recognize Bolivia as a sovereign state until 1848. Furthermore, Bolivia was the last republic in South America to be visited by a US diplomatic or consular agent. For the remainder of the nineteenth century, the US role in Bolivian foreign policy was sporadic. During the War of the Pacific, the United States was one of several governments involved in mediation efforts, none of which had a significant impact on the outcome of the dispute, and the amateurish diplomacy of the United States left Bolivians generally hostile to US mediation efforts. After World War I, a short but intense depression in Bolivia led to a heavy insertion of US banking and financial systems, an experiment which ended when the Great Depression hit the United States. In this period, Bolivia again turned to the United States in the hope it would use its good offices in support of a sovereign outlet to the Pacific. Following abortive plebiscitary proceedings in Tacna and Arica, Secretary of State Kellogg called for the cession of Tacna and Arica to Bolivia. Peru soon blocked this initiative; nevertheless, Bolivians welcomed the proposal as an indication of US support for their cause. Consequently, they were disappointed when Bolivia was excluded from bilateral talks between Chile and Peru, talks held under US auspices, which led to the Treaty of Lima.

During World War II, the depth and breadth of economic, military, and political relations between Bolivia and the United States expanded in what became the second distinct period in bilateral relations. In the course of the war, the United States agreed to provide development assistance to Bolivia, the first time it had granted a significant amount of economic aid to a developing country. The two countries also agreed to their first military assistance pact. The US government lent a sympathetic ear to Bolivian arguments for a sovereign port on the Pacific but failed to support concrete initiatives. In the immediate post-war period, the US commitment to the economic and political development of Bolivia waned for a short period before resuming in 1951. US support for the MNR government during the National Revolution proved to be the one and only time the United States provided sustained support for a genuine social revolution. With Bolivia increasingly dependent on US largesse, US involvement in the internal and external affairs of Bolivia continued to increase. Over the next 50 years, the Bolivia–US relationship can be subdivided into several periods; however, the dominant theme throughout remained the growing economic, military, and political dependence of Bolivia on the United States. By the end of the century, Bolivia had become the most dramatic case of dependence in the hemisphere with extreme dependence impacting on virtually every aspect of its political economy. This high level of dependence limited the policy options available to Bolivia, especially in times of crisis. It also increased the salience of external decision-making centers, like the US government, International Monetary Fund, and World Bank, on internal decision making. To receive essential external aid, Bolivia was forced to accept externally designed programs like the IMF-stabilization program, US-imposed drug policies, and Washington Consensus. Not surprisingly, the dominant role of the United States in Bolivia for more than a half century generated considerable pushback from the Bolivian body politic.

Standard interpretations of the relationship between Bolivia and the United States in the second half of the twentieth century tend to stress US control over Bolivian affairs. A more nuanced view highlights the extent to which Bolivia decision-makers enjoyed a degree of control over bilateral relations with their North American counterparts. Throughout the second half of the last century, Bolivia remained in a dependent relationship with the United States but that did not mean Bolivian officials accepted unquestioningly every US policy action. On the contrary, Bolivian decision-makers often managed to persuade US officials to agree to policies which reflected Bolivian calculations of self-interest. Long engaged in a dependent relationship, Bolivian officials often proved skillful in subtly manipulating the patron–client relationship to their own ends. During the Cold War, for example, Bolivia leaders occasionally reached out to the Soviet Union and the East Bloc as part of a strategy to increase US assistance by playing on Washington's fear of communism. The first two Paz Estenssoro administrations and the military governments which followed exemplify sustained periods in which Bolivia succeeded in moderating US intentions. More recently, successive Bolivian governments have used the US fixation on the supply side of the war on drugs to leverage additional economic and military aid from Washington.

In this regard, it is important to remember that the foreign policy of Bolivia has remained closely tied to domestic interests, structures, and policies. From the outset of the independence era, violence was an integral part of the Bolivian political system with internal conflict often disrupting external policy to the point that the latter was merely a reflection of the former. The prolonged influence of militarism, *caudillismo*, and ideology remains clear, and as new political forces and movements surfaced, new actors participated in the political system and impacted on its foreign policy. Bolivian exporters in league with both civilian and military governments heavily influenced central tenets of Bolivian foreign policy for much of the nineteenth century. In the twentieth century, important new actors included labor unions like the *Central Obrero Boliviano* (COB), *Confederación Sindical Única de Trabajadores Campesinos de Bolivia* (CSUTCB), and *Federación Sindical de Trabajadores Mineros de Bolivia* (FSTMB); nontraditional political parties like the *Movimiento Indígena Pachakuti* (MIP), *Movimiento Revolucionario Tupac Katari de Liberación* (MRTKL), and *Movimiento al Socialismo* (MAS); other social movements and organizations like the *Confederación de Pueblos Indígenas de Bolivia* (CIDOB), *Confederación Sindical de Comunidades Interculturales de Bolivia* (CSCIB), and *Federación de Juntas Vecinales* (FEJUVE); and social activists like Silvia Rivera Cusicanqui. The National Assembly also has played a long-term role both in determining the nation's leadership and in approving or disapproving conventions, pacts, and treaties, often influencing if not dictating the state's foreign policy in the process. In recent years, all of these domestic forces, bodies, and movements have continued to bear upon Bolivian foreign policy.

It is also important to recognize the full extent to which Bolivian governments have exploited the maritime and related issues to generate domestic support. For example, the diplomatic initiative launched by Bolivia in 1950 exemplified both the popularity of the maritime issue with the body politic and recognition by Bolivian leaders of the domestic political value of stressing it. A similar observation applies to the hardline position on the maritime and Lauca River issues taken by Bolivia in 1966, a period in which the Barrientos administration was eager to divert public opinion from domestic issues, including the guerrilla war launched by Ché Guevara. Domestic turmoil after 1971 continued to compromise foreign policy initiatives and to offer new opportunities for the Bolivian government to launch foreign policy initiatives in part to divert public attention from domestic woes. Most recently, the activist foreign policy of the Morales administration, with its opposition to colonialism, imperialism, and neoliberalism and its concomitant support for the environment, indigenous rights, and Mother Earth, was strongly influenced by domestic factors, elements, and conditions.

By 2005, the shortcomings of the neoliberal economic policies and hard-line drug programs advocated by the United States were clear for all to see, and the newly elected Morales administration seized on the moment to reorient domestic and foreign policy away from the long-standing, heavy-handed influence of the US government. For a short time, Washington attempted to pursue a conciliatory policy but that quickly proved impossible. Instead, a series of moves and countermoves by Bolivia and the United States inexorably led to a progressive decline in the power and influence of the latter in Bolivia. On the US side, the bundling of the drug war and trade issues left little room for compromise. On the Bolivian side, a strong economy and a changing neighborhood reduced its need for US support and assistance. As a new century dawned, a wave of left-leaning governments won election in a Latin America which was increasingly democratic, prosperous, and self-confident. As regional groupings proliferated, over-arching Pan-American partnerships long dominated by the United States, like the Organization of American States, were less relevant. At the same time, US hegemony gave way to multi-polarity in which the United States was not the only game in town. Increasingly, China in particular acted as an investor, lender, and trading partner to Latin America. In the face of these dramatic changes, the influence of the United States declined in Bolivia and elsewhere in the region. By the time President Morales in 2018 began his campaign for a fourth term in office, the United States had less influence in Latin America than at any time in the past century.

In the process, a growing number of external actors impacted on Bolivian foreign policy. The Standard Oil Company was an early player before the Toro government seized its assets in 1937. Since that time, Bolivia has nationalized/renationalized hydrocarbon companies on two more occasions, a record for a developing country. Other multinational corporations which have impacted on external relations include the Antofagasta Nitrate and Railroad Company, Archer Daniels Midland (ADM), Bechtel Corporation, Bolivian Syndicate of New York, BP Group, Cargill, Glencore International, Royal Dutch Shell, and Total. As Bolivian public finance moved from crisis to crisis, the International Monetary Fund, World Bank, and international banking community increased their involvement in Bolivia, frequently generating controversy and resentment because of their impact on domestic and foreign policies. Outside human rights groups, like Amnesty International and the Andean Commission of Jurists, teamed with local actors, like the Catholic Church and the Permanent Human Rights Assembly of Bolivia, to pressure the government on democratization and human rights issues. More recently, a growing number of other international organizations, including the United

Nations, Andean Group, and Bolivarian Alliance for the Peoples of Our America, to name a few, influenced the direction and content of Bolivian foreign policy. Under the Morales government, Chinese aid, investment, and trade also has made a major contribution to the redirection of external policy. Finally, in an example of people's diplomacy, the Aymara community on the borders of Bolivia has engaged to an unprecedented extent in recent years in cross-border relations with related communities in Chile and Peru. All of these groups, movements, organizations, and parties impact on Bolivian foreign policy either directly or indirectly through their impact on domestic policy.

## Economic Independence

The search for economic independence dominated Bolivian foreign policy from the outset of the republican period to the present time. In the colonial era, the mining centers of the former Viceroyalty of Peru, which included the Audiencia of Charcas, were serviced for the most part by Pacific ports. At independence, the former Audiencia of Charcas, which was the basis for nineteenth century Bolivia, contained nothing beyond an awkward outlet to the Pacific Ocean through a narrow corridor in the Atacama Desert. While this corridor included a tiny port at Cobija, the difficult and expensive journey to this inhospitable stretch of shoreline left Bolivia's export economy dependent on Peruvian ports, notably Arica. For more than a century after independence, Bolivian foreign policy pushed for a sovereign outlet to the Pacific with Arica as its primary target. The Arica for Bolivia movement finally ended in 1929 when the Treaty of Lima ended any realistic hope that Bolivia could obtain Arica. In the interim, Bolivia ceded to Chile in perpetuity the ports of Antofagasta, Cobija, Mejillones, and Tocopilla in 1904. The Chilean ports of Arica, Antofagasta, and Mejillones are the main ports used by Bolivia today, but the Peruvian port of Ilo promises to be more important in the future.

With a few exceptions, Bolivian governments after 1825 embraced a policy of export-led growth with silver, tin, oil, and natural gas at different times the drivers of that policy. The reliance on export-led growth left the nation highly vulnerable to the vagaries of international economic cycles with often severe consequences for the national economy. When global demand and prices for these commodities were high, the effects of the policy were generally favorable. Examples of good times include the first Montes government when rising tin exports led to an economic boom and World War II when there was another boom in the demand and price for tin. Most recently, the export of natural gas made Bolivia the energy center for the southern cone of South America. When the reverse was true, the global economic system limited economic independence, restraining budgets and policy options. The first half-century of independence, a period in which Bolivia faced economic stagnation, is an example of bad times. The steep drop in the output and price of silver at the end of the nineteenth century and the sharp decline in the price of tin preceding the Great Depression and in the aftermath of World War II also exemplify the economic cycles which have plagued the Bolivian economy. Bolivian governments often portrayed the periodical debt crises resulting from a drop in export-led growth as unfortunate and unique. On the contrary, they constituted a pattern which cursed Bolivia from independence.

From the beginning, the export-led nature of the Bolivian economy meant that trade policy would have a major influence on foreign policy. The Spanish American Empire acted as a mercantilist customs union, and with its demise, successive Bolivian governments debated the relative merits of protectionism versus free trade. The appropriate role of foreign investment in economic development was another source of ongoing debate. Early trade policies were bound to regional rivalries and frequently were a source of controversy and conflict. In the Bolivian case, this was especially true with neighboring Brazil, Chile, and Peru as all of these states maneuvered aggressively for commercial advantage. In an environment in which money was always short, *caudillo*-led governments too often sacrificed the national interest for personal gain. The discovery mid-nineteenth-century of guano, nitrates, and other minerals in the littoral appeared to promise an era of greater prosperity; instead, it led to a disastrous war in which Chile occupied the entire Bolivian coastline. Economic, financial, and trade policies assumed new dimensions in the twentieth century when Bolivia turned increasingly to the industrialized world to provide the capital investment necessary to promote economic growth. Hydrocarbons helped provoke the largest and most destructive war in twentieth century Latin America, fueled the state after the 1952 revolution, and became the cornerstone for the state capitalist economy. Natural gas supplies are a central element in contemporary Bolivian relations with Argentina and Brazil and to a lesser extent Paraguay. In recent years, the potential export of Bolivian natural gas through Chile or Peru also impacted on Bolivia's bilateral relations with those states.

## Prisoner of Geography

When Bolivians refer to their country as the classic case of a landlocked developing state, they generally miss the point. Bolivia is a classic example of the economic challenges faced by any landlocked developing state; however, its insistence on a sovereign outlet to the ocean as a solution to those challenges is unique. In common with landlocked developing countries, serious structural limitations limit Bolivian access to world markets, restricting the impact foreign trade can have on the remainder of the economy. The ability of Bolivia to connect with an increasingly integrated world economy is heavily compromised by its dependence on the transit of most of its exports and imports through a single country, one with which it has had a long and conflicted relationship. In this regard, Bolivia shares similar economic challenges with other landlocked developing states, but it is singular in that it is the only one seeking to resolve its difficulties through a sovereign outlet to the ocean.

The remainder of the 32 landlocked developing states have long concentrated on improved transit rights and facilities to improve their trade picture.

Economically, independent studies have suggested that Bolivia's GDP would have been as much as 20 percent higher if it enjoyed sovereign access to the sea, and the Bolivian government has estimated its GDP would increase 1 percent per annum if it had direct access to the Pacific. While the details of such statistics can be – and have been – called into question, independent observers agree they are directionally correct. Absent a sovereign outlet to the Pacific, Bolivia clearly is a prisoner of geography and will remain at an economic disadvantage vis-à-vis its neighbors as long as it does not enjoy freer access to markets and new technologies. In this context, Bolivia has long complained that Chile has been unnecessarily restrictive in Bolivian use of Chilean ports even though the ports of Antofagasta, Arica, and Iquique remain the primary outlets for Bolivian exports to Asia and the United States. The privatization of Chilean ports at the end of the twentieth century amplified long-standing Bolivian complaints in areas like cross-border relations, inadequate infrastructure and associated time delays, and bureaucratic administration practices. In response, Bolivia has pushed for the return of the administration of Chilean ports to the Chilean government while working at the same time to improve the infrastructure and administration of those ports to improve transit times. Bolivia also has taken steps to reduce its dependence on Chilean ports, including the development of an alternate route to the Pacific via the Peruvian port of Ilo and improved access to the Atlantic through the Hidrovía Paraguay–Paraná and Puerto Busch on the Paraguay River.

Today, Bolivia's quest for a sovereign outlet to the Pacific continues to retard regional economic growth in western Bolivia, northern Chile, and southern Peru. Until such time as Bolivia and Chile resume full diplomatic relations, a condition tied to the maritime issue, it will remain difficult for Bolivia, Chile, and Peru to implement fully an integrated development strategy for the region. In the interim, the challenges of a global economy appear to be modifying the character and context of the maritime dispute, and this evolution could offer Bolivia new opportunities to fulfill its cherished ambition of improved access to the Pacific. In the new millennium, frontiers increasingly have become less areas of exclusive space that rigidly define the territorial limits of a given state and more privileged centers of interstate complementarity and cooperation. With the decreasing relevance of national boundaries, frontiers also have become a more complex and dynamic phenomenon, offering fresh opportunities for well-developed strategies of cross-border integration and development. Modern concepts of frontiers, through the promotion of increased commerce and wider economic growth, often improve inter-state relations by encouraging peace and development in borderlands which in the past were centers of controversy and conflict.

The five factors most often identified as critical to the success of economic growth triangles in Asia are economic complementarity, geographical proximity, political commitment, policy coordination, and infrastructure. All of these factors are present or could be created in the region surrounding the Bolivia–Chile–Peru tripoint. Moreover, the development of a regional growth triangle as part of a broader process designed to address Bolivia's quest for improved access to the Pacific would clearly benefit the regional economies of the three parties linked to the question. It would also remove Bolivia's maritime issue from a zero sum game in which one side loses if the other side gains and place it within the context of a new era of trinational cooperation on the Pacific coast of South America. Enhanced trinational integration and cooperation offers potential for accelerated economic development and improved regional well-being which eventually could satisfy the long-term aspirations of Bolivia, Chile, and Peru in the tripoint region.

At independence, the core goals of Bolivian foreign policy were similar to those of the other newly independent South American republics. Bolivia was less successful than its neighbors in the pursuit of sovereignty, national security, continental solidarity, territorial integrity, and economic independence for a multitude of reasons. From the outset, internal and external concerns were closely linked with domestic considerations often dictating the nation's international posture. In a political system prone to violence, foreign policy often was the handmaiden of domestic policy. Regionalism also influenced both domestic and foreign policy from the beginning. Moreover, the limited ability of the nation to defend itself often was compromised by poor governance, limited state capacity, and a fixation on the maritime issue. The size and location of Bolivia, together with the structure and state of its economy and the relationships developed with regional and extra-regional powers, also impacted on its conduct of foreign affairs. All of these considerations continued to limit Bolivian foreign policy in the twentieth century, and by this time, Bolivia was reduced to less than half its original size. The creation of the Bolivian Diplomatic Academy in 1954 contributed to the development of an increasingly competent and professional diplomatic corps; consequently, Bolivian diplomacy in the second half of the twentieth century was increasingly effective in promoting the external interests of the state. By the end of the century, Bolivian diplomats were doing an excellent job of explaining to the international community their case for a sovereign outlet to the Pacific; unfortunately, few individuals or states were interested in listening to their story. This was particularly true in the case of the other landlocked developing states of the world. Sympathetic to the Bolivian dilemma, their focus remained on improved transit rights and facilities. Most recently, Bolivia has taken advantage of reduced global bipolarity to expand economic, political, and social ties. It has done so in the belief that a more active role in a broader range of movements and organizations will contribute to an alternative world order grounded in more equality, increased participation, and greater social justice. Wider involvement in the international system has created new opportunities, but it also imposed new challenges and constraints.

# Bibliography

**Articles, books, documents, papers, and reports**

Abecia Baldivieso, Valentín (1986) *Las relaciones internacionales en la historia de Bolivia*. 2nd edn. 3 vols. La Paz and Cochabamba: Editorial Los Amigos del Libro.

Achtenberg, Emily (2017) "Financial Sovereignty or A New Dependency? How China is Remaking Bolivia." North American Congress on Latin America (NACLA) (10 September): 1–7. https://nacla.org/blog/2017/08/11/financial-sovereignty-or-new-dependency-how-china-remaking-bolivia. Accessed 25 November 2018.

Agramont Lechín, Daniel and José Alejandro Peres-Cajías (2016) *Bolivia un país privado de Litoral: apuntes para un debate pendiente*. La Paz: OXFAM and Plural editores. https://www.researchgate.net/publication/322086849_Bolivia_un_pais_privado_de_Litoral_apuntes_para_un_debate_pendiente. Accessed 28 November 2018.

Agramont Lechín, Daniel and Gustavo Bonifaz (2018) "The Growing Chinese Presence in Latin America and its (Geo)political Manifestations in Bolivia." London School of Economics, Global South Unit, Working Paper No. 2. http://eprints.lse.ac.uk/88088/1/Working%20Paper%20No.%202.%202018%20%28Agramont%20and%20Bonifaz%29.pdf. Accessed 17 February 2019.

Albarracín Millán, Juan (2005) *La dominación perpetua de Bolivia: La vision chilena de Bolivia en el Tratado de 1904*. La Paz: Plural editores.

Alexander, Robert J. (1982) *Bolivia: Past, Present, and Future of Its Politics*. New York: Praeger.

Alurralde Tejada, Juan Carlos, Jorge Molina, Elena Villarroel, Paula Pacheco (2011) "Science Helps To Solve International Water Conflicts Case: The Mauri River." Paper presented at XIV World Water Congress, Pernambuco, Brazil (September). Mimeograph copy.

Alvarado A., Julio G. (2013) "Bolivia: tan cerca y tan lejos del Pacífico." In *Debate Boliviano: la demanda marítima ante La Haya*, 28–34. La Paz: Ediciones Pazos Kanki.

Alvarez, Elena H. (1995) "Economic Development, Restructuring, and the Illicit Drug Sector in Bolivia and Peru: Current Policies." *Journal of Interamerican Studies and World Affairs* 37, 3 (Fall): 125–149.

Andaluz, Horacio (2002) *Bases jurídicas para la reintegración marítima de Bolivia: La regla pacta sunt servanda como punto cero*. Santa Cruz: Universidad Privada de Santa Cruz de la Sierra.

Andrade, Victor (1976) *My Missions for Revolutionary Bolivia, 1944–1962*. Pittsburgh, PA: University of Pittsburgh Press.

Andreas, Peter (1995) "Free Market Reform and Drug Market Prohibition: U.S. Policies at Cross-purposes in Latin America." *Third World Quarterly* 16, 1 (Spring): 75–87.
Aninat, Augusto (1978) "El programa de liberación y el arancel externo común." In *Pacto Andino: Carácter y perspectivas*, ed. Ernesto Tironi, 111–183. Lima: Instituto de Estudios Peruanos.
Araníbar Quiroga, Antonio (2001) "Gas por el Pacífico: ¿Chile o Perú? La alternativa: Arica Trinacional." *Semanario PULSO* (December). Mimeograph copy.
Araníbar Quiroga, Antonio, et al. (2001) *Hacia un enfoque trinacional de las relaciones entre Bolivia, Chile y Perú*. La Paz: Plural Editores.
Araya Leüpin, Eduardo (2017) "Notas para un historia de relaciones vecinales de Chile en el siglo xx." *Revista Chilena de Relaciones Internacionales* 1, 1 (January–June): 73–99. https://rchri.cl/articulo/notas-para-una-historia-de-las-relaciones-vecinales-de-chile-en-el-siglo-xx/. Accessed 9 February 2019.
Arguedas, Alcides (1922) *Historia general de Bolivia (El proceso de la nacionalidad), 1809–1921*. La Paz: Arnó Hermanos editores.
Arguedas, Alcides (1981) *Historia de Bolivia*. 5 vols. La Paz: Libreria Editorial Juventud.
Arnade, Charles W. (1957) *The Emergence of the Republic of Bolivia*. Tallahassee, FL: University of Florida Press.
Artaraz, Kepa (2012) *Bolivia: Refounding the Nation*. London: Pluto Press.
Arze Quiroga, Eduardo (1991) *La relaciones internacionales de Bolivia, 1825–1990*. La Paz and Cochabamba: Editorial Los Amigos del Libro.
Avery, William P. (1983) "The Politics of Crisis and Cooperation in the Andean Group." *The Journal of Developing Areas* 17, 2 (January): 155–183.
Bákula Patiño, Juan Miguel (2002) *Perú: Entre la Realidad y la Utopía, 180 Años de Política Exterior*. 2 vols. Lima: Fondo de Cultura Económica.
Baptista Gumucio, Mariano, ed. (1978) *Tamayo y la Reivindicación Marítima de Bolivia*. La Paz: Editorial Casa Municipal de la Cultura "Franz Tamayo."
Barragán, Rossana (2008) "Oppressed or Privileged Regions? Some Historical Reflections on the Use of State Resources." In *Unresolved Tensions: Bolivia Past and Present*, ed. John Crabtree and Laurence Whitehead, 83–103. Pittsburgh, PA: University of Pittsburgh Press.
Barrenechea y Raygada, Oscar (1942) *El congreso de Panamá*. Lima: Ministerio de Relaciones Exteriores.
Barrenechea y Raygada, Oscar (1947) *Congresos y conferencias internacionales celebrados en Lima, 1847–1894*. Buenos Aires: Peuser.
Barrios Morón, Raúl (1995) "Bolivia y Paraguay: Construyendo una historia cooperativa." In *Política exterior boliviana: tendencias y desafíos*, ed. Raúl Barrios Morón et al., 275–289. La Paz: Unidad de Análisis de Política Exterior.
Barrios Morón, Raúl (1997) "Las relaciones de Bolivia con los países de Asia-Pacífico." Paper presented at Reunión de América Latina y el Caribe de Centros de Estudios sobre Asia-Pacífico, Caracas, Venezuela (17–18 July). Mimeograph copy.
Barros Borgoño, Luís (1897) *La negociación chileno-boliviana de 1895*. Santiago de Chile: Imprenta y Encuadernación Barcelona.
Barros Borgoño, Luís (1922) *La Cuestión del Pacífico y Las Nuevas Orientaciones de Bolivia*. Santiago de Chile: Imprenta Universitaria.
Barros Borgoño, Luís (1924) *The Problem of the Pacific and the New Policies of Bolivia*. Baltimore, MD: The Sun Job Printing Office.

Basadre, Jorge (1948) *Chile, Perú y Bolivia independientes*. Barcelona: Salvat Editores.
Basadre, Jorge (1968) *Historia de la república del Perú, 1822–1933*. 6th edn. 16 vols. Lima: Editorial Universitaria.
Basile, Clemente (1943) *Una guerra poca conocida*. 2 vols. Buenos Aires: Círculo Militar.
Bazoberry Quiroga, Antonio (2003) *El mito del Silala*. La Paz: Plural editores.
Becerra de la Roca, Rodolfo (2002) *El tratado de 1904: la gran estafa*. La Paz and Cochabamba: Editorial Los Amigos del Libro.
Bello Codesido, Emilio (1919) *Anotaciones para la historia de las negociaciones diplomáticas con el Perú y Bolivia, 1900–1904*. Santiago de Chile: La Ilustración.
Bieber, Enrique León (1984) *Las relaciones económicas de Bolivia con Alemania, 1880–1920*. Berlin: Colloquium Verlag.
Bieber, Enrique León (2004) *Pugna por influencia y hegemonía: La rivalidad germano-estadounidense en Bolivia, 1936–1946*. Frankfurt: Peter Lang.
Binetti, Bruno and Ben Raderstorf (2018) "A Requiem for UNASUR." *Global Americas* (25 April): 1–5. https://theglobalamericans.org/tag/unasur/. Accessed 25 November 2018.
Blasier, Cole (1971) "The United States and the Revolution." In *Beyond the Revolution: Bolivia since 1952*, ed. James M. Malloy and Richard S. Thorn, 53–109. Pittsburgh, PA: University of Pittsburgh Press.
Boas, Frank (1959) "Landlocked Countries and the Law of the Sea." *International Comparative Law Bulletin* 4, 1 (December): 22–27.
Bolivia. Ministerio de Relaciones Exteriores y Culto (1976) *Memoria del Ministerio de Relaciones Exteriores: Correspondiente a 1975*. La Paz. Mimeograph copy.
Bolivia. Ministerio de Relaciones Exteriores y Culto (1977) *Fundamentos del Derecho de Bolivia de Retorno al Mar (23 de Marzo de 1977)*. La Paz. Mimeograph copy.
Bolivia. Ministerio de Relaciones Exteriores y Culto (1979a) "Exposición del Misión Permanente de Bolivia ante la Organización del los Estados Americanos." 14 February 1979. Mimeograph copy.
Bolivia. Ministerio de Relaciones Exteriores y Culto (1979b) *Discursos Inaugurales: IX Asamblea General Ordinaria de la O.E.A. (22 de Octubre de 1979)*. La Paz. Mimeograph copy.
Bolivia. Ministerio de Relaciones Exteriores y Culto (1979c) *Mediterraneidad de Bolivia: IX Asamblea General Ordinaria de la O.E.A. (22 de Octubre de 1979)*. La Paz. Mimeograph copy.
Bolivia. Ministerio de Relaciones Exteriores y Culto (1983) "Informe sobre el Problema Maritimo de Bolivia." 18 November 1983. La Paz.Mimeograph copy.
Bolivia. Ministerio de Relaciones Exteriores y Culto (1987) "Planteamietos Bolivianos: Memorandums 1 & 2," 18 April 1987; "Preguntas de la Delegación de Chile en Relación a los Planteamientos Formulados por Bolivia con Fecha 21 de Abril de 1987," 22 April 1987; "Respuestas de la Delegación de Bolivia al Cuestionario Presentado por la Delegación de Chile en el Documento de Fecha 22 de Abril de 1987," 22 April 1987. *Relaciones Internacionales: Revista Boliviana* 2, 3 (April): 99–107.
Bolivia. Ministerio de Relaciones Exteriores y Culto (1988) *Tricolor: Historia y Proyecciones de Paz, Desarrollo e Integración del Diferendo Marítimo Boliviano-Chileno*. La Paz and Cochabamba: Editorial Los Amigos del Libro.
Bolivia. Ministerio de Relaciones Exteriores y Culto (1997) *Las Relaciones Boliviano-Chilenas: Diagnóstico y Perspectivas*, 30 July 1997. La Paz. Mimeograph copy.

## 214  Bibliography

Bolivia. Ministerio de Relaciones Exteriores y Culto (1998) *Aspectos de la política exterior boliviana 1998*. La Paz: Editorial Hisbol.

Bolivia. Ministerio de Relaciones Exteriores y Culto (2004) *El libro azul: La demanda marítima boliviana*. La Paz: Dirección de Informaciones de la Presidencia de la República y Ministerio de Relaciones Exteriores.

Bolivia. Ministerio de Relaciones Exteriores y Culto (2009) *El acuedo inicial sobre el Silala, o Siloli* (*The Initial Agreement on Silala, or Siloli*). La Paz: Dirección de Informaciones de la Presidencia de la República y Ministerio de Relaciones Exteriores. https://www.internationalwaterlaw.org/documents/regionaldocs/Silala/SilalaAgreement2009_Spanish.pdf. Accessed 22 September 2018.

Bolivia. Ministerio de Relaciones Exteriores y Culto (2014) *El libro del mar (The Book of the Sea)*, 2nd edn. La Paz: Dirección Estratégica de Reivindicación Marítima.

Bonilla, Heraclio (1980) *Un siglo a la deriva: Ensayos sobre el Perú, Bolivia y la guerra*. Lima: Instituto de Estudios Peruanos.

Bórquez Galleguillos, Rodolfo and Javier Hernán Sáez Moraga (2016). "Los convenios de mayo de 1895 entre Chile y Bolivia: Estudio histórico-jurídico." Memoria para optar al grado de licenciado en ciencias jurídicas. Universidad de Chile. http://repositorio.uchile.cl/bitstream/handle/2250/140394/Los-convenios-de-mayo-de-1895-entre-Chile-y-Bolivia.pdf?sequence=1&isAllowed=y. Accessed 22 May 2017.

Botelho Gosalvez, Raúl (1980) *El litoral boliviano: perspectiva histórica y geopolítica*. Buenos Aires: El Cid Editor.

Briceño-Ruiz, José and Isidro Morales (2017) "Introduction." In *Post-hegemonic Regionalism in the Americas: Toward a Pacific-Atlantic Divide?*, ed. José Briceño-Ruiz and Isidro Morales, 1–15. London and New York: Routledge.

Burr, Robert N. (1967) *By Reason or Force: Chile and the Balancing of Power in South America, 1830–1905*. Berkeley and Los Angeles, CA: University of California Press.

Bustos, Carlos (2003) *Chile y Bolivia: Un largo camino*. Santiago de Chile: Editorial Puerto de Palos.

Cajías, Lupe (2014) "1977–1985: Transition between Dictatorships and Democracy." In *From Military Dictatorships to Evo Morales Populism: Three Decades of Intense Bolivian History*, ed. Raúl Peñaranda, 7–14. La Paz: Página Siete.

Cajías de la Vega, Fernando (1975) *La provincia de Atacama (1825–1842)*. La Paz: Instituto Boliviano de Cultura.

Calderón, Félix (2000) *El tratado de 1929: La otra historia*. Lima: Fondo Editorial del Congreso del Perú.

Camacho Omiste, Edgar (1981) *Bolivia y la integración andina*. 2nd edn. La Paz and Cochabamba: Editorial Los Amigos del Libro.

Camacho Omiste, Edgar (2000) "Nuevas perspectivas de la cuestión marítima." In *Bolivia: Temas de la Agenda Internacional*, ed. Alberto Zelada, 345–370. La Paz: Unidad de Análisis de Política Exterior.

Carlsen, Laura (2008) "The Failure of U.S. 'Democracy Promotion' in Bolivia." *Center for International Policy, Americas Program* (31 October). Mimeograph copy.

Carranza, Mario E. (2017) "Resilient or declining? Mercosur and the Future of Post-neoliberal Regionalism in Latin America." In *Post-hegemonic Regionalism in the Americas: Toward a Pacific-Atlantic Divide?*, ed. José Briceño-Ruiz and Isidro Morales, 125–140. London and New York: Routledge.

Carrasco, José (1920) *Bolivia's Case for the League of Nations*. London: Selwyn & Blount.

Carter, Jimmy (2003) "President Carter's Bolivia Trip Report: Dec. 16–21, 2003." Atlanta, GA: The Carter Center. https://www.cartercenter.org/news/documents/doc1571.html. Accessed 2 August 2018.
Cayoja Riart, Humberto (1998) *El Expansionismo de Chile en el cono sur.* La Paz: Editorial Proinsa.
Chan-Sánchez, Julio J. (1995) "Economic Integration in Latin America: The Andean Group in the 1990s." Paper delivered at the Nineteenth Latin American Studies Association Meeting, Washington, DC (28–30 September). Mimeograph copy.
Checa Drouet, B. (1936) *La doctrina americana de uti possidetis de 1810.* Lima: Librería e Imprenta Gil.
Chesterton, Bridget María (2016) "Introduction: An Overview of the Chaco War." In *The Chaco War: Environment, Ethnicity, and Nationalism*, ed. Bridget María Chesterton, 1–20. London and New York: Bloomsbury.
Chile. Ministerio de Relaciones Exteriores (1975) *Memoria del Ministerio de Relaciones Exteriores: Correspondiente al año 1975.* Santiago de Chile. Mimeograph copy.
Chile. Ministerio de Relaciones Exteriores (1976) *Memoria del Ministerio de Relaciones Exteriores: Correspondiente al año 1976.* Santiago de Chile. Mimeograph copy.
Chile. Ministerio de Relaciones Exteriores (1977) *Memoria del Ministerio de Relaciones Exteriores: Correspondiente al año 1977.* Santiago de Chile. Mimeograph copy.
Chile. Ministerio de Relaciones Exteriores (1978) *Memoria del Ministerio de Relaciones Exteriores: Correspondiente al año 1978.* Santiago de Chile. Mimeograph copy.
Chile. Ministerio de Relaciones Exteriores (1979) *Memoria del Ministerio de Relaciones Exteriores: Correspondiente al año 1979.* Santiago de Chile. Mimeograph copy.
Chile. Ministerio de Relaciones Exteriores (2007) "Acta de la XVII reunion del mecanismo de consultas políticas Chile-Bolivia." Press Release. 19 October.Santiago de Chile. http://www.minrel.gob.cl/minrel/site/artic/20080716/pags/20080716180444.html. Accessed 14 December 2018.
Chile. Ministerio de Relaciones Exteriores (2014) "Chile y la aspiración marítima boliviana: mito y realidad." June. Santiago de Chile. https://www.mitoyrealidad.cl/mitoyrealidad/site/artic/20141230/asocfile/20141230145007/presentaci__n.pdf. Accessed 24 June 2015.
Chile. Ministerio de Relaciones Exteriores (2015) "El libre transito de Bolivia: la realidad." 26 January.Santiago de Chile: Ministerio de Relaciones Exteriores.
Concha Robles, José Miguel (2011) *Iniciativas chilenas para una alianza estratégica con Bolivia (1879–1899).* La Paz: Plural editores.
Concha Robles, José Miguel and Cristian Garay Vera (2013) *El Tratado de 1904: Negociaciones e intereses involucrados.* La Paz: Plural editores.
Correa, Vera Loreto and Viviana García Pinzón (2012) "Aunque las aguas nos dividan: las relaciones chileno-bolivianas y la construcción de una agenda común." *Latinoamérica* 54 (January–June): 75–100. http://www.revistadeestlat.unam.mx/index.php/latino/article/view/56469/50119. Accessed 9 February 2019.
Cote, Stephen (2016a) "Bolivian Oil Nationalism and the Chaco War." In *The Chaco War: Environment, Ethnicity, and Nationalism*, ed. Bridget María Chesterton, 157–175. London and New York: Bloomsbury.
Cote, Stephen (2016b) *Oil and Nation: A History of Bolivia's Petroleum Sector.* Morgantown, WV: West Virginia University Press.
Crabtree, John and Laurence Whitehead (2008) "On Regionalism." In *Unresolved Tensions: Bolivia Past and Present*, ed. John Crabtree and Laurence Whitehead, 61–64, Pittsburgh, PA: University of Pittsburgh Press.

## Bibliography

Crabtree, John and Ann Chaplin (2013) *Bolivia: Processes of Change*. London: Zed Books.
Crandall, Russell C. (2008) *The United States and Latin America after the Cold War*. Cambridge: Cambridge University Press.
Crespo, Alfonso (1979) *Santa Cruz: El Condor Indio*. La Paz: Librería y Editorial Juventud.
Crespo, Alfonso (1997) *Hernán Siles Zuazo: el hombre de abril*. La Paz: Plural editores.
Crosby, Kenneth Ward (1949) "The Diplomacy of the United States in Relation to the War of the Pacific, 1879–1884." Ph.D. diss., George Washington University.
Cuevas Cancino, Francisco (1976) *Del congreso de Panamá a la conferencia de Caracas*. Caracas: Oficina Central de Información.
Dangl, Benjamin (2007) *The Price of Fire: Resource Wars and Social Movements in Bolivia*. Oakland, CA: AK Press.
Davis, William Columbus (1950) *The Last Conquistadores: The Spanish Intervention in Peru and Chile, 1863–1866*. Athens, GA: University of Georgia Press.
De Cossío Klüver, Manuel Augusto (2011) "Tierra por agua: Las negociaciones marítima boliviano-chilenas (1946–1952)." M.A. thesis, Universidad Católica Boliviana "San Pablo."
Delaney, Robert W. (1962) "General Miller and the Confederación Perú-Boliviana." *The Americas* 18 (January): 213–242.
Delgado, Ana Carolina T. and Clayton M. Cunha Filho (2016) "Bolivia-Brazil: Internal Dynamics, Sovereignty Drive, and Integrationist Ideology." In *Foreign Policy Responses to the Rise of Brazil: Balancing Power in Emerging States*, ed. Gian Luca Gardini and Maria Herminia, 129–144. London: Palgrave Macmillan.
Denegri Luna, Félix (1988) "Perú-Bolivia: una etapa histórica de sus complejas relaciones (1919–1929)." In *Relaciones del Perú con las paises vecinos*, ed. Eduardo Ferrero Costa, 97–127. Lima: Centro Peruano de Estudios Internacionales.
Dennis, William Jefferson (1931) *Tacna and Arica: An Account of the Chile-Peru Boundary Dispute and of the Arbitrations by the United States*. New Haven, CT: Yale University Press.
Deustua Caravedo, Alejandro (1999) "Los Convenios de Ilo y Su Impacto Regional." In *El Desarrollo del Sur del Perú: Realidad y desafíos*, ed. Drago Kisic and Ramón Bahamonde, 27–37. Lima: Centro Peruano de Estudios Internacionales.
Dorn, Glenn J. (2011) *The Truman Administration and Bolivia: Making the World Safe for Liberal Constitutional Oligarchy*. University Park, PA: University of Pennsylvania Press.
Dunkerley, James (1984) *Rebellion in the Veins: Political Struggle in Bolivia, 1952–1982*. London: Verso Editions.
Dunkerley, James (2007) *Bolivia: Revolution and the Power of History in the Present*. London: Institute for the Study of the Americas.
Eckstein, Susan (1976) *The Impact of Revolution: A Comparative Analysis of Mexico and Bolivia*. London: Sage Publications.
Ellis, R. Evan (2009) *China in Latin America: The Whats and Wherefores*. Boulder, CO: Routledge.
Ellis, R. Evan (2017) "Chinese Engagement with Bolivia: Resources, Business Opportunities, and Strategic Location." *Air & Space Power Journal* (2 February): 3–19. http://www.au.af.mil/au/afri/aspj/apjinternational/apj-s/2016/2016-2/2016_2_03_ellis_s_eng.pdf. Accessed 18 November 2018.

Ellis, R. Evan (2018) "It's Time to Think Strategically about Countering Chinese Advances in Latin America." *Global Americas* (2 February): 1–12. https://the globalamericans.org/2018/02/time-think-strategically-countering-chinese-advances-la tin-america/. Accessed 25 November 2018.
Encina, Francisco A. (1956) *Resumen de la Historia de Chile*. 2d edn. 3 vols. Santiago de Chile: Empresa Editora Zig-Zag.
Encina, Francisco A. (1963) *Las Relaciones entre Chile y Bolivia, 1841–1963*. Santiago de Chile: Editorial Nascimento.
Ergueta Avila, Edgar (2000) "ILO: Diagnóstico y Proyecciones." In *Bolivia: Temas de la Agenda Internacional*, ed. Alberto Zelada Castedo, 93–120. La Paz: Unidad de Análisis de Política Exterior.
Escobari Cusicanqui, Jorge (1969) *El desvio del Rio Mauri: Integración y reintegración marítima 3 conferencias*. La Paz: Universidad Mayor de San Andrés.
Escobari Cusicanqui, Jorge (1982) *Historia diplomática de Bolivia*. 2 vols. 4th edn. Lima: Industrial.
Escobari Cusicanqui, Jorge. (1986a) "Enunciados para una política internacional boliviana." *Relaciones Internacionales: Revista Boliviana* 1, 1 (primer trimestre): 25–41.
Escobari Cusicanqui, Jorge (1986b) "El diálogo con Chile." *Relaciones Internacionales: Revista Boliviana* 1, 2 (segundo trimestre): 53–66.
Escobari Cusicanqui, Jorge (1988) *El derecho al mar: las diez evasivas chilenas (de 1895 a 1987)*. 3rd edn. La Paz: Librería Editorial Juventud.
Espinosa Moraga, Oscar (1964) *La cuestión del Lauca*. Santiago de Chile: Editorial Nascimento.
Espinosa Moraga, Oscar (1965) *Bolivia y el mar, 1810–1964*. Santiago de Chile: Editorial Nascimento.
Farcau, Bruce W. (1996) *The Chaco War: Bolivia and Paraguay, 1932–1935*. New York: Praeger.
Farcau, Bruce W. (2000) *The Ten Cents War: Chile, Peru, and Bolivia in the War of the Pacific, 1879–1884*. Westport, CT: Praeger.
Farthing, Linda C. (2018) "A Surprise Win for the Victims of Bolivia's Gas War." North American Congress on Latin Ameica (NACLA) (6 April). https://nacla.org/news/2018/04/06/surprise-win-victims-bolivia%E2%80%99s-gas-war. Accessed 8 November 2018.
Farthing, Linda C. and Benjamin H. Kohl (2014) *Evo's Bolivia: Continuity and Change*. Austin, TX: University of Texas Press.
Faye, Michael L., John W. McArthur, Jeffrey D. Sachs, and Thomas Snow (2004) "The Challenges Facing Landlocked Developing Countries." *Journal of Human Development* 5, 1 (March): 31–68.
Fellmann Velarde, José (1967) *Memorandum sobre política exterior boliviana*. La Paz: Libreria Editorial Juventud.
Ferrero Costa, Eduardo (1987) "Peruvian Foreign Policy: Current Trends, Constraints and Opportunities." *Journal of Interamerican Studies and World Affairs* 29, 2 (Summer): 55–78.
Ferris, Elizabeth G. (1979) "Foreign Investment as an Influence on Foreign Policy Behavior: The Andean Pact." *Inter-American Economic Affairs* 33, 2 (Autumn): 45–69.
Field, Thomas C., Jr. (2014) *From Development to Dictatorship: Bolivia and the Alliance for Progress in the Kennedy Era*. Cornell, NY: Cornell University Press.

## Bibliography

Fifer, J. Valerie (1972) *Bolivia: Land, Location, and Politics since 1825*. Cambridge: Cambridge University Press.

Finot, Enrique (1980) *Nueva Historia del Bolivia: Ensayo de Interpretación Sociológica de Tiwanaku a 1930*. 7th edn. La Paz: Gisbert & Cía S.A.

Fontaine, Roger W. (1977) *The Andean Pact: A Political Analysis*. Washington Papers, vol. 5, Center for Strategic and International Studies, Georgetown University. Beverly Hills, CA and London: Sage Publications.

Francaviglia, Richard V. (2018) *Imagining the Atacama Desert: A Five-Hundred-Year Journey of Discovery*. Salt Lake City, UT: University of Utah Press.

Galarza, Ernest (1971) "Debts, Dictatorship and Revolution in Bolivia and Peru." *Foreign Policy Reports* 7 (May 13): 101–118.

Galindo Quiroga, Eudoro (1977) *Litoral andino: Retrospección y perspectivas en torno al problema marítimo*. La Paz and Cochabamba: Editorial Los Amigos del Libro.

Gamarra, Eduardo A. (2005) "State, Drug Policy, and Democracy in the Andes." *Andean Working Paper,* Inter-American Dialogue (June): 1–13.

Gamarra, Eduardo A. (2007) "Bolivia on the Brink." The Center for Preventive Action, Council on Foreign Relations, Council Special Report 24 (February).

Gamarra, Eduardo A. (2016) "U.S.-Bolivian Relations in Times of Change." In *The Obama Doctrine in the Americas: Security in the Americas in the Twenty-First Century*, ed. Hanna S. Kassab and Jonathan D. Rosen, 185–212. Lanham, NJ: Lexington Books.

Ganzert, Frederic William (1934) "The Boundary Controversy in the Upper Amazon between Brazil, Bolivia, and Peru, 1903–1909." *Hispanic American Historical Review* 14, 4 (November): 427–449.

Garay Vera, Cristián (2008) "El Acre y los 'Asuntos del Pacífico' Bolivia, Brasil, Chile y Estados Unidos, 1898–1909." *Historia* 2, 41 (July–December): 341–369.

García-Corrochano, Luis (2012) "La política exterior del Perú respecto de Bolivia y Chile (1992–2012)." In *Veinte años de política exterior peruana (1991–2011)*, ed. Fabián Novak, 75–94. Lima: Fondo Editorial de la Pontificia Universedad Católica del Perú.

García Salazar, Arturo (1928) *Resumen de historia diplomática del Perú, 1820–1884*. Lima: Talleres Gráficas Sanmartí y Cía.

Garibaldi, Rosa (2003) *La política exterior del Perú en la era de Ramón Castilla: Defensa hemisférica y defense de la jurisdicción nacional*. Lima: Fondo Editorial Fundación Academia Diplomática del Perú.

Gironda Cabrera, Eusebio (2001) *Coca immortal*. La Paz: Plural editores.

Gisbert, Teresa (2001) "La independencia, 1800–1828." In *Historia de Bolivia*, 4th edn., ed. José de Mesa, Teresa Gisbert, and Carlos D. Mesa Gisbert, 307–369. La Paz: Editorial Gisbert.

Glassner, Martin Ira (1964) "Bolivia and an Access to the Sea." M.A. thesis, California State College at Fullerton.

Glassner, Martin Ira (1970a) *Access to the Sea for Developing Land-Locked States*. Dordrecht: Martinus Nijhoff.

Glassner, Martin Ira (1970b) "The Río Lauca: Dispute over an International River." *The Geographical Review* 60, 2 (April): 192–207.

Glassner, Martin Ira (1988) "Bolivia's Orientation: Toward the Atlantic or the Pacific?" In *Geopolitics of the Southern Cone and Antarctica*, ed. Philip Kelly and Jack Child, 154–169. Boulder, CO: Lynne Rienner.

Gómez, Juan Pablo (1980) *Vida, pasión y muerte del General Mariano Melgarejo*. La Paz: Ediciones Puerte del Sol.

González Zelaya, Jaime (1986) "Cuestiones comerciales con Chile y la causa marítima." *Relaciones Internacionales: Revista Boliviana* 1, 2 (segundo trimestre): 23–29.
Gootenberg, Paul (1989) *Between Silver and Guano: Commercial Policy and the State in Postindependence Peru*. Princeton, NJ: Princeton University Press.
Gordon, Dennis R. (1979) "The Question of the Pacific: Current Perspectives on a Long-Standing Dispute." *World Affairs* 141, 4 (Spring): 321–335.
Guachalla, Luis Fernando (1976) *La cuestión portuaria y las negociaciones de 1950*. La Paz and Cochabamba: Editorial Los Amigos del Libro.
Guachalla, Luis Fernando (1982) *Bolivia-Chile: La negociación marítima, 1975–1978*. La Paz: Empresa Editoria Siglo.
Guevara Arze, Walter (1978) *Radiografía de la negociación con Chile*. Cochabamba: Universo.
Guillermo Elío, Tomás (1986) "La mediterraneidad boliviana: Un límite a su desarrollo." *Relaciones Internacionales: Revista Boliviana* 1, 2 (segundo trimestre): 7–20.
Gumucio Granier, Jorge (1997) "Alberto Ostria y el pacto con el Perú de 1936." *Agenda Internacional* 4, 9 (julio/diciembre): 97–106.
Gumucio Granier, Jorge (2005) *Estados Unidos y el mar boliviano: Testimonios para la historia*. La Paz: Plural editores. The English translation is *United States and the Bolivian Seacoast*. http://www.boliviaweb.com/mar/sea/.
Gutiérrez Moscoso, Fernando (2000) "Régimen de Libre Tránsito." In *Bolivia: Temas de la Agenda Internacional*, ed. Alberto Zelada, 69–92. La Paz: Unidad de Análisis de Política Exterior.
Guzmán, Augusto (1998) *Historia de Bolivia*. 8th edn. La Paz and Cochabamba: Editorial Los Amigos del Libro.
Guzmán Escobari, Andrés (2015a) *Un mar de promesas incumplidas: La historia del problema marítimo boliviano (1879–2015)*. La Paz: Plural editores.
Guzmán Escobari, Andrés (2015b) "The Role of Master Narratives of Bolivia and Chile in the Formation of Their National Identities." Master's thesis, University of Amsterdam.
Hausmann, Ricardo (2001) "Prisoners of Geography." *Foreign Policy* (January/February): 45–53.
Healy, Kevin (1988) "Coca, the State, and the Peasantry in Bolivia, 1982–1988." *Journal of Interamerican Studies and World Affairs* 30, 2&3 (Summer/Fall): 105–126.
Heilman, Lawrence C. (2017) *USAID in Bolivia: Partner or Patrón?* Boulder, CO: Lynne Rienner.
Henderson, Peter V. N. (2013) *The Course of Andean History*. Albuquerque, NM: University of New Mexico Press.
Herrera Alarcón, Dante (1961) *Rebeliones que intentaron desmembrar el sur del Perú*. Lima: Imprenta Colegio Militar Leoncio Prado.
Hillman, John (1984) "The Emergence of the Tin Industry in Bolivia." *Journal of Latin American Studies* 16, 2 (November): 403–437.
Hindery, Derrick (2013) *From Enron to Evo: Pipeline Politics, Global Environmentalism, and Indigenous Rights in Bolivia*. Tucson, AZ: University of Arizona Press.
Holland, E. James (1975) "Bolivia." In *Latin American Foreign Policies: An Analysis*, ed. Harold Eugene Davis and Larman C. Wilson, 338–359. Baltimore, MD: Johns Hopkins University Press.
Hylton, Forrest and Sinclair Thomson (2007) *Revolutionary Horizons: Past and Present in Bolivian Politics*. London: Verso.

Inman, Samuel Guy (1965) *Inter-American Conferences, 1826–1954: History and Problems*. Washington, DC: University Press.

International Court of Justice (2012) "Public Sitting Held on Friday 14 December 2012, at 10 a.m., at the Peace Palace, President Tomka Presiding, in the Case Concerning the Maritime Dispute (Peru v. Chile)." 14 December. http://www.icj-cij.org/docket/files/137/17230.pdf. Accessed 7 September 2018.

International Court of Justice (2013) "Application Instituting Proceedings. Obligation to Negotiate Access to the Pacific (Bolivia v. Chile)." 24 April. https://www.icj-cij.org/files/case-related/153/17338.pdf. Accessed 7 September 2018.

International Court of Justice (2014) "Maritime Dispute (Peru v. Chile). Summary of the Judgment of 27 January." https://www.icj-cij.org/files/case-related/137/17958.pdf. Accessed 7 September 2018.

International Court of Justice (2015a) "Public Sitting Held on Monday 4 May 2015, at 3 p.m., at the Peace Palace, President Abraham Presiding, in the Case Concerning Obligation to Negotiate Access to the Pacific Ocean (Bolivia v. Chile). Preliminary Objection [First Round of Oral Argument]." CR 2015/18. 4 May. http://www.icj-cij.org/docket/files/153/18628.pdf. Accessed 7 September 2018.

International Court of Justice (2015b) "Public Sitting Held on Wednesday 6 May 2015, at 10 a.m., at the Peace Palace, President Abraham Presiding, in the Case Concerning Obligation to Negotiate Access to the Pacific Ocean (Bolivia v. Chile). Preliminary Objection [First Round of Oral Argument]." CR 2015/19. 6 May. http://www.icj-cij.org/docket/files/153/18636.pdf. Accessed 7 September 2018.

International Court of Justice (2015c) "Public Sitting Held on Thursday 7 May 2015, at 4:30 p.m., at the Peace Palace, President Abraham Presiding, in the Case Concerning Obligation to Negotiate Access to the Pacific Ocean (Bolivia v. Chile). Preliminary Objection [Second Round of Oral Argument]." CR 2015/20. 7 May. http://www.icj-cij.org/docket/files/153/18644.pdf. Accessed 7 September 2018.

International Court of Justice (2015d) "Public Sitting Held on Friday 8 May 2015, at 3 p.m., at the Peace Palace, President Abraham Presiding, in the Case Concerning Obligation to Negotiate Access to the Pacific Ocean (Bolivia v. Chile). Preliminary Objection [Second Round of Oral Argument]." CR 2015/21. 8 May. http://www.icj-cij.org/docket/files/153/18644.pdf. Accessed 7 September 2018.

International Court of Justice (2015e) "Obligation to Negotiate Access to the Pacific Ocean (Bolivia v. Chile). Judgment. The Court rejects the Preliminary Objections Raised by Chile and Finds that it Has Jurisdiction to Entertain the Application Filed by Bolivia on 24 April 2013." General List No. 153. 24 September (http://www.icj-cij.org/docket/files/153/18746.pdf). Accessed 7 September 2018.

International Court of Justice (2016a) "Application Instituting Proceedings. Dispute over the Status and Use of the Waters of the Silala (Chile v. Bolivia)." 6 June. https://www.icj-cij.org/files/case-related/162/162-20160606-APP-01-00-EN.pdf. Accessed 7 September 2018.

International Court of Justice (2016b) "Obligation to Negotiate Access to the Pacific Ocean (Bolivia v. Chile). Counter-Memorial of the Republic of Chile." 6 volumes. 13 July. https://www.icj-cij.org/files/case-related/153/153-20160713-WRI-01-00-EN.pdf. Accessed 15 September 2018.

International Court of Justice (2017a) "Obligation to Negotiate Access to the Pacific Ocean (Bolivia v. Chile). Reply of the Government of the Plurinational State of Bolivia." 5 volumes. 21 March. https://www.icj-cij.org/files/case-related/153/153-20170321-WRI-01-00-EN.pdf. Accessed 15 September 2018.

International Court of Justice (2017b) "Obligation to Negotiate Access to the Pacific Ocean (Bolivia v. Chile). Rejoiner of the Republic of Chile." 3 volumes. 15 September. https://www.icj-cij.org/files/case-related/153/153-20170915-WRI-01-00-EN.pdf. Accessed 15 September 2018.

International Court of Justice (2018a) "Obligation to Negotiate Access to the Pacific Ocean (Bolivia v. Chile). Conclusion of the Public Hearings. The Court to Begin its Deliberation." Press Release No. 2018/16. 28 March. https://www.icj-cij.org/files/case-related/153/153-20180328-PRE-01-00-EN.pdf. Accessed 15 September 2018.

International Court of Justice (2018b) "Obligation to Negotiate Access to the Pacific Ocean (Bolivia v. Chile)." Judgment. 1 October. https://www.icj-cij.org/files/case-related/153/153-20181001-JUD-01-00-EN.pdf. Accessed 2 October 2018.

International Court of Justice (2018c) "Dispute over the Status and Use of the Waters of the Silala (Chile v. Bolivia)." 15 November. https://www.icj-cij.org/files/case-related/162/162-20181115-ORD-01-00-EN.pdf. Accessed 29 January 2019.

Iturralde Chinel, Luis (1963) *La desviación del rio Lauca por Chile*. La Paz: Empresa Industrial Gráfica E. Burillo.

James, Daniel, ed. (1968) *The Complete Bolivian Diaries of Ché Guevara and Other Captured Documents*. New York, NY: Stein and Day.

Jordán Pozo, Rolando (1999) "Minería: Siglo xx, la era del estaño." In *Bolivia en el siglo xx: La formación de la Bolivia contemporánea*, ed. Fernando Campero Prudencio, 219–239. La Paz: Harvard Club of Bolivia.

Kendall, Lane Carter (1936) "Andrés Santa Cruz and the Peru-Bolivian Confederation." *Hispanic American Historical Review* 16, 1 (February): 29–48.

Kiernan, V. G. (1955) "Foreign Interests in the War of the Pacific." *Hispanic American Historical Review* 35, 1 (February): 14–36.

Klein, Herbert S. (1969) *Parties and Political Change in Bolivia, 1880–1952*. Cambridge: Cambridge University Press.

Klein, Herbert S. (2011) *A Concise History of Bolivia*. 2nd edn. Cambridge: Cambridge University Press.

Klein, Herbert S. and José Alejandro Peres-Cajías (2014) "Bolivian Oil and Natural Gas under State and Private Control, 1920–2010." *Bolivian Studies Journal* 20: 141–164.

Kohl, Benjamin and Linda Farthing (2006) *Impasse in Bolivia: Neoliberal Hegemony and Popular Resistance*. London: Zed Books.

Kriener, Florian (2017) "Determining an International Watercourse: The Dispute of Chile v. Bolivia concerning the Silala." *Revista Tribuna Internacional* 6, 12: 1–17.

Krueger, Chris (2017–18) "Conversing with Lawrence C. Heilman's USAID in Bolivia: Partner or Patrón?" *Bolivian Studies Journal* 23–24: 151–187. https://bsj.pitt.edu/ojs/index.php/bsj/article/view/182. Accessed 31 January 2019.

Lagos Carmona, Guillermo (1981) *Historia de las fronteras de Chile: Los tratados de limites con Bolivia*. 2nd edn. Santiago de Chile: Editorial Andrés Bello.

La Marca, Arianna (2017) "Chinese FDI in Bolivia: Help or Hindrance to National Development?" Council on Hemispheric Affairs (COHA) (31 August): 1–5. http://www.coha.org/chinese-fdi-in-bolivia-help-or-hindrance-to-national-development/. Accessed 25 November 2018.

Lamberg, Robert F. (1970) "Che in Bolivia: The 'Revolution' that Failed." *Problems of Communism* 19, 4 (July): 25–37.

Larrain, Sara and Colombina Schaeffer (2010) "Conflicts over Water in Chile: Between Human Rights and Market Rules." Programa Chile Sustentable (September). http://

## 222   Bibliography

www.chilesustentable.net/wp-content/uploads/2015/06/Conflicts-over-Water-in-Chile. pdf. Accessed 26 May 2017.
Lavaud, Jean-Pierre (2003) *La dictadura minada*. La Paz: Plural editores.
Lecaros Villavisencio, Fernando (1983) *La Guerra con Chile en sus Documentos*. 3rd edn. Lima: Ediciones Rikchay Perú.
Ledebur, Kathryn (2002) *Coca and Conflict in the Chapare*. Washington, DC: Washington Office on Latin America (July).
Ledebur, Kathryn and John Walsh (2009) "Obama's Bolivia ATPDEA Decision: Blast from the Past or Wave of the Future?" Washington Office on Latin America (August).
Lehman, Kenneth D. (1999) *Bolivia and the United States: A Limited Partnership*. Athens, GA: University of Georgia Press.
Lehman, Kenneth D. (2003) "Braked but not Broken: Mexico and Bolivia – Factoring the United States into the Revolutionary Equation." In *Proclaiming Revolution: Bolivia in Comparative Perspective*, ed. Merilee S. Grindle and Pilar Domingo, 91–113. Cambridge, MA: Harvard University Press.
Lehman, Kenneth D. (2016) "Completing the Revolution? The United States and Bolivia's Long Revolution." *Bolivian Studies Journal* 22: 4–35. http://bsj.pitt.edu/ojs/index.php/bsj/article/view/154. Accessed 5 December 2017.
Lincoln, Jennie K. (1984) "Peruvian Foreign Policy since the Return to Democratic Rule." In *The Dynamics of Latin American Foreign Policies: Challenges for the 1980s*, ed. Jennie K. Lincoln and Elizabeth G. Ferris, 137–149. Boulder, CO: Westview Press.
Lindsay, Reed (2005) "Exporting Gas and Importing Democracy in Bolivia." *NACLA Report on the Americas* 39, 3 (December): 5–11, 40.
Loveman, Brian (2001) *Chile: The Legacy of Hispanic Capitalism*. 3rd edn. Oxford: Oxford University Press, 2001.
Lucas Jaimes, Julio (Brocha Gorda) (1893) *Asuntos internacionales: Epílogo de la Guerra del Pacífico*. Buenos Aires: Argus.
Macías, Silvio (1936) *La guerra del Chaco: Paraguay versus Bolivia (1932–1935)*. Asunción: Editorial La Tribuna.
McNicoll, Robert Edwards (1937) "Peruvian-American Relations in the Era of the Civilist Party." Ph.D. diss, Duke University.
Maihold, Günther (2006) "The Vienna Summit between Latin America/the Caribbean and the EU: Relative Success despite Low Expectations." Real Instituto Elcano de Estudios Internacionales y Estratégicos (3 July). Mimeograph copy.
Maihold, Günther (2008) "The Lima Summit: A Meeting of Euro-Latin American Asymmetry". Real Instituto Elcano de Estudios Internacionales y Estratégicos (8 July). Mimeograph copy.
Malamud, Carlos (2006a) "Venezuela's Withdrawal from the Andean Community of Nations and the Consequences for Regional Integration (Part I)." Real Instituto Elcano de Estudios Internacionales y Estratégicos (30 May). Mimeograph copy.
Malamud, Carlos (2006b) "Venezuela's Withdrawal from the CAN (Andean Community of Nations) and Its Effects on Regional Integration (Part II: The Impact on Mercosur)." Real Instituto Elcano de Estudios Internacionales y Estratégicos (16 June). Mimeograph copy.
Malamud-Goti, Jaime (1990) "Soldiers, Politicians and the War on Drugs in Bolivia." *American University International Law Review* 6, 1: 35–55.
Maldonado Prieto, Carlos (2005) *Chile versus Perú y Bolivia: Una relación vecinal conflictiva*. Santiago de Chile: Friedrich Ebert Stiftung.

Mallin, Jay (1968) "'Che' Guevara: Some Documentary Puzzles at the End of a Long Journey." *Journal of Inter-American Studies* 10, 1 (January): 74–84.
Malloy, James M. (1970) *Bolivia: The Uncompleted Revolution.* Pittsburgh, PA: University of Pittsburgh Press.
Malloy, James M. (1982) "Bolivia: The Sad and Corrupt End of the Revolution." Universities Field Staff International. *UFSI Report* 3: 1–9.
Malloy, James M. and Eduardo Gamarra (1988) *Revolution and Reaction: Bolivia, 1964–1985.* New Brunswick, NJ: Transaction Publishers.
Mann, Arthur J. and Manuel Pastor, Jr. (1989) "Orthodox and Heterodox Stabilization Policies in Bolivia and Peru, 1985–1988." *Journal of Interamerican Studies and World Affairs* 31, 4 (Winter): 163–192.
Marsh, Margaret Alexander (1928) *The Bankers in Bolivia: A Study in American Foreign Investment.* New York: Vanguard Press.
Martínez, Cástulo (1990) *El Mar de Bolivia: Reflexiones de un ciudadano chileno.* La Paz: Librería Editorial Juventud, 1990.
Martínez, Cástulo (2001) *Chile depredador.* La Paz: Librería Editorial Juventud.
Martínez, Cástulo (2002) *Las aguas del Silala: crónica de un despojo.* La Paz: Librería Editorial Juventud.
Mayorga Ugarte, J. Antonio (2007) *Gonismo: Discurso y poder.* 2nd edn. La Paz: Plural editores.
Medeiros Querejazu, Gustavo (1975) "III conferencia de las Naciones Unidas sobre el derecho al mar." *Kollasuyo* 88 (first semester): 76–93.
Melo Lecaros, Luis (1963) "International Rivers – The Lauca Case." *The Indian Journal of International Law* 3: 133–150.
Mercado Jarrín, Edgardo (1979) *Política y estrategia en la guerra de Chile.* Lima: n.p.
Mercado Moreira, Miguel (1916) *Historia internacional de Bolivia: Cuestiones de límites.* Cochabamba: González y Medina.
Mesa, José de and Carlos D. Mesa Gisbert (2001) "La república: Los cimientos de la nación, los años de confusión, 1829–1880." In *Historia de Bolivia*, 4th edn., ed. José de Mesa, Teresa Gisbert, and Carlos D. Mesa Gisbert, 371–481. La Paz: Editorial Gisbert.
Mesa, José de and Teresa Gisbert (2001) "El virreinato: La sociedad mestiza, 1700–1800." In *Historia de Bolivia*, 4th edn., ed. José de Mesa, Teresa Gisbert, and Carlos D. Mesa Gisbert, 233–306. La Paz: Editorial Gisbert.
Mesa Gisbert, Carlos D. (2001a) "La república: La construcción de la nación oligárquica, el gérman del nacionalismo, 1880–1952." In *Historia de Bolivia*, 4th edn., ed. José de Mesa, Teresa Gisbert, and Carlos D. Mesa Gisbert, 483–646. La Paz: Editorial Gisbert.
Mesa Gisbert, Carlos D. (2001b) "La república: Revolución, militarismo y democracia, 1952–2000." In *Historia de Bolivia*, 4th edn., ed. José de Mesa, Teresa Gisbert, and Carlos D. Mesa Gisbert, 647–818. La Paz: Editorial Gisbert.
Mesa Gisbert, Carlos D. (2003) *Presidentes de Bolivia: Entre Urnas y Fusiles.* 3rd edn. La Paz: Editorial Gisbert.
Mesa Gisbert, Carlos D. (2016) *La historia del mar boliviano.* La Paz: Editorial Gisbert.
Miguel Concha, José (2011) *Iniciativas chilenas para una alianza estratégica con Bolivia (1879–1899).* La Paz: Plural editores.
Mihaly, Aaron M. (2006) "¿Por qué se ha caído Goni? Explicando la renuncia forzada del Presidente Sánchez de Lozada en octobre de 2003." In *Conflictos políticos y*

*movimientos sociales en Bolivia*, ed. Nicholas A. Robins, 95–119. La Paz: Plural editores.

Milic, Milenko (1981) "Access of Land-Locked States to and from the Sea." *Case Western Reserve Journal of International Law* 13, 3: 501–516.

Millington, Thomas (1992) *Debt Politics after Independence: The Funding Conflict in Bolivia*. Gainesville, FL: University of Florida Press.

Miranda Pacheco, Carlos (1999) "Petróleo: Del descubrimiento Petrolífero a la explosión del gas." In *Bolivia en el siglo xx: La formación de la Bolivia contemporánea*, ed. Fernando Campero Prudencio, 241–267. La Paz: Harvard Club of Bolivia.

Mitchell, Christopher (1977) *The Legacy of Populism in Bolivia: From the MNR to Military Rule*. New York, NY: Praeger.

Molina, George Gray (2008) "Bolivia's Long and Winding Road." Andean Region Working Paper, Inter-American Dialogue (July).

Molina, George Gray (2011) "U.S.-Bolivian Relations: Behind the Impasse." In *Shifting the Balance: Obama and the Americas*, ed. Abraham F. Lowenthal, Theodore J. Piccone, and Laurence Whitehead, 86–99. Washington, D.C.: Brookings Institution Press.

Montenegro, Wálter (1987) *Oportunidades perdidas: Bolivia y el mar*. La Paz and Cochabamba: Editorial Los Amigos del Libro.

Monteón, Michael (1982) *Chile in the Nitrate Era: The Evolution of Economic Dependence, 1880–1930*. Madison, WI: University of Wisconsin Press.

Moore, John Bassett (1904) *Brazil and Peru Boundary Question*. New York: Knickerbocker Press.

Morales, José Agustín (1925) *Los primeros cien años de la República de Bolivia, 1825–1925*. 3 vols. La Paz: Empresa Editora Veglia & Edelman.

Morales, Juan Antonio and Carlos Machicado (1978) "Problemas y perspectivas del desarrollo económico boliviano y la integración andina." In *Pacto Andino: Desarrollo nacional e integración andina*, ed. Ernesto Tironi, 17–78. Lima: Instituto de Estudios Peruanos.

Morales, Waltraud Queiser (1984) "Bolivian Foreign Policy: The Struggle for Sovereignty." In *The Dynamics of Latin American Foreign Policies: Challenges for the 1980s*, ed. Jennie K. Lincoln and Elizabeth G. Ferris, 171–191. Boulder, CO: Westview Press.

Morales, Waltraud Queiser (1986) "La Geopolítica de la Política Exterior de Bolivia." *Relaciones Internacionales: Revista Boliviana* 1, 2 (abril–junio): 69–95.

Morales, Waltraud Queiser (1992a) "Militarising the Drug War in Bolivia." *Third World Quarterly* 13, 2: 353–370.

Morales, Waltraud Queiser (1992b) *Bolivia: Land of Struggle*. Boulder, CO: Westview Press.

Morales, Waltraud Queiser (2001) "Political Economy of Bolivia's Foreign Policy." *Bolivian Studies Journal* 9 (Fall): 111–131.

Morales, Waltraud Queiser (2002) "Toward a New Bolivian Foreign Policy?: The Past, Present and Future State Capacity and Bolivian Foreign Policy." *Bolivian Research Review* 2, 1 (February): 4–36.

Morales, Waltraud Queiser (2009) "Bolivia." In *Politics of Latin America: The Power Game*, 3rd edn., ed. Harry E. Vanden and Gary Prevost, 557–588. Oxford: Oxford University Press.

Bibliography 225

Morales, Waltraud Queiser (2010) *Brief History of Bolivia*. 2nd edn. New York, NY: Checkmark Books.
Morales, Waltraud Queiser (2016) "Bolivia's Foreign Policy toward the Middle East (2000–2015): Promoting a Populist and Radical Agenda Abroad." In *Latin American Foreign Policies towards the Middle East: Actors, Contexts, and Trends*, ed. Marta Tawil Kuri, 179–200. New York: Palgrave Macmillan.
Morales Anaya, Juan Antonio and Mario Napoleón Pacheco Torrico (1999) "Economía: El retorno de los liberals." In *Bolivia en el siglo xx: La formación de la Bolivia contemporánea*, ed. Fernando Campero Prudencio, 155–192. La Paz: Harvard Club of Bolivia.
Mouline, Sophie (2013) "21st Century Regionalism: Where is Latin America Headed?" Council on Hemispheric Affairs (COHA). (3 September): 1–11. http://www.coha.org/21st-century-regionalism-where-is-latin-america-headed/. Accessed 27 November 2018.
Moya Quiroga López, Rolando (1962) *Momento internacional: Desviación de las aguas del rio Lauca*. La Paz: Gutemberg.
Mulligan, B. M. and G. E. Eckstein (2011) "The Silala/Siloli Watershed: Dispute over the most Vulnerable Basin in South America." *Water Resources Development* 27, 3 (September): 595–606.
Murillo de la Rocha, Javier (1999) *Discursos*. La Paz: Editorial General.
Nalavala, Nosh, ed. (2014) "Latin America Reviews Progress Towards Second United Nations Conference on the Landlocked Developing Countries." *The Commitment* (Spring): 5–7. Mimeograph copy.
Nash, June (1979) "Bolivia: The Consolidation (and Breakdown?) of a Militaristic Regime." *LASA Newsletter* 10, 3 (September): 37–43.
Navarro, Gustavo (1968) "Ensayo sobre la confederación Perú-Boliviana: 'El crucismo.'" *Journal of Inter-American Studies* 10, 1 (January): 53–73.
Navia Ribera, Carlos (1984) *Los Estados Unidos y la revolución nacional: entre el pragmatismo y el sometimiento*. Cochabamba: Centro de Informacíon y Documentación para el Desarrollo Regional.
Novak, Fabián (2000) *Las Conversaciones entre Perú y Chile para la Ejecución del Tratado de 1929*. Lima: Fondo Editorial, 2000.
Novak, Fabián and Sandra Namihas (2013) *Las relaciones entre el Perú y Bolivia (1826–2013)*. Lima: Konrad Adenauer Stiftung and Instituto de Estudios Internacionales Pontificia Universidad Católica del Perú.
Oblitas Fernández, Edgar (2001) *Historia secreta de la Guerra del Pacifico de 1879 a 1904*. La Paz and Cochabamba: Editorial Los Amigos del Libro.
O'Brien, Thomas F. (1979) "Chilean Elites and Foreign Investors: Chilean Nitrate Policy, 1880–1882." *Journal of Latin American Studies* 11, 1 (May), 101–121.
Olivera, Oscar (2004) *Cochabamba: Water War in Bolivia*. Cambridge, MA: South End Press.
Orias Arredondo, Ramiro (1998) *Opiniones y análisis: "El Régimen de los paises sin litoral en el derecho del mar y las perspectivas para Bolivia."* La Paz: Fundemos.
Orias Arredondo, Ramiro (2000) "Bolivia: La Diplomacia del Mar en la OEA." In *Bolivia: Temas de la Agenda Internacional*, ed. Alberto Zelada Casteđo, 387–413. La Paz: Unidad de Análysis de Política de Exterior.
Orias Arredondo, Ramiro (2001) "Bolivia y Perú: Construyendo un interés compartido." In *Bolivia, país de contactos: Un análisis de la política vicinal contemporánea*, ed. Orias Arredondo, Ramiro, AlfredoSeoane Flores and William Torres Armas,

273–309. La Paz: Fundación Boliviana para la Capacitacón Democrática y la Investigación.
Orias Arredondo, Ramiro (2004) "Bolivia-Chile: la cuestión de la mediterraneidad. Algunas consideraciones desde el derecho internacional." *Revista Fuerzas Armadas y Sociedad* 18, 1–2 (enero/junio): 51–73.
Orias Arredondo, Ramiro, Alfredo Seoane Flores and William Torres Armas (2001) "Bolivia-Chile: una agenda para el diálogo." In *Bolivia, país de contactos: Un análisis de la política vicinal contemporánea*, ed. Orias Arredondo, Ramiro, Alfredo Seoane Flores and William Torres Armas, 161–215. La Paz: Fundación Boliviana para la Capacitacón Democrática y la Investigación.
Ortega, Luis (1984) "Nitrates, Chilean Entrepreneurs and the Origins of the War of the Pacific." *Journal of Latin American Studies* 16, 2 (November): 337–380.
Ortiz de Zevallos Paz Soldán, Carlos, ed. (various years) *Archivo diplomático peruano*. 9 vols. Lima: various publishers.
Ostria Gutiérrez, Alberto (1958) *The Tragedy of Bolivia: A People Crucified*. New York, NY: The Devin-Adair Company.
Palacios Rodríguez, Raúl (1974) *La Chilenización de Tacna y Arica, 1883–1929*. Lima: Editorial Arica.
Parkerson, Phillip Taylor (1979) "Sub-Regional Integration in Nineteenth Century South America: Andres Santa Cruz and the Peru-Bolivia Confederation, 1835–1839." PhD diss., University of Florida.
Peñaloza Cordero, Luis (1984) *Nueva historia económica de Bolivia: La Guerra del Pacífico*. 3rd edn. La Paz and Cochabamba: Editorial Los Amigos del Libro.
Pérez del Castillo, Alvaro (1980) *Bolivia, Colombia, Chile y el Perú*. La Paz and Cochabamba: Editorial Los Amigos del Libro.
Perú. Ministerio de Relaciones Exteriores (1934–36) *Memoria del Relaciones Exteriores del Perú*. Lima: Ministerio de Relaciones Exteriores.
Perú. Ministerio de Relaciones Exteriores (1936) *Tratados, Convenciones y Acuerdos vigentes entre el Perú y otros Estados*. 2 vols. Lima: Imprenta Torres Aguirre.
Perú. Ministerio de Relaciones Exteriores (1937–39) *Memoria del Relaciones Exteriores del Perú*. Lima: Ministerio de Relaciones.
Perú. Ministerio de Relaciones Exteriores (2011) *Memoria del Ministerio de Relaciones Exteriores, julio 2006 – julio 2011*. Lima: Ministerio de Relaciones Exteriores. http://rree.gob.pe/politicaexterior/Documents/MEMORIA-del-MRE-Jul-2006-Jul2011.pdf. Accessed 3 September 2017.
Perú. Ministerio de Relaciones Exteriores (2013) *Memoria institucional del 28 de julio de 2011 al 15 de mayo del 2013*. Lima: Ministerio de Relaciones Exteriores. Mimeograph copy.
Perú. Ministerio de Relaciones Exteriores (2014) *Memoria institucional de 15 de mayo de 2013 al 24 de junio de 2014*. Lima: Ministerio de Relaciones Exteriores. http://transparencia.rree.gob.pe/index.php/2-planeamiento-y-organizacion/2-5-memoria-institucional/8019-3-memoria-institucional-de-eda-rivas-franchini-2013-2014/file. Accessed 3 September 2017.
Peterson, Dale William (1969) "The Diplomatic and Commercial Relations between the United States and Peru from 1883 to 1918." Ph.D. diss., University of Minnesota.
Philip, George and Francisco Panizza (2011) *The Triumph of Politics: The Return of the Left in Venezuela, Bolivia and Ecuador*. Cambridge: Polity Press.
Phillips, Richard Snyder, Jr. (1973) "Bolivia in the War of the Pacific, 1879–1884." Ph.D. diss., University of Virginia.

Phillips, Tony (2008) "The Bolivian Crisis, the OAS, and UNASUR." America Policy Program Discussion Paper (30 September). https://www.americas.org/5567/. Accessed 3 February 2019.
Pike, Fredrick B. (1963) *Chile and the United States, 1880–1962: The Emergence of Chile's Social Crisis and the Challenge to United States Diplomacy*. Notre Dame, IN: University of Notre Dame Press.
Pike, Fredrick B. (1967) *The Modern History of Peru*. New York: Praeger.
Pike, Fredrick B. (1977) *The United States and the Andean Republics: Peru, Bolivia, and Ecuador*. Cambridge, MA: Harvard University Press.
Pinochet de la Barra, Oscar (2000) "La diplomacia chileno-boliviana antes de la Guerra del Pacífico." *Revista Diplomacia* 83 (abril/junio): 21–26.
Pinto Cascán, Darwin and Roberto Navia Gabriel (2007) *...un tal Evo: Biografía no autorizada*. 2nd edn. Santa Cruz de la Sierra: Editorial El País.
Pittman, Howard (1984) "Chilean Foreign Policy: The Pragmatic Pursuit of Geopolitical Goals." In *The Dynamics of Latin American Foreign Policies: Challenges for the 1980s*, ed. Jennie K. Lincoln and Elizabeth G. Ferris, 125–135. Boulder, CO: Westview Press.
Ponce Caballero, Jaime (1998) *Geopolítica chilena y mar boliviano*. La Paz: P.G.D. Impresiones.
Prado Salmon, Gary (1984) *Poder y fuerzas armadas, 1949–1982*. La Paz and Cochabamba: Editorial Los Amigos del Libro.
Prudencio Lizón, Ramiro (1975) "La nota de König y otros antecedents del Tratado de 1904 con Chile." *Kollasuyo* 88 (primer semestre): 94–123.
Prudencio Lizón, Ramiro (2004) "El problema marítimo boliviano." *Revista Agenda Internacional* 11, 21: 27–45.
Prudencio Lizón, Ramiro (2011) *Historia de la negociación de Charaña: La más importante negociación del siglo XX sobre el problema marítima boliviano*. La Paz: Plural editores.
Prudencio Romecín, Roberto (1975) "Nuestro Problema Marítimo." *Kollasuyo* 88 (primer semestre): 5–37.
Puente Radbill, José de la (1989) "La mediterraneidad de Bolivia." In *Relaciones del Perú con Chile y Bolivia*, ed. Eduardo Ferrero Costa, 39–58. Lima: Centro Peruano de Estudios Internacionales.
Querejazu Calvo, Roberto (1973) *Bolivia y los ingleses, 1825–1948*. La Paz and Cochabamba: Editorial Los Amigos del Libro.
Querejazu Calvo, Roberto (1979) *Guano, salitre, sangre: Historia de la Guerra del Pacífico*. La Paz and Cochabamba: Editorial Los Amigos del Libro.
Querejazu Calvo, Roberto (1983) *La Guerra del Pacífico: Síntesis histórica de sus antecedentes, desarrollo y consecuencias*. La Paz and Cochabamba: Editorial Los Amigos del Libro.
Querejazu Calvo, Roberto (1992) *Masamaclay: Historia, política, diplomática y militar de la Guerra del Chaco*. 5th edn. La Paz and Cochabamba: Editorial Los Amigos del Libro.
Querejazu Calvo, Roberto ed. (1996) *Oposición en Bolivia a la Confederación Perú-Boliviana: Cartas del Vicepresidente Mariano Enrique Calvo y el Presidente Andrés Santa Cruz*. Sucre: Editorial Judicial.
Quiroga, Yesko (2003) *ALCA: El debate boliviano*. La Paz: Plural ediciones.
Ríos Gallardo, Conrado (1959) *Chile y Perú: Los pactos de 1929*. Santiago de Chile: Editorial Nascimento.

## 228  Bibliography

Ríos Gallardo, Conrado (1963) *Chile y Bolivia definen sus fronteras 1842–1904.* Santiago de Chile: Editorial Andres Bello.

Rippy, J.Fred (1953) "British Investments in Paraguay, Bolivia and Peru." *Inter-American Economic Affairs* 6, 4 (Spring): 38–48.

Rivera, Salvador (2014) *Latin American Unification: A History of Political and Economic Integration Efforts.* Jefferson, NC: McFarland & Company.

Roca, José Luis (1980) *Fisonomía del regionalismo boliviano.* La Paz: Plural editores.

Roca, José Luis (2004) "1904: Un tratado que restableció la paz pero no la amistad." In *A cien años del tratado de paz y amistad de 1904 entre Bolivia y Chile,* 11–61. La Paz: Editorial Garza Azul.

Roca, José Luis (2008) "Regionalism Revisited." In *Unresolved Tensions: Bolivia Past and Present,* ed. John Crabtree and Laurence Whitehead, 65–82. Pittsburgh, PA: University of Pittsburgh Press.

Rodríguez Ostia, Gustavo (1994) *Elites, mercado y cuestión regional en Bolivia (Cochabamba).* Quito: Facultad Latinoamericana de Ciencias Sociales (FLACSO).

RomeroA. G., Gonzalo (1986) "Geopolítica de problema marítimo." *Relaciones Internacionales: Revista Boliviana* 1, 2 (segundo trimestre): 33–50.

Ross Orellana, César (2016) "La política chilena hacia Bolivia, 1900–1930: la constitución de un discurso estructural." *Si Somos Americanos* 16, 1 (enero–junio): 181–210.

Rossi, Christopher R. (2017) "The Transboundary Dispute over the Waters of the Silala/Siloli: Legal Vandalism and Goffmanian Metaphor." *Stanford Journal of International Law* 53, 1 (Winter): 55–87.

Rout, Jr. Leslie B. (1970) *Politics of the Chaco Peace Conference, 1935–1939.* Latin American Monographs, No. 19. Institute of Latin American Studies, University of Texas at Austin. Austin and London: University of Texas Press.

Ryan, Henry Butterfield (1998) *The Fall of Che Guevara: A Story of Soldiers, Spies, and Diplomats.* Oxford: Oxford University Press.

Sachs, Jeffrey D. (1987) "The Bolivian Hyperinflation and Stabilization." *American Economic Review* 77, 2 (May): 279–283.

Sachs, Jeffrey D. (1999) "Latinoamérica y el Desarrollo Económico Global." In *Bolivia en el siglo xx: La formación de la Bolivia contemporánea,* ed. Fernando Campero Prudencio, 23–45. La Paz: Harvard Club of Bolivia.

St John, Ronald Bruce (1977) "Hacia el Mar: Bolivia's Quest for a Pacific Port." *Inter-American Economic Affairs* 31, 3 (Winter): 41–73.

St John, Ronald Bruce (1980) "Marxist-Leninist Theory and Organization in South Vietnam." *Asian Survey* 20, 8 (August): 812–828.

St John, Ronald Bruce (1984) "Peru: Democracy under Siege." *The World Today* 40, 7 (July): 299–306.

St John, Ronald Bruce (1992a) *The Foreign Policy of Peru.* Boulder, CO: Lynne Rienner.

St John, Ronald Bruce (1992b) *Boundaries, Trade and Seaports: Power Politics in the Atacama Desert.* Occasional Paper Series No. 28, Program in Latin American Studies, University of Massachusetts at Amherst.

St John, Ronald Bruce (1994a) "Stalemate in the Atacama." *IBRU Boundary and Security Bulletin* 2, 1 (April): 64–68.

St John, Ronald Bruce (1994b) *The Bolivia-Chile-Peru Dispute in the Atacama Desert.* International Boundaries Research Unit, Boundary & Territory Briefing 1, 6.

St John, Ronald Bruce (1996) "Peru: Atypical External Behavior." In *Foreign Policy and Regionalism in the Americas*, ed. Gordon Mace and Jean-Philippe Thérien, 121–136. Boulder, CO and London: Lynne Rienner.

St John, Ronald Bruce (1999) *La Política Exterior del Perú*. Lima: Asociación de Funcionarios del Servicio Diplomática del Perú.

St John, Ronald Bruce (2000) "Chile, Peru and the Treaty of 1929: The Final Settlement." *IBRU Boundary and Security Bulletin* 8, 1 (Summer): 91–100.

St John, Ronald Bruce (2001) "Same Space, Different Dreams: Bolivia's Quest for a Pacific Port." *The Bolivian Research Review* 1, 1 (July): 1–22. http://www.bolivianstudies.org/revista/2001_07.htm#SameSpace,Different Dreams. Accessed 22 May 2017.

St John, Ronald Bruce (2003) "Learning from an Ousted President." *Foreign Policy in Focus* (10 December). http://www.contexto.org/docs/politica04.html. Accessed 2 February 2018.

St John, Ronald Bruce (2004) "Bolivia's Referendum about More than Gas." *Foreign Policy in Focus* (30 August). https://fpif.org/bolivias_referendum_about_more_than_gas/. Accessed 22 May 2017.

St John, Ronald Bruce (2005a) "Bolivia Steps Back from the Abyss." *Foreign Policy in Focus* (15 July). Mimeograph copy.

St John, Ronald Bruce (2005b) "So What if Morales Wins in Bolivia." *Foreign Policy in Focus* (14 December). http://web.archive.org/web/20051215224938/http://www.fpif.org/fpiftxt/2988. Accessed 7 June 2018.

St John, Ronald Bruce (2006) "Evo Morales No Che Guevara." *Foreign Policy in Focus* (9 January). http://www.contexto.org/docs/politica23.html. Accessed 13 August 2018.

St John, Ronald Bruce (2010) *Toledo's Peru: Vision and Reality*. Gainesville, FL: University of Florida Press.

St John, Ronald Bruce (2012) "Peru: A Model for Latin American Diplomacy and Statecraft." In *Routledge Handbook of Diplomacy and Statecraft*, ed. B. J. C. McKercher, 181–191. London and New York: Routledge.

St John, Ronald Bruce (2015a) "Bolivia v. Chile: Old Story, New Chapter." *Council on Hemispheric Affairs* (5 June). http://www.coha.org/bolivia-v-chile-old-story-new-chapter/. Accessed 13 August 2018.

St John, Ronald Bruce (2015b) "Bolivia Takes Its Case to International Court Why Now?" *Center for International Policy, Americas Program* (27 June). https://www.americas.org/bolivia-takes-its-case-to-international-court-at-the-icj-why-now/ Accessed 13 August 2018.

St John, Ronald Bruce (2015c) "World Court Accepts Jurisdiction in Bolivia-Chile Dispute." *Center for International Policy, Americas Program* (12 October). Mimeograph copy.

St John, Ronald Bruce (2017) "Peruvian Foreign Policy in the New Millennium: Continuity and Change." *Revista del Instituto Riva-Agüero* 2, 2: 65–119.

St John, Ronald Bruce and Stephen M. Gorman (1982) "Challenges to Peruvian Foreign Policy." In *Post-Revolutionary Peru: The Politics of Transformation*, ed. Stephen M. Gorman, 179–196. Boulder, CO: Westview Press.

Salazar Paredes, Fernando (2000) *Hacía una nueva política exterior boliviana*. La Paz: El Centro para el Estudio de las Relaciones Internacionales y el Desarrollo/Plural editores.

Salazar Paredes, Fernando, Jorge Gumucio Granier, Franz Orozco Padilla and Lorena Salazar Machicado (2001) *Charaña: Una negociación boliviana, 1975–1978*. La Paz: El Centro para el Estudio de las Relaciones Internacionales y el Desarrollo.

Salinas Baldivieso, Carlos Alberto (1938) *Historia diplomática de Bolivia.* Sucre: Editorial Charcas.
Salman, Tom (2007) "Bolivia and the Paradoxes of Democratic Consolidation." *Latin American Perspectives* 34, 6 (November): 111–130.
Sanchez, W. Alejandro (2015) "More Pragmatic, Less Ideological: Bringing the U.S. and Bolivia Together?" Council on Hemispheric Affairs (COHA)4 March. Mimeograph copy.
Sanders, Thomas G. (1986) "Bolivia's Turbulent Experiment with Democracy." Universities Field Staff International, *UFSI Report* 27: 1–8.
Sanders, Thomas G. (1989–90) "Bolivia: From Victor Paz to Jaime Paz." Universities Field Staff International, *UFSI Report* 9: 1–10.
Sater, William F. (1986) *Chile and the War of the Pacific.* Lincoln, NE: University of Nebraska Press.
Sater, William F. (2007) *Andean Tragedy: Fighting the War of the Pacific, 1879–1884.* Lincoln, NE: University of Nebraska Press.
Scott, James Brown, ed. (1931) *The International Conference of American States, 1889–1928.* New York, NY: Oxford University Press.
Seckinger, Ron L. (1974) "The Chiquitos Affair: An Aborted Crisis in Brazilian-Bolivian Relations." *Luso-Brazilian Review* 11, 1 (Summer): 19–40.
Seckinger, Ron L. (1976) "South American Power Politics during the 1820s." *Hispanic American Historical Review* 56, 2 (May): 241–267.
Seiferheld, Alfredo (1983) *Economía y petróleo durante la guerra del Chaco: Apuntes para una historia económica del conflict Paraguayo-Boliviano.* Asunción: Instituto Paraguayo de Estudios Geopolíticos e Internacionales.
Seoane Flores, Alfredo (2000a) "Oportunidades y asimetrías en la integración hemisférica." In *Bolivia: Temas de la Agenda Internacional,* ed. Alberto Zelada Castedo, 207–238. La Paz: Unidad de Análisis de Política Exterior.
Seoane Flores, Alfredo (2000b) "Estado actual y proyecciones de la Comunidad Andina de Naciones." In *Bolivia: Temas de la Agenda Internacional,* ed. Alberto Zelada Castedo, 291–312. La Paz: Unidad de Análisis de Política Exterior.
Seoane Flores, Alfredo (2000c) "Ampliación y profundización de la relación especial con el MERCOSUR." In *Bolivia: Temas de la Agenda Internacional,* ed. Alberto Zelada Castedo, 265–289. La Paz: Unidad de Análisis de Política Exterior.
Seoane Flores, Alfredo (2001) "Relaciones Bolivia-Brasil: Interdependencia y asociación estratégica." In *Bolivia, país de contactos: Un análisis de la política vicinal contemporánea,* ed. Ramiro Orias Arredondo, Alfredo Seoane Flores, and William G. Torres Armas, 107–158. La Paz: Fundación Boliviana para la Capacitacón Democrática y la Investigación.
Seoane Flores, Alfredo, Humberto Zambrana, Fernando Jiménez and Rafael González (1997). *Bolivia y Chile: complementación económica y asimetrías.* La Paz: Unidad de Análisis de Política Exterior.
Shultz, Jim (2008a) "The Cochabamba Water Revolt and Its Aftermath." In *Dignity and Defiance: Stories from Bolivia's Challenge to Globalization,* ed. Jim Shultz and Melissa Crane Draper, 9–42. Berkeley, CA: University of California Press.
Shultz, Jim (2008b) "Lessons in Blood and Fire: The Deadly Consequences of IMF Economics." In *Dignity and Defiance: Stories from Bolivia's Challenge to Globalization,* ed. Jim Shultz and Melissa Crane Draper, 117–143. Berkeley, CA: University of California Press.

Shumavon, Douglas H. (1981) "Bolivia: Salida al Mar." In *Latin American Foreign Policies: Global and Regional Dimensions*, ed. Elizabeth G. Ferris and Jennie K. Lincoln, 179–190. Boulder, CO: Westview Press.

Sicotte, Richard, Catalina Vizcarra, and Kirsten Wandschneider (2009) "The Fiscal Impact of the War of the Pacific." *Cliometrica* 3, 2 (June): 97–121.

Siekmeier, James F. (2011) *The Bolivian Revolution and the United States: 1952 to the Present*. University Park, PA: Pennsylvania State University Press.

Sivak, Martín (2002) *El dictador elegido: Biografía no autorizada de Hugo Banzer Suárez*. 3rd edn. La Paz: Plural ediciones.

Soder, Jr., John Phillip (1970) "The Impact of the Tacna-Arica Dispute on the Pan-American Movement." Ph.D. diss., Georgetown University.

Tapia, Luis (2017) "Analysis of Bolivia." In *Latin America, Mobilization, and a Move to the Right: Four Country Analyses*, 26–36. Quito: Andean Regional Office, Rosa Luxemburg Foundation. https://rosalux.org.ec/pdfs/LATIN%20AMERICA,%20MOBILIZATION,%20AND%20A%20MOVE%20TO%20THE%20RIGHT.pdf. Accessed 9 February 2019.

Téllez Lúgaro, Eduardo (1989) *Historia general de la frontera de Chile con Perú y Bolivia 1825–1929*. Santiago de Chile: Colección Terra Nostra.

Tini, María Natalia (2008) "La distancia sobre la cercanía: la política exterior argentina hacia Bolivia y Paraguay." *Relaciones Internacionales* 17, 34 (mayo): 197–221.

Tironi, Ernesto (1978) "Políticas frente al capital extranjero: la Decisión 24." In *Pacto Andino: Carácter y perspectivas*, ed. Ernesto Tironi, 71–110. Lima: Instituto de Estudios Peruanos.

Tomasek, Robert D. (1967) "The Chilean-Bolivian Lauca River Dispute and the O.A.S." *Journal of Inter-American Studies* 9, 3 (July): 351–366.

Torres Armas, William G. (1997) *Bolivia y la región asiática de la Cuenca del Pacífico: Una agenda para el siglo XXI*. La Paz: Unidad de Análisis de Política Exterior.

Torres Armas, William G. (2000a) "Bolivia y sus fronteras: La búsqueda de una política centrada en el desarrollo, la cooperación y la integración." In *Desarrollo fronterizo: construyendo una nueva agenda*, ed. Alfredo Seoane Flores, Ramiro Orias Arredondo, and William Torres Armas, 179–276. La Paz: Universidad de la Cordillera.

Torres Armas, William G. (2000b) "Bolivia: Núcleo de distribución y abastecimiento de energía en el Cono Sur." In *Bolivia: Temas de la Agenda Internacional*, ed. Alberto Zelada Castedo, 313–341. La Paz: Unidad de Análisis de Política Exterior.

Torres Armas, William G. (2000c) "La reforma del consejo de seguridad." In *Bolivia: Temas de la Agenda Internacional*, ed. Alberto Zelada Castedo, 159–178. La Paz: Unidad de Análisis de Política Exterior.

Torres Armas, William G. (2001a) "Bolivia y Argentina: La búsqueda de los nuevos ejes estructurantes de la relación bilateral." In *Bolivia, país de contactos: Un análisis de la política vicinal contemporánea*, ed. Ramiro Orias Arredondo, Alfredo Seoane Flores, and William G. Torres Armas, 43–101. La Paz: Fundación Boliviana para la Capacitacón Democrática y la Investigación.

Torres Armas, William G. (2001b) "Bolivia-Paraguay: el reencuentro de dos voluntades." In *Bolivia, país de contactos: Un análisis de la política vicinal contemporánea*, ed. Ramiro Orias Arredondo, Alfredo Seoane Flores, and William G. Torres Armas, 219–270. La Paz: Fundación Boliviana para la Capacitación Democrática y la Investigación.

Traverso, Jorge (1986) "Bolivia y la convención sobre el derecho del mar." *Relaciones Internacionales: Revista Boliviana* 1, 2 (segundo trimestre): 121–130.

## 232  Bibliography

Tredinnick, Felipe (1998) *Geopolítica del mar*. La Paz and Cochabamba: Editorial Los Amigos del Libro.

Tudela, Francisco (1998–99) "Entrevista a Francisco Tudela." *Debate* 20, 104 (diciembre–enero): 12–20.

Tyler, Alice Felt (1927) *The Foreign Policy of James G. Blaine*. Minneapolis, MN: University of Minnesota Press.

Ugarteche, Oscar (1986) *El estado deudor: Economía política de la deuda: Perú y Bolivia, 1968–1984*. Lima: Instituto de Estudios Peruanos.

Ulloa Sotomayor, Alberto (1938) *Congresos Americanos de Lima*. 2 vols. Lima: Imprenta Aguirre.

Ulloa Sotomayor, Alberto (1941) *Posición Internacional del Perú*. Lima: Imprenta Torres Aguirre.

Ulloa Sotomayor, Alberto (1987) *Chile: Para la Historia Internacional y Diplomática del Perú*. Lima: Editorial Atlantida.

United Nations (1958a) United Nations Conference on the Law of the Sea (UNCLOS), 24 February to 27 April 1958, Volume I: Preparatory Documents, "Question of Free Access to the Sea of Land-Locked Countries," A/CONF.13/29 and Add.1. http://legal.un.org/diplomaticconferences/1958_los/vol1.shtml. Accessed 12 December 2018.

United Nations (1958b) United Nations Conference on the Law of the Sea (UNCLOS), 24 February to 27 April 1958, Volume VII: Fifth Committee, "Question of Free Access to the Sea of Land-locked Countries, Summary records of meetings and Annexes," A/CONF.13.43. http://legal.un.org/docs/?path=../diplomaticconferences/1958_los/docs/english/vol_7.pdf&lang=E. Accessed 12 December 2018.

United Nations (1958c) United Nations Conference on the Law of the Sea (UNCLOS), 24 February to 27 April 1958, Volume VII: Fifth Committee. "Question of Free Access to the Sea of Land-locked Countries, Summary records of the 6th to 10th meetings of the Fifth Committee," A/CONF.13/C.5/SR.6–10. http://legal.un.org/docs/?path=../diplomaticconferences/1958_los/docs/english/vol_7.pdf&lang=E. Accessed 12 December 2018.

United Nations (1963) Treaty Series, Volume 450, Numbers 6464–6481, "Final Act of the United Nations Conference on the Law of the Sea, held at the European Office of the United Nations, at Geneva, from 24 February to 27 April 1958 (with annexed resolutions); and Convention on the High Seas, 29 April 1958." https://treaties.un.org/doc/publication/unts/volume%20450/v450.pdf. Accessed 12 December 2018.

United Nations (1968) Treaty Series, Volume 597, Numbers 8641–8652, "Final Act of the United Nations Conference on Transit Trade of Land-locked Countries (with annexed resolutions), and Convention on Transit Trade of Land-locked Countries, both done at New York, on 8 July 1965." https://treaties.un.org/doc/publication/UNTS/Volume%20597/v597.pdf. Accessed 12 December 2018.

United Nations (1997) *Convention on the Law of the Non-Navigational Uses of International Watercourses (1997)*. http://legal.un.org/ilc/texts/instruments/english/conventions/8_3_1997.pdf. Accessed 27 August 2018.

United Nations (2003) United Nations Conference on Trade and Development (UNCTAD) *Report of the International Ministerial Conference of Landlocked and Transit Developing Countries and Donor Countries and International Financial and Development Institutions on Transit Transport Cooperation*. Almaty, Kazakhstan. 28 and 29 August. A/CONF.202/3. http://unctad.org/en/docs/aconf202d3_en.pdf. Accessed 27 August 2018.

## Bibliography 233

United Nations (2007) United Nations Environment Programme (UNEP) *Hydropolitical Vulnerability and Resilience along International Waters: Latin America and the Caribbean*. Nairobi: UNEP Publications. http://wedocs.unep.org/bitstream/handle/20.500.11822/7803/-Hydropolitical%20Vulnerability%20and%20Resilience%20Along%20International%20Waters%20_%20Latin%20America%20and%20the%20Caribbean-2008858.pdf?sequence=4&isAllowed=y. Accessed 27 August 2018.

United Nations (2013) Office of the High Representative for the Least Developed Countries, Landlocked Developing Countries, and Small Island Developing States (UN-OHRLLS), *Landlocked Developing Countries: Things to Know, Things to Do*. New York. https://unohrlls.org/custom-content/uploads/2016/06/LLDC_Things_To_Know-Do_2016.pdf. Accessed 27 August 2018.

Uprety, Kishor (2006) *The Transit Regime for Landlocked States*. Washington, DC: The World Bank.

Urquidi Barrau, Fernando (2005) "Recursos hídricos en la frontera boliviano-chilena (Silala y Lauca)." In *Política Exterior en Materia de Recursos Hídricos*, 37–70. La Paz: UDAPEX-PNUD.

Vaca Guzmán Moyano, Santiago (1879) *Bolivia y Chile: Sus tratados de límites*. Buenos Aires: Imprenta de Pablo E. Coni.

Valdez, Jorge (2012) "Las relaciones del Perú con la Europa comunitaria." In *Veinte años de política exterior peruana (1991–2011)*, ed. Fabián Novak, 161–174. Lima: Fondo Editorial de la Pontificia Universidad Católica del Perú.

Vargas-Hidalgo, Rafael (1979) "The Crisis of the Andean Pact: Lessons for Integration among Developing Countries." *Journal of Common Market Studies* 17, 3 (March): 213–226.

Vargas Ugarte, Rubén (1962) *Ramón Castilla*. Buenos Aires: Imprenta López.

Vázquez-Machicado, Humberto (1990) *Para una historia de los límites entre Bolivia y el Brasil*. La Paz: Libreria Editorial Juventud.

Vial Solar, Javier (1900) *Páginas diplomáticas*. Santiago de Chile: Imprenta Litografía y Encuadernación Barcelona.

Vucíc, Mihajlo (2017) "Silala Basin Dispute – Implications for the Interpretation of the Concept of International Watercourse." *Belgrade Law Review* 65, 4 (September): 91–111.

Wagner de Reyna, Alberto (1964) *Historia Diplomática del Perú (1900–1945)*. 2 vols. Lima: Ediciones Peruanas.

Wagner Tizón, Allan (1999) "Comentarios," In *El Desarrollo del Sur del Perú: Realidad y desafíos*, ed. Drago Kisic and Ramón Bahamonde, 135–137. Lima: Centro Peruano de Estudios Internacionales.

Weinstein, Barbara (1983) *The Amazon Rubber Boom, 1850–1920*. Stanford, CA: Stanford University Press.

Whitaker, Arthur P. (1948) *The United States and South America: The Northern Republics*. Cambridge, MA: Harvard University Press.

Whitehead, Laurence (1970) "Bolivia's Conflict with the United States." *The World Today* 26, 4 (April): 167–178.

Wikileaks Cablegate (2006) "Economic Roots of Bolivia's Social Revolution." 17 May. ID: 06LAPAZ1332. U.S. Embassy in La Paz. Mimeograph copy.

Wilgus, A.Curtis (1931) "The Second International American Conference at Mexico City." *Hispanic American Historical Review* 11, 1 (February): 32–40.

Wilgus, A.Curtis (1932) "The Third International American Conference at Rio de Janeiro, 1906." *Hispanic American Historical Review* 12, 4 (November): 443–448.

Wood, Bryce (1966) *The United States and Latin American Wars, 1932–1942.* New York, NY: Columbia University Press.
Worcester, Donald E. (1963) "Naval Strategy in the War of the Pacific." *Journal of Inter-American Studies* 5, 1 (January): 31–37.
Yepes, Ernesto (1999) *"Un plebiscito imposible…" Tacna-Arica 1925–1926: El Informe Pershing-Lassiter.* Lima: Ediciones Análisis.
Yepes, J. M. (1955) *Del congreso de Panamá a la conferencia de Caracas, 1826–1954.* 2 vols. Caracas: CROMOTIP.
Young, Kevin A. (2017) *Blood of the Earth: Resource Nationalism, Revolution, and Empire in Bolivia.* Austin, TX: University of Texas Press.
Zambrana Marchetti, Juan Carlos (2017–18) "Soft 'Nation-Building': The Economic Weapon Developed by the US in Bolivia." *Bolivian Studies Journal* 23–24: 188–338. https://bsj.pitt.edu/ojs/index.php/bsj/article/view/184. Accessed 31 January 2019.
Zelada Castedo, Alberto, ed. (2000) *Bolivia: Temas de la Agenda Internacional.* La Paz: Unidad de Análisis de Política de Exterior.
Zibechi, Raúl (2005) "Two Opposing Views of Social Change in Bolivia." *Center for International Policy, Americas Program* (14 December). Mimeograph copy.
Zook, David H. (1960) *The Conduct of the Chaco War.* New York, NY: Bookman Associates.

**Interviews**

Aranibar Quiroga, Antonio. Foreign minister of Bolivia (1993–1997). La Paz, 13 March 2001; via e-mail, 11 May 2001, 26 June 2001, 12 July 2001, 29 November 2001.
Belaúnde Terry, Fernando. President of Peru (1963–1968, 1980–1985). Denver, CO, 16 May 1969; Lima, 11 July 1983.
García Belaúnde, José Antonio. Foreign minister of Peru (2006–2011). Lima, 14 January 2014.
Gumucio Granier, Jorge. Bolivian ambassador to Peru (1994–2000), vice minister of foreign affairs (1988–1989, 1993–1994, 2003–2006). Lima, 1 September 1999; La Paz, 13 March 2001; via e-mail, 4 March 2000, 18 April 2001, 10 May 2005, 11 January 2006, 1 August 2013, 3 August 2014.
Maúrtua de Romaña, Oscar. Foreign minister of Peru (2005–2006). Lima, 11 July 1983, 18 April 2006.
Rodríguez Cuadros, José Manuel. Foreign minister of Peru (2003–2005). Lima, 14 March 2008.
Roncagliolo Orbegoso, Rafael. Foreign minister of Peru (2011–2013). Lima, via e-mail, 20 October 2014.
Sánchez de Lozada, Gonzalo. President of Bolivia (1993–1997, 2002–2003). Bloomington, IL, 9 September 2003.
Toledo Manrique, Alejandro Celestino. President of Peru (2001–2006). Lima, 9 May 2003, 19 April 2006; Palo Alto, CA, 12 September 2008; via telephone, 10 July, 20 July, 28 July, 10 August 2009; via e-mail, 28 August 2009.
Wagner Tizón, Allan. Foreign minister of Peru (1985–1988, 2002–2003), secretary general of the Andean Community (2004–2006), minister of defense (2006–2008). Lima, 9 May 2003.

## Newspapers, news agencies, magazines

*Bolivian Times* (La Paz, Bolivia)
*El Comercio* (Lima, Peru)
*El Diario* (La Paz, Bolivia)
*El Mercurio* (Santiago, Chile)
*El Mundo* (Santa Cruz de la Sierra, Bolivia)
*El Peruano* (Lima, Peru)
*Financial Times* (*FT*) (London, England)
*International Herald Tribune* (IHT) (Paris, France)
*La Razón* (La Paz, Bolivia)
*La República* (Lima, Peru)
*La Tercera* (Santiago, Chile)
*Latin American Herald Tribune* (*LAHT*) (Caracas, Venezuela)
*Los Tiempos* (Cochabamba, Bolivia)
*Miami Herald* (*MH*) (Miami, Florida)
*New York Times* (*NYT*) (New York, New York)
*Opinión* (Cochabamba, Bolivia)
*Perú21* (Lima, Peru)
*Presencia* (La Paz, Bolivia)
*Reuters* (New York, New York)
*Wall Street Journal* (*WSJ*) (New York, New York)
*Washington Post* (*WP*) (Washington, DC)
*Xinhua* (Beijing, China)

## Websites

Academia Diplomática Plurinacional (http://www.academiadiplomatica.gob.bo/pagina_adp/)
Bolivian Studies Journal (https://bsj.pitt.edu/ojs/index.php/bsj)
Instituto de Estudios Internacionales (https://ideibo.weebly.com/)
Ministry of Foreign Affairs of Bolivia (http://www.cancilleria.gob.bo/webmre/)

# Index

Page numbers in *italics* refer to figures.

Achá, José María 33–34, 36
Acre region 62, 64–66
Adams, Charles 55
Adriázola Valda, Óscar 137
Age of the Caudillos 4, 7, 32–34
Aguas del Illimani 149
Aguas del Tunari 148
Aguirre, Joaquín 37
Ahmadinejad, Mahmoud 180
Akhavan, Payan 186
Allende, Salvador 130, 131, 138
Alliance for Progress 121
*Almirante Cochrane* (warship) 44, 46, 48, 53
Álvarez, Mariano 57
Álvarez, Mariano Alejo 18
Amazon Cooperation Treaty Organization (*Organización del Tratado de Cooperación Amazónica*, OTCA) 140
Amazon River 65, 90
American Popular Revolutionary Alliance (*Alianza Popular Revolucionaria Americana*, APRA) 109
American Treaty on Pacific Settlement *see* Pact of Bogotá
Amnesty International 206
Ampuero, Roberto 189
Andean Commission of Jurists 206
Andean Community of Nations (*Comunidad Andina de Naciones*, CAN) 161, 162, 163, 166, 174, 175, 176, 194
Andean Group (*Group Andino*) 138–140, 160–161, 201, 207

Andean Pact (*Pacto Andino*) *see* Andean Group (*Group Andino*)
Andean Passport 161
Andean Trade Promotion and Drug Enforcement Act (ATPDEA) 173, 183
Andean Zone of Peace (*Zona de Paz Andina*) 162
Andes Mountains 1, 75, 91, 95, 116, 131
Andrade, Víctor 101, 119
Annan, Kofi 163
anti-narcotics programs 147; *see also* drug control; war on drugs
Antofagasta 45, 47, 60, 72, 85, 116, 155
Antofagasta and Bolivia Railway Company 75, 112, 157, 158
Antofagasta Nitrate and Railroad Company 34, 45, 46, 47–48, 51
Appleton, John 29
Araníbar Quiroga, Antonio 154, 155
arbitration, and Pan-American Conferences 78, 79–80, 200–201
Arce, Aniceto 61, 66, 67, 202
Arequipa 24, 111
Argentina 4, 8, 10, 16, 30, 63, 128, 195; and arbitration 79; and Brazil 45; economic crisis (2018) 196; exporting Bolivian oil through 76; and Madre de Dios region issue 88; and Pan-American Conferences 79; and Peru 18; and Peru–Bolivia Confederation 24, 25; and Treaty of Defensive Alliance (1873) 44–45, 46
Argentina–Bolivia relations 44, 67, 80, 93–94, 158–159, 200, 202; bilateral agreements 144; and Chaco War 98, 102; and Madre de Dios region issue 88; and Morales administration 196;

natural gas exports 144, 158, 159, 170, 184, 196; oil pipeline proposal of Bolivia 95, 102; Paraguay River issue 91; Tarija 16, 67, 93, 196, 202; trade pacts 102; Vaca Guzmán–Quirino Costa treaty (1889) 67
Argentina–Chile relations: bilateral talks 72; Pactos de Mayo (1902) 71
Argentina–Paraguay relations: and Chaco War 98, 102, 108; Treaty of Limits, Commerce, and Navigation (1852) 91
Arguedas, Alcides 31, 33
Arguedas, Antonio 121
Arguedas, Juan Bautista 28
Arica 11, 12, 13, 17, 18, 19, 20, 28, 29, 37, 40, 54, 56, 58–60, 66, 67, 68, 69, 70, 71, 72, 73, 79, 81, 82, 83, 86, 87, 109, 110, 111, 131, 132, 155, 204, 207
Arthur, Chester A. 56
Atacama Desert 7, 11, 13, *14*, 17; *El Proyecto Trinacional* 132; guano deposits in 13, 33, 36–37, 50, 58; nitrate deposits in 33, 34, 38–40, *39*, 42–43, 46, 49–51, 55; Silala River dispute 111–112, *112*, 157–158, 189–190
Atacama littoral 1–2, 29, *59*
Audiencia of Charcas 8, 9, 11, *12*, 15, 63, 207
austerity/stabilization program 106, 120, 129, 204
Aylwin, Patricio 153

Bachelet, Michelle 184, 187, 192
Badani Lenz, Jorge 156
Ballivián, Adolfo 34
Ballivián, José 28, 32, 33
Ballivián Rojas, Hugo 105
Balmaceda, José Manuel 56, 66, 67
Balta Montero, José 42
Banzer Suárez, Hugo 108, 127–128, 129, 131, 132, 134, 136, 137, 138, 143, 144, 146, 147–148, 150, 151, 154, 156, 158, 159, 167
Baptista, Mariano 61, 68–69
barbarous *caudillos* 31, 33
Barrenechea, José Antonio 41
Barrientos Ortuño, René 107, 108, 116, 121, 122, 158, 205
Battle of Angamos 53
Battle of Ayacucho 9
Battle of Callao 38
Battle of Ingavi 28, 29, 30, 198
Battle of Tacna 53–54
Battle of Tumusla 10
Battle of Yungay 27
Battle of Zepita 9
Bechtel Corporation 148
Bedregal Gutiérrez, Guillermo 143
Bello Codesido, Emilio 83
Bello Codesido–Gutiérrez treaty (1904) 2, 72, 74, 82, 141, 154, 185, 186, 192
Belzu, Manuel Isidoro 33
Benavides, Óscar R. 109
Berzaín, Sánchez 183
Betancur, Belisario 142
Bioceanic Railway Corridor Project 178, *178*, 180, 195
Blaine, James G. 55–56, 78, 79
*Blanco Encalada* (warship) 47, 48, 53
Blanco Encalada, Manuel 24, 25
Bolívar, Simón 9, 10, 13, 16, 18, 22, 31, 142, 199
Bolivarian Alliance for the Peoples of Our America (*Alianza Bolivariana para los Pueblos de Nuestra América*, ALBA) 174, 184, 201, 207
Bolivarian regime, end of 16–21
Bolivian Diplomatic Academy 210
Bolivian Gulf Oil 108, 122, 169
Bolivian National Assembly 17, 20, 26, 29, 34, 35, 40, 42, 43, 54, 67, 69, 72, 83, 205
Bolivian National Revolution (1952) 105–108, 119, 198, 204
Bolivian Socialist Falange (*Falange Socialista Boliviana*, FSB) 104
Bolivian Mining Corporation (*Corporación Minera de Bolivia*, COMIBOL) 106
Bolivian Syndicate of New York 64–65
Bonaparte, Napoleon 8
Brazil 4, 52, 128, 185, 195; and Argentina 45; and Chaco War 98; and Chile 45; mediation, in Madre de Dios region issue 88; and Pan-American Conferences 80; and Paraguay River issue 91; and Treaty of Defensive Alliance (1873) 45
Brazil–Bolivia relations 202; Acre region 64–65; economic agreements 143–144; Gasbol pipeline 159; and Morales administration 169–170; Muñoz-Netto convention 40–42; natural gas exports 159, 195–196; and Paraguay River issue 91; Roboré Agreements 102; supply and export of Bolivian

## 238  Index

petroleum 102; Treaty of Petrópolis (1903) 65, 74, 90, 94, 202
Brazil–Peru relations *see* Peru–Brazil relations
brokered democracy 164
Buchanan, James 29
Bulnes Prieto, Manuel 26, 27, 37
Busch, Germán 104
Bush, George W. 171, 172, 173, 180, 194, 196
Bustillo Montesinos, Mariano Rafael 32

Cabrera, Ladislao 55
Camacho, Eliodoro 61, 63
Campero, Narciso 54, 57, 60
Cardoso, Fernando Henrique 159
Carrillo, Juan Crisóstomo 57, 62
Cartagena Agreement (1969) 123, 138, 140
Carter, James Earl "Jimmy" 128, 137, 165–166
Cartes, Horacio 196
Carvajal Prado, Patricio 132–133
Castilla, Ramón 27, 35–36
Castro, Fidel 165, 171, 174, 177
*caudillismo* 31, 199, 205
*caudillos* 31, 46, 47, 208
Central Bank of Bolivia 78
Chaco Austral 91
Chaco Boreal 74, 91, 93, 94, 95, 96, 97, 100, 101, 102
Chaco Central 91
Chaco War (1932–1935) 4, 76, 97–101, 108, 203; Bolivia–Paraguay boundary (1938) *99*; competing narratives about 101–103; postwar politics 103–105; and Royal Dutch Shell 102; and Standard Oil Company 101–103; and United States 102–103
Charles IV 8
Chávez, Hugo 163, 165, 171–172, 174, 175, 176, 193, 197
Chile 2, 4, 8, 30, 124, 167; and Brazil 45; and Chaco War 108; civil war in 67; and Declaration of Bogotá 138; and guano deposits in Atacama Desert 13, 33–34, 36–37, 50, 58; mediation in Bolivia–Peru trade conflict 19–20; and Melgarejo administration 34; navy 44, 46, 52; and Pan-American Conferences 78, 79, 80–81, 200–201; and Peru–Bolivia Confederation 22–23, 24–26, 27; population of 52; privatization of ports 155, 192, 209; and Treaty of Defensive Alliance (1873) 44, 46; war with Spain 38; withdrawal from Cartagena Agreement 138
Chile–Argentina relations *see* Argentina–Chile relations
Chile–Bolivia relations 13, 45, 46, 71–73, 93, 108, 119, 200, 208; and Achá administration 33–34; and Antofagasta Nitrate and Railroad Company 47–48, 51; Bello Codesido–Gutiérrez treaty (1904) 72, 74, 82, 141, 154, 185, 186, 192; Bolivian littoral 68, 69, 70, 71, 72, 85; Charaña talks 128, 130–137, 141, 145; Chilean occupation of Bolivian littoral 48, 49, 56, 60, 202; December 1895 protocol 69; Declaration of Algarve 156; and drop in Bolivian exports 139; foreign trade 22–23, 83; Fresh Approach (*Enfoque Fresco*) 143; gas por mar 157; and guano deposits in Atacama Desert 36–37; König memorandum 71; land-sea corridor proposal of Chile 133–134, *133*, 203; Lauca River dispute 112, *113*, 114–117, 192; and League of Nations 84–85; Lindsay–Corral protocol (1872) 43, 45; Line of Concordance (*Línea de la Concordia*) 132; Matta–Reyes Ortiz protocol (1891) 67; Maurí River dispute 117; May 1895 treaties and protocols 69–70; mediation efforts of United States 121; and Morales administration 171; nitrate deposits in Atacama Desert 33, 38–40, *39*, 42–43, 50–51; October 1890 proposal 66, 67; Pando administration 70–71, 72; postwar 66–67, 68–69, 70; seaport issue 72, 82, 83, 84, 85, 86, 109, 110, 116, 125, 131, 132–134, 141–142, 143, 153, 154, 156, 157, 162, 184, 185–189, 203, 209; Sica Sica–Arica oil pipeline 109; Silala River dispute 111–112, *112*, 157–158, 189–190; silver mines at Caracoles 43, 48; strategic relationship 154; ten centavos tax on nitrates exports 47, 50, 51; Third Summit of the Americas 156; Treaty of Mutual Benefits (1866) 38–40, *39*, 43, 51, 202; Treaty of Sucre (1874) 34, 45–46, 47, 51; Trucco Memorandum 110; *see also* War of the Pacific (1879–1884)

Chile–Peru relations 42, 74; Act of Execution (1999) 150–151; *Aquiles* incident 23; bilateral talks (1928–1929) 86–87; Billinghurst–Latorre protocol (1898) 70; and Freire military expedition 23; Jiménez–Vial Solar accord (1894) 68; and League of Nations 84; and Morales administration 176; nitrate mining 49–50; plebiscite for Tacna and Arica 58, 59, 60, 66, 68, 69, 70, 73, 86; postwar 66, 67–68, 69–70; seaports issue 81, 86, 136, 186–187; treaty of friendship, commerce, and navigation (1876) 46; Treaty of Lima (1929) 74, 87, 96, 102, 103, 109, 110, 117, 134, 136, 150, 186, 202, 204, 207; Viña del Mar protocol (1882) 56; Washington Conference (1922) 85–86, 87; *see also* War of the Pacific (1879–1884)

China–Bolivia relations 82, 172, 179–180, 196, 207; lithium reserves 180; military relations 179; strategic implications 180; trade relations 180

Chincha Islands, Spanish occupation of 37–38

Chiquitos 15

Choquehuanca, David 179, 192

Chungará Lake 192

Chuquicamata copper mine 112

Chuquisaca 9, 26

Cobija 13, 19, 20, 29, 38, 43, 48, 110, 207

coca production 130, 147–148, 166

Cochabamba 148

Cold War 205

Colombia 19, 176, 199; free trade agreement of 174, 176; and La Mar administration 17; mediation, in Chile–Bolivia seaport issue 142; and treaty of limits (1826) 17

Communist Party of Bolivia 107

Community of Latin American and Caribbean States (*Comunidad de Estados Latinoamericanos y Caribeños*, CELAC) 140, 176, 180, 196, 201

Complementary Economic Agreement (*Acuerdo de Complementación Económica*, ACE) 140, 144, 160, 161

compulsory arbitration 78, 79–80, 200, 201

Concordance (*La Concordancia*) 105

Congress of Panama *see* Panama Congress (1826)

Conservative Party (Bolivia) 61, 62

Constituent Assembly 10, 17

continental solidarity 31–32, 51, 199–201

Convention and Statute on Freedom of Transit (1921) 123, 124

Convention and Statute on the Regime of Navigable Waterways of International Concern (1921) 124

Convention on the High Seas (1958) 124–125

Convention on the Territorial Sea and Contiguous Zone (1958) 124

Convention on Transit Trade of Land-Locked States (1965) 126

Coolidge, Calvin 86

Copacabana Peninsula 108

Cordillera Occidental 1, 13, 87

Cordillera Oriental 1, 13

Cordillera Real *see* Cordillera Oriental

Córdova, Jorge 33, 36

Correa, Rafael 176, 197

corruption 121, 129, 148, 169

Cotacotani Lagoon wetlands 192

coup d'état *see golpe de estado*

Covenant of the League of Nations 84, 123

Crespo Gutiérrez, Alberto 136–137

Cuba: and Bolivia, relations 171, 193; and United States 183

Cuban missile crisis (1963) 121

cultured *caudillos* 31, 33

Customs Mutual Assistance Agreement (CMAA) 183

Cuzco Consensus 163

Day of the Sea (*Día del Mar*) 136

Daza, Hilarión 34, 42, 47–48, 53, 54

Declaration of Ayacucho (1974) 132

Declaration of Bogotá 138

Declaration of Ilo (2010) 194

Declaration of La Moneda 175

Declaration of Montevideo on the Industrial and Agricultural Use of International Rivers 114, 115, 117

Declaration of Sucre (2016) 195

Declaration on Security in the Americas 162

Decree 21060 130

democracy 128, 129, 130, 163, 164, 165, 168, 171, 198

Desaguadero River 117

Diez de Medina, Eduardo 86

Dignity Plan (*Plan Dignidad*) 147

Dillon, Read, and Company 78

## Index

drug control 164–165, 167, 182, 183, 195; *see also* war on drugs
Drug Enforcement Agency (DEA) 164, 173, 182
drug trade 128, 129, 130, 147, 165
DUCTEC SRL 158
Dulles, John Foster 120

East Bloc 120, 121, 129, 205
Echenique, José Rufino 35, 36
Economic Commission for Latin America (*Comisión Económica para la América Latina*, CEPAL) 137, 201
economy of Bolivia 6, 7, 31; aid from United States 106, 118, 120; Andean Pact 138–140; and Banzer administration 127–128; and Barrientos administration 107; decline in 77–78; Decree 21060 130; economic crisis 144; economic depression 11; economic independence 4, 207–208; economic stabilization plan 106; export-led growth 207, 208; fiscal reforms 78; foreign debt 77–78, 129; and landlocked position 2, 125, 154–155, 189, 208, 209, 210; loans 74–75, 76, 78, 129; organized labor 139; petroleum 76–77; privatization 147, 148; railways 75; resource nationalism 77; and Siles Reyes administration 77; and Siles Zuazo administration 129; tin exports 74, 77–78, 103, 118, 139, 207; trinational integration 210
Ecuador 19, 30, 176, 177, 197, 199–200; and Andean Pact 139; and Pan-American Conferences 79, 80; and Peru–Bolivia Confederation 24; war with Spain 38
Egaña, Mariano 23, 24, 27
Eisenhower, Dwight David 106, 120
Elías, Domingo 35
Elío Bustillos, Tomás Manuel 118
Equitable Trust Company 78
Errázuriz Echaurren, Federico 70, 71
Escobari Cusicanqui, Jorge 4, 3, 155
European Union (EU) 175–176, 177
Evarts, William Maxwell 55
Export-Import Bank of the United States (EXIM) 118

Farcau, Bruce W. 103
Federación Boliviana 16
Federal Revolution 62, 198
Federation of the Andes 10, 22, 199
Fellmann Velarde, José 115, 116, 125
Ferdinand VII 8, 9
Fernández Alonso, Severo 61
Fernández y Fernández, Joaquín 119
Ferreyros y de la Mata, Manuel 19
Fifer, J. Valerie 17
Fifth Pan-American Conference, Santiago (1923) 80
First Ladies of the Americas (*Primeras Damas de las Américas*) 163
First Pan-American Conference, Washington (1889–1890) 78–79, 200
Flores, Juan José 19
Fontaine, Roger W. 138
Ford, Gerald 136–137
foreign investment 31, 33, 36, 50, 76, 77, 128, 138, 159, 169, 170, 208
Fourth International 104
Fourth Pan-American Conference, Buenos Aires (1910) 80, 94
France 38, 82, 172; and Bolivia 29; investment in Latin America 50; and Morales administration 170, 178
freedom of transit 123, 125, 127
free trade 7, 33, 54, 60, 208; agreements 174, 175–176, 193, 194; area/zone 160–161
Free Trade Area of the Americas (*Área de Libre Comerico de las Américas*, ALCA) 161
Frei, Eduardo 130
Freire, Ramón 23
Frelinghuysen, Frederick T. 56, 57
Freyre, Ricardo Jaime 85
Frías Ametller, Tomás 34, 44
Friendship Bridge (*Puente de la Amistad*) 159
Fujimori, Alberto 143, 150, 160

Gamarra, Agustín 17, 18, 19, 21, 26, 28, 29
García Belaúnde, José Antonio 194
García Calderón, Francisco 57
García Linera, Alvaro 171
García Meza Tejada, Luis 128–129, 140, 141, 144
García Pérez, Alan 142, 143, 176, 193–194
García Sayán, Diego 151
Garfield, James A. 55, 56
Gas War 149
Gaviria, César 162
Gazprom 178, 179

Geisel, Ernesto Beckmann 131
General Agreement on Tariffs and Trade (GATT) 140
Germany–Bolivia relations 82, 178
Glassner, Martin 116
globalization 129, 153, 175
Goldberg, Philip S. 173
*golpe de estado* 11, 23, 32, 84, 85, 97, 104, 107, 121, 127, 131, 144, 199
Gran Chaco 91
Gran Colombia 10, 17
Great Britain 38, 42, 88; investment in Latin America 50; and Morales administration 170; and Nazi Putsch 118; and Peru–Bolivia Confederation 29
Great Depression 78, 97, 103, 122, 203, 208
Greenlee, David 165, 171
Group of 77 (*Grupo de los 77,* G-77) 138, 142, 177, 201
Guachalla, Fernando 71
guano deposits, in Atacama Desert 13, 33, 36–37, 50, 58
guerrilla forces 107
Guevara, Ernesto "Che" 107, 121, 205
Guevara Arze, Walter 124
Gutiérrez, Carlos 83
Gutiérrez Guerra, José 76, 82, 83–84
Gutiérrez Vea Murguía, Guillermo 132
Guzmán Saldaña, Mario Gustavo 173

Harding, Warren G. 85–86
Hayes, Rutherford B. 55, 91
Hertzog, Enrique 105
Hicks, George 47
*Huáscar* (warship) 53
Hu Jintao 172
Hull, Cordell 118, 119
Humala Tasso, Ollanta 194, 195
human rights 128, 148, 166, 173, 206

Ibáñez y Gutierrez, Adolfo 46
Ilo 150, 151, 157, 209
independence, Bolivia at 1–2, 11–16
Initiative for Integration of Regional Infrastructure in South America (*Iniciativa para la Integración de la Infraestructura Regional Suramericana,* IIRSA) 159, 185
Insulza, José Miguel 154, 163
Intendencia of Potosí 11, 16
Intendencia of Puno 15

Inter-American Commission on Human Rights (IACHR) 176
Inter-American Democratic Charter 163
Inter-American Development Bank (IDB) 116, 137–138, 150
Inter-American Treaty of Reciprocal Assistance 176
International Conference of American States on Conciliation and Arbitration, Washington (1928) 95
International Court of Justice (ICJ) 2, 4, 158, 168, 184–189, 191, 194
International Criminal Court (ICC) 172, 180
International Law Conference, Buenos Aires (1925) 80
International Monetary Fund (IMF) 106, 120, 129, 147, 164, 204, 206
International Union of American Republics 78, 79, 80, 200
international watercourse, definition of 190
Iran–Bolivia relations 180
Irigoyen, Manuel 44
Irigoyen, Pedro 49
Irisarri, Antonio José de 24
Israel–Bolivia relations 180–181

Japan 82, 179, 181

Kampala Declaration 126
Kellogg, Frank B. 86, 204
Kemmerer, Edwin W. 78
Kemmerer Mission 78
Kennedy, John F. 121
Kirchner, Cristina Fernández de 197
Kirchner, Néstor 159, 196, 197
Kissinger, Henry 137
König Velásquez, Abraham 71, 81
Kuczynski, Pedro Pablo 195

La Fuente, Antonio Gutierrez de 17
Lagos, Ricardo 156, 184
Lake Titicaca 109, 111, 116, 119, 143, 150, 202
Lake Titicaca Binational Agency 150
La Mar, José de 17
Lanza, José Miguel 9
Laos–Bolivia relations 181
La Paz Treaty (1996) 159
Larrabure y Unánue, Eugenio 67
Latin American and Caribbean Economic System (*Sistema Económico*

*Latinoamericano y del Caribe,* SELA) 140, 201
Latin American Free Trade Association (*Asociación Latinoamericana de Libre Comercio,* ALALC) 138, 201
Latin American Integration Association (*Asociación Latinoamericana de Integración,* ALADI) 138
Lauca National Park 192
Lauca River dispute 112, *113*, 114–117, 192
Lavalle, José Antonio de 48–49
League of Nations 82, 84–85, 201
Lechín, Juan 106
Leguía, Augusto B. 83
Lehman, Kenneth D. 164
Lenz, Jorge Badani 156
Liberal Party (Bolivia) 61, 62, 69, 75, 76
Libya–Bolivia relations 180
Lima-Callao 22
Linares, José María 33, 36
Lindsay–Corral protocol (1872) 43, 45
Line of Concordance (*Línea de la Concordia*) 132
literature on foreign policy of Bolivia 3, 5
lithium industry 178, 180
Logan, Cornelius A. 57
Long, Huey 102–103
López de Romaña, Eduardo 71
López Netto, Felipe 41
Lower Peru 9, 10, 11
Lugo, Fernando 196
Lula da Silva, Luiz Inácio 159, 169, 196, 197

Macías, Silvio 103
MacLean Abaroa, Ronald 162
Madre de Dios region 63, 88, *89*, 90, 202
Maduro, Nicolás 174, 197
Maney, George 57
Manzono, Omar 157
Mariátegui, Javier 18
Maritime Commission 131, 132
Martínez Sotomayor, Carlos 116
Matarani 111
Mato Grosso 15
Matta, Juan Gonzalo 67
Matte Memorandum 86
Maurí River dispute 117, 192–193
*media luna* 170–171, 173, 198
Mejillones 33, 36, 37, 40, 42, 45, 48, 116, 157
Melgarejo, Mariano 34, 38, 41, 42, 43, 47, 202

Mercado Moreira, Miguel 3
mercantilism 33
Merino, José Toribio 143
Merkel, Angela 176
Mesa Gisbert, Carlos Diego 149, 150, 152, 157, 159, 163, 164, 165, 167, 169, 187
Mexico, and Pan-American Conferences 79
militarism 199, 205
military socialism 104
mining industry 33, 34, 36–37, 38–40, *39*, 42–43, 46, 76, 106, 112
Montero Flores, Lizardo 57
Montes, Ismael 62, 72, 74, 75, 81, 207
Montt, Jorge 69
Montt, Manuel 37
Morales, Agustín 34, 43
Morales, Waltraud Queiser 129
Morales Ayma, Juan Evo 148, 149, 165, 166, 167, 168–169, 176, 196, 197, 198, 206; and Andean Community 174, 175; anti-imperialist military school 173; and Argentina–Bolivia relations 196; axis of good 172; and Brazil–Bolivia relations 169–170; and Chile–Bolivia relations 184; and China–Bolivia relations 179–180, 207; and Constitution (2009) 170; energy sector, nationalization of 169–170; and European Union economic aid 177–177; and foreign military bases 175; and Iran–Bolivia relations 181; and Israel–Bolivia relations 181–182; and Japan–Bolivia relations 181; and Laos–Bolivia relations 181; Lauca River dispute 192; and Libya–Bolivia relations 181; and October Agenda 169; and Organization of American States 176; and Paraguay–Bolivia relations 196; and Peru–Bolivia relations 193–195; rejection of privatization program 170; and Russia 178–179; and seaport issue 184, 187, 188, 189; Silala River dispute 189–190, 191; and South Korea–Bolivia relations 181; Summit of Latin America, the Caribbean, and the European Union 174–175; and United States 171, 172–173, 182–183
Morales Bermúdez, Remigio 68
Morla Vicuña, Carlos 79
Moscoso, Teodoro 116

Movement toward Socialism (*Movimiento al Socialismo,* MAS) 168, 170
Muñoz, Mariano Donato 41
Muñoz-Netto convention 40–42, 91
Muñoz Reyes, Víctor 82
Murillo de la Rocha, Javier 154–155, 156, 162

National Copper Corporation (*Corporación Nacional del Cobre,* CODELCO) 112, 158
nationalism 97, 107, 121, 122, 200
Nationalist Revolutionary Movement (*Movimiento Nacionalista Revolucionario,* MNR) 104, 105, 106, 119, 120, 121, 204
nationalization: of Bolivian Gulf Oil 122; of energy sector 149, 169–170, 195, 196, 206; of Standard Oil Company 102, 103, 169; of tin mines 106
National Maritime Council (*Consejo Nacional Marítimo,* CONAMAR) 134
national security 202
natural gas 108, 144, 148, 149, 150, 151–152, 157, 160, 166, 178, 184, 195–196, 207, 208
Nazi Putsch 118
neoliberal economic policies 129, 130, 164, 166, 168, 197, 206
New Economic Policy (*Nueva Política Económica*) 130
New Granada 32
nitrate deposits in Atacama Desert 33, 34, 38–40, *39*, 42–43, 46, 49–51, 55
Nixon, Richard M. 120
Non-Aligned Movement (NAM) 140, 142, 201

Obama, Barack 177, 182, 196
obligatory arbitration *see* compulsory arbitration
October Agenda 169
*O'Higgins* (warship) 48
Olañeta, Casimiro 19, 23, 37
Operation Condor 128, 144, 148
Orbegoso, Luís José de 20, 21, 23, 26–27
Organization of American States (OAS) 78, 115, 141–142, 154, 162–163, 176, 182, 184, 200, 201, 206
Ortiz de Zevallos, Ignacio 16
Ostria Gutiérrez, Alberto 109
Ovando Candía, Alfredo 107, 108, 122, 127

Pacheco, Gregorio 61, 62
Pacific Alliance 176–177, 184
Pact of Bogotá 185, 186, 187
Pactos de Mayo (1902) 71
Palestine Liberation Organization 129
Panama Congress (1826) 31–32, 199
Pan-American Conferences 78–81
Pan-Americanism 31, 71, 199
Pando, José Manuel 62, 70–71, 72, 202
Paraguay–Bolivia relations 4, 159–160; Chaco War (1932–1935) 4, 76, 97–101, *99*; and Morales administration 196; oil pipeline across Chaco Boreal 103; and Paraguay River issue 93, 94–95, 202–203
Paraguay River 15, 65, 74, 91, *92*, 93, 94, 102, 202–203, 209
Paris Peace Conference (1919) 82
Party of the Revolutionary Left (*Partido de la Izquierda Revolucionaria,* PIR) 104
Paz Estenssoro, Víctor 104, 105, 106, 107, 115, 121, 130, 143, 144, 146, 179, 205
Paz Zamora, Jaime 146, 147, 150, 152–153, 162
Peace Corps, expulsion of 122, 173
Peñaranda del Castillo, Enrique 105, 118
Permanent Court of Arbitration 79, 201
Peru 1, 4, 8, 10, 12, 17–18; and Andean Group 160, 161; and arbitration 79; Assembly of Northern Departments 20, 21; Assembly of Southern Departments 20, 21, 29; and Bello Codesido–Gutiérrez treaty (1904) 73; and Bolivia, unification of 16, 17, 18, 19, 20; and Chaco War 98, 108; Chincha Islands, Spanish occupation of 37–38; free trade agreement of 174, 176, 193, 194; and Muñoz-Netto convention 41; nitrate monopoly 49–50; and Pan-American Conferences 79, 80; rebellions in 20–21; war with Spain 38
Peru–Bolivia Confederation 21–24, 29, 203; and Argentina 24, 25; and Chile 22–23, 24–25, 27; dissolution of 24–27; establishment of 21–22; internal opposition to 22, 26; and Orbegoso 21, 23, 26–27; Treaty of Paucarpata (1837) 24–25; war of Chile with 23–24, 25–26, 27
Peru–Bolivia relations 41, 42, 90, 108, 142–143, 199–200; arbitration treaty

## 244  Index

(1901) 63; bilateral talks 18–19; Bolivian invasion of Peru (1841) 28; boundary, defining 88, *89*; Candamo–Terrazas protocol 63; commercial issues 63–64; foreign trade between 19, 34–36; Ilo 150, 151, 157, 209; joint declaration (1955) 111; labor migration 151; Lake Titicaca 109, 111, 143, 202; Madre de Dios region 63, 88, *89*, 90, 202; Maurí River dispute 117, 192–193; and Morales administration 174, 193–194; natural gas exports 148, 149, 151–152; peace agreements 20, 28, 35; Peruvian invasion of Bolivia (1828) 18; Peruvian invasion of Bolivia (1841) 28; Polo–Sánchez Bustamante Protocol (1909) 88; postwar relations, War of Pacific 62–64; seaport issue 67, 82–83, 131, 132, 135–136, *135*, 150, 151, 152, 154, 157, 194, 204; strategic alliance 195; Treaty of Defensive Alliance (1873) 43–44, 46, 47, 48, 49, 51; treaty of limits (1826) 16–17; treaty of limits (1886) 63; Ulloa–Ostria treaty (1936) 109; war debts 62–63; and War of the Pacific (1879–1884) 54, 57
Peru–Brazil relations 18, 45, 64, 65–66
Peru–Chile relations *see* Chile–Peru relations
Petrobrás 159, 169, 195–196
petroleum 76–77, 95, 101, 104, 106
Pettis, Newton 55
Piérola, Nicolás de 70
Piñera, Sebastián 184, 188, 189
Pinilla, Claudio 94
Pinochet, Augusto 131, 148
Pinto Garmendia, Aníbal 47, 48, 49
Pisagua 37
Polisario Liberation Front 129
Polo–Sánchez Bustamante Protocol (1909) 88
Popolizio, Néstor 188, 195
Prado, Mariano Ignacio 46, 48, 49
Presidential Certification 165
presidential politics of Bolivia 146–150
privatization 147; rejection, during Morales administration 170; of seaports 155, 192, 209; water 148
protectionism 11, 31, 208
public works 74, 75, 78
Puna de Atacama 67, 69, 93, 202
Putin, Vladimir 178–179

Querejazu Calvo, Roberto 40, 103
Quintanilla Quiroga, Carlos 105
Quiroga, Ovidio 105
Quiroga Ramírez, Jorge 148, 151, 158, 163, 167, 180

railways 2, 4, 70, 74, 81–82, 112; Arica–La Paz 72, 73, 74, 82, 83, 132, 134; Bioceanic Railway Corridor Project 178, *178*, 180, 195; La Paz–Antofagasta 62, 75; La Paz–Guaqui 75; Madeira–Mamoré 90
Ramos, Sebastián 15
Reagan, Ronald 129
Reason of the Fatherland (*Razón de Patria,* RADEPA) 105
regional autonomy 146, 149, 167, 169, 170–171
regional cooperation 4, 123, 137–140, 155, 160–164, 174
regional integration 4, 21–24, 102, 123, 137–140, 155, 156, 160–164, 173, 174–176
regionalism 3, 22, 77, 128, 145, 173, 175, 177, 198, 210
representative democracy 165
Republican Party (Bolivia) 75–76
Resolution 426 141–142
Resolution 989 162
resource nationalism 77, 106, 122
Revolutionary Workers' Party (*Partido Obrero Revolucionario,* POR) 104
Reyes Ortiz, Serapio 48, 67
Ribeyro, Ramón 63
Riesco Errázuriz, Germán 70
Rio Branco, Baron do 65
Río de la Plata system 67
Rio Group (*Grupo Río,* G-Río) 140, 163
Ríos Gallardo, Conrado 87
Rio Treaty of Reciprocal Defense (1947) 115
Rivera Cusicanqui, Silvia 205
Roboré Agreements 102
Rocafuerte, Vicente 24
Rocha, Manuel 165
Rodríguez Cuadros, José Manuel 194
Rodríguez Veltzé, Eduardo 150, 157, 171, 186, 187
Romero, Gonzalo 141
Roncagliolo Orbegoso, Rafael 195
Roosevelt, Franklin Delano 118, 119
Rosas, Juan Manuel de 24
Rosneft 179
Royal Dutch Shell 76, 95, 102

Royal Geographical Society 88
rubber plantations, in Acre region 62, 64–66
Ruck Uriburu, Franz 130
Russia–Bolivia relations 178–179

Saavedra, Bautista 76–77, 78, 84, 85
Saavedra Bruno, Carlos Armando 152
Salado River 202
Salamanca Urey, Daniel 95, 97, 98, 102, 104
Salaverry, Felipe Santiago 20, 21, 23
Salazar y Mazarredo, Eusebio de 37
Salinas Baldivieso, Carlos Alberto 3
Salta (Argentina) 16
Sánchez Bustamante Vásquez, Daniel 81
Sánchez de Lozada, Gonzalo ("Goni") 146, 147, 148, 149, 151, 152, 154, 157, 158, 160, 163, 167, 169, 172, 179, 182, 183
San Martín, José de 9, 22
Santa Cruz, Andrés 9, 16, 17, 18, 19, 20, 21, 22, 24, 25–27, 28, 30, 197
Santa María, Domingo 59, 66
sea, access to 2, 11–13, 30, 43, 52, 116, 123, 142, 201, 205, 207, 208, 209, 210; Act of Cochabamba 131; Antofagasta 45, 47, 60, 72, 85, 116, 155; Arequipa 24, 111; Arica 11, 12, 13, 17, 18, 19, 20, 28, 29, 37, 40, 54, 56, 58–60, 66, 67, 68, 69, 70, 71, 72, 73, 79, 81, 82, 83, 86, 87, 109, 110, 111, 131, 132, 155, 204, 207; bilateral and multilateral initiatives 140–143; *Blue Book, The* 163; *Book of the Sea, The* 185; Cobija 13, 19, 20, 29, 38, 43, 48, 110, 207; Colombian mediation 142; Ilo 150, 151, 157, 209; inherent right of state to outlet to sea 82; International Court of Justice 184, 185–189; issue, tripartite nature of 110–111, 131, 136, 137; Kampala Declaration 126; and League of Nations 84, 85; Lima-Callao 22; Matarani 111; Mejillones 33, 36, 37, 40, 45, 48, 116, 157; and Organization of American States 141–142, 154, 162; Peruvian proposal of tripartite zone (1976) 135–136, *135*; Pisagua 37; privatization of ports 155; Tacna 56, 58–60, 66, 67, 68, 69, 70, 71, 72, 79, 81, 82, 83, 86, 87, 109, 204; Tocopilla 48; UN Conference on the Law of the Sea (1958) 124–125; UN Conference on the Law of the Sea (1973) 126–127; UN Conference on Trade and Development (UNCTAD) 125; UN Conference on Transit Trade of Land-locked Countries 125, 126; and United Nations 163; and United States 118–119, 204; Valparaiso 23; and War of the Pacific *see* War of the Pacific (1879–1884)
Second Latin American Conference, Lima (1847) 32, 200
Second Pan-American Conference, Mexico City (1901) 79–80, 201
VII Summit of the Americas, Panama (2015) 177
Shannon, Thomas 182
Silala River dispute 111–112, *112*, 157–158, 189–190
Siles Reyes, Hernando 77–78, 86, 87, 97
Siles Salinas, Luis Adolfo 108
Siles Zuazo, Hernán 106, 120, 129, 142, 144, 179
Silva Cimma, Enrique 153, 162
silver mines 43, 48
Single Convention on Narcotic Drugs (1961) 129
Sixth Pan-American Conference, Havana (1928) 80–81
Snowden, Edward 183
Solana, Javier 172
Soler, Adolfo 94
Sotomayor, Emilio 48
South American Community of Nations (*Comunidad Sudamericana de Naciones,* CSN) 163, 175, 201
South American Energy Summit (2007) 175
Southern Common Market (*Mercado Común del Sur,* MERCOSUR) 160, 161, 166, 174, 176–177, 182, 196
South Korea–Bolivia relations 181
sovereignty of Bolivia 4, 29, 32, 37, 50, 67, 104, 134, 173, 203–207
Soviet Union 108, 129, 205
Spain: and Bolivia 29; colonialism 198; intervention in Latin America 37–42; and Morales administration 170; occupation of Chincha Islands 37–38
Spencer, Trask, and Company 78
Speyer and Company 75
Standard Oil Company 76, 77, 95, 97, 104, 118, 206; and Chaco War 101–103; nationalization of 102, 103, 169

Stifel-Nicolaus Investment Company 76, 78
Stroessner, Alfredo 160
Sucre, Antonio José de 9–10, 10–11, 12, 13, 16, 17, 18
Summit of Latin America, the Caribbean, and the European Union (*Cumbre de América Latina, el Caribe y la Unión Europea*, ALC-UE) 174–176, 201
Summit of the Americas for Sustainable Development (*Cumbre de las Américas para el Desarrollo Sostenible*) 163

Tacna 56, 58–60, 66, 67, 68, 69, 70, 71, 72, 79, 81, 82, 83, 86, 87, 109, 204
Taiwan 179
Tarija 15–16, 24, 67, 93, 149, 196, 202
Technical Cooperation Agreement (1951) 119
Tejada Sorzano, José Luis 104
territorial integrity 202–203
Third Pan-American Conference, Rio de Janeiro (1906) 80, 201
Third Summit of the Americas 156
tin exports 74, 77–78, 103, 118, 139, 207
Tocopilla 48
Toledo Manrique, Alejandro Celestino 151, 152, 159, 174, 193
Toro, David 102, 104, 109, 206
Torres Gonzales, Juan José 108, 122, 127, 173
Treaty of Acora (1842) 34
Treaty of Amazon Cooperation (1978) 144
Treaty of Ancón (1883) 57–58, 63, 66, 68, 69, 86
Treaty of Arequipa (1831) 20
Treaty of Arequipa (1847) 35
Treaty of Defensive Alliance (1873) 43–44, 46, 47, 48, 49, 51
Treaty of La Paz (1835) 21
Treaty of Lima (1929) 74, 87, 96, 102, 103, 109, 110, 117, 134, 136, 150, 186, 202, 204, 207
Treaty of Madrid (1750) 14
Treaty of Mutual Benefits (1866) 34, 38–40, *39*, 43, 51, 202
Treaty of Paucarpata (1837) 24–25
Treaty of Peace, Friendship, and Commerce (1904) *see* Bello Codesido–Gutiérrez treaty (1904)
Treaty of Petrópolis (1903) 65, 74, 90, 94, 202
Treaty of Piquiza (1828) 18
Treaty of San Ildefonso (1777) 14, *15*
Treaty of Santiago (1845) 27
Treaty of Sucre (1874) 34, 45–46, 47, 51
Treaty of Tacna (1837) 22, 26
Treaty of the Rio de la Plata Basin, 1969 (*Tratado de la Cuenca del Plata*) 140, 144
Trescot, William Henry 56–57
Trinational Project (*Proyecto Trinacional*) 155–156
Triple Alliance 45
Trotsky, Leon 104
Trucco, Manuel 110
Trucco Memorandum 110
Truman, Harry S. 119, 120
Trump, Donald J. 183–184

Ulloa–Ostria treaty (1936) 109
UN Conference on the Law of the Sea (1958) 124–125
UN Conference on the Law of the Sea (1973) 126–127
UN Conference on Trade and Development (UNCTAD) 125, 164
UN Conference on Transit Trade of Land-locked Countries 125, 126
UN Convention on the Law of the Non-Navigational Uses of International Watercourses 190–191
UN Convention on the Law of the Sea (1982) 126–127
UN General Assembly 124, 125, 153, 154–155, 163, 187, 201
Union of South American Nations (*Unión de Naciones Suramericanas*, UNASUR) 175, 177, 196
United Kingdom *see* Great Britain
United Nations 163, 201, 206–207
United Provinces of the Río de la Plata 16
United States 4, 6, 38, 83, 88, 97, 107, 176, 200; and Andean Community 174, 175; and Banzer administration 127–128; and Bolivia 29, 85–86, 117–122, 127–128, 145, 147, 164–166, 167, 182–184, 203–205, 206; and Bolivian Gulf Oil 108, 122; and Chaco War 102–103; companies, investment in petroleum in Bolivia 76, 77; economic aid to Bolivia 106, 118, 120; and First Pan-American Conference (1889–1890) 78, 79; free trade agreements of 174, 176, 193, 194;

mediation efforts between Bolivia and Chile 71; military bases 175; and Morales administration 171, 172–173, 182; and Pan-American Conferences 79, 80–81; personnel, immunity agreements for 165; and Peru–Bolivia Confederation 29, 203; and seaport issue of Bolivia 82, 85, 86, 136–137; and Tacna/Arica dispute 86–87; 3 Ds 164–165; and War of the Pacific (1879–1884) 55–57, 203; Washington talks with Chile and Peru (1922) 85–86
United States Agency for International Development (USAID) 173, 183
Upper Peru 1, 8, 9, 11; declaration of independence 9; and degree of Sucre 9–10; liberation of 9, 10; ports 11
Uribe, Álvaro 174, 176
Urriolagoitía, Mamerto 105, 109, 119
Uruguay 91
URUPABOL Group (*Grupo URUPABOL*) 138
US Army School of the Americas *see* Western Hemisphere Institute for Security Cooperation (WHINSEC)
*uti possidetis de jure de 1810* 1, 10, 11, 16, 37, 41, 63, 202

Vaca Guzmán–Quirino Costa treaty (1889) 67
Valdés Soublette, Juan Gabriel 156
Valle, Manuel María del 62
Valparaiso 23
*Valparaíso* (warship) 46
Velarde, Juan Francisco 78
Velasco Alvarado, Juan 108
Venezuela 9, 17, 163, 165, 171–172, 174, 176, 177, 180, 193, 194, 195, 197
Viceroyalty of Buenos Aires 63
Viceroyalty of New Granada 8
Viceroyalty of Peru 1, 8, 9, 11, 63, 207
Viceroyalty of Río de la Plata 1, 8, 9, 10
Villarroel, Gualberto 105
Villazón, Eliodoro 72
Viña del Mar protocol (1882) 56
Vizcarra, Martín Alberto 195
voluntary arbitration 80

Wagner Tizón, Allan 142, 151, 152, 155, 162, 174
War of the Pacific (1879–1884) 2, 3, 7, 17, 34, 46, 134, 141, 203; Battle of Angamos 53; Battle of Tacna 53–54; Bolivian declaration of war on Chile 49; capture of Arica 54; Chilean occupation of Bolivian littoral 48, 49, 202; Chile's efforts to detach Bolivia from Peru 53, 55; confederation protocols between Bolivia and Peru 54; Conference of Arica (1880) 55; European support for Chile 50; final settlements 57–60; fiscal impact of 58; and guano/nitrate mining 58; mediation efforts 54–57, 203; nitrate monopoly 49–50; outbreak of hostilities, reasons for 51; peace talks of Bolivia with Chile (1883–1884) 58–60; postwar politics 60–62; protocols of Bolivia and Peru 52–53; Tacna and Arica 56, 58–60; truce agreement 60; Viña del Mar protocol (1882) 56
War of the Triple Alliance (1864–70) 91
war on drugs 129, 164, 171, 172, 173, 205, 206
Washington Consensus 130, 164, 204
Wasmosy, Juan Carlos 160
water privatization 148
weak money 35, 36
Western Hemisphere Institute for Security Cooperation (WHINSEC) 172–173
Whitaker, Arthur P. 103
Wilson, Belford H. 27
Wilson, Woodrow 82, 83
Wood, Bryce 103
World Bank 147, 164, 204, 206
World Trade Organization (WTO) 140, 201
World War II 117–118, 204, 208

Xi Jinping 180
Xinjiang TBEA Group 180

*Yacimientos Petrolíferos Fiscales Bolivianos* (YPFB) 102, 104, 106, 147, 169, 172

"Zero Coca" campaign *see* Dignity Plan (Plan Dignidad)
Zilvetti, Pedro José 56, 57
Zook, David H. 103

Printed in the United States
by Baker & Taylor Publisher Services